M000316152

"If you are passionate—or even just curious—about equality in our country, read this book. It offers the economic grounding to debate the most pressing issues of our time: Education, health care, taxes, housing, labor policies—practically every issue in our country has an important element tied to the Black-white wealth gap. Just as Thomas Piketty's *Capital* shed new light and broad interest on the subject, *Fifteen Cents on the Dollar* will catalyze broad and thoughtful conversations about the Black-white wealth gap."

—Janelle Jones, vice president of policy and advocacy
at the Washington Center for Equitable Growth
and former chief economist of the Department of Labor

"A brilliant and disturbing book that exposes and explains the pernicious nexus between the American economic system and American racism. It should be required reading for anyone seeking to understand the persistence of the wealth gap in our nation."

—Jill Abramson, author of *The Merchants of Truth:*
The Business of News and the Fight for Facts and
former executive editor of the *New York Times*

"Story and Reed have written one of the most poignant and insightful accounts of race, wealth, and poverty in the United States I have come across in the last twenty years. The stories they tell, the data they show, and the conclusions they draw are all compelling, disturbing, and convincing. Here is a book ready for policy makers, activists, community leaders and everyone interested in addressing the insidious interweaving of poverty and race in America."

—Willie James Jennings, associate professor of
systemic theology and Africana studies at Yale Divinity School,
and author of *After Whiteness: An Education in Belonging*

"Wealth is where history shows up in your wallet. *Fifteen Cents on the Dollar* is an unforgettable look into how the racial wealth divide impacts families, our economy, and our society as a whole. This pivotal work is a must-read for those hoping to understand how today's inequalities are the result of a system built on a legacy of oppression."

—Heather McGhee, *New York Times* bestselling author of *The Sum of Us:*
What Racism Costs Everyone and How We Can Prosper Together

"As a Black man who's experienced some of the issues of the people in these pages, I felt seen reading this book. As a journalist, I was thrilled to see such powerful reporting and storytelling be harnessed for explaining one of the most convoluted yet consequential topics in American history. *Fifteen Cents on the Dollar* is accessible, compelling, eye-opening, moving, and, at times, very sobering. It's a weighty message but not a heavy read. It's an important read."

—Jared Council, founding editor of *For(bes)*
The Culture and former *Wall Street Journal* reporter

"*Fifteen Cents on the Dollar* will challenge everything you thought you knew about the Black-white wealth gap. It hits differently when you see it through the eyes of those who have struggled to endure and overcome it. This book is insightful, inspiring, and enraging—in a word, a revelation."

—William J. Kole, author of *The Big 100: The New World of Super-Aging* and former Associated Press editor

"A compelling exploration of America's racial wealth divide with an exceptional blend of rigorous data and profound human emotion. At a moment when discussions about inequality are vital, this book offers a journey that engages the mind and the heart. Whether in the boardroom, within our communities, or around the dinner table, these insights offer a more nuanced, informed, and empathetic perspective on personal and professional growth, and how we can do better."

—Charles Duhigg, *New York Times* bestselling author of
The Power of Habit: Why We Do What We Do in Life and Business and
Supercommunicators: How to Unlock the Secret Language of Connection

"Story and Reed say wealth is financial power accumulated over time, then show how the Black community has been blocked for centuries in the game. Pay attention. This isn't just history; the problem could get worse in an age of widening inequality."

—Jon Hilsenrath, former chief economics correspondent for the *Wall Street Journal*
and author of *Yellen: The Trailblazing Economist Who Navigated an Era of Upheaval*

"Louise Story and Ebony Reed have written an expertly reported and deeply moving book. . . . I can't tell you the number of times I thought, 'Oh, no, Tandreia!' as she repeatedly got her hopes up, only to have them dashed again. I was so concerned when the authors couldn't get in touch with Lovelace. And I loved getting to know Killer Mike, Brook Bacon, James Woodall, and many others. By telling the stories of these individuals and their families, Louise and Ebony offer fresh and much-needed insight. This is reporting and storytelling of the highest order."

—Stephen Wisnefski, executive editor of Investopedia

FIFTEEN CENTS ON THE DOLLAR

FIFTEEN CENTS ON THE DOLLAR

How Americans Made the Black-White Wealth Gap

LOUISE STORY AND **EBONY REED**

HARPER

An Imprint of HarperCollinsPublishers

FIFTEEN CENTS ON THE DOLLAR. Copyright © 2024 by Louise Story and Ebony Reed. All rights reserved. Printed in the United States of America. No part of this book may be used or reproduced in any manner whatsoever without written permission except in the case of brief quotations embodied in critical articles and reviews. For information, address HarperCollins Publishers, 195 Broadway, New York, NY 10007.

HarperCollins books may be purchased for educational, business, or sales promotional use. For information, please email the Special Markets Department at SPsales@harpercollins.com.

FIRST EDITION

Designed by Michele Cameron

Library of Congress Cataloging-in-Publication Data has been applied for.

ISBN 978-0-06-323472-7

24 25 26 27 28 LBC 5 4 3 2 1

Louise Story has donated and will continue to donate all her profits from this book to nonprofit organizations, and Ebony Reed has donated a share of hers. These nonprofits support education, women's empowerment, and journalism, with a strong focus on Black Americans.

Please visit the website for this book at www.15cents.info to find out about these donations, to contact the authors, and to learn more about their teaching, speaking events, and journalism careers.

For Terez A. Paylor and our relatives past, present, and future
—Ebony Reed

For my children, and for yours
—Louise Story

America has given the Negro people a bad check, a check which has come back marked "insufficient funds."

—Dr. Martin Luther King Jr.

CONTENTS

PREFACE

It was about 1 a.m. on April 12, 2022, as he stood outside his home crying tears of rage and disbelief. There wasn't anything to say, really. Nearly twenty years of his life had been spent there. He had fought for it. He had won and lost and won and lost again. Standing in front of his house just after the fire, this was Lovelace.

Lovelace watched the smoke, looked upon the ashes of his dreams. The old man he'd been sheltering had been hauled into an ambulance. When, soon afterward, the man arrived at Grady Hospital, a local news station carried the story. "We don't have his age or his name," the anchor reported on air. "We do know that he was alive when he showed up here at Grady."

The man's name was Carl Phillips, and he had once been a familiar face at the nearby Shepherd's Inn homeless shelter. Located in downtown Atlanta, a two-minute walk from the National Center for Civil and Human Rights museum, the shelter welcomed around four hundred men per night. Most were Black, like Phillips. Covid-19 had brought more unhoused people to the shelter, some as young as eighteen. They were not all Atlanta natives. A good number of people had come to Atlanta because of its reputation as "the Black Mecca." "I heard Atlanta was a place for me," they would say to shelter staff.

"They come to our doors because they have nobody else to turn to," Rachel Reynolds, a manager at the shelter, told us. "Whether that's something that's been done to them or something they have done," she added, "it doesn't really matter."

Phillips, the man taken to Grady, was partially blind. He had been sleeping on the streets of Bankhead, a once-white area near downtown that, over time, had become mainly Black and, in recent times, had become famous among rap fans as the rough neighborhood of the late rapper Shawty Lo. There was a drive-by shooting in the weeks before the fire that sent Phillips to the hospital—but there was also the local dry cleaner shop that had kept track of Phillips's disability card for safekeeping and helped him buy groceries for a while. And there was the Black Bankhead homeowner James Lewis Lovelace III, who had recently gotten Phillips off the street. After at first putting a couch on the front porch for him, Lovelace had eventually taken him in, letting him sleep in a bedroom.

That homeowner, Lovelace, had a complex personal story himself. He was born and raised in Atlanta, and grew up with little privilege. By his early forties, he was spending his afternoons and nights running a small barbecue stand next to a gas station. He had been in and out of prison. He had children. He had dreams. He had fought hard for everything he had and was willing to share it—and then, one night, everything he had was gone.

*   *   *

Nine days later, Tandreia Dixon was visiting her cousin in Washington, D.C. It was a much-needed break from the one-stoplight town in North Carolina where she lived with her mother to save money.

The last few years had been trying for Tandreia. When she finished graduate school, earning a master's in industrial technology, she was left with significant student debt. Then her father died. She kept trying to move forward, but the jobs she took wore her down to the point where she fainted on a warehouse floor. A move to the Atlanta area made her life so expensive, she couldn't save money. Then the pandemic hit. She set up a company to be an entrepreneur and, not gaining traction, she reversed course. Covid-19 struck her family. She ended up moving back to North Carolina to live with her mother.

It was her thirty-third birthday, and Tandreia had split from her cousin for a solitary outing to the National Museum of African American History and Culture. She'd been once before, but she hadn't seen it all. Now she felt a pull to go back. She felt the work she was trying to do "to change the trajectory" for herself and her family demanded that she remember the steps of her forebears. She took out her cell phone to photograph the things in the museum that caught her attention.

First, she photographed a map of the major ports of the slave trade, including a harbor in the Carolinas where her family had long lived. Then she spotted a section of the museum on the business of the slave trade and moved in. Tandreia was endlessly interested in the intersection of race and money. "To Pick a Bale of Cotton: The labor of enslaved Americans fueled the rapid growth of the national economy," a sign read. "African Americans, often malnourished and sleep deprived, used extraordinary skill to catapult the United States into the global economy." She saw historic advertisements for the enslaved: "Jessee, aged about 20 years, fine field hand; CAN PICK 500 LBS. COTTON; INVALUABLE BOY," one ad from 1855 read.

Snap, snap—she wanted all these on her phone. Another title card noted that "Slavery harnessed to cotton created wealth, and wealthy Americans created tools to protect and expand upon their investments. The Bank of the United States sold bonds in slaves that helped finance roads, levees, canals, and railroads. Insurance companies sold policies to guarantee the 'soundness' of enslaved people's bodies. Even the U.S. Postal Service played a role by delivering financial news around the world regarding the price of enslaved African Americans."

Another title card: "$2,500,000." That was the amount of slave-based bonds that European investors had purchased in just the year 1828. Another: "$25,700,000." That was the amount of slave-backed mortgages that banks had issued in Louisiana in just 1859.

Mounted to the wall was a weathered piece of paper from the mid-1860s, when the federal government granted land to some formerly enslaved people. The document showed details of land given to a Black man in Georgia in a program that has become known as "forty acres and a mule." But this man and others would soon lose their land. The government reneged on the land grants soon afterward.

"I just feel this pulling" to be at the museum, Tandreia explained to us. "This pull and this desire to be here. I'm preparing to own my own property, trying to change the trajectory for myself and my family. I'm back in this one-stoplight town, saving and working, you know, *work-*

ing. I just needed a reminder, like, *Man, I really got to give this thing all I got.*"

These thoughts were repeating in her head as she passed more images. *All I got.* It had become a mantra for Tandreia as she tried to become a millionaire. And she believed she would get there through hard work, careful planning, and strategic trade-offs. *All I got.*

She snapped a photo of a display on Madam C. J. Walker, who in the early 1900s founded a beauty products company for Black Americans, becoming a self-made millionaire. The Walker display was lit brightly to show off Walker's canisters of pressing oil and grower gel. So bright were the lights that Tandreia showed up in the reflection. Average height, librarian-like in her horn-rimmed glasses, dressed casually in a gray T-shirt and a long cardigan sweater. Her hair was cut very short, with her natural wave just barely visible. This had not always been her look—she used to wear long braids and focus more on fashion, but as she committed herself more to her professional life and to saving money, she had moved into this no-nonsense style. (Braids can be expensive.)

Away from friends and family, Tandreia had no need to smile or try to make other people comfortable, something she was good at doing. Instead, she focused on the exhibit. "African people—this is the foundation of building up the United States," she told us. "Bonds and mortgages and things like that, off of the backs of slaves. This is the foundation of the United States."

A title card for an image of the One Cent Savings Bank of Nashville, Tennessee, said it was one of the oldest Black American banks still in operation. Founded in 1904, by 2022 it was called Citizens Bank. Tandreia paused before the title card in part because she had recently become a customer of a new Black-focused banking company.

After George Floyd was killed in 2020, Black-owned banking had garnered renewed attention as a potential solution to the country's racial inequities. A few weeks before Tandreia's trip to the African American museum, *Bloomberg Businessweek* had run an article about Greenwood Bank. Tandreia was a new customer there, so she read it with interest. "Greenwood Aims to Repair Centuries of Racist Banking," the headline said. It was a big statement, and Greenwood executives were quick to expand on it, posting on social media that their mission was to end racism and racial wealth gaps. One Greenwood founder wrote on Instagram, "Creating and building generational wealth." Another posted, "700,000 people have joined the Greenwood community on a journey to fix the financial inequity that has been around for centuries."

Tandreia wondered if Greenwood Bank was taking a swipe at Wells Fargo Bank. In data analyzed in the Bloomberg story, the Black-white lending gap at Wells Fargo was stark: the bank turned down 53 percent of Black home mortgage refinancing applicants, but when it came to white applicants, it turned down only 28 percent. Discrepancies like this must have been what Greenwood was referring to with "racist banking," Tandreia thought.

And yet, the idea that any entity could end racism, even just racism in banking, was hard to believe—for Tandreia, at least. "Greenwood making a statement like that? I respect it," she marveled. "But my goodness. It's like me trying to eat an elephant, you know?"

*   *   *

Two days later, Brook Bacon was celebrating his wife's birthday.

Out on a walk, the two stopped for her to pose in front of a mural on a brick wall. Brook's blond, trim wife, dressed casually, walked up to the wall. A black shark more than two times her size loomed behind her, its sharp-toothed mouth open, ready to take a bite. She posed proudly, one hand on her hip, radiating positive energy around turning forty.

Brook, who had turned forty just before the Covid-19 pandemic began, snapped the photo. His skin was light brown, though dark compared to hers. He wore his hair grown out naturally, Afro-style—a rarity in the often white-dominated workplaces of his career in finance and in their mostly white small town in New Hampshire.

Turning forty is a time of self-reflection for many people, but this was especially so for Brook. His father had been killed by a white police trooper two years before. Since then, Brook had reexamined practically every element of his life, family, and financial experience as a Black person in America. He had been awakened to patterns of racism he had once ignored and had realized that his biracial marriage and his small, mostly white New Hampshire town was only a piece of who he was. Once something he had avoided, his family's roots in Georgia had become important to him.

His roots had also just made him wealthy: the state government had awarded a settlement for his father's death. Though the money had come at a terrible cost, Brook could now worry less about his finances. At forty-two, and after years of personal setbacks tied at least partly to his race, he could worry less about his job as a mid-level business analyst. He could pay off his student debt. He could offer his two children more schooling options—an elite private school, even, like their mother had attended. He and his wife could invite more family on their annual trips to Hilton Head, South Carolina. They could move to a larger home if they wanted.

But money couldn't bring people back or make up for lost time. Money couldn't serve as punishment, either, when it came from the state. What Brook wanted was not financial. He wanted justice: prison time for the man who had killed his father. He was determined to keep pushing.

Would people listen?

*   *   *

April 2022 was a time of pride for James Woodall. His first book was now available for pre-order.

Wired for Racism? How Evolution and Faith Move Us to Challenge Racial Idolatry was a policy-oriented book he had coauthored with an older white pastor. James, at twenty-eight, was one of the very few Black Americans featured on his publisher's website. Black Americans, who often do not have the personal savings needed to fund the research and writing of books, have been underrepresented in the book publishing industry.

James was modest about what he had accomplished, especially given that he had worked on the book while serving as president of the Georgia NAACP. "It was a large undertaking considering the times that we were in and the work I was doing," he told us. "It was a relief to get it done."

After the murder of George Floyd, James had been among the fastest-rising young leaders in the NAACP. He helped catalyze numerous large donations for the progress of Black Americans. He inspired young people across the state of Georgia to speak out and push for progress on civil justice and the racial wealth gap. He held the hands of family members across the state when their loved ones were killed by police. And he did all this while working on his new book—and while just trying to get by.

Despite his growing public career, James had been struggling to pay his bills. He had tens of thousands of dollars in student debt and a negative net worth. He didn't have parents who could subsidize his life. He wouldn't benefit from substantial inheritance or generational wealth. And his high-profile NAACP appointment, while long on prestige, was short on pay: his position as state president came with no salary.

Rubbing shoulders with the NAACP's Black elite, James might have given the impression of being from an elite background himself. He was tall and lean, with close-cut hair and a runner's physique. That and his impeccable formal attire helped him blend into the world of privilege. But he did not grow up with privilege. His father was in prison by the time James was a teenager. His uncle on one side of his family worked in the illegal drug business. His great-grandfather had been incarcerated for a murder. Financially, James's mother had struggled as far back as he could remember, juggling her own student loans, a lack of a college degree, and housing insecurity. She filed for bankruptcy twice while he was growing up, was evicted from apartments four times, and when money was tight, the solution was a payday loan. She moved James and his three younger siblings every few years, and sometimes every few months, around the Atlanta metropolitan area. At times, she used her children's Social Security numbers to get credit for herself, leaving James and his siblings with smudged credit histories before they were in their twenties. Seeking structure and support, James served in the military reserve; his friends would call him Major. He sought out religion and became a Baptist preacher.

None of this is detailed in James's book. There is only a quick description of his childhood: "Imagine," James and his coauthor wrote, "growing up with a single mother who must work nonstop to provide for four children and herself while your father is in prison for the rest of his life. That's [James's] background, and he is not unique. . . . In families like [his], a 'normal' life for young people includes poverty, pregnancy, and even prison."

James, "in particular, because he is Black, recognizes all too well the experience of grief and darkness associated with being the target of racism," the authors noted, adding that James and other Black people have been "expected to exist without being fully human" because of "their experience of terror over police brutality and systemic inequity."

As the coauthors described it, James began as the student of his coauthor, seventy-two-year-old Mark Ellingsen. But the more the two got to know each other, the more James became the teacher. "Let me say some things he has taught," Ellingsen told us. "Simple things like the risks of driving while Black. Like the risks of shopping while Black—how you're going to get those dirty looks."

Being Black in America, Ellingsen said, means living outside the opportunities that white Americans have. And the leaps Black Americans have had to make to gain opportunities are gut-wrenching. "It can produce anger," he said. "It can produce despair . . . It's in my gut now. It's in my heart."

Despite inspiring Ellingsen's reflections, James told us it was only when the book was finished that he stopped and thought about what being an author meant for his life. "Wow," he said. "I'm the first in my family to do this."

*   *   *

We got to know James, Brook, Tandreia, and Lovelace between 2020 and 2023. They were Black Americans with family ties to Georgia, where we based much of our reporting. They were professionals and entrepreneurs with life experiences and family that connected them to many walks of life. They were born between 1979 and 1994, roughly the years of the Millennial generation. They were all strongly motivated to lift their families' places in the economy.

We connected with them while conducting hundreds of in-depth interviews with Black Americans to understand both their views on race and money and the dollars and cents of their own financial situation. We followed the roots and branches of their family trees to trace their generational wealth or, in many cases, lack of wealth. We talked to dozens of their family members and pulled court records going back two hundred years. We contextualized what they told us with our broader interviews, with findings from a national poll we commissioned, and with a review of scholarly research.

At the same time, we followed the progress of a handful of new companies that were formed with the explicit goal of creating a world with more racial equity. Many of the people getting the most attention for trying to address the Black-white wealth gap in 2020 were businesspeople. We wanted to understand their companies' opportunities and challenges—and the people behind these companies. The businesses we followed included a Black-focused television news channel, a Black-owned food business, and a Black-focused financial company. All three (and more) feature in these pages, but it is the last, the financial company called Greenwood Bank, that we came to see as a through line for the examination we undertook of race and money in the United States.

Greenwood Bank was founded in 2020 by three well-known Atlanta-based businessmen: Andrew Jackson Young Jr., the former mayor of Atlanta and a Civil Rights leader; Michael Render, the rapper also known as Killer Mike; and Ryan Glover, the founder of Black-focused content businesses, including Bounce TV and Noontime Records. The young people we feature in this book intersect with Greenwood Bank and its stated ethos: Tandrèia Dixon was one of Greenwood's customers; James Woodall connected with Greenwood's founders through political circles; and Brook Bacon and James Lovelace represent a range of the customers Greenwood was aiming to attract. In the course of our research, the founders of Greenwood Bank also emerged as central subjects of this book, not least because of the remarkable stories of their own lives and family trees.

Our book explores the history and present reality of the Black-white wealth gap through the lives and histories of these seven Black individuals, all of whom we found to be insightful, interesting, and, at times, inspiring. Alongside their stories, we investigate new and historical scholarship, data, and the public debate over wealth gaps, seeking to understand the history of race and money and to evaluate current business practices for their impact on equity.

A note about names: Because we will say a lot about the personal lives of our seven principal subjects, we will use their given names throughout the book, except we will call James Lovelace by his surname, "Lovelace," to avoid confusion with James Woodall. For all other people in the book—except where family members with identical last names are discussed together—we use surnames.

A note on terms: We use the term *enslaved people* rather than *slaves* because enslavement was something forced on Black people, not something inherent to their identity as people. They were *people* who were enslaved. We capitalize *Black* when referring to Black Americans because this has become the standard in most journalism; *white* is kept in lowercase in journalism practices, as this book later explains. We generally use the phrase "the Black-white wealth gap" rather than "the racial wealth gap" because there are gaps in wealth between other races. When we use "racial wealth gaps," in the plural, we are speaking broadly about inequities in race and money among many races. The Black-white racial wealth gap is unique in the role that enslaved Black Americans played in creating the U.S. economy, but history is full of economic injustices against Latinos, Asian Americans, Native Americans, and other groups. While our focus is on one group's legacy of injustice, their stories hold lessons for a more inclusive future for everyone.

And a note about us: Like many of the people profiled in our book, we both grew up in the 1980s and '90s, the post–Civil Rights era. By then, opportunity supposedly existed for everyone. We both had fathers who were first-generation college graduates, and we both were told stories of their self-made success. Working on this book together has been an intimate journey of listening and thinking during which conversations between us about our interviews, the data, and lessons from history also turned personal.

We have studied the Black-white wealth gap, but, we realized, we have also lived it. Ebony and her fiancé, both Black, lived in Kansas

City, Missouri, in part to save money—well before the Covid-19 pandemic. They believed that earning East Coast salaries while living in the Midwest was a good way to build generational wealth. We talked about the 2008 financial crisis, which Louise, who is white, had reported on from Wall Street while Ebony edited stories of foreclosures in Detroit. (Ebony had also dealt with her own short sale and financial mistreatment.) We talked about the GI Bill and about who in our families had benefited and who had not. We talked about medical school and how Louise's father had been able to attend, but how, just a few years before him, Black students had not been welcomed at his school. We talked about our childhoods and how race had figured in where our parents had chosen to settle their families and, ultimately, in Ebony's having to take out student loans while Louise did not. Through our partnership, we came to better understand the ways race, class, and money have affected our own lives. We came to reconsider how we think about capitalism, wealth, meritocracy, and the financial system. And we learned from people all around us about the gravity of wealth gaps.

We hope this book will take you on a similar journey.

INTRODUCTION

THE BLACK-WHITE
WEALTH GAP

Sadie T. M. Alexander, the first Black economics PhD in the United States, often recounted a story about the first day of a sociology course she took as an undergraduate at the University of Pennsylvania back in the 1910s. The professor asked Alexander and the other students to write down which races were inferior and which were superior. Most of the students wrote that white people were superior; some Black students wrote that as well. When asked why, the white students pointed to "wealth" as the reason.

Wealth—what is it, really? We asked MBA students in the course we teach at Yale for their definition, and we heard many different answers. Some gave variations on the definition used by the Federal Reserve.

- Wealth is what you own less what you owe.
- Wealth is the value of all assets minus debts.
- Wealth is the total value of all assets minus all liabilities.

A few students neglected to specify that debt be subtracted from assets, echoing a common misperception in which people assume that someone with visible assets is wealthy—even though those assets may be dwarfed by debt:

- Wealth is the accumulation of assets and access to spend them.
- Wealth is the value of assets owned by an individual.

Other students took care to distinguish wealth from income:

- Wealth is the accumulation of assets that provide financial comfort, income notwithstanding.
- Wealth is economic resources not attained directly through employment.

Others discussed wealth in terms of what it could achieve for people:

- Wealth is something that can provide for a human being.
- Wealth is what you can pass on from generation to generation.
- Wealth is having the financial and physical means and the mental and emotional well-being to pursue a fulfilling life.
- Wealth is money and happiness.
- Wealth is an accumulated, quantifiable return on past privilege; access to opportunities; and individual merit and fortune that promote social and economic mobility.
- Wealth is financial security, stability, and independence.
- Wealth is financial power accumulated over time.

This last series of definitions in some ways was the most interesting, because it showed the emotions that get wrapped up in money. Wealth is a "fulfilling life." Wealth is "happiness." Wealth is "stability and independence." Wealth is "power."

The Yale students were a narrow group, and a wider survey of Americans would likely reveal even wider divergence on the definition of wealth. It's something most people think they know about, but few discuss it with precision—some people even confuse it with income. Wealth is also personal, and fraught with opportunity for judgment. Whereas income is earned in a way that at least to some degree feels meritocratic, wealth is something built over time or, often, something given to someone. Whether someone *deserves* wealth—or not—is subjective and sometimes fiercely debated. Beyond that, with all the ways people can choose to show wealth or keep it from view, there is ambiguity even among close friends about how much wealth someone *really* has. To further complicate matters, wealth is highly localized in how people perceive it. Someone who is deemed wealthy in one community might not seem as wealthy in another.

Understanding trends in wealth and, by extension, racial wealth gaps entails looking at the present but also at history. It's difficult for people to assess the past. For all these reasons—people's secrecy around their wealth; the need to understand things in history that haven't been well covered; and the variety of ways that wealth is defined by different people—racial wealth gaps are not fully understood by most Americans. Indeed, studies have found that Americans overestimate how much Black-white gaps have improved. Americans think progress in reducing racial income gaps immediately translates to reducing wealth gaps. It doesn't. And they think both income and wealth gaps are far smaller than they really are. Across our extensive interviews and discussions, we found that Black people know there is a wealth gap but often do not appreciate how severe it is. White people have a range of understandings about the gap, but it was not uncommon for them to tell us that the Black-white gaps had disappeared. These misperceptions are is not surprising: Americans of all racial backgrounds are often overly optimistic. We love the idea of progress. There are many successful, financially stable Black Americans who have climbed the corporate ladder, become celebrities, or created successful companies.

But harbingers of change do not mean that that change has been widely achieved.

It is in part because of Americans' misperceptions about the economic status of Black Americans that we wrote this book. How can Americans discuss issues like affirmative action, student loan forgiveness, and corporate diversity and inclusion policies if they do not know the size of the Black-white wealth gap or whether it is closing or growing wider? How can they discuss generational wealth—which is to say, inherited wealth—if they have not looked at the arc of the history of racial wealth inequities? How can a person even evaluate their family's story and understand their own financial history without knowing the broader picture of America's unequal pie?

The data in this book follow the financial definition used by the Federal Reserve: that wealth is the total sum of all that a person owns minus the amount of debt they owe. In other words: wealth = assets - liabilities.

There is no long-running government dataset available to study wealth over the history of the United States. Old reports taken on wealth by the U.S. Census were ended by 1880, and newer reports measure slightly different things and are not run every year. This has created a gap in public discourse. Imagine if there were a monthly "wealth report." Like the Employment Situation Summary that the Bureau of Labor Statistics releases on the first Friday of every month, a "wealth report" or, better, a "wealth gap report" would provide regular updates on the status of people's wealth and how it compares among different groups of Americans.

Without a recurring wealth gap report, we look to the datasets that do exist. Most helpful is the Federal Reserve's Survey of Consumer Finances, a broad report that includes a section on household assets, liabilities, and gifts and inheritances received. This survey has been carried out every three years since 1989, and it includes race. It is the central dataset this book uses for statements about the wealth gap since 1989. In addition, we will include older datasets that were pieced together in an excellent 2023 research paper by Ellora Derenoncourt of Princeton University along with three scholars from the University of Bonn.

Let's start with data from over the past twenty years. When you look at how much wealth the typical, or "median," Black American has compared with the median white American, you see that the typical white family has consistently had upward of $100,000 more in wealth than the typical Black family. This has meant that consistently since 1989, between 77 and 86 percent of Black families have had less wealth than the median white family.

When examined in graph form, white wealth versus Black wealth is far from an image of equality. Plotted over the last thirty years, the white wealth line floats along like a cluster of clouds, while Black wealth sits on the ground below, watching the clouds pass by. This gap holds true whether you look at the median wealth or the average levels of wealth. The numbers? The average level of white wealth in the 2022 government survey was $1,361,810 per household. The average level of Black wealth was $211,600.

This gap equates to striking differences in Black and white wealth, especially when you look at average levels of wealth, which (in contrast to measuring by the median) capture the gaping inequities on the high end. Because wealth in the hands of the wealthiest white Americans is so high and poverty among Black Americans is so common, the total share of wealth in the hands of white families is much higher than their share of the population. Taking 2022 data as an example, Black families, on average, had $1,150,210 less wealth than the average for white families.

The Spread Between White and Black Wealth

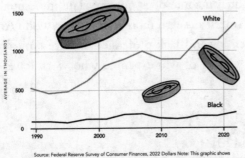

Source: Federal Reserve Survey of Consumer Finances, 2022 Dollars Note: This graphic shows the average wealth of white families over time compared to the average wealth of Black families.

Dividing the average Black family's wealth by the average white family's wealth gives us 15.5 percent. The same is true when you compare median (or "typical") white and Black families, indicating this is not a phenomenon tied only to the wealth of a few white people at the top. The Black-white wealth gap is broad based. Numerically, as of 2022, for every dollar held by the typical white family, the typical Black family had 15.5 cents. That's an 84.5-cent gap.

Put another way, Black families have just over fifteen cents for every white dollar.

Some people point out that there is a general growing wealth gap between the richest Americans and everyone else, regardless of race. Most white Americans have far less wealth than the richest Americans, they point out. This is true, and there are numerous excellent books on the broader wealth gap, including Thomas Piketty's *Capital in the Twenty-First Century*. But the overall gap has nuances that are specific to subsets of people. In particular, there's the persistent problem of racial wealth gaps in the United States. Black Americans are overrepresented among lower-wealth Americans and have continued falling behind as the overall gap has grown. For many, that means having no wealth at all. About one quarter of Black households in 2021 had no wealth at all (or they had so much debt that their wealth was negative). Only 11 percent of white households that year had no wealth.

The Black-white wealth gap is visible in just about any comparison you make along the economic spectrum. When you look at white and Black Americans within the same income bracket, you still see gaping disparities: Equal income does not translate into equal wealth. Even when Black Americans earn more money than white Americans, their wealth is often lower. Black professionals have typically one third to one half the wealth of white people who work lower-paying, blue-collar jobs.

Historical Data

The most comprehensive historical data on the Black-white wealth gap appeared in a 2023 working paper from economists at Princeton and the University of Bonn. Ellora Derenoncourt, the Princeton economist, noted that most policy discussions about the gap focus on small-bore solutions that, in her view, would not come anywhere close to closing it. "History is not always present in our minds when we're thinking about some of these economic gaps," she told us. "People want to find a solution in terms of what end up being pretty marginal factors in terms of actually closing the gap. So you might hear talk of, you know, financial literacy. And it's true when you look at things, at those kinds of statistics, you do see that Black Americans, on average, have less invested in stocks compared to the average white American, etc. So I can see how those policy ideas come up."

The problem is, Derenoncourt's research found, simply increasing the savings rate of Black Americans through more stock ownership or other investment tactics would not significantly narrow the Black-white wealth gap over a few decades. The gap began at such a large point— white wealth was nearly sixty times greater than Black wealth at the end of the Civil War, her research found—that such incremental progress would not remove it. As of the 1980s, white wealth stood at six times Black wealth, she and the other researchers discovered, but the gap was stuck there; and it remained at the same level moving into the 2020s.

White Families Still Have More

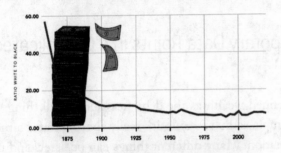

Sources: Ellora Derenoncourt, Chi Hyun Kim, Moritz Kuhn, Moritz Schularick, Wealth of Two Nations: The U.S. Racial Wealth Gap, 1860-2020, The Quarterly Journal of Economics, 2023; Federal Reserve Survey of Consumer Finances. Note: This graphic shows the average wealth of white families divided by the average wealth of Black families.

To create this long-running dataset, Derenoncourt and her coauthors painstakingly pieced together more than a dozen other datasets. Among them were census records from 1860 and 1870, as well as state tax records and a historical survey that was a precursor to the Federal Reserve's modern-day Survey of Consumer Finances. It's worthwhile to notice the slopes on the graph. The steeper the line points downward, the faster the progress toward closing, or "converging," as economists say, the wealth gap. Notice that this convergence shown in the above graph has been largely flat since 1950. Notice also that convergence turned to slight divergence in the years leading into 2020.

And notice that when the graph is flipped around to show the ratio of Black to white since 1860, the ratio climbs upward but sputters out—it's a molehill next to the mountain of white family wealth.

Black Cents on the White Dollar

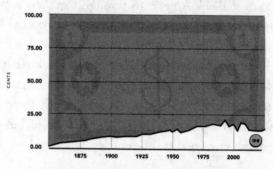

Sources: Ellora Derenoncourt, Chi Hyun Kim, Moritz Kuhn, Moritz Schularick, Wealth of Two Nations: The U.S. Racial Wealth Gap, 1860-2020, The Quarterly Journal of Economics, 2023; Federal Reserve Survey of Consumer Finances. Note: This graphic shows the average wealth of Black families divided by the average wealth of white families, expressed as cents on the dollar.

Contemporary Data Points in a Complicated Equation

We have defined wealth as the debt-free value of all things a person owns. As simple as that sounds, it's really shorthand for a more complicated equation. Many different things can be assets and many can be liabilities.

Let's rewrite

Wealth = Assets - Liabilities
    in fuller form as:
    Wealth =
(**Assets** like House + Land or Properties + Car + Business Ownership +
    Stock Holdings + Bonds + Crypto + Collectibles + Cash + Other Assets)

- (**Liabilities** like Mortgages + Auto Loans + Credit Card Bills + Student
    Loans + Other Loans and Debt)

While assets are better than liabilities, wealth is often built through the smart use of liabilities. Loans can, for example, fuel a person's ability to start a company, or they can enable the purchase of a home whose value may appreciate. And all assets are not created equal—some assets hold value better than others.

The equation we've just given spells out more details on wealth, but in terms of the Black-white wealth *gap*, it's also not simple. To understand the gap, one has to look at the past as well as the present, at the setbacks Black families experienced as well as the good things that happened for many white families' wealth. The inputs to the gap are also often outputs of the gap, creating a cycle that's difficult to break. For instance, banking is both a factor in creating the gap and a symptom of the gap. Whether a bank like Wells Fargo issues a mortgage to a family is a factor in that family's wealth trajectory. But whether Wells Fargo's loan officers believe a family should have a loan is tied in part to that family's financial situation, which is tied to the history of the racial wealth gap, to generational wealth, and even to the bank's past decisions to avoid lending to Black families.

A word about income: Pay is an important factor that allows people to purchase assets that build their wealth and to save money. This book covers research and stories that pertain to the income gap, and pay equity matters. But as later sections of the book show, income gaps and wealth gaps do not always move in tandem. Even where income gaps have gotten smaller, wealth gaps remain because of larger factors like inheritance, discriminatory lending, and investment patterns.

Words to Remember

Data can appear faceless and remote, but there are personal stories behind the numbers—stories of parents, grandparents, and great-grandparents striving for more, sometimes achieving it and, often, having setbacks. For many Black Americans, historic shifts in the trajectory of Black wealth are personalized in the loss of land; in challenges to homeownership or to a family business; in banking discrimination; in the jobs that were closed to them and the schools they could not attend. These stories are passed down generationally, and just about every Black American we interviewed had direct family ties to a historic economic injustice. The people we feature in this book were trying to better their families' finances in the years 2020–23. We show you their lives during that period and also their familial connections to wealth gap history.

As the book unfolds, you will read through historical moments that we consider turning points in the story of the Black-white wealth gap. We suggest you read those sections with the following framework in mind:

- **Expropriation**—also known as "taking" or "extraction." This is when white Americans took things from Black Americans. At the most extreme level, it included enslaving them. Later in U.S. history, it included coercing Black Americans into turning over their land.
- **Exclusion**—also known as "closure" or "opportunity hoarding." This is when white Americans do not allow Black Americans to share in opportunities.
- **Exploitation**—sometimes, in a present-day context, synonymous with "subordination." In this category, Black Americans are "let in" to a situation by white Americans, but they are not treated fairly or given their fair share of economic benefits. This term is used in some labor situations, but we view it as too gentle a term to apply to slavery.

Most of the time that expropriation, exclusion, or exploitation occurs, as we will show, the people involved justify their actions with what we refer to as "money-over-morals thinking." Time and again, U.S. citizens and leaders have rationalized unethical actions with financial justifications. Mid-twentieth-century white suburbanites who were resistant to Black people moving in next door, for example, often said they *personally* didn't mind Black neighbors, but that they feared for their own homes' property value. Today, insurance companies say they are happy to provide auto insurance to people without regard to race, but they also charge more for people living in areas that experience higher levels of crime, ignoring the racial impact of such a policy. This is a financialization of ethics.

When money triumphs over morals, equality loses.

Another pattern is Americans' oscillation between believing there should be race-specific institutions and then, in contrast, thinking that all races should be integrated into the same institutions. There have been repeated movements and efforts, from both inside and outside the Black community, to create Black-focused companies, nonprofits, and government programs. This book puts a strong focus on examining what it means to be a Black-owned company.

Another common pattern involves the failure to monitor the results of policies and make adjustments with racial equity in mind. Time and again, companies and arms of government offer products or benefits that, in theory, are open to all people but, in practice, are not equitably distributed. Color-blind policies often do not lead to equitable results.

Finally, it's worth remembering that progress comes in fits and starts. After the Civil War, Black Americans' wealth improved dramatically for decades compared to white wealth—in part because Black wealth was starting from such a low base; in part because of the loss of southern white wealth; and in part because Black Americans in some areas obtained land. That narrowing of the gap continued into the early twentieth century, but faced challenges as white residents attacked the progress of local Black businesses and cities were segregated. In the mid-1900s, Black Americans continued to make slow progress through the Civil Rights Movement, but the improvements in the gap slowed in the 1990s, and following the 2007 recession, years of progress were lost. Society entered a new period of focus on racial equity in 2020, and a small gain in Black wealth—for the typical Black family—was reported in 2023. But, as of the printing of this book in 2024, it was not clear that these trends would continue or that any of the reforms or initiatives introduced after George Floyd was killed would remain in place, or that the reforms were having any effect in closing the gap. In fact, by 2024, a fierce pushback against race-based social programs had emerged. In some ways, the clouds of white wealth up in the sky seemed farther than ever from the ground.

Who's to Blame, Government or Business?

In the course of our research, people often asked us if racial wealth gaps are caused by the government or by private industry. The answer, this book will show, is that both public and private interests have played a role and continue to do so.

The gap began with slavery, itself an alliance of public and private action, as enslaved Black Americans helped build the early American economy while being denied its fruits. The gap remained beyond emancipation through a combination of government, business, and individual action. First was the lack of economic assistance or land to Black Americans and then the mistreatment of formerly enslaved people by insurance companies and banks, including by a bank set up by the federal government. Jim Crow's barriers, too, were often formed by business and government alliances. Black Americans lost land through the actions of private individuals, business developers, and unfavorable government regulations alike. The gap was held open in part by wrongful imprisonment throughout history and by the financial toll of the justice system. Black Americans were excluded from large-scale government subsidies to white Americans, including New Deal programs and the GI Bill. Then there was zoning and redlining—set up by governments but also supported by businesses. And segregation at universities was enabled by federal law, but businesses also segregated employees. Eminent domain, too, often relied on government-private actions. Governments in many places pushed Black people to leave their properties, after lobbying by businesses.

In recent years, the combination of public and private setbacks has continued. Predatory lending and the events of the 2008 financial crisis were yet another set of harms brought by the government and private industry. Then there is the case of student loan debt, one of the most pressing current private-public problems, which has strong racial implications. Discrimination in hiring and promotions at private companies and unequal pay levels among racial groups are mostly business actions, but government agencies also haven't been great in their human resource practices. And then there's the differing access and behaviors around investing in the stock market and in building companies that go public, which have business and education wound up within them. Like the backs of enslaved people, who were whipped and scarred uncountable times, the difference in wealth between white and Black Americans is tied to many economic lashes, old and new.

America, and Americans, made the Black-white wealth gap. And our society continues to hold it in place.

To take one example of an insidious, ongoing factor in the making of racial wealth gaps, as of 2024, plenty of federal tax policies, while appearing race neutral, have racialized effects. The U.S. Treasury Department ran an examination of the ways its tax policies affected people by race and found strong racial patterns. Several of the largest so-called tax expenditures disproportionately help white families. Among the tax deductions in the 2023 report in which white Americans made up a higher percentage of the beneficiaries than their share of the population: the charitable contributions deduction, the preferential tax rates for capital gains and dividends, and the ability to deduct home mortgage interest from taxes. There was only one category in the report in which Black families benefited more than their share of the population: the Earned Income Tax Credit, which is for low- and moderate-income earners.

Tax benefits for wealthy people mostly went to white people, the government data made clear, and the ones for poor people went disproportionately to Black people, Latino Americans, and other minority groups. Here's the rub: There were more tax expenditures in existence for *wealthy* people. This meant that, in effect, there were more of these benefits for *white* people. Modern-day tax policy as of 2024 was undermining what is supposed to be a progressive income tax system . . . and widening the Black-white wealth gap.

The Black Dollar

It says a lot about American society that most the of time, when businesses talk about people of color, they talk about their "buying power." In the case of Black Americans, that buying power is known as the Black dollar.

Many companies justify their investments in diversity in part based on goals to make more money by selling their products to more diverse people. Marketers cite lots of statistics about the supposedly large amounts of money, or "purchasing power," in the hands of Black people. In the early 2020s, many Black-owned businesses adopted this language, saying they would reach the Black dollar and urging investors, often white investors, to fund their businesses.

But we question how powerful Black Americans really are in the economy. However high their purchasing power is, white Americans' is higher, in aggregate and per capita. Talking about an absolute amount of money, even if it sounds like a high amount, ignores the comparison to other groups of people. There's a gap in purchasing power between white and Black Americans that does not equal their representation in the population. Moreover, the total amount of purchasing power held by a group—in this case, Black Americans—also ignores the distribution of money within that group. There are Black Americans who have broken through and amassed wealth. That does not mean that many Black Americans have come close to parity with the typical white American.

The *Black dollar* is a marketing term, pure and simple. If it is not money-over-morals language, it's at least money out of context. That context is the wealth gap: that the median, or "typical," Black family has just about fifteen cents for every white dollar. The Black dollar, an idea originally meant to tout purchasing power, is actually a mirage. It obscures the fact that the ratio of a typical Black family's wealth to a typical white family's wealth is a poor one, not a powerful one.

While the Black dollar had long been a concept peddled by white marketers, it moved aggressively to being used also by Black founders to fuel their new companies. They used the concept to raise money from angel investors and venture capitalists and to talk about social change through shopping. They pointed to recirculation of Black dollars as an answer for the Black-white wealth gap. And they urged Black people to patronize them out of racial loyalty.

In an era in which segregation has been banned in public schools and pretty much all other settings, the segregation of money has remained a popular economic idea. A new wave of Black-owned businesses, market watchers, and activists are asking: Could Black Americans segregate their money? Should they? Is it possible for Black businesses to grow and scale with only Black funding, Black employees, and Black customers? And if Black dollars could, indeed, recirculate and empower these businesses, would this create real change for a broad base of Black Americans or only for those, Black or otherwise, at the top?

The Many Tentacles of the Gap

We have a lot to cover in the upcoming chapters: housing, capital markets, student loans, credit card debt, bankruptcy, insurance, small business and entrepreneurship, banking, diversity in the workplace, the criminal justice system, and more. Taken in isolation, the facts in this book may seem to have plausible explanations. Many Americans think that in an era in which we've had a Black president, any person who struggles to get ahead has only their own actions to blame. When one looks at the many tentacles of the Black-white wealth gap, however, its systemic nature becomes hard to explain away. For example, as of 2023:

- Black Americans have the lowest homeownership rate;
- The unemployment rate of Black Americans is consistently 1.5 to 2 times the unemployment rate of white Americans;
- The average Black household earns only about half the income of the average white household;
- Black Americans are about half as likely to own stocks as are white Americans;
- Black college graduates on average owe $25,000 more in student loans than white college graduates;
- 59 percent of the Black students who start college don't finish within six years (compared to 33 percent of white Americans);
- Dismissed bankruptcy cases are far more common among

Black Americans than white Americans, with the result that Black Americans who enter bankruptcy do not get to wipe away their debts as often as white Americans;

- Black Americans own about 10 percent of the businesses tracked by the U.S. Census, but their firms account for only half of 1 percent of all the revenue generated by tracked companies;

- Within professional workplaces, where higher wages can typically be earned, Black Americans under-index their percentage of the total workforce in every sector other than social service. That means they are underrepresented in management, finance, engineering, medicine, law, and many other fields;

- Only 18 banks are owned by Black Americans in this country, out of around 4,000 FDIC-insured banks;

- In the criminal justice system, the arrest rate for many misdemeanors is twice as high or more for Black Americans as it is for white Americans; and

- Black Americans are shot and killed by police at more than twice the rate of white Americans.

After George Floyd was killed, the two of us started discussing the financial stories of people who had been killed by the police. We quickly found a connection between violent deaths and the history of the Black-white wealth gap and, through this, many other connections. When you overlay maps showing the locations of victims of such shootings with maps of redlined areas—that is, where the government categorized neighborhoods back in the 1930s by level of financial risk to mortgage lenders and insurers—clear patterns emerge. For instance, in 2021, the *Philadelphia Inquirer* showed the pattern on maps in its city—the very city that was home to our nation's founding. A quick glance showed how the "red dots" indicating areas with frequent shootings also happened to be mainly in the old, redlined neighborhoods. Those are the neighborhoods the U.S. government labeled as "hazardous" in 1937, cementing discriminatory lending practices in the area.

In Minneapolis, according to a 1930s Minneapolis zoning map, the street corner where George Floyd was killed lay on the edge of a redlined, so-called hazardous, zone. Cup Foods, the corner store where Floyd allegedly presented a fake twenty-dollar bill, sits at the intersection of two Minneapolis neighborhoods. The demographics of the neighborhoods that collide here are telling: On the east side of Cup Foods, the neighborhood of Bancroft is about 73 percent white and about 10 percent Black. On the west side of Cup Foods, the neighborhood of Bryant is about 48 percent white and about 21 percent Black.

This clash of neighborhoods along a boundary line is typical in Minneapolis, which went from being an integrated city to a segregated one in the early 1900s due to a proliferation of racially restrictive covenants. Typical language inserted into deeds back then by white homeowners included that a property "shall not at any time be conveyed, mortgaged or leased to any person or persons of Chinese, Japanese, Moorish, Turkish, Negro, Mongolian or African blood or descent." As of 2020, Minneapolis had become the U.S. city with the lowest homeownership rate among Black residents. Here is yet another cost of segregation.

To Leslie Redmond, the president of the NAACP in Minneapolis in 2020, the national attention that followed Floyd's murder was an opportunity for the broader country to learn what many Black people saw every day—that the Black community didn't have access to the same opportunities as many white people. Her state, Redmond told us, had "some of the worst racial disparities in the nation for Black people. But if you look at it for white people, it's the best. Great education. You have more Fortune 500 companies per capita than any other state. You have good health care, you have good parks and recreation, and everything is good for white people in Minnesota."

To Redmond and many other people hitting the streets for those 2020 demonstrations, the reality was obscured by signs of progress in the hands of a few Black Americans and not shared by all. As she said, "It's like, if you don't look at it too hard, you're not going to be able to see it for what it really is."

The Black Mecca?

Wealth is often invisible, but real estate is one place where it's made visible. Among all the tentacles of the wealth gap, housing and land-ownership are among the most important. Beyond the safety, shelter, and comfort of housing, real estate is a financial matter. It makes a difference in economic well-being whether a person is paying rent they can afford. It makes a difference in wealth building whether they can purchase a home and whether they receive home loans on fair terms. It makes such a difference that land was a critical discussion as the Civil War ended. At the time, Union general William Sherman issued an order to grant all formerly enslaved people up to forty acres of land. That promise—soon broken by President Andrew Johnson—is what inspired Spike Lee to name his film production company 40 Acres and a Mule Filmworks. Now the expression "forty acres and a mule" signifies the many promises made to Black Americans, then broken.

To see the Black-white wealth gap on display, we went to Atlanta. There, housing has been a persistent problem both for poor Black Americans and for people in the middle class trying to build wealth. And, just as in Minneapolis and Philadelphia, the location of where a Black person lives can mean the difference between life and death. Many sections of this book explore land and home-ownership and the evolution of real estate policy, telling somewhat chronologically what occurred in this important wealth-building area that left Black Americans so far behind white Americans. We set those storylines in Atlanta.

Economically, Atlanta had larger groups of well-off Black Americans than many other cities for much of modern history. The city was central to the Civil Rights Movement, and city leaders had pushed for the inclusion of Black business owners in the awarding of city contracts. By 2020, Black Americans had become a major force in city government and in local policymaking, and Atlanta had long been called the Black Mecca.

Still, in 2020, the Black-white wealth gap was an important undercurrent in Atlanta's racial demonstrations, with protestors pointing to the gap between the city's reputation as the Black Mecca and the day-in, day-out reality for many Black Americans living there. In a 2022 study of large cities, Atlanta would be ranked as the city with the nation's highest income inequality. It was driven by, the local paper would say, "the city's entrenched racial disparities which took root generations ago."

A Better World

We undertook our reporting for this book with optimism. We looked to Atlanta and to Greenwood Bank as case studies in the progress that might occur. Atlanta had a head start on the rest of the country, it seemed, due to its relatively large Black upper class; and nationally, there was momentum for greater support for Black Americans following the murder of George Floyd. Greenwood, based in Atlanta but marketed nationally, seemed like a promising engine for change. It was founded in 2020 by such luminaries as former Atlanta mayor Andrew Young and the rapper Killer Mike, and it was named after the once-booming Greenwood business district in Tulsa, Oklahoma. It drew on the proud legacy of Black banking, especially banks like Freedom National Bank, once run by baseball star Jackie Robinson. On top of all that, Greenwood's marketing played up the company's promise to eradicate the Black-white wealth gap.

We followed along with Greenwood's founders and its customers through extensive interviews. And we added our names to Greenwood's customer waiting list and then, once let in, we registered a bank account so we could keep abreast of the institution's developments. But over the next few years, it became clear that Greenwood was more complicated than we had expected.

Greenwood's trajectory became more muddled as there was a push and pull in society for and against progress. Just as Greenwood was gaining traction, the public was becoming more polarized on racial equity programs. A pushback against diversity efforts within companies grew, and the U.S. Supreme Court banned affirmative action in education in 2023. It was dizzying—the pushback grew even as state and city reparations programs gained their greatest traction ever. Books addressing diversity were being banned at the same time that they were most in demand among some people. Efforts like Greenwood's mission to close the Black-white wealth gap increasingly sat squat in the middle of a divisive ideological battle.

Beyond the broader polarization, we came to realize that "closing the Black-white wealth gap" meant different things to different people. In particular, among Greenwood's founders and customers, we saw that beyond the Black-white wealth gap, there was also a Black-Black wealth gap. Black Atlantans who had "made it" had lifestyles and opportunities far removed from those of other Black families in the Atlanta area, even as those wealthier Black individuals served as evidence, to some observers, that Black economic progress was on track. But as affirmative action and other policies came under question, the role of class within the debates on race also became clearer.

As we researched what should occur to help create more opportunities for Black Americans, we kept running into solutions that would help primarily Black Americans at the top. This made us question what exactly advocates of closing racial wealth gaps hoped would occur when they said the Black-white wealth gap should be closed. If only the Black elite got richer and richer, mirroring the extreme wealth of the white elite, would that fulfill what companies like Greenwood had set out to achieve? Such a shift could "close the racial wealth gap" while still maintaining two Black Americas. In statistical terms, putting more wealth into the hands of a few Black Americans could close the "mean" (or average) Black-white wealth gap while still leaving a large racial divide between median (or typical) Black and white families. Examining exactly what businesspeople like the Greenwood founders meant when they said they wanted to close the Black-white gap became a driving force for us. Headlines and hype do not always translate into widespread results.

What was clear to us throughout our reporting was that most of the Black Americans we interviewed viewed closing the Black-white gap as an effort that should help *all* Black Americans. From James Lovelace, who just wanted steady support to build a BBQ business; to Tandreia Dixon, who tattooed "Dream Big" on her arm and hoped her expensive university degrees would enable her to build financial freedom; to Brook Bacon, who wanted to see people in rural Georgia, where his father was killed, be treated more fairly by the system; to James Woodall, who wanted to work among Black social change leaders at places like the NAACP but couldn't afford to—all these individuals lived in various parts of the Black economic spectrum, but none was at the very top. They wanted the gap closed not just for themselves but for their cousins, their classmates, and their communities.

Like them, we knew there had to be something better than a world of fifteen cents on the dollar.

CHAPTER 1

MEET GREENWOOD BANK

Remember that every time you #SwipeGreenwood, you help close the wealth gap and create generational wealth in the Black community.

—Greenwood Bank advertisement

Ryan Glover was still riding high from the sale of Bounce TV, the television network he had cofounded with Dr. Martin Luther King Jr.'s son. He was enjoying retirement and spending more time with his family. He thought he might coach kids' football, now that he had the time. One of his sons, also named Ryan Glover, was rising in the ranks as a quarterback at the University of Pennsylvania.

Based in Atlanta, Ryan had been an active player in celebrity circles for more than two decades, first as a music producer and then as a television executive. An aggressive negotiator, he had fought his share of contentious business deals yet remained well networked among Black celebrities and Black political circles. He had been in the headlines years earlier when his eleven-year-old son was run over and killed by a Jet Ski while in a lake, after which Ryan and his ex-wife (a celebrity stylist who was also the ex-wife of the rapper Usher) fought vigorously for justice. Middle-aged now, with a beard and a genteel style, Ryan had become a social media influencer along with his new wife, with the two posting photos of their glitzy fashion- and travel-filled lives. Ryan often spoke in a hoarse voice, probably from talking over all the loud social gatherings the two attended.

To celebrate his fiftieth birthday in early 2020, Ryan traveled to South Africa for a safari party. It was just as the Covid-19 lockdown was beginning in the United States and months before Americans would refocus on racial justice following the killing of George Floyd. Ryan and friends partied in Cape Town; hiked to the Cape of Good Hope, jumping out from behind rocks to startle one another; and ventured in search of impalas, gazelles, and giraffes in an open-air Land Cruiser operated by their hotel, the Royal Malewane, one of the most elite hotels in the Greater Kruger National Park and, reportedly, a favorite spot for Elton John. Even as the world focused on the spreading coronavirus, Ryan and his friends enjoyed the big life. "#NoFearHere," one of them posted on social media.

In attendance on the safari were several well-connected, wealthy Black Americans from Atlanta, where Ryan lived, including a Black technology investor who often hosted start-up battles in the city that attracted budding companies and aspiring entrepreneurs; and his girlfriend, a woman featured on the *Real Housewives of Atlanta* reality television program.

In a private moment, the investor sat with Ryan to tell him he was too young to retire and that he should put his connections within Black culture to use for good. "You have far too many resources and relationships in the culture to just swim off into the abyss and not utilize your relationships or resources to help the culture," he said. "You can't just walk off into the sunset."

Ryan asked, "Well, what do we do?"

"Have you heard of neobanking?" the friend replied.

Ryan had not heard of it. So he started researching this subsection of financial services that eschews brick-and-mortar locations in favor of digital-only mobile banking. At the same time, he reflected on his family's life. His grandmother had used her mattress as her safe-deposit box. Other relatives had lost land to white people in Oklahoma. He also reflected on his own path to founding a record label and a television network, both of which he had funded with personal capital and by turning to friends and family, rather than seeking out banks. "I never even thought about using financial institutions' money to build any of the businesses," he recalled. In contrast, he added, "I have friends who are non–African Americans who *only* use banking capital to build their businesses and their brands."

Ryan's wheels were turning. The conversation during his safari party, he realized, had "stimulated something very ancestrally important," and it was "forcing me to start Greenwood."

*   *   *

Michael Render had moved just south of Atlanta in recent years to a comfortable but not lavish home off a country road. But when he visited his sister, he retraced steps to his grandparents' home in the city. The modest house sits inside a historic Black community near the corner of Collier Drive NW and Hamilton E. Holmes Drive. It is part of Collier Heights, a historic Black neighborhood built by Black developers in the mid-1900s, with Black financing and for Black residents. This was where Michael grew up and became the rapper-activist-businessman better known as Killer Mike.

After breaking through at a young age on the OutKast album *Stankonia*, Michael had found his groove in rap music as partner to a white rapper in a group called Run the Jewels. He had also found his groove in the national discourse as a cheerleader for Atlanta and for liberal politicians like Bernie Sanders. He routinely took stands on police brutality, free speech in music, gun laws, marijuana, and systemic racism through intellectual writings and news talk shows and also through his searing, history-laden lyrics. He was a powerfully built person with a commanding presence. He invested in vintage cars as a hobby and in businesses in Atlanta as a passion. Unlike the swanky attire of Ryan Glover, Michael often dressed in baggy pants and a baggy T-shirt, usually all in one color. What stood out about his appearance were his chunky necklaces, bright sneakers, and warm, welcoming smile.

Michael's childhood home in Collier Heights offered him a comfortable upbringing, but it was on the edge of poorer areas. Just a few hundred yards away, as of the 2020s, was the Berean Outreach Ministry, a food and clothing pantry that provided help to eight hundred local families a week.

One summer afternoon in 2022, twenty-five cars were lined up outside the pantry, so many that they overflowed into a lot across the street. We wanted to see what residents of Michael's childhood stomping grounds were experiencing in their financial lives.

It was a sorry picture. A man who called himself Lamar May, sixty-five and retired, said he owned a home and was on a fixed income. He had learned about the Berean food pantry from a homeless man who lived near the edge of his property. Santrella Brinkley, fifty-four and a mother of three, said she was homeless; she was in line that day for clothing, food, and anything she might offer to friends and family who were providing her with a place to sleep. Shecky Benham, fifty-two, worked in security, but he supported his father and helped support his nephew, who had just finished college and was looking for work. Benham owned his home and his Nissan Altima, but he was having trouble making ends meet, in part due to rising grocery prices. "Chicken is expensive," he said. "Last week, I think they had leg quarters. So, every little bit that you can save here can definitely help you, you know, pay other things, whether or not you're going to divert that money toward paying the bills."

Lecario Glass stood out to us. At twenty-three, he was far younger than the others in line, and he was at the food pantry for the first time. Until recently, he had been living with his mother and could find food at her place, but now he was on his own. He didn't have a particular item in mind that he needed—anything would help, so long as it fit into the storage space under the seat on his bright-yellow scooter. Glass was proud to be out on his own and to be able to pay the rent on a one-bedroom apartment, just around the corner, on Martin Luther King Jr. Drive SW. It had been a difficult few years, though he had been able to hold down jobs. During the Covid-19 pandemic, his job at a Dollar Tree was considered "essential" and was not cut. By the time we met him at the food pantry, Glass was working at AutoZone. He knew more about cars than many car owners. "I don't have a car, but I know how to change everybody's batteries," he said. "They pay me ten dollars an hour to change everybody's battery."

He made a point of saying he was going to change jobs soon. Money mattered to Glass, and he was trying to make careful financial choices to advance in life, he said. Like his choice of transportation:

he was riding an Eagle-150cc scooter, and because it didn't go as fast as an automobile, he believed he didn't need to get a license to ride it, or insurance. And he didn't regularly use a bank. He had opened an account a while back with Wells Fargo, but he had yet to use it. "I'm out on my own, but I'm taking baby steps," he said. "As long as you take any steps, it matters."

MLK Drive, where Glass lived, was one of the places that tended to get Michael Render talking. Certain topics and places got Michael stirred up, we found in conversations with him, and this street was one of them. "Martin Luther King Jr. Drive, where I grew up, is now absent a bank," the rapper told us. "As they build new Chases around Atlanta, in the Midtown area, they're taking Chases out of the west side of Atlanta, which is a shame to me."

It wasn't all that long ago that Michael had himself worked at Auto-Zone. In fact, he often brought up the auto parts chain in conversation to underscore his working-class roots. Explaining his first reaction to Ryan Glover's idea to create a digital bank, Michael told us, "I have been that person making two hundred bucks working at AutoZone, so I instantly understood. . . . It allows people who had used check-cashing places to stop being fleeced. So, you make a two-hundred-dollar check, and if you're being charged, you know, twenty percent of what it costs to cash a check, you'd be charged forty bucks. You walk out with one hundred sixty bucks. That keeps you right there, right there at poverty. I can't save anything."

Michael trusted Ryan, noting that he had "an impeccable business reputation." He had known Ryan for years from the music business. How, exactly? "Black people in music who sing and dance hang out in Atlanta," he said simply. Ryan had shared his business smarts over the years with Michael and other rappers. "He was one of the guys who helped us understand what we were doing," Michael said. "You know, we were just happy to get one-hundred-and-some thousand dollars and buy a new car and then party. He was the guy that was telling us, 'You should be investing, you should be thinking about this . . . you should think of yourself as a brand.'"

Beyond Michael's musical career in which, as Killer Mike—so named for "killing" the microphone—he had alternately alienated and endeared himself to people by wearing T-shirts that read, "Kill Your Masters," he had also helped lead a modern movement around Black banking. This pulled on ideas that have come in and out of vogue many times in history, as Black Americans have toggled between setting up their own institutions and trying to meld into white ones. Michael's involvement with banking started in a big way in the summer of 2014, after a New York City police officer killed Eric Garner on a sidewalk in Staten Island using an illegal choke hold. In response, Michael called on other musicians, like T.I., Young Dolph, and Usher, to help him encourage people to move their money to Black-owned banks, arguing that money talked.

As of 2014, there were only 24 Black-owned banks out of 5,607 banks in the United States, and this figure would fall over the next decade. But in advocating for Black ownership of banks, Michael was joining a social dialogue that, for a century and a half, has raised foundational questions about the mission of banks in general. It is a discussion that goes as far back as Frederick Douglass, the nineteenth-century abolitionist who noted that a Reconstruction-era bank aimed at Black people was supposed to "show our people the road to a share of the wealth and well-being of the world."

For Michael, Black banking was a form of social protest. "There are two things you can do to get America's attention," he told us. "You can affect money, and you can affect through violence. This country has been formed from money and violence. And that's not just Black people . . . That's since the original thirteen colonies that were meant to send money back to the United Kingdom. At some point, those people, as a form of protest, said, 'No, and we're willing to be violent to help you explicitly understand "no."'" So, money and violence have a peculiar marriage in this country."

Michael said that while his "gut" wanted violence—"because there's nothing like an 'eye for an eye' to help you understand how much you hurt me"—he knew it "wasn't the right thing to do. It simply sets Black people up to be slaughtered by the state. The right thing to do to get the state's attention was to move money."

Michael was proud of what he and others had accomplished back in 2014. They had urged Black Americans to move their money into Black-owned banks like Citizens Trust, an Atlanta-based bank founded in 1921 that Michael remembered his grandparents using when he was a child. "We got so much money moved to Citizens Trust that Wells Fargo started a sixty-million-dollar Black mortgage program. We moved so much money that we saw big banks start to pay attention," he said.

It's not clear if Wells Fargo and other banks took action in direct response to the Black banking movement, but the whole experience was energizing to Michael. This time around, in 2020 with Greenwood Bank, he would not just be a cheerleader; he would be an owner. "What really made me jump on board," he said, "is ownership. You know, they didn't just offer me 'Here's a sponsorship.' No. They said, 'We want you as part of the board and ownership.'"

On top of that, Michael's longtime mentor, Atlanta's former two-term mayor, Andrew Young, was involved. The rapper and the politician talked about it and, for a model, turned to digital banking businesses in India that had helped masses of people with banking cards that were simple and cheap to use. Michael decided to move forward. "I said, 'Okay, this makes sense as a card,'" he told us. "It beats the check-cashing places and liquor stores. It allows people to partner with us, real banks, and get people real accounts to start to build real financial literacy. It allows people to really build credit."

* * *

Andrew Young and his son, Andrew Young III, lived on opposite ends of Atlanta. The elder Andrew lived in an unassuming ranch-style house on the west side, where Black Americans had moved in the middle of the twentieth century as the city's neighborhoods became more segregated.

His namesake, who goes by "Bo," lived in Buckhead, on the other side of the city, in Atlanta's northwest corner. Buckhead has some of the city's most expensive real estate and counts many prominent white business leaders as residents.

A drive through Bo's neighborhood in 2022 showed us that he lived in a divided community. Every few houses had signs in their yard advocating that Buckhead should secede from Atlanta and become its own city. The issue was highly controversial within Buckhead and in the broader Atlanta area. On the one hand, Buckhead had not always been part of Atlanta: a large area with its own commercial district and heavily white population, it was annexed in the 1950s as part of Atlanta's white mayor's efforts to ensure the city's population included a large group of white voters. On the other hand, for Buckhead to leave Atlanta in the 2020s would eat into Atlanta's tax base. The debate over the Buckhead secession had racial connotations, too, given that Buckhead sat on the edge of a city that had long been called the Black Mecca.

Bo Young's seven-bedroom house, featuring a castle-like turret, stands back from the street, with a driveway that dips down and around to the house a bit like a concrete moat. When we were there, Bo had a sign in his yard supporting the election for U.S. Senate of Raphael Warnock, the pastor at Ebenezer Baptist Church, where Martin Luther King Jr.'s father was a longtime minister—but no sign supporting Buckhead's secession.

Bo was a businessman and also sometimes the link between his father and businesses. He had helped launch Bounce TV with Ryan Glover by bringing in his father and Martin Luther King III as well-known founders who could legitimize the new Black TV network and draw publicity. And as the summer of 2020 got going, he was actively involved in discussions around Greenwood Bank, where he would become a board member. Father and son, clearly close, mutually respectful, and similar in their preppy appearances, with close-cut hair and light skin, were in fact quite different from each other. While Andrew was a perennial ambassador comfortable in the spotlight, Bo worked hard to avoid attention. Andrew had centered his life's work on social progress, continuing what he viewed as the important missions of the Civil Rights Movement; Bo had centered his life on building wealth in order to free himself, he told us, to spend time with his family. Money, to him, bought time.

The name "Greenwood" appealed to all the founders. It was a nod to the Greenwood business district in Tulsa, Oklahoma, where in 1921, successful Black-owned businesses and Black people were attacked by a white mob in what has come to be called the Tulsa Race Massacre. More than memorializing that tragedy, the name also suggested a return to the grand promise of the historical Greenwood. Known as the "Black Wall Street," the Greenwood district had been a thriving community in every sense before its destruction. It had many banks, businesses, and well-off homeowners as well as a robust Black-owned newspaper, the *Tulsa Star*. It was the success of this community on its own terms, despite the rising injustices of the Jim Crow era, that had inspired Ryan to settle on the name "Greenwood Bank."

Greenwood's founders all liked the idea of innovating using digital technology. They wouldn't simply be catching up to white businesspeople with a Black-owned bank. Rather, because traditional banking had not worked well for many Black Americans, they wanted to create something new and tech-savvy. They would focus heavily on mobile technology, building community among customers, and marketing Black-owned businesses around the country. They hoped to loan money to Black individuals and Black businesses, feeding directly into Black wealth. They liked the idea of "neobanking," and digital-only mobile banking. Their hope was that their new approaches could be as transformative as microfinance had been in India. For them, the American version of microfinance would be a platform that created economic equality across races.

Andrew Young had long believed there could not be racial justice without economic equality, he told us. The bank intrigued him as a legacy project as he approached ninety years old. (In July 2020, he was eighty-eight.) All his years as a Civil Rights leader, politician, and diplomat had convinced him that race and money were inseparable. "Slavery was about money," he told us. "Slaves were actually monetized. So, they were 'a money.'" He continued with a reference to Martin Luther King Jr., with whom he had spent much of the 1960s as a key partner in the Civil Rights Movement. "One of Martin's phrases was 'It's a cruel thing just to monetize a people as money and don't let them make any themselves.'"

Business-wise, the moment of 2020 seemed right to create Greenwood Bank. Many Americans were searching for new ways to make the world more fair and equitable. The streets of Atlanta and other cities had been full of demonstrators upset over the murder of George Floyd. The Black-white wealth gap was glaring and was not improving.

As the summer of 2020 continued, and Greenwood's founders developed their plans, Andrew raised a concern with his cofounders Ryan Glover and Michael Render. Where would Greenwood Bank get its start-up capital, and would he be expected to contribute? "Look, I can't keep up with you guys. I will be your adviser and your mentor. But I don't have this kind of money to be a part of Greenwood," he told them. "Remember, I didn't make but fifty thousand dollars a year for eight years as mayor."

"Damn," Michael replied.

"What's the matter?" the former mayor asked.

"My wife made me turn down a gig for that much money that was one week, because she didn't want me to travel," Michael said. "In one week, I turned down that much money."

For our part, as soon as we heard about Greenwood Bank, we decided to watch its progress, to learn everything we could about the historic, personal, and financial forces that had brought together this rapper, this entertainment executive, and this longtime politician–Civil Rights leader. Would they be able to use banking to tackle the Black-white wealth gap? Would their hopes and hard work add up to any widespread progress for Black Americans? What would someone looking to solve the Black-white wealth gap need to know about the gap's history and its present reality?

CHAPTER 2

MICHAEL RENDER AND THE FRACTURING OF A CITY

Blacks . . . should be quarantined in isolated slums in order to reduce the incidents of civil disturbance, to prevent the spread of communicable disease into the nearby white neighborhoods, and to protect property values among the white majority.
—J. Barry Mahool, mayor of Baltimore, 1910

Four days after George Floyd was killed, Michael Render joined Atlanta's mayor, Keisha Lance Bottoms, in a televised press conference. The rapper had been posting on social media over the past week, but even as large demonstrations broke out in his hometown, this was his first public speech about what had occurred.

The mayor opened by condemning the tenor of the demonstrations, especially the recent vandalization of CNN's headquarters, and encouraging people to funnel their frustrations into voting, not vandalism.

Then Michael Render came onstage. He wore a chunky gold necklace and a black T-shirt with prominent white letters that read "Kill Your Masters." The mayor and police chief flanked him. "I didn't want to come, and I don't want to be here," Michael said slowly. "I'm the son of an Atlanta city police officer," he continued. "My cousin is an Atlanta city police officer. And my other cousin, an East Point police officer. And I got a lot of love and respect for the police officers down to the 'original eight,'" he said, referring to the first Black officers in Atlanta, "that, even after becoming police, had to dress in a YMCA because white officers didn't want to get dressed with niggers. And here we are, eighty years later, and I watched a white officer assassinate a Black man." He started to cry and wiped away a tear.

"I know that tore your heart out, and I know it's crippling," he continued. "I am duty bound to be here to simply say that it is your duty not to burn your own house down for anger with an enemy. It is your duty to fortify your own house so that you may be a house of refuge in times of organization. And now is the time to plot, plan, strategize, organize, and mobilize."

His speech continued for eight minutes. It captured Michael's boundary-breaking way of communicating. Within seconds, he moved from discussing the racism in a speech made by the vice president of the Confederacy to comparing the officer who had killed George Floyd to a wild animal. "He casually put his knee on a human being's neck for nine minutes as he died," Michael said, "like a zebra in the clutch of a lion's jaw."

Michael called for systemic change. "We don't want to see one officer charged," he said. "We want to see four officers prosecuted and sentenced. We don't want to see Targets burning, we want to see the system that sets up for systemic racism burnt to the ground." And he called out the power of consumer boycotts to effect change. "Atlanta said, 'Coca-Cola, we love you. But if you don't pull out of South Africa, we're gonna leave. We're not gonna drink Coca-Cola anymore' . . . and apartheid ended."

Celebrities watching online reacted in real time. "MANDATORY LIS-TEN!!!" LeBron James tweeted. "@KillerMike always on point!" tweeted comedian Sarah Silverman. "@KillerMike is a leader I hope to vote for one day." And Qasim Rashid, then running for Congress in Virginia, tweeted, "This is mandatory viewing. You won't regret it."

Some non-celebrity listeners felt Michael Render spoke on their behalf, and some felt he didn't, which was fitting for a man who makes a point of telling people to think about who speaks for them. Ment Nelson, a Black artist in South Carolina, posted, "The whole country needs to stop right now and listen to Killer Mike. He's verbalizing what a lot of us don't know how to express." Others weren't so positive: "Killer Mike, usually I respect you but not this time. Forget all that. Stop burning stores and burn government buildings and police stations. Burn police cars and beat any officer that tries to detain one of you."

Still emotional, Michael concluded his remarks, saying, "We have to be better than this moment. We have to be better than burning down our own homes, because if we lose Atlanta, what else have we got?"

Michael Render was speaking to the world and to his neighbors, and he was speaking to Black Americans. His presence onstage that day, saying those words, brought us into his and his family's story, which goes back more than 160 years and ends in Atlanta—and which, along the way, traces the contours of injustice embedded in the Black-white wealth gap. The rapper-businessman-activist descended from families who were *expropriated* in the worst possible sense of the word, as enslaved people. They were then *excluded* from equal access to schools, neighborhoods, and other public benefits because of their race. They were *exploited* as sharecroppers, in workplaces, and by financial institutions. Their land, in some cases, and even their bodies would be *expropriated* for years to come.

All this took place, across generations, in and around a city sometimes known as the Black Mecca. To walk Atlanta's streets in the 2020s with Michael Render's history in mind is to dig back into our country's legacy of slavery, the fits and starts of racial progress, and the debates over integration that have played out for more than 150 years in this city.

The Path to Segregation

Atlanta has been significant to the entire history of our country on issues of race and money. Before the Civil War, Atlanta had a small Black population, because enslavers were generally based in rural areas of the state. Of the 400,000 enslaved people in Georgia at the end of slavery, only about 2,500 lived in Atlanta as of 1863 (along with about 25 free Black residents).

In the post–Civil War years, all this changed rapidly. Recently freed slaves marched proudly with General William Sherman when he arrived in Atlanta in 1864. Many resettled in the city. Over time, these new residents were joined by an influx of f formerly enslaved people who had been working on Georgia's farms, as scores of new factories and mills opened in Atlanta and drought and depression hit rural Georgia.

By the 1880s, Atlanta began generating attention as a place that had a plan for moving forward. "The New South," an expression coined in 1886 by the managing editor of the *Atlanta Constitution* newspaper, Henry Grady, became a tagline for progress in the minds of many public figures and businesspeople. It was an idea meant to bring harmony among old southern white residents, white businesspeople migrating in from the North, and also the formerly enslaved. The nickname urged harmony without equality. As Henry Grady said, "The supremacy of the white race of the South must be maintained forever, and the domination of the Negro race resisted at all points and at all hazards because the white race is the superior race. . . . [This declaration] shall run forever with the blood that feeds Anglo-Saxon hearts."

Atlanta would, nevertheless, be the seat of important moments in Black intellectual history. It was there in 1895 that Booker T. Washington delivered what came to be called the Atlanta Compromise, saying, "In all things that are purely social we can be as separate as the fingers, yet one as the hand in all things essential to mutual progress." It was a statement that many took as advocacy for segregation. Part of the intellectual nexus was the burgeoning group of Black-focused universities set up in Atlanta in the decades following the war. These universities, now known as HBCUs, for Historically Black Colleges and Universities, were able to educate some Black Americans over time, though many Black Americans did not have enough elementary and high school education to attend.

W. E. B. Du Bois taught at one of Atlanta's Black universities, and he strongly disagreed with Booker T. Washington's advice that Black Americans remain separate. Thus began a long-running dispute among Black leaders about how much Black businesspeople and workers should integrate versus create their own enterprises. Du Bois had mixed feelings about the city, and he famously used the word *Atalanta* in an essay about the corruption of race in America. The word, which means "equal in weight" in Greek, was also the name for the Greek goddess who would only marry someone who could outdo her. When Du Bois wrote that "swarthy Atalanta, tall and wild, would marry only him who out-raced her," the implication was that the city, which Du Bois said should have been named after the goddess (it wasn't), was overly interested in status, wealth, and materialism.

Today, Atlanta is a place where racial lines often run smack-dab in the middle of crosswalks. The crosswalk leading to Michael Render's childhood home sits on Hamilton E. Holmes Drive NW, a street named after the first Black man to attend the University of Georgia. Before Holmes made his historic move into the state university in 1961, the street was called Hightower Road. This was, in the 1950s, a border between white and Black Atlanta.

While Atlanta's leaders desperately tried to control who lived where, life on the ground revealed a community in turmoil. A typical story just off Hightower Road: On a Saturday in February 1956, Jewell Stewart Jr. moved into a new home. A thirty-one-year-old father, Stewart had paid eight thousand dollars to purchase the small A-frame house, with two thousand dollars down. This was a hefty amount for an auto parts worker, but Stewart wanted space for his wife and five-year-old daughter. His family was among five Black families who had just purchased in the neighborhood, even though it was a "contested area" in which it was unclear whether Blacks would be welcomed. The Stewarts were the first Black family to move in, and their move came after a hard month—their daughter had been out of school three weeks with scarlet fever. Now, finally, it seemed that a new phase had begun for them. Their boxes arrived, and they started unpacking, dreaming of their future and taking comfort in knowing that within weeks, another Black family would be residing across the street. That first day, they ate dinner and settled in for the night.

Hours later, there was a boom. "I was in the house when the bomb exploded. We had the blinds closed and couldn't see who did it," Stewart said at the time. Some two hundred white people quickly gathered outside his house. By the next day, the number of people gathered had grown to six hundred.

Stewart rushed his daughter to a friend's home for safety. Then he took his wife to a doctor; shell-shocked, she had to be carried because her nerves were too bad for her to walk on her own. He called his boss at work that Monday and said he couldn't come in. Then he started trying to figure out if he could get his money back and move his family away.

White residents in the neighborhood, meanwhile, were on a witch hunt to figure out who had sold the house to the Stewarts. Many pointed fingers at up-and-coming, Black-run real estate firms. Some white residents called Black brokers and asked if they'd come sell their houses, too—they said they wanted to leave if the dominant race of the neighborhood was changing. The furor over who was to blame for the Stewarts' home purchase became so intense that the local city planning officer felt he had to clarify the matter. The Stewarts' house, he told the local paper, "was sold by a white firm. I think the story was unfair in placing the responsibility on Negro dealers."

Decades later, the incident remained a sore point in family memories. When we reached out to one of Stewart's children to discuss it, she replied, "STOP." The family sold the house just two months after purchasing it, to the West Side Development Company, which then took sixteen years to resell it. It would be two years before the Stewart family purchased a new home.

A few blocks to the west of the Stewarts' house is 2615 Collier Drive NW. There, back from the road, stands a one-story 1,056-square-foot white house with light-blue trim. A magnolia tree and carefully maintained plants line the yard. Built in 1950, the house was purchased by a Black family in 1954, as white residents fled to the other side of the Hightower Road divide. This is the home Killer Mike grew up in long before "Killer" was attached to his name.

Collier Heights was developed in the late 1940s, after decades of significant debate over what local residents declared to be the proper, and improper, places for Black Americans to live—and after an earlier history that was less segregated. Following the post–Civil War influx of both white and Black residents, Atlanta's booming industrial companies built housing for their new workers, but by the 1890s, investor money poured in to build rentals. At that time, Black residents made

up about 40 percent of Atlanta's population, which almost tripled between 1880 and 1906, and rentals were common for the working class,
no matter their race. Rather than steering Black workers to different
neighborhoods, property owners often designated certain houses right
next to each other as being for either Black or white renters. Black
residents lived in all four quadrants of Atlanta in both 1891 and 1899,
and on almost every block, according to in-depth studies of housing
maps by urban historian LeeAnn Lands. This was in a period that
preceded segregation-focused zoning rules and restrictive covenants in
deeds. And that meant there were not many large single-race neighborhoods in the city at the time.

Atlanta at the turn of the twentieth century was, as Lands put it, "a
city unconcerned with residential segregation, neighborhood aesthetics and property control." Though Black Americans were far from even
in their footing with white Atlantans, this was a time when the city
was not yet outrightly *excluding* Black Americans from living in particular neighborhoods. This changed fairly abruptly following the race
riot of 1906, an event that has never left Atlanta's collective memory.

On the night of Saturday, September 22 of that year, after an intense month of conflict over disputed attacks on local white women, a
mass of white people, mostly men, gathered in downtown Atlanta at
Five Points, a convergence of thoroughfares that is generally considered the center of town. The men discussed lynchings and other possible acts of violence against Black residents. The mayor heard about the
gathering and came out and encouraged people to go home. A voice
rang out telling the mayor to go home himself, adding, "We're going
to get some niggers!"

At least five thousand white men gathered that night, the former
editor in chief of *Atlanta Magazine*, Rebecca Burns, wrote in *Rage
in the Gate City*, a detailed history of the riots. The men killed dozens of Black men—local shopkeepers, commuters on streetcars, and
passersby—by beating, shooting, stabbing, and slaying them with axes,
glass bottles, and knives. Black businesses, where success had been
hard-earned, were destroyed. The attacks continued the next few days
and spread to an Atlanta suburb and to Brownsville, a neighborhood
of mainly Black residents near the Black universities. "What happened

during those days in September 1906 marks a shameful chapter in white Atlanta's history, and a painful one for Black Atlanta," Burns wrote. "Its impact is etched into the city's streets and into Atlantans' collective experience."

Black business leaders in the following years began creating businesses that were more Black-focused, clustered on Auburn Avenue, to provide for their own in ways white businesses were not doing. Prominent among them would be Heman E. Perry, who in 1908 would move to Atlanta and set up influential Black-owned businesses, including an insurance business, a bank that would later become Citizens Trust Bank, and a printing company whose equipment would later print early editions of the *Atlanta Daily World*. The result of the 1906 riots was a stronger form of neighborhood segregation that would have a lasting effect in Atlanta.

This was kicked off in part by a meeting on the Tuesday morning after the attacks. The city organized the meeting and spoke about it in the *Constitution* as being open to "prominent citizens." Seven prominent Black businessmen and ministers were included in the meeting, along with a group of white politicians and businessmen. The group agreed that the Black attendees would work to convince their communities to be "good Negroes," and the white attendees said the police would protect them. The Black leaders urged the white leaders to ease some Jim Crow restrictions—a wish that would not come to fruition. In fact, Jim Crow gained momentum following the attacks, and new rules would be added—like one restricting restaurants from serving both white and Black diners—over the next few years. These rules played a strong role in segregating Black and white money.

The lasting result would be that members of Atlanta's Black elite were left divided over the right way to move forward to raise economic prospects for their communities—whether to build their own institutions or attempt to meld into white businesses and neighborhoods. Some white residents, meanwhile, took it upon themselves to establish racial boundaries. In 1910, a group of white residents in a neighborhood in central Atlanta met up at the city's Grace Methodist Church and issued a written notice. It read:

Whereas, we deem it for the best interest of both the white people and the colored people that there be a separation of the races and that, in the interest of friendship and harmony, the limits should be defined within which it is proper that each should reside....

[It was] therefore resolved by the citizens of the portion of the Fourth Ward known as "Jackson Hill" that the following boundary line be and that it is hereby drawn within which it shall not be proper for Negroes to reside, or own, or rent property except as servants or as tenants on the rear of the premises of white owners.

This particular resolution, similar to others that would follow, listed the streets along the boundary and noted that the information would be distributed to all local real estate agents.

These residents were charting boundaries at a time when public thinking about property use was evolving. City planning didn't emerge as a discipline or a major feature of public governance until the 1910s. In some ways, the very idea of urban planning went against the very American values of individualism and the right to do as you please with your own property.

Racial segregation was a factor in the new urban planning from day one. Early movers included New York City, Baltimore, and Washington. In Baltimore in 1910, after a Black family moved onto the all-white McCulloh Street and vandalism ensued, a white neighbor took an idea for a residential segregation law to the City Council. The law, passed later that year, was the first of its kind in the United States. It said that Black residents could not move onto city blocks that were more than half white; it also banned white residents from moving onto largely Black blocks.

The City of Atlanta jumped into the fray in 1913 with its first segregation ordinance, which prescribed the race for each city block. In 1917, however, the U.S. Supreme Court ruled segregation ordinances unconstitutional, and Atlanta looked for other means. It found an answer in zoning.

With zoning, the city would be dictating property usage rules without passing segregation laws per se. New York City passed its first significant zoning ordinances in 1916, and a central group of planning experts traveled city to city helping various cities map out their land use. In 1918, Harland Bartholomew, the nation's first full-time city planner, who started in Newark but quickly ended up in St. Louis, became an evangelist for the practice. Bartholomew invited the likes of landscape architect Frederick Law Olmsted and Herbert Swan, the executive secretary for zoning in New York City, to St. Louis to discuss land use in light of the Supreme Court's decision. As Bartholomew explained at a gathering, one of "the biggest things that brought zoning about in St. Louis" was that residential districts were "invaded" by colored people and boardinghouses.

Atlanta moved more aggressively to create zoning rules in 1922 by hiring a consultant named Robert Whitten. Whitten had been a member of New York City's zoning committee and had just completed a plan in Cleveland. Whitten's views on race and zoning were openly stated. "Home neighborhoods had to be protected from any further damage to values resulting from inappropriate uses, including the encroachment of the colored race," he wrote to Atlanta officials. His manual for Atlanta said that "race zoning is essential in the interest of public peace, order and security and will promote the welfare and prosperity of both the white and colored race." Whitten's map broke up areas of the city into racial zones: "colored" and "undetermined."

Once again, the courts intervened. Two years later, Georgia's Supreme Court ruled that race-based zoning was illegal. Still, the ruling didn't really matter in practice. Whitten's racial map was cemented as a model that Atlanta officials and the real estate industry continued to follow.

As time went by, Atlanta began to look more and more like Whitten's map. When Black residents moved into "undetermined" or "white" neighborhoods, white residents there were highly divided over what to do. In the mid-1920s, Bankhead, a neighborhood slightly west of downtown Atlanta, became a point of focus. Whitten's map had designated the area for white residents, but some white residents wanted to have freedom to rent their properties to Black tenants. A woman named Alice Link had to go to court to get a restraint on city zoning rules (that were still being enforced despite the Georgia Supreme Court ruling) so that she could rent a home she owned to a Black family.

Twenty-three years later, in 1947, Bankhead remained in turmoil. Three blocks from Alice Link's home, dynamite was thrown onto a new Black resident's porch on Ashby Street. The attacks continued for months on houses purchased by Black residents, with multiple homes hit on some nights. In one instance, about two dozen windows of homes near the Black-owned houses were knocked out by a bomb.

These sorts of attacks were happening all over the country, and Black community news outlets regularly covered them. Within days of the Ashby Street bombing in 1947, a Black-owned newspaper reported another incident, in Knoxville, Tennessee. There, local residents had placed a twelve-foot-tall burning cross on the lawn of a house that had recently been purchased by a Black physician. Using property values as a justification for harsh words and harsh actions—a financialization of ethics—the people involved in the Knoxville attack wrote to the physician:

> Your audacity of asserting your legal rights has, to our dismay, made us revert to primitive instincts.... The reason we can never feel good toward you is by the very fact that you are a Negro, which is no sin itself—but it is a fact that our property values took a slide.... Money might move you in, but money can't change your color.

Other Black home purchasers attacked by white mobs around this time included: Harvey and Johnetta Clark in 1951 in Cicero, Illinois; Wilbur Gary in 1952 in Richmond, California; Andrew and Charlotte Wade in 1954 in Shively, Kentucky, which is near Louisville; and Bill and Daisy Myers in 1957 in Levittown, Pennsylvania. And the attacks continued into recent decades. Robert and Martha Marshall's house in a white neighborhood in Louisville was firebombed when they moved in . . . in 1985.

In Atlanta, it was clear that white leaders had fixed ideas on where they wanted Black people to live, and they used public facilities, like schools, to put them there. In 1924, for instance, Atlanta opened Booker T. Washington High School, the first high school for Black Americans in the city. Before this, Black students had access to public education only through elementary school or, in a few cases, private high school. Booker T. Washington High was a political settlement of sorts—the city needed Black voters to support a bond issue, and it built the high school in exchange. The location, west of the city's center, changed where Black residents ended up living.

As Ethington Lewis, a longtime, original teacher at the high school, recalled, "The white power structure" picked the west side location for a reason. "That was the direction in which they wanted the Negroes to move," Lewis said in an interview in 1979. "If the Negroes had moved farther eastward he would run into a very fine white section called Inman Park, going to the area of Grant Park, out towards Decatur, out towards Ponce de Leon Avenue. That was where your rich white people were living. So, the only way that they figured that the Negroes should move was in the southwest section and you had all kinds of vacant land. . . . That was, naturally, the way in which the power structure wanted the Negro to move: away from the whites. And to tell you the truth, we weren't particular about moving into white areas anyways. All we wanted was some nice section in which to live and a good school."

A small Black neighborhood would later crop up around the new high school. The name of the neighborhood, which spoke to the land grab of the time, was "Just Us." A little over a mile west of that was Mozley Park, a neighborhood of Victorian-style homes built from 1920 to 1940. Mozley Park featured a twenty-eight-acre park complete with two ponds, large gardens, and a community center based in a stately mansion. Parks were designated as being for one race or another, and this was a "white park."

In 1948, a new home went up on the corner of Mozley Place and Chappell Road, just across the street from the park. The notable thing about this particular home was that it was being built by William A. Scott III, the son of the founder of the *Atlanta Daily World*, a Black-focused newspaper. Its construction came just as the U.S. Supreme Court was hearing a case on race-based housing covenants. Such provisions, which had been commonly inserted into home deeds since the early 1900s, forbade the owner of a home from selling it to a person of another race. The case before federal justices involved a Black couple from Missouri, the Shelleys, who had purchased a home in St. Louis, only to have a neighbor sue to block them from moving into it. That neighbor pointed to a covenant in the deed created in 1911 that banned "people of the Negro or Mongolian Race." The Supreme Court, acting with a partial bench—three justices had recused themselves due to, some have suggested, their ownership of homes that had race-based restrictions—ruled that private parties could abide by their own agreements. But, the Court said, the government would not enforce such covenants because doing so would be discriminatory and would violate the Equal Protection Clause of the Fourteenth Amendment.

The Supreme Court case was a positive development for equity in America: The government was not supposed to promote segregation and its exclusionary effects. But it was also utterly American to leave it up to individuals to govern their neighborhoods, an idea steeped in the logic that private citizens could do what they liked with private property. Not only has property ownership long been an American right (for white men), but protecting property *values* has been almost as sacred.

This elevation of "property value rights" fueled money-over-morals behavior. This would continue to be the case in Atlanta in neighborhoods like Mozley Park and other areas on the west side.

As the *Atlanta Daily World* founder's son settled into his home in Mozley Park, another notable Black resident moved in early the following year, 1949. William Weatherspool, a Baptist minister who had used his faith to reach across racial lines, moved to Mozley Drive with a steely determination to stay there. At this point, Black residents of Atlanta were increasingly buying homes—between 1940 and 1950, homeownership among the city's Black residents increased 117 percent, faster than it had for the white population—but by the end of the decade, the proportion of Black Atlantans who owned homes was still only 24 percent in contrast to 47 percent of white Atlantans. And most purchases were within a small subset of areas.

After Weatherspool moved to Mozley Drive, two hundred white residents stormed the Georgia governor's office. The governor was sympathetic to them and supported revoking the license of the broker who had sold the house to Weatherspool. Soon, with support from the governor (and despite the U.S. Supreme Court ruling), the Black real estate agent who had sold Weatherspool the house was arrested. His crime? Selling a home in an area not open to Black buyers. Next, the white residents stormed the mayor's office demanding rules that would "protect our homes." Many of them rallied around Weatherspool's home night after night, and police protection had to be brought in.

The Mozley Park protest was only one more entry in Atlanta's ugly history of neighborhood mob riots, but this incident marked a turn in the city's approach to racial segregation. The white mayor, William Hartsfield, created a biracial committee to set racial boundaries and named six prominent Atlanta residents to examine Mozley Park and "establish a line at which encroachments will stop," as the *Atlanta Constitution* put it at the time. Hartsfield went farther in 1952, forming a group called the West Side Mutual Development Committee—with three prominent Black leaders and three white leaders—to drive the racial geography of western Atlanta. The group set out not so much to determine the future, but to "discover an objective truth," as historian Kevin Kruse has put it, about "whether a neighborhood was solidly white or surely becoming Black."

The rule of thumb for this committee was whether a neighborhood had what it called "community integrity." When a journalist asked a member of the committee whether "community integrity" was "merely a polite way of masking segregation," that committee member said, "It has gotten away from the idea of fixed boundary lines, buffer zones, and all the rest. I couldn't sell that to Negroes. But we can buy the idea of community integrity."

While that process played out with the mayor, another group of Black businessmen worked behind the scenes on their own project. Beginning in the mid-1940s, Black leaders—including the co-chair of the Atlanta Negro Voters League and the ascending publisher of the *Atlanta Daily World*, the Black newspaper—began meeting to discuss new housing for the Black population, which was rising quickly again as more people left Georgia farmland.

In 1951, "Project X" began. While Atlanta's white political and business community set rules around boundaries and expectations for the Black community, Project X was about flipping the storyline. A group of roughly two dozen Black investors put money into an anonymous company and set out on a land-buying spree on the west side of Atlanta. The neighborhood they had chosen was called Collier Heights. It was sparsely populated, which made it conducive to quiet land purchases.

The Birth of Collier Heights

Along the way, the leaders of Project X continued to try to keep their work quiet. As Robert A. Thompson, a Black community leader who led Project X, explained, "Atlanta had witnessed a race riot before (in 1906). We were determined for that not to occur again."

The mayor's West Side Mutual Development Committee was at the time working with neighborhoods adjacent to Collier Heights to determine the "community integrity" of their blocks. Bordering Collier Heights to the south is an area called Adamsville, and starting around 1954, white residents there asked the development committee to intervene. "We are deeply concerned with the continued infiltration of Negroes," one civic club in Adamsville wrote. "This movement is beginning to pose as a threat to some adjoining white communities." As the Adamsville Civic Club put it, it was time for "a new 'Gentleman's Agreement Line.'" Even a local pastor wrote with alarm, saying "the colored people are moving closer week by week." Among the development committee's responses was to usher out Black buyers. When real estate agents sent in inquiries on behalf of Black buyers, the mayor's committee sent a letter that read, "You will notice from the map the location of the northern boundary of Adamsville," explaining that the line would remain in place until "a clear majority of the property owners" wanted to welcome Black buyers. The city was building an expressway (later called I-20) along that boundary anyway, and it would serve, in the words of the committee, as "the boundary between the white and Negro communities."

The intervention from the mayor's committee even got personal with individual homebuyers. In 1957, when a Black man named M. C. Jackson purchased a home there and neighbors did not want him to stay, the development committee used connections to get Jackson a new home, this time in public housing. Then the committee facilitated neighbors' buying back Jackson's home, even though it had been burned to the ground by people who didn't want him there.

All this was happening just a few blocks from Project X and the site of Collier Drive, where Michael Render would grow up. There, in 1959, Michael's mother, Druzella "Denise" Clonts, was born. Her parents, Arthur and Bettie, had moved to 2615 Collier Drive a few years earlier, in 1954, after Arthur served a few months in the military. Arthur was listed in Atlanta city records at the time as a "laborer" and a "cement finisher." Bettie, raised in Macon, Alabama, where her family members were once enslaved, had moved to Atlanta and become a nurse.

The Clonts family was growing as Collier Heights was coming into its own. From 1950 to 1970, fifty-four subdivisions were built in Collier Heights, with a total of 1,700 homes. Because so much of the land had been pre-purchased by the team behind Project X, Black-focused builders got a jump start before white residents in the area became alarmed.

By the time the Black-funded building came to the attention of white residents in 1954, the horse had left the barn. As Thompson, the leader of Project X, said, "The whites, when they found out that Blacks owned the land, they like to have died, but they couldn't do a damn thing about it." Soon, another member of Thompson's group bought 125 acres. When the nearby white residents found out, Thompson said, "They ran. They squawked and raised hell, but they couldn't do a damned thing about that. Blacks had bought the land."

The Collier Heights Civic Club tried to reverse this trend, sending a letter to its members discouraging them from selling to Black buyers: "Take the time to thoroughly think through and consider just what you as an individual stand to lose both *financially* and *morally* by the action of several people in the community selling to colored and leaving you or your neighbor in a predicament created by this selfish few," the letter urged. "REMEMBER THAT COLORED CANNOT BUY UNLESS THE WHITE MAN SELLS."

Soon, the mayor's development committee got involved in Collier Heights. The committee asked the white residents to vote on whether they would sell to Black buyers or stay put—with the idea that all residents would follow the elected outcome. The tallied votes showed that just over half wanted to stay put and attempt to keep the area white. Many neighbors, however, didn't cast a vote and simply wrote in commentary. "I won't stay here and be surrounded by Negroes regardless of any decision," one neighbor wrote, signaling that the outcome wouldn't be as simple as holding a vote.

The civic club leaders became convinced that most white residents were going to move, and so, they organized the neighborhood to sell simultaneously. Within three months, the small population of white residents who had lived around Collier Heights had almost entirely moved. From 1954 to 1955, about three hundred white owners sold their homes to Black buyers.

Project X had succeeded in its mission. As Thompson described it, the group had "leapfrog[ged]" over the flood of white residents who were also spreading out farther from the city's center.

The Clontses were happy beneficiaries of Project X's vision. Their new home was on Collier Drive, the eponymous street of Collier Heights and a prime location in Atlanta. Situated on about four thousand acres seven miles from downtown, Collier boasted hilly, winding, tree-lined roads that left behind the city's boxy property grid. From the start, the new residents took care of their homes with pride. Lawns were well maintained. In the backyards, children played and BBQ grills were fired up. Cars were parked on the street or under carports. It was a place where people were proud to do things in what they felt was a proper manner, an upper-class manner, away from view, in the privacy of their backyards.

"You never saw the children in the front yard," recalled Minnette Coleman, a longtime resident. "Sometimes you didn't even know if people had children in their house. We played in the backyard . . . Your friends came over, you played in your backyard. But who were your friends? Your friends were kids who were probably going to grow up and go to college. And have professional jobs, and this was what our middle-class parents viewed as fulfilling the Du Bois prophecy for having sired members of 'the talented tenth.' So whenever I think of Collier Heights, when I was a kid, I think you had to play in a backyard."

The "talented tenth" concept, circulating in Collier Heights at the time, was a civic-minded idea from W. E. B. Du Bois. It suggested that the top tenth of Black Americans, after acquiring education and success, should become leaders of their communities, giving back to others. Collier Heights had that aspirational quality, that it was a neighborhood on the rise that could lift many Black Americans.

Soon, people far and wide began paying attention to Collier Heights. In 1958, the United Press International declared that "Atlanta has an answer to Negro Housing." The article said that "a Negro can stand at a certain spot in Atlanta and as far as his eye can see there is space for him to live. That's perhaps the most significant victory yet for the Negro in this Deep South metropolis."

In August 1959, the *New York Times* declared that "the true center of the Negro's Southern middle class is Atlanta" and ran a photo of a ranch-style home in Collier Heights. The next month, *Time* magazine included Collier Heights in a story about African American suburbs: "These developments are all peopled by the newly prospering Negro middle class, who all seem to have one thing in common: a fever for good living," the article said. "They settle where the air is clean and the schools good, join the PTA, buy power lawn mowers, curse the crab grass, endure the rigors of commuting, barbecue their steaks, buy second cars and second TV sets, grumble about taxes."

A lot was changing in Atlanta by the time the Clontses adopted Denise's younger brother, Demagio, who was born in 1965. Battles had been playing out over school desegregation, which was by no means smooth or welcomed by all parties. Parks and golf courses had also had several rounds of challenges and pushes to welcome Black residents. The Civil Rights Movement was in full swing, and some of its leaders often met in homes within Collier Heights to plan meetings. Martin Luther King Jr.'s father, the leading reverend at Ebenezer Baptist Church, had moved in, and the neighborhood became a stopping point for well-wishers after King's assassination.

These well-wishers were at times surprised by their surroundings. Christine King Farris, King's sister, described how "when my brother Martin was taken, Richard Nixon came down to express his condolences," and upon arriving at her father's home, Nixon "looked around and said, 'I think you call this a '*split-level*' . . . I think he was surprised to see what we had in Collier Heights."

It wasn't just presidents and dignitaries who were impressed. Many Black families were in awe when they visited Collier Heights. Myrna Clayton remembered making her way to a friend's house for a sleepover in 1971: "It was almost like foresty. And so it was lots of trees and lots of houses. And it seemed like the houses, as you got closer and closer, got bigger and bigger and bigger. . . . For a second grader, you know, it was like going to Disneyland." Clayton's family moved from their more modest neighborhood to Collier Heights soon afterward.

Abandonment

For the Clontses, Collier Heights was a point of pride, but the kids also felt awkward among the elite. As Denise put it, "I grew up in Atlanta's historic Collier Heights. That don't mean we were uppity[,] as we are really country folk, but [it] sounds cool."

Arthur Clonts died in March 1970, after a long struggle with injuries he suffered from an explosion in a manual labor job. He was forty years old. To officiate at his funeral, Bettie chose Rev. William Weatherspool, the man whose home purchase in Mozley Park had set off the protests at the governor's and mayor's offices decades earlier and who, since then, had only grown in stature. When the reverend moved his church's location westward in 1955, following the migration of Black Atlantans, his congregation had joined him in a public procession through Atlanta from the old location to the new. The procession drew attention: Black Atlantans were walking away from downtown and charging into their own, new area of the city.

Denise was only eleven years old when her father died, and she was shaken. She had been her "daddy's princess," she would later write. "A daddy's girl. I loved and adored my father and was shaken by his death when I was still a child. I was lonely at times. I missed my ole man but never forgot his love."

A few years later, Denise met Michael Lee Render. He had also lost his father at a young age, when he was ten. By the time their lives intersected, Denise was sixteen, and Michael was eighteen. They had a son together, born April 20, 1975. They named him Michael Santiago Render.

Denise, by her own account, wanted a life of creativity and adventure. She had "zero interest in becoming a nurse"—her mother's career—"working in health, or finding a good job. I was an artist!" She loved partying with her cousins and friends, she loved music, and she cultivated a "creative crowd." When Michael was born, motherhood was not the only thing on her mind.

Denise moved to nearby Decatur, leaving her son with Bettie in Collier Heights. She would go on to open a floral business, marry another man, and have two daughters. She was proud to make a home that was "lively and festive," as she put it, and that was a "place of refuge" for friends and family going through tough times. She also weathered tough times herself, using drugs and being arrested for petty crimes. Though Denise often spent weekends with Michael, she felt sorry throughout her life that she had lost so much time with her son—she would tell him that she had not wanted to leave him, that her mother had demanded it, and that it was a hard sacrifice for her. "Like a hole in my heart," Michael later rapped about the abandonment. *Like a hole in my heart.*

Michael's father, Michael Lee Render, was on his own path and also not regularly present for his son. In the early 1980s, he was arrested for abandoning a dependent child. It was a scary time for Black children in Atlanta. In 1982, the time of the charge against Michael Lee Render, there had been murders of poor Black kids occurring in town. Some of their bodies were being dumped over a bridge not too far from young Michael's grandmother's house in Collier Heights.

For a city run by its second Black mayor in a row, many non-elite Black residents nonetheless felt betrayed, ignored, cast away. They felt the city had deserted them, that no one cared that there was a serial killer in town. Next, crack cocaine would be the local killer. It was a time of one step forward, two steps backward for Black Atlantans and Black Americans generally. More doors were open, but drugs were on the streets, and police were stepping up arrests. Amid all this, in 1986, the federal government created a holiday to celebrate Martin Luther King Jr.

During the 1980s, Michael's father married, started a new family, and joined the police force. He continued to be only partially present for his first child, but Michael's father's mother, Mary Long Render, who lived just west of Collier Heights, became a welcome presence in her grandson's life. The family believed that Mary's lineage could be traced back to Dr. Crawford Long, a prominent (white, slave-owning) Georgian doctor credited with inventing anesthesia. Michael Render would speak fondly of his paternal grandmother later in life.

It was Bettie Clonts, though, his maternal grandmother, who provided Michael with the stable household of his childhood. Soon, she found a new partner, Willie Burke Sherwood, who also took on Michael's parenting and shared stories about Black inventors, like the Black man who had taught Jasper "Jack" Daniel to make whiskey. Bettie had worked as a nurse, but at Sherwood's urging, she quit that job to watch out for Michael as levels of drug use and crime rose nearby.

Michael loved Bettie's grits, eggs, and bacon. As friends and family remembered her after her passing, Bettie was known for her strong Christian faith and for her "birthday cards with $1 in them, the Christmas cards, the phone calls, the prayers, the songs and most of all just being there." She was the sort of grandmother who would fuss at the kids for getting tattoos and remind them to keep their hair in order. She also taught Michael about history. Specifically, she liked to talk about local Black business history, Michael told us.

The Clontses kept their money with Citizens Trust, a Black-owned bank. Michael's grandmother had done so from the time she moved to Atlanta at a young age, Michael told us proudly. His grandparents took him and his sisters to get accounts, too, at around age six, he said. None of Collier Heights, he told us, could have been built without the success of Black-owned financial companies, including Citizens Trust, which itself dates back to the companies Heman Perry formed around Auburn Avenue after the 1906 racial attacks. Indeed, in Atlanta city property records from the 1950s and '60s, Citizens Trust is printed on row after row as the mortgage issuer for homeowners in Collier Heights.

Michael also brought up one of the prominent builders of Collier Heights, Herman Russell, as a source of inspiration. "I would argue that had it not been for Herman Russell, who was at one point the largest Black developer in the country . . . I would not have had the quality of education that I got at Collier Heights Elementary," he said. Russell's company had spotted the opportunity in Collier Heights and invested in building homes there for Black Americans, helping to create a neighborhood of safe streets and good schools.

Michael had a foot outside Collier's neat lawns, however. Feelings of insecurity plagued his childhood and teenage years, and as he saw different models of people in his life, he turned toward what he has called "defiant" behavior. As Michael put it on the cover of a 2012 album, he was among the people who were "readers of the books, leaders of the crooks." Though Collier Heights was a stable neighborhood, and though he was furthering his education at Frederick Douglass High School, there were crime-ridden areas nearby. He was exploring two worlds—learning to hustle the streets while also studying history and looking for answers for the future.

Michael made friends one summer at a camp for teenagers founded, in part, to assuage Black Atlantans' concerns after the murders of local Black children. One camp friend was Asha Jackson, who also attended Frederick Douglass. Jackson, who went on to become a local judge, told us about Michael's bifurcated childhood. "His dad was a police officer, and his mom was a drug addict, and they kind of hooked up. His grandmother was really influential, and her house was right on Collier Road." One might question, Jackson said, why Michael ever "needed to be a hustler," given his background and potential for a better trajectory. "[It was] because that was what was acceptable, you know, for a Black male from that community, and [it was about] survival."

When Michael was fifteen, he had a religious awakening, spurred by conversations with his father, and joined the Nation of Islam. His new faith put him at odds with people like his teachers at school, who viewed the group as radical. Relevant to Michael's blossoming thoughts on race and money, the Nation preached ideas of Black separatism, including ideas from Marcus Garvey's early 1900s advocacy for Black Americans to build their own economy and businesses separate from the white economy. (Some Nation of Islam leaders have made anti-Semitic statements, which complicates the effectiveness of their messages about Black empowerment.) These Black separatist ideas would be highly relevant to the Bank Black Movement that Michael joined in 2014 and to the founding of Greenwood Bank.

When Michael's grandmother Bettie left her job to stay home and watch out for him, he told us, the neighborhood was crawling with crack dealers. Looking for something better, Michael organized a group of friends to petition the City of Atlanta for assistance for the city's youth. He and the group showed up at the mayor's office and said they represented kids from four nearby counties. They wanted support for teenagers to meet and talk about social change. They wanted access to gathering places. Michael was quickly developing as the teen in town who would rally peers after events, as he would later after the beating of Rodney King. Michael told the mayor, "We have one requirement, and that's just that adults shut up and listen to kids for a change."

This was early 1990, and the mayor was Andrew Young, the Civil Rights leader. Andrew was winding up his two terms leading the city, and he would go on to represent Atlanta in its successful bid to host the 1996 Summer Olympic Games.

When Michael and his group refused to leave the mayor's office without funding, the mayor told them, "I've got a thousand dollars." Michael's reply: "We'll take it, along with some free access to public venues."

And they were off. This work put Michael into higher visibility with the uber-wealthy of Atlanta and with the Black political elite. The Young family would help fund Michael's first year at Morehouse, a private Black college in the city. And one day down the road, after the killing of George Floyd, Michael would be standing next to another Atlanta mayor and saying, "If we lose Atlanta, what else have we got?"

Black Americans *had* Atlanta, but it had been a complicated relationship from the start. They had been welcomed after the Civil War and housed in the same neighborhoods as white families, but then they were aggressively pushed to relocate and consolidate on the city's west side. Black Americans nevertheless triumphed in many chapters of the city's history, wresting control of neighborhoods like Collier Heights and driving their own destiny with financing and support from Black-owned banks and Black-owned businesses. They had come into power running much of the city's politics.

At every step of the way, they had been tested by forces bigger than merely those in Atlanta. Programs from the federal government, like redlining, had also played a central role in the Black-white wealth gap locally. And federal programs played a role in what Andrew Young and other Black politicians felt hindered some of what they could achieve for Black Americans. Black Americans *had* Atlanta even back in the early 1990s, but over the next thirty years, the economic distribution of all wealth was becoming more complicated.

CHAPTER 3

ANDREW YOUNG AND FINANCE FOR THE FREEDMEN

To get the right to vote in Democracy and not have access to capital is to only be: halfway free.

—Andrew Young

It was January 2016, and Andrew Young had been called to speak at a meeting at the Treasury Department in Washington, D.C. The federal government was renaming an annex of the Treasury Building "the Freedman's Bank Building," after one of the nation's historic financial scandals, and Andrew was, in many ways, an ideal spokesman for the building. "When we look at the history of the African American integration into America," he said from the podium, "the one thing that's been most difficult for us is to *desegregate the money*."

First, he wanted to set some history straight: There were Black Americans with money just after the Civil War, Andrew said emphatically, but it was the decades that followed the war that made it increasingly difficult for Black Americans to build wealth. Money, he said, became segregated. This occurred because of exclusion but also because of withdrawal. Yes, there was an unjust push from white Americans, but there was also a pull by some Black Americans who envisioned separate community-focused institutions.

The question of how to desegregate money was so difficult, Andrew went on, that Civil Rights leaders in the 1960s sometimes avoided the topic. "It wasn't an accident that we didn't talk about—much about—money," Andrew said. "Dr. King always said to us that, you know, 'to be free, you've got to overcome the love of wealth and the fear of death.' And so, we didn't talk much about either. Though we knew that both were very significant in creating the world in which we live."

On the subject of the gathering, Andrew said that "the Freedman's Bank is a significant part of our economic legacy." He said economies need to be "inclusive" to grow, and then he added a prescription for the future. "It's not that we need more boots on the ground. We need more Ferragamo's on the ground," he said. "We need bankers. We need investors. We need people to create jobs."

The Original Failed "Black" Bank

The roots of Black banking reach back to the Freedman's Savings and Trust Company, often called Freedman's Bank.

In January 1865, several months before the end of the Civil War, a white minister named John Alvord met in New York City with business leaders to discuss an idea for a Black bank. It was part of a broader discussion on how to help even the path for Black Americans along with the ill-fated "forty acres and a mule" order.

The Black bank had stronger backing than the land grants—it had the backing of business. Alvord had been a Union Army chaplain, working with soldiers during the war, and Black soldiers would be the initial focus for the bank. They had been receiving military pay, and many of them had no place to deposit it. In Alvord's words, these soldiers needed a "benevolent" bank that would help them with "thrift." The idea borrowed on initiatives in the South by which Union generals had set up banks for Black soldiers, including the Free Labor Bank in Louisiana and the Military Savings Bank in South Carolina. Soon, several congressmen proposed a bill to create the Freedman's Savings and Trust Company. President Abraham Lincoln signed the bill into law in March 1865, just over a month before the Confederate general Robert Lee surrendered in Appomattox, Virginia.

The Freedman's Bank charter said that the money would be invested in "stocks, bonds, Treasury notes, or other securities of the United States," but it did not contain a mandate to lend the funds back to Black Americans. The point of the bank was not to spur economic development or to create wealth for Black communities; it was simply to hold their money. The bank wrote in an advertisement in 1865: "This then, being a National Institution in the hands of these good men, it is as safe as the Government can make it, and, therefore, there can be no safer place in the country to deposit." At the same time Freedman's Bank was rolling out, the U.S. government also set up the Freedmen's Bureau to administer aid to formerly enslaved people. The bureau encouraged Black Americans, including schoolchildren and members of churches and civic groups, to put their money in the bank.

Andrew Young, Michael Render, and Ryan Glover, bank founders-to-be many years later, have all talked about the landmark nature of Freedman's Bank. What none of them knew until our research uncovered it was that Andrew Young was a descendant of several Freedman's Bank depositors.

And we found that connection in an unexpected part of the family. Andrew and his family talked to us at length about their history, but there was one grandparent they didn't talk about much. That was Andrew's maternal grandfather, Joseph H. Fuller. As Andrew's younger brother, Walter, put it, "I don't know much about my grandfather [Joseph H. Fuller] because he was, well, he was sort of a rounder that—a rolling stone that probably was involved in gambling and illicit activities that were not discussed around children." Andrew Young used the same phrase for Fuller: "We saw him as a rolling stone."

Joseph Fuller was born around 1858 in New Orleans to Joseph and Hannah Fuller, who had recently moved from Donaldsonville, Louisiana, an area with sugar plantations. They had an older daughter, Adaline. After the Civil War, Adaline was the first in the family to apply for an account at Freedman's Bank, opening one in 1866. At this time, she was already married with a son. She listed her brother, Joseph Fuller, as a family member. The bank also asked a puzzling question, given that slavery had ended. It asked for the name of her "master" and plantation. Adaline left those lines blank.

By 1867, the bank had twenty branches around the country. Though it had been initially chartered two years earlier with strict controls around investments, Congress later loosened these restrictions. This came after lobbying by white trustees who had ties to the banking industry. It meant that Freedman's could start making loans and high-risk investments in things like speculative new companies. This decision would ultimately doom the bank. Yet its marketing to ordinary depositors like Adaline did not indicate any risks.

The bank "misleadingly promoted itself as benefiting from a government guarantee," according to historians Claire Célérier of the University of Toronto and Purnoor Tak of the London Business School. Célérier and Tak ran Freedman's advertisements through algorithms to identify misleading statements and found that Freedman's had issued more than other contemporary banks. They also found that the bank used racial stereotypes in ads. One ad from 1871 read, "Cut off your vices—don't smoke—don't drink—don't buy lottery tickets. Put the money you save into the FREEDMAN'S SAVINGS BANK."

By the time Joseph Fuller turned twelve, around 1870, he was a domestic servant, living with his white employers in New Orleans. In April 1873, Fuller walked into Freedman's Bank and applied for an account. He was listed as being sixteen years old and having a "yellow complexion." Throughout his life, he worked as a laborer, porter, bartender, and in other low-level jobs, records show. In one job, he was listed as a laborer at the U.S. Mint, the only wellspring of wealth he would ever see.

When Fuller deposited his savings at Freedman's in 1873, the bank had more than thirty-seven branches in seventeen states and the District of Columbia. More than seventy thousand people had opened accounts, and the bank's deposits had grown to more than $57 million. That same year, during an economic downturn, a banker named Henry Cooke, the finance chairman of Freedman's board of directors, took advantage of the bank. In one of the most shameful banking scams in U.S. history, Cooke used Freedman's to off-load bad investments from other banks. These included his brother's private bank in Philadelphia, Jay Cooke and Company, and a commercial bank that would collapse later that year. Jay, the brother, had been an adviser to the U.S. Treasury

Department during the Civil War and had helped raise money for the Union by selling war bonds. Both brothers were well connected politically. The Cookes used Freedman's Bank money for risky investments in real estate and railroads and to make loans to friends without collateral, and they had Freedman's assume responsibility for souring loans that Freedman's trustees had offered at other banks under their supervision. Soon, Freedman's Bank was in severe financial trouble.

Congress brought in regulators to examine the bank, but the intervention came too late. As a last-ditch effort, the U.S. government asked Frederick Douglass to take over the bank. Wealthy from property holdings in Baltimore and elsewhere, Douglass invested ten thousand dollars of his own money as a show of confidence. But only three months after taking over, Douglass declared the matter hopeless. The trustees closed the bank on June 29, 1874, a little over a year after Joseph Fuller, Andrew Young's grandfather, deposited his savings.

Fuller was one of 61,144 depositors who collectively saw nearly $3 million in losses at the bank at the time it collapsed. Congress reimbursed some depositors, but they had to request their money, which many didn't know to do. In the end, only about half the depositors got money back, and they got on average $18.51 apiece—eventually amounting to 62 percent of their outstanding balances.

In a statement to the depositors of Freedman's Bank just before it collapsed, Douglass laid out the reasons the bank's liabilities had ended up higher than its assets. First, he said, managers had erred in trying to compete with older and more established banks by offering higher interest rates on savings than the bank could afford. Second, he said managers had been "tempted into a sort of banking missionary movement" and had established branches in remote areas that could not be profitable in the near future. And third, he cited a detrimental "feeling of caste" and a "race malignity." "This institution," he said, "conspicuously and pre-eminently represents the idea of progress, and elevation of a people who are just now emerging from the ignorance, degradation, and destitution entailed upon them by more than two centuries of slavery. *A people who are hated not because they have injured others, but because others have injured them.*"

Douglass wrote many impactful texts during his life, but his words on the Freedman's Bank are among his most moving and prescient. He focused on the tensions between running a bank for profit versus serving as a missionary movement.

Far from departing from capitalism or America's tendency to distribute wealth unequally, Douglass said that Black Americans should be able to have a pyramid of wealth, just as white Americans did—that, indeed, "a wealthy class" was needed. "No people can well rise to a high degree of mental or even moral excellence without wealth," he wrote, lamenting the loss of Freedman's Bank as a ladder toward this. "A people, uniformly poor, and compelled to struggle for barely a physical existence, will be dependent and despised by their neighbors, and will finally despise themselves. While it is impossible that every individual of any race shall be rich—and no man may be despised for merely being poor—yet *no people can be respected which does not produce a wealthy class*. Such a people will only be the hewers of wood and drawers of water, and will not rise above a mere animal existence."

Douglass's contention, that Black people should have a wealthy class just like white people, foreshadows a debate that is still alive today: Is the goal to create more economic equality among all Black Americans or to elevate a few rich ones, in the same way that white Americans have extreme wealth in the hands of a few?

Freedman's Bank made clear what happens when you start something without a consistent mission. The bank's goals kept changing, and that was part of the problem. There were Douglass's ambitious words, but there was also its founders' original vision and all the marketing in between. Was the bank meant to create a class of wealthy Black Americans, as its final chairman suggested? Or was it to keep formerly enslaved people's money safe, as its early founders suggested?

The bank's collapse was sealed by the risky investments that trustees like Henry Cooke had made, which were not even focused on benefiting the bank's customers. As Douglass later described it, Freedman's Bank was "the Black man's cow, but the white man's milk." This practice of taking Black individuals' money and investing it in white-owned companies was not a matter of poor execution of the mission; it was a problem at the heart of the conception of Freedman's Bank. The U.S. government in the 1860s failed to realize that banking is about more than keeping depositors' money safe; it's also about lending and investing money. Any effort to "help" the Black community with a Black bank that used their money to invest entirely outside their community was, in our view, exploitative. Letting Black Americans into banking, but then not treating them fairly, is exploitation.

What does it actually mean to be a Black bank? The answer to this question has varied ever since Freedman's Bank, and a lack of thoughtfulness around what it should mean has been at the center of other failed efforts. A bank's key criteria for evaluation, in our view, should be:

- Depositors: Who are your customers? Are you receiving money from Black individuals?
- Borrowers: To whom are you lending money? Are you lending to Black borrowers?
- Investment recipients: Where are you investing the money that you do not lend? Are these Black-controlled entities?
- Employees: How representative of your customer base are your employees? Do you hire Black employees?
- Managers/leaders: Do you hire Black leaders?
- Owners: Who owns or invests in your bank? Are they Black?

How did Freedman's Bank do in these areas? About 90 percent of Freedman's Bank depositors were Black, as were some of the bank's frontline employees. But on every other measure, Freedman's Bank wasn't really all that "Black." The bank did not make a significant effort to lend money to the Black community, with 80 percent of its loans going to white people. Moreover, money was loaned mainly to entities in Washington, D.C., which meant depositors' money was pulled out of local communities across the country but not reinvested there. In terms of investments, Freedman's money was invested in white-owned businesses. In terms of leadership, Frederick Douglass had come in only at the end; most of the leadership over time was white. And last, in terms of ownership, the charter of Freedman's Bank said it was owned by its depositors, but the depositors had no input in or control over the bank and no ability to sell their "investment." In practice, the ownership was the U.S. government.

Several scholars have studied Freedman's Bank and questioned whether it ultimately helped or harmed Black communities. Luke C. D. Stein of Babson College and Constantine Yannelis of the University of Chicago concluded that Freedman's Bank increased the wealth of Black Americans served by the bank. The school attendance rates, literacy rates, real estate holdings, and income of Black Americans were typically higher for people who had Freedman's Bank accounts.

Finance scholars Célérier and Tak dispute this finding, however, saying that Black wealth was more likely a preexisting factor in communities with Freedman's branches: The branches had been placed there because these were already promising communities. Freedman's Bank grew quickly mainly due to misleading marketing and overstatements, they wrote, arguing that the whole enterprise amounted to a wealth transfer from Black Americans to white Americans, given that the deposits were mainly from Black individuals, but the loans were largely to white people.

Beyond the question of how the bank affected Black wealth, there is the question of how it affected Black Americans' trust in financial institutions. This was answered in the years following Freedman's collapse by both W. E. B. Du Bois and Booker T. Washington. The two men, who often disagreed on matters, agreed on this point. Du Bois later wrote:

Then in one sad day came the crash—all the hard-earned dollars of the freedmen disappeared; but that was the least of the loss—all the faith in saving went too, and much of the faith in men; and that was a loss that a Nation which to-day sneers at Negro shiftlessness has never yet made good.

And Washington concurred:

When they found out that they had lost, or been swindled out of all their savings, they lost faith in savings banks, and it was a long time after this before it was possible to mention a savings bank for Negroes without some reference being made to the disaster of [the Freedman's Bank].

The Freedman's debacle would remain a sore point for Black Americans for years to come. Nearly thirty years after the bank collapsed, the *Chicago Defender*, a Black newspaper, wrote that the lesson of the bank was that Black Americans need to "be careful in who they get to handle their business for them: they should remember that a man who would institute Jim Crow [train] cars, and rape his daughters and make a grandfather clause for him, is not the one to handle his business."

Freedman's Bank was still a national scandal in 1876, when Joseph Fuller married Louisa Czarnowski. The two would become the parents of Andrew Young's mother, Daisy Fuller Andrew. When they married, money was tight, and the most money Fuller stood to receive immediately from Freedman's Bank was 20 percent of his deposit (more would be paid back, slowly, over several decades).

For Louisa Czarnowski's family, wealth had already been lost due to discrimination. Her grandfather was a white ship's captain, and her grandmother was an enslaved person, set free by the white captain during their relationship. Shipping had been a lucrative business in New Orleans, and at the time of his death, the captain left the family with properties there. But, ultimately, these were taken away because locals didn't recognize the property rights of enslaved people. Like her grandmother, Louisa's mother also had children with a white man, whom she married. These relationships led to light skin, and some family members disassociated themselves from their Black roots, blending into the light-skinned Creole community. Louisa, however, married Joseph Fuller, a Black American. Even four years into their marriage, in 1880, she and Joseph were living with Joseph's older sister, the census for that year shows.

It took until 1883 for Congress to pay more money back to Freedman's Bank depositors, and, at that time, it was only about sixty cents on the dollar. It's unclear whether Joseph Fuller ever got his money back. As late as 1905, notices still ran in Black newspapers about unclaimed deposits from the bank. At the time, Joseph and Louisa had had nine children, including three-year-old Daisy. Money would remain tight. Using probate records, we discovered that beyond his grandfather and his great-aunt Adaline, Andrew had three other family members on his father's side with Freedman's Bank accounts. All three opened their accounts in Atlanta.

When we told Andrew and his son, Bo, that five of their relatives had been depositors with Freedman's Bank, Andrew said, "Ah-haaaa." And Bo said, "That's incredible." The two men listened not with anger, but with a sense of pride at having ancestors who were savvy enough to go to a bank in the 1870s. "I've been telling my dad for forty years that we needed to be in business, not politics," Bo said. "This proved that I was right and that we have business in our DNA. And so, it's refreshing. Finally, I get to prove them wrong on something."

Andrew was matter-of-fact in his reaction. He said he had known he was probably connected to the bank, but he hadn't known what the ties were. He added that he was mainly surprised to find out that the ancestor he had dismissed as a "rolling stone" had even had money to deposit. "I never knew of any organized wealth or disciplined wealth on the Fuller side," Andrew said. "That was all on the Young side."

Unfair Insurance

The resources of the Young side of the family came from insurance— despite the insurance industry's being unfair to Black Americans in the late 1800s. As with the dawn of Black banking, early exploitative practices in insurance led not only to missed opportunities for wealth, but also an erosion of trust within the Black community, a legacy still alive in the insurance industry of the 2020s.

Let's start with a little history. The enslaved were the first group of people in our country's early history to be commonly insured. But, crucially, they were not insured to the benefit of their own families. They were insured to the benefit of their owners who wanted a payout if their "property" passed away. In fact, in early American history, some white families were not keen on insurance for themselves because they viewed it as being at odds with religion and their god's will.

From the inception of the insurance industry's involvement with slavery, Black lives were valued differently. The premiums to insure them were often twice the price on white lives. In the mid-1850s, insurance companies began marketing insurance more to white Americans as a badge of personal responsibility. The insurance industry grew rapidly after the war. By 1870, the number of policies in the state of New York, for instance, had increased from 50,000 to 650,000 in just ten years. Many insurers sold only expensive policies, but one company, Prudential, began marketing policies more broadly. The company led the way in creating policies that cost small sums and paid out just enough for burials and death expenses. Prudential would also lead the way in creating race-based pricing.

There was some legislative support to protect Black Americans. In 1884, a Black state senator in Massachusetts, Julius Caesar Chappelle, introduced a bill to bar discrimination by life insurance companies. He had noticed that some insurance companies were paying out one third less to Black families than to white families. According to Benjamin Wiggins's excellent book *Calculating Race*, Chappelle said that many Black families were unaware of this discrepancy. The bill to ban life insurers from racial discrimination in Massachusetts passed within months. Within the next seven years, ten other states passed similar bills. "But with each anti-discrimination intervention," Wiggins wrote, "insurers developed sophisticated measures to circumvent such policies."

In 1894, the industry found a statistician to publish research supporting racist underwriting. The State of New Jersey had just passed its version of an anti-discrimination bill for insurers, and Prudential, based in that state, was concerned. The company contacted Frederick Hoffman, a statistician who had been compiling data on Black Americans and writing about it in insurance journals. In one article, he wrote that Black Americans were likely to face extinction. "Something must be radically wrong in a constitution thus subject to decay," Hoffman wrote about the Black man. "Even if he be placed on equal grounds [to a white man] he still will exhibit what an eminent writer calls 'his race proclivity to disease and death.'"

Prudential brought Hoffman, about twenty-nine years old, to its headquarters and hired him. Within two years of working there, he published a report that set off decades of policies. Called *Race Traits and Tendencies of the American Negro*, his 330-page report was full of statistics that he said backed up the differential pricing for Black Americans. The report had an immediate and lasting impact on the industry. As historian Megan Wolff wrote in a 2006 paper, Hoffman's "application of mathematical tools to a social debate set a precedent for the use of statistics and actuarial science—two fields then in their infancies, which absorbed the biases and errors of their early participants. . . . Hoffman's work embedded racial ideologies within its approach to actuarial data, a legacy that remains with the field today."

At the heart of the argument of *Race Traits and Tendencies* were data showing higher levels of sickness and death among Black Americans than white Americans. The problem was that the data Hoffman used didn't isolate environmental and economic effects. Formerly enslaved people were a large part of his dataset, yet Hoffman didn't account for the fact that many had grown up in conditions far less healthy than those of white Americans. Contemporary Black scholars immediately noticed the gaps in the analysis. W. E. B. Du Bois said that "most of the conclusions drawn from these facts are of doubtful value, on account of the character of the material, the extent of the field, and the unscientific use of the statistical method." The supposed health gap wouldn't exist, Du Bois noted, if Black Americans had been compared to other poor, "immigrant" groups.

Prudential and other insurance firms used the *Race Traits and Tendencies* to justify paying out less for Black lives and, at times, refusing to pay commissions to agents who brought in Black clients. Exploitation met eventual exclusion in the insurers' policy approach: by 1940, a survey found that over 40 percent of insurance companies did not accept Black people as customers.

The American Economic Association ran *Race Traits and Tendencies* in one of its publications, and though the report has been discredited, as of 2023, the association's president and publications officers were unresponsive when we asked them if the association would retract the paper. Over time, the Hoffman work has left a lingering stench in contemporary business. Race remains a factor in insurance models, at least behind the scenes. Take modern auto insurance: Most insurers charge a premium for people who live in higher-crime zip codes. In that case, the input to the insurer's model is the zip code, not race—but Black people often live in higher-crime zip codes because of the wealth gap and past practices like redlining. So, even when race is not overtly a factor, it is inherently a factor, with zip code acting as a stand-in for race. Thus, Black people often pay more for auto insurance.

Market-based thinking would say that these higher rates are appropriate: cars in higher-crime areas could present insurers with higher claims and costs. But this leaves behind individuals in those areas who are trying to work hard to find success.

Consider Lecario Glass, the twenty-three-year-old we met at the Berean Outreach Ministry food pantry in Atlanta. As of 2022, he was riding a scooter, in part because he didn't have enough money to pay for auto insurance, he told us. But when he moves on from AutoZone and into a higher-paying job, perhaps he might save up to purchase a car. That would be a financial milestone, and it could open doors for him, allowing him to take a job farther away for higher pay. And yet, because of where he lived, he would still pay more for auto insurance than a person in a more white-dominant neighborhood. It's debatable whether this is fair. In terms of history, this line of risk-based thinking can be traced back to Hoffman's *Race Traits and Tendencies* report, along with broader trends in model-based pricing.

And so, it's no wonder that for generations, Black Americans have remained hesitant to apply for insurance. Even as late as the 2000s, funerals were often more difficult in the Black community. It was normal for Black families to ask friends and family to chip in for funeral expenses, because a relative died without life insurance.

For Andrew Young, the insurance industry was more complicated. Andrew's father's father played a role in the evolution of life insurance, but the effort would end in disappointment.

That grandfather, Frank Smith Young, was the relative whom Andrew Young mentioned the most in interviews with us. Frank was born in 1860, in Franklin, Louisiana, and Andrew told us that by 1910 or so, "he had four or five million dollars in the bank in Franklin, Louisiana." Smith Young never said it was his own money, Andrew told us. "He wouldn't pay my daddy's tuition to college because he said, 'This is not our money.' . . . And he had—and I don't know how he got this way, that's what bothers me—he had an account for something called the

Knights of the Pythias. He had an account for Prince Hall Masons. And an account for [the Independent Order of] Odd Fellows, and a burial society."

Smith Young was managing the accounts of fraternal organizations he belonged to in Franklin, Louisiana, when Andrew was born in 1932. Over the next few years, as the Depression continued, much of that money went away, Andrew told us. As we talked with Andrew about our project, he said he wanted us to find out what happened to those millions of dollars his grandfather had managed. We dug into that research and ended up finding that his grandfather's story was a bit of the "other side of the coin" to Prudential's avoidance of Black Americans as customers. It was a story of what some Black Americans did when they were not welcomed by white America.

Frank Smith Young's family owned land in Franklin when he was born, assets his descendants believe were tied to relatives who fought in New Orleans in the War of 1812. During that war with Britain, General Andrew Jackson offered land to Black people who joined his troops, and some of Frank Smith Young's descendants believe the family was among those who benefited.

In 1888, Smith Young married Hattie Epps, who had moved to New Orleans from Atlanta. Epps was a Civil Rights activist in the post–Civil War period, focusing on some laws around segregation in private businesses. The 1875 Civil Rights Act had said that businesses should treat all people equally when dealing with them. But business owners were not following the law and were frequently discouraging entry by Black Americans or separating them. And so, on February 3, 1883, Epps and two other Black Americans entered DeGive's Opera House in Atlanta and sat down in the first gallery rather than in the area reserved for Black attendees. The opera house owner asked the police to tell them to move. Epps and the others refused, and they were arrested. Their sit-in yielded results: the opera house owner was arrested for violating the Civil Rights Act. This effort was part of a concerted push by Black Americans to force business owners to treat them equally. Decades before the sit-ins of the 1950s and '60s, Epps was sitting in. Her efforts were too early in one sense: that fall in 1883, the U.S. Supreme Court ruled that the 1875 law requiring businesses to treat all people equally was unconstitutional and infringed on business owners' rights, making Epps's efforts moot at that point. The spirit that Epps showed, however, led us to think about how people pushing for change today often have parents, grandparents, and great-grandparents who once did so themselves.

Andrew Young's grandfather Frank Smith Young first appeared in news clippings as a planter in Franklin, chiming in at times to report the weather. In 1894, for instance, he wrote, "The past week was favorable for farmwork. The crops are growing nicely. Corn planting is nearly completed. Planters are now preparing to sow pens.—Frank S. Young." These clippings did not relay the importance Smith Young played in organizations that included the Knights of Honor, the Pythians, and the Odd Fellows. After Frederick Hoffman's *Race Traits and Tendencies* study, life insurance companies like Prudential were turning Black Americans away with increased vigor. This propelled Black people to find their own way to provide insurance for their communities, by pooling money within community organizations—just one example of a separate financial system made by and for Black neighbors. This idea of a separate economy and separate financial institutions would come in and out of vogue among Black leaders. In Frank Smith Young's life, Marcus Garvey would become a vocal proponent of building a separate, Black-focused economy.

In Atlanta, around the time of the 1906 racial attacks, insurance and banking were prominent among the newly formed Black-focused enterprises. In 1905, Alonzo Franklin Herndon turned his earnings from a barber business into a successful insurance company, and Heman E. Perry's empire included both the precursor to Citizens Trust Bank and an insurance business. In 1913, the Atlanta State Savings Bank became the first Black bank to be chartered in Georgia. The idea that all these businessmen were pursuing was called "the double dollar." The logic was that the dollar had double weight when you spent it at companies that hired and supported your community. This idea remained relevant in the 2020s for start-ups like Greenwood Bank.

In Louisiana, Frank Smith Young was a leading figure in building the separate insurance economy for Black Americans. Fraternal organizations like the ones Andrew Young described to us would gather their members' funds into an informal insurance pool that Smith Young managed and paid out as claims came in. This put Smith Young in control of substantial funds and made him influential with large banks and even Louisiana's political leaders. When the state was opening a charity hospital in New Orleans but was not hiring Black nurses, Smith Young was able to call Governor Huey Long and convince him to add Black nurses, Andrew told us. When police and some leaders in Franklin were discriminating against Black residents, Smith Young was able to get them to back off by threatening to move the money he managed out of Franklin banks and into New Orleans banks.

By the middle of his life, Frank Smith Young was among local leaders publicly expressing support for the ideas put forward by Booker T. Washington, that Black Americans should operate their businesses separately and not compete with the white economy. In 1910, Smith Young was among the local leaders who created a business league that adopted the resolutions of Booker T. Washington's National Negro Business League. The local league agreed to call "attention of the Negro to the fact that there are vast areas of unoccupied soil which can be tilled by him," as one local news item put it. The local league also focused its meeting that year on a movement for a chain of Black banks.

In Atlanta, Standard Life, the insurance company set up by Heman Perry, expanded greatly throughout the 1910s. That company, however, ran into financial problems in the 1920s, and eventually, Perry was forced to turn the company over to white ownership. The reversal of fortune was disillusioning to many. As one account of Standard Life's collapse said, "News of the loss of this company cast a pall of gloom over colored Atlanta. Women wept and men who had invested their all on their confidence in Perry now swore vengeance on him." It was an early example of how disappointed Black communities can be when a Black-focused institution runs into trouble.

For Frank Smith Young, the moment of fate came when the Great Depression hit. Throughout his life, Smith Young had remained influential in several fraternal groups—at one point holding the title "grand dictator and protector" of the Knights and Ladies of Honor of America. When the Depression hit, according to his grandson Walter Young, Smith Young chose to disperse the substantial insurance funds of the groups he managed back to the groups' members. This move may have ended some of those insurance pool schemes, but it helped those families in a difficult period.

By the mid-1930s, Smith Young was working in the corporate world as a vice president for Douglas Life Insurance Company, an insurer focused on Black customers. It was a departure from the fraternal world of insurance. A few years later, in the fall of 1940, he passed away. His death certificate listed nephritis, a kidney condition, as the cause. Filings with the probate court show that he left his second wife—he had been a widower—and four children a bank account worth $315, Douglas Life corporate shares worth $1,800, and some land in Franklin worth $2,000.

Andrew Young deeply admired his grandfather. As an adult well into his successful career in politics, Andrew met a well-known preacher in Brooklyn who knew he was from Louisiana and asked if he knew Frank Smith Young. "That's my grandfather," Andrew told him. And the preacher said, "Well, he would sure be proud of you—as the first Black congressman from the South in a hundred years. But you've got a long way to go to catch up with him."

CHAPTER 4

RYAN GLOVER AND THE HISTORIC GREENWOOD

You have used our forefathers as you do now your horses and mules, but the time shall never come when the present generation shall be treated thus. It is true that you once had him as property, but now he is on equality with you.
—From a column in the *Muskogee Phoenix*

In the 1940s, Ryan Glover's parents had a make-or-break choice. They could stick it out in Oklahoma, where their family owned land but where they felt racism was unbearable, or they could leave and move to housing projects in California. "The times were so horrible," Ryan's mother, Fern, told us.

Fifty years earlier, two decades after the end of the Civil War, the outlook had seemed more promising for Ryan's family. In the mid-1800s, two of his great-great-grandparents, Morris and Katie Rentie, had been enslaved by Native Americans in the Indian Territory. Following the war, like most enslaved people in their region, the Renties were freed and welcomed to farm more or less as equals with their former enslavers.

The Renties' early experience after the Civil War stood in stark contrast to most Black Americans' experiences. Around the country, many local governments introduced laws and regulations—often known as

Black Codes or Jim Crow rules—to limit the rights of Black Americans. These rules codified segregation, limited Black people's abilities to work in certain professions, required in some cases that they work for white people, dictated where they could live, prohibited marriage to white people, and even restricted their ability to convene in large groups. All this, along with the Freedman's Bank collapse and the broken promise of "forty acres and a mule," was far from the Renties' initial experience. As Isparhecher, a political leader of the Creek Nation, where the Renties lived, liked to say after the war, "I will recognize all people as equals whether white, red, or Black."

Over time, the Renties managed to become owners of large tracts of land—and they weren't alone. The postwar situation in Oklahoma was unique, but the story of Black families obtaining land—an important form of wealth—in the late 1800s is the story of a national upswing in Black wealth that started to aggressively conquer the Black-white wealth gap. That is to say that despite the odds elsewhere in the country, the Renties weren't alone in building wealth post-emancipation. But the backlash was soon to follow.

As they acquired land and influence, Ryan's ancestors were active in local debates among Black Americans about buying into American capitalism. They chose the side of business, and Black businessmen like them would feed into the boom that became the Greenwood district of Tulsa, Oklahoma, otherwise known as Black Wall Street.

That is, until all this progress was torn down by hate.

The Trail of Enslaved People's Tears

Ryan Glover's great-great-great-grandfather Renty McIntosh Rentie was likely born in West Africa around the year 1800. British slave registries show he spent years enslaved in the Bahamas before he was brought to Alabama in the 1830s. There he was enslaved by the Creek Indian tribe (also known as the Muscogee tribe), which counted 902 enslaved people among its 22,694 members, according to an 1833 census. When gold was discovered in Georgia, President Andrew Jackson led Congress in passing the Indian Removal Act of 1830. To provide land to white people, the law forced around 70,000 members of Native tribes to move west, and the refugees included about 7,000 Black people who were enslaved by the tribe. In addition to undertaking the treacherous "Trail of Tears" walk, the enslaved people were cooking, cleaning, and otherwise serving their tribal masters. As one Cherokee would later say, "My grandparents were helped and protected by very faithful Negro slaves who . . . went ahead of the wagons and killed any wild beast who came along."

Renty McIntosh Rentie began fatherhood along the Trail of Tears. In the locations of his children's births, one can also see the terrible journey that sent Native Americans and their enslaved people walking an average of five thousand miles apiece. First, Renty's children were born in Alabama, then Georgia; by 1838, his children were being born in the new "Indian Territory," which was mainly in the yet-to-be-formed state of Oklahoma. There, Renty fathered eleven more children, including Morris, around 1847.

Though Morris was not alive during the Trail of Tears, he may have heard stories about it from his father. Even seventy years later, freed Black people in the Native American territory would talk about how they had witnessed the broken promises of the U.S. government to the tribes during the 1830s and how they had suffered alongside the Native Americans.

Many of the Renties were owned by John Yargee, who kept sixteen enslaved people as of 1860, including two men, two women, and twelve children, one of whom was Morris. As the Civil War began, Yargee took Morris's brothers John and Solomon to fight on the Southern battlefields. Morris, at around thirteen years old, was too young to fight, so he stayed home to farm and take care of the livestock. This was a time when the Rentie family was torn between "masters" and living on different sides of the war. Morris's father, Renty, and some of Morris's half-siblings had been living with a Creek chief who fled to Union territory during the war. Renty fled with the chief and three of his own young children, at times carrying them on his back for the journey.

In 1866, a treaty between the Creek Nation and the U.S. government evened the playing field between enslaved people and their enslavers.

The treaty reaffirmed the tribe's independence but also required it to give up some land to the U.S. government and to recognize the formerly enslaved people as full citizens of the tribe. "The institution of slavery, which has existed among several of the Tribes, must be forthwith abolished, and measures taken for the unconditional emancipation of all persons held in bondage, and for their incorporation into the Tribes on an equal footing with the original members, or suitably provided for," the federal government commission on the treaty wrote.

It's hard to overlook the irony of the U.S. government insisting that Native American tribes treat formerly enslaved people as equal citizens. This stood in contrast to the inequities the U.S. government continued to allow between races around the rest of the country.

Despite the tribal nation's active participation in slavery, Black Americans found good standing in the Indian Territory after the Civil War. They served as council members, ministers, and judges there. Jesse Franklin, a Black American who was born into slavery within the tribes in Alabama, was named to the Creek tribe's Supreme Court in 1874—nearly one hundred years before the U.S. Supreme Court welcomed its first Black justice. The journalist Ida B. Wells wrote in awe of the equality she saw in the tribal communities after the Civil War, saying that she saw "the chance [Black people] had of developing manhood and womanhood in this new territory." In areas with mixed Black-white populations, Black children were attending school with white children as late as 1900. These signs of political inclusion attracted Black migrants to the tribal land over the next few decades. To some Black Americans, it seemed like an escape from the violence and discrimination they faced elsewhere. Some locals began setting up all-Black towns to attract Black residents from across the South.

Morris Rentie, approaching twenty at the end of the Civil War, became a farmer of cattle, horses, goats, and sheep. At first, like other tribal members, he farmed on communal land. "Every citizen had the right to establish his home anywhere in the Creek Nation that he wanted to," Morris's son Louis recalled, "provided somebody else didn't have a home already on it."

In time, Morris came to own a lot of land—as much, in fact, as his former owner, John Yargee.

It wasn't an accident that these formerly enslaved people eventually enjoyed equal footing with their former masters. In 1887, the U.S. government initiated a sweeping plan to bring members of the Creek Nation and other tribes into official government records. The plan removed tribal ownership of all land and named individuals within the tribe as owners; it also made them U.S. citizens.

Individual landownership was highly controversial among Native Americans. Many preferred to maintain tribal unity and feared that individual landownership would slowly erode their community. It was also controversial among some Black members of the tribes, who did not trust the federal government. Within the Creek tribe, Black freed people remembered that the U.S. government had broken its promises in its 1832 treaty with the Creek Nation. These Black tribal members warned that allotment might actually be a trick to take land from the tribe. As one asserted, participating in the U.S. government's program would end with "people with packs and bundles on their backs having to leave their homes."

Still, other Black Americans, including the Rentie family, liked the idea that the U.S. government was offering them landownership. The Black editor of the newspaper the *Muskogee Pioneer* advocated to allocate land to former Creek Nation "freedmen" and urged them to enroll. The newspaper also supported an initiative led by Morris Rentie's half brother Warrior to create an Inter-National Afro-American League that would unite Black Americans across different tribes. Warrior, also known as W. A. Rentie, was one of the half-siblings enslaved by the Creek tribe's chief, Roley McIntosh, and carried on his father's back to the wartime refugee camp as a ten-month-old baby. Warrior had benefited greatly from the semblance of equality that followed the Civil War and attended college at the Nashville Normal and Theological Institute, a Black Baptist school founded just after the war. By the 1890s, after working as a teacher at a Creek school, he went into politics and quickly became one of the strongest voices for the freedmen of the tribes. Land, he argued, should be allocated to the Black members of a tribe at a level equal to what the Native Americans received. Increasingly, Warrior found himself arguing against his former enslaver, the tribal chief.

As the pressure for land allotments grew, tensions developed between Native Americans and the freedmen. Some Native Americans in the tribe suggested that the Black members be disenfranchised (something not possible under the 1866 treaty). One Native American described the people she had formerly enslaved as "intruders" who were now "robbing our children of land and money." The surging fear of giving too much to Black Americans even spread to Isparhecher, the tribal leader who had previously spoken in favor of treating Black members equally. Isparhecher proposed an uneven land division, saying that if allotment occurred, Native Americans should receive 160 acres apiece and Black tribe members 40. Chief McIntosh, Warrior's former owner, helped lead discussions about disenfranchising Black tribal members or otherwise slowing "the ascendancy of the Negro race in the [Creek] Nation."

This desire of tribal leaders to protect what they believed was *theirs* was yet another attempt to exclude Black Americans from the full benefits of equality. Native American history had been replete with mistreatment by European settlers, including murdered family members and stolen land. Still, some of the tribal members did not want Black people to share in the land equally—yet they held the land in Oklahoma in part due to the labor of the people they had enslaved. The sweat of Black people lined the Trail of Tears, and even as freedmen, the formerly enslaved Black Americans continued to help the Native community build wealth. Any exclusionary effort was an affront to history and ignored the reality that more growth, wealth, and progress came from inclusion. "You have used our forefathers as you do now your horses and mules," an infuriated column in the *Muskogee Phoenix* read, "but the time shall never come when the present generation shall be treated thus. It is true that you once had him as property, but now he is on equality with you." The column is believed to have been written by Warrior Rentie.

For the Rentie family, the U.S. government's program—which ultimately allocated land to Black and Native people equally—was a positive path forward. When some Native Americans who opposed individual landownership rose up in a violent demonstration known as the Crazy Snake Uprising, the Renties did not participate. They wanted to own, explained Louis Rentie, a son of Morris and Katie. "We believed in allotment," he said. And he noted that his father, Morris, was a "businessman with an eye to the future."

When land allocation was done, Morris Rentie's family owned 2,400 acres. That land was spread among fifteen family members, who each received 160 acres. The Renties' fifteen plots were located in the town of Henryetta, about fifty-four miles south of Tulsa, a city originally settled as a Creek tribal town but incorporated by white settlers in 1898. The broader Rentie family, including Morris, Warrior, and all their siblings, received at least 10,000 acres in total, our research found. Not only did the Renties become landowners, but they also became U.S. citizens. Harkening back to the Jeffersonian ideal of the landowning citizen, the U.S. government married the two.

This was how Morris's and Warrior's families came to be treated as equals to their former owners.

The Homestead Gap

When discussing anything "given" to Black Americans—like the acres allocated to the Rentie family—it's worth pausing to understand how much land was given to white Americans. The Black-white wealth gap is not only about the movement in the Black wealth line. It's also about the events that put the white wealth line up in the sky.

Before the Civil War, decades of land giveaways and subsidies sprang from federal government programs. These programs, which focused on new states or regions such as Ohio or Florida, were generally for white people. In Congress, some lawmakers said there should be laws specifying that the land grants were for white people, while others replied that such a law would be superfluous because Black individuals were not citizens (a view confirmed by the U.S. Supreme Court in the 1857 *Dred Scott* decision). Obtaining federal land was a benefit for citizens.

In 1862, far more land went up for grabs. Under the newly passed Homestead Act, the U.S. government expanded land grants, allocating 160 acres of land per recipient. Over the next eighty years, 1.5 million families would receive 240 million acres. Though this program was post-emancipation, only 5,000 of those 1.5 million families were Black.

Another program, the 1866 Southern Homestead Act, was set up specifically to help the formerly enslaved population of the South. The press at the time referred to it as the "Negro Homestead Bill," and leaders in Congress spoke passionately about how Black Americans *deserved* some land to get a fair start. According to Samuel Pomeroy, chairman of the Senate Committee on Public Lands, "They have been stripped of everything. True, thank God! They are free, but they have nothing but their hands to rely upon for support, and they want land."

"Every nation is weakened when its citizens have no homes," U.S. representative John Shanks of Indiana concurred. Though opponents of the bill warned that it would deprive plantation owners of labor needed to continue to grow cotton, the bill passed.

But there were many problems with the program. Much of the available acreage was not great farmland. And some was tied up in old deals with railroad companies, leaving land grant officials uncertain as to whether they could even give away the titles to it. In addition, some local officers of the program were ensnared in fraudulent grants. Still other land was claimed by timber investors who would claim it, strip the timber, and then move away. Just ten years into the program, despite the federal government's introducing timber agents to police the matter, timber investors successfully lobbied congressmen to release the land to them rather than to the homestead program. With that, Congress voted to repeal the law altogether.

In the end, the aborted Southern Homestead Act granted land to only four thousand Black families. It was nowhere near the broad impact that advocates of "forty acres and a mule" had hoped to have before that program was annulled. On top of that, many of the land recipients somehow turned out to be white: in Mississippi, historian Michael Lanza studied a sample of the grants and found that 70.7 percent in this "Negro Homestead" program went to white people.

Perhaps the main upshot of the government's homestead programs was that they lured many white Americans to move out west. This meant those white families left or sold land they had previously held dear on the East Coast. This opened up some areas for Black Americans to purchase property, which they did, as we'll see in chapter 8. While purchasing the land is not as much of a wealth transfer as receiving it as a gift, the land shift that occurred leading into the 1900s meant a shift in the wealth gap as well.

An Eye for Business

The two million acres the United States awarded to Black tribal members was, *Smithsonian Magazine* said, "the largest transfer of land wealth to Black people in the history of the United States."

The Rentie family wanted to put their new assets to good use. Along with Morris's eye for business, his half brother Warrior brought to bear the training of a lawyer, politician, and businessman. While many freedmen were farmers with little education, Warrior stood out, and scholar Gary Zellar has written that Warrior typified the formerly enslaved person that an Arkansas politician was talking about in 1904 when he said, "I can say for the Negroes of the [Creek Nation] Indian Territory that—as a body of people—they are in advance of any body of colored people that I know of in any of the States. They have had the benefit of free schools and colleges for more than half a century. They are educated, they are self-assertive, they are aggressive." Records with the federal body in charge of allotments, known as the Dawes Commission, show that the Rentie family was aggressive in filing claims for what they viewed as the best land. They also worked hard to keep their plots clustered next to each other.

Warrior looked to banking to secure the financial future of his family and broader community. In 1905, more than one hundred years before Ryan Glover would start Greenwood Bank, Ryan's ancestor cofounded the Creek Citizens Bank. The *Topeka Plaindealer* described the bank that year as "one of the strongest and best financial institutions in that portion of the territory." The bank was included in W. E. B. Du Bois's 1907 study of Black banks across the country. At the time, people spoke of it with awe. "This was the first Negro bank with a Negro president and other officers that we ever saw," the *Topeka Plaindealer* article continued. "So much of interest did we see in connection with this bank that we can never forget it. There was a large, steel safe, with time-lock vaults, a fine roll-top desk and revolving chair and other fixtures, and so much cash! The Negro president discussing loans and discounts, while customers were coming and going. The men who are connected with this bank are worth more than a quarter of a million dollars."

Warrior Rentie's wealth was on display in press coverage of the Creek Citizens Bank. The *Plaindealer* made a point of noting that Rentie and his children owned 880 acres of land. It was a large amount of land, though not quite as much as his older brother Morris owned.

Morris and Warrior had a bond in political activism and fighting for equality. The same year that Warrior founded the Creek Citizens Bank, Morris attended the Sequoyah Convention, a failed effort by Native Americans to convince the U.S. government to create a Native American state separate from the incipient state of Oklahoma. Soon after, when Oklahoma's state constitution defined Black Americans as a distinct group of people, paving the way for Jim Crow laws there, Warrior represented Black freedmen in a visit with President Theodore Roosevelt. Warrior urged the president to refuse to support Oklahoma's constitution. The president told Warrior and the others to take their concerns to the Justice Department. Oklahoma became a state in 1907.

For the Renties, the riches of their land, the bank, and other developing businesses would be stymied by an influx of white businesspeople, the rise of Jim Crow, and a backlash against Black Americans in the new state. When oil was found on local land, the practice of "grifting" emerged, as businessmen developed deals aimed at taking over people's properties. Some grifting focused heavily on Black Americans because the federal government allowed Black Americans to sell large portions of their land without the restrictions it had imposed on Native Americans. In the years between 1910 and the start of the Great Depression, the Rentie family ended up in many legal battles over their land and, consequently, even over the custody of their children.

"Graft and exploitation became widespread practices in Indian Territory and Oklahoma Territory," according to *Smithsonian Magazine*.

"Given implicit permission by the federal government, white professionals continued a wide-ranging effort to dismantle Black wealth in the region." Some of the practices *Smithsonian* highlighted included predatory contracts to sell land, the theft of land, and the coercion of Black Americans to leave town. The worst grifting happened through guardianships.

Because the federal government allocated land to children under the age of eighteen, non-family members saw these riches in the hands of children and emerged to argue that the parents were incompetent, in order to then petition to take on guardianships of the children. This sort of grifting got even more feverish when oil was found on the children's land. Sarah Rector was once called "the richest colored girl" in the country for the oil found on her land. Rector's oil deals were with various oil companies, including Prairie Oil and Gas, one of the main players in the crude oil business in the Midwest and a subsidiary of the Rockefellers' Standard Oil. Rector received a $300,000 signing bonus and then 12.5 percent in royalties. She lived in a shack on her property while her white guardian became rich. The Black press finally exposed her situation, and Rector got more control of her money and moved away to Kansas City, Missouri, where she lived in a mansion. But according to the *Muskogee Times-Democrat*, some 143 Black children in the Muskogee area ended up in orphanages in 1910 when their guardians accepted similar deals on the children's parcels. Andrew J. Smitherman, a leading Black journalist in Oklahoma, found that more than 3,000 Black and Native American children were put into guardianships in this era, almost entirely with white Americans as guardians. These guardians, he found, took $100 million from the children they were supposed to protect. "The biggest game of graft in the state today is the guardianship graft," Smitherman said at the time. "They have 'Jim Crowed' us, attempted to disenfranchise us, taxed us without giving us representation, and after doing all of this, they are clamoring to be guardians of our children—the children of the race they have so grossly wronged."

The troubles began for the Rentie family in 1910, when oil was discovered on land owned by Warrior and his children. Rather than giving Warrior the option to be the guardian of his own children, he was simply notified that a guardian had been appointed for them. The oil would bring in $120,000 per year, a sizable sum. Warrior was perplexed as to why he could not be his children's guardian—after all, he was their father and an educated, successful businessman. He visited the man who was set to be appointed by the court as his children's new guardian and told him, "The day you are appointed guardian of my children is the day you will die." The next day, Warrior was arrested. Eventually, after a battle, the court renamed him guardian of his children.

The troubles then moved to Morris's oldest son, Isaac. In 1916, Isaac lost guardianship of his daughter Henrietta, age thirteen. A white man named William Harrower was named guardian. It's unclear to us why Harrower, often called "W.H." in the records, was considered more qualified to oversee Henrietta's affairs than her own father. According to census records, Harrower had only a fourth-grade education—Henrietta herself had completed the sixth grade—and a patchwork résumé as a farmer and traveling grocer. Harrower's guardianship of Henrietta lasted two years before her parents got their rights restored. But the experience was surely traumatic emotionally and financially. By 1940, Harrower owned a wholesale oil and gas company as well as his own home. As of 1940, Henrietta lived in a rental home.

Next up in the guardian shuffle was Esther Rentie, a niece of Morris's. Her father was her guardian until sixteen days before her eighteenth birthday. Over the course of those sixteen days, three other guardians were named in quick succession. By 1923, a fourth man was named, as the local court decided that even though Esther was older than eighteen, she still needed a guardian. All this activity was about who would control the right to profit from Esther's land. The land was rented to Prairie Oil and Gas for thirty thousand dollars a year.

At least some of the money went to Esther, and she was able to acquire property elsewhere: In 1930, she owned a home in Kansas City, directly across the street from the mansion of Sarah Rector, once "the richest colored girl" in the country. There Esther rented out rooms to nine boarders. She died in 1939, at thirty-five. By 2023, a two-family redbrick town house sat at her old address.

Oil industry records show numerous mentions of oil wells on Rentie-owned land in the 1920s. Contemporaneous newspaper accounts and court files show that guardians continued to run affairs for several Rentie children. The activity became so egregious that Andrew Smitherman decided to start the Negro Guardianship League to battle abusive guardians, with Smitherman playing a dual role as journalist and advocate. (These dual roles were common among the press back then.) Warrior Rentie provided the funding for Smitherman's organization.

As he fought on behalf of Black parents, Smitherman moved from Muskogee, where the Rentie family was largely based, to Tulsa, to start a newspaper. His paper, the *Tulsa Star*, was headquartered in the Greenwood district, where Black people ran a slew of businesses. Those Black businessmen had purchased the land for the district from a Native American, using funds from their own land allotments. Some of the Rentie family moved to Greenwood, too, including descendants of one of Morris's younger brothers. Morris's name was passed down this line of the family as they raised their children in Greenwood's booming period. As one of these family members, also named Morris Rentie, would recall about Greenwood, "It was something to see the way people got along together." Business, he said, "was swinging."

Black Wall Street

Guardianships and corrupt deals around oil fields notwithstanding, some Black and Native Americans gained oil wealth and started using it to build business districts. A member of the Rentie family, William, donated twenty acres to help build the downtown of a new all-Black town called Rentiesville. Another Rentie, Stephen and his children, founded Rentie Grove, a neighborhood on the Tulsa city border.

Just a few miles away, in Tulsa, the Greenwood district flourished with so many banks, businesses, and well-off homeowners that it became known as Black Wall Street. This was an area with bustling commerce, churches, hundreds of businesses, handsome buildings with bright window displays and well-dressed clientele, and families raising children with an air and promise of upward mobility.

At the same time, Jim Crow laws were being passed in Oklahoma.

For a while, Greenwood residents operated relatively unbothered. They did much of their shopping in the district, and many of them worked there. This put their money into a circular motion, insulating at least some funds to *some* degree and protecting that money from immediately leaving the community. As Eli Grayson, one descendant of a Black Creek tribe member, recalls, "Back in those days, because of Jim Crow laws, Black people could only spend money among Black people. They couldn't go to the white store, Macy's. They had to spend it in the Black communities. And that dime that they spent there on a Saturday morning or Saturday afternoon went into that community, stayed in that community, rotated in that community up to nineteen times."

This "recirculation" concept is one we will return to, and question, as we follow the story of the contemporary Greenwood Bank. It's a bit like the "double dollar" concept that appealed to Atlanta entrepreneurs around the same time, and to businessmen like Frank Smith Young in Louisiana. In the case of Black Wall Street, other circumstances intervened.

Life in Greenwood came to a tragic halt in May 1921, after accusations of the rape of a white woman were lodged against a Black teenager. A large group of white men stormed the jailhouse where the accused teen was being held. When local Black residents tried to help the police protect the jail, the white men flooded the streets of Greenwood in retaliation. Tulsa descended into racial conflict. The white mob destroyed nearly every building, including the printing presses of the *Tulsa Star*. Up to three hundred people were murdered. An eyewitness (a white woman who was a girl at the time) described the scene this way:

> Cattle trucks heavily laden with bloody, dead, Black bodies…some were naked, some dressed only in pants…. They looked like they had been thrown upon the truck beds haphazardly for arms and legs were sticking out through the slats…. On the second truck, lying spread-eagled atop the high pile of corpses, I saw the body of a little Black boy, barefooted, just about my age…. Suddenly, the truck hit a manhole in the street. His head rolled over, facing me, staring as though he had been frightened to death.

Greenwood residents fled their homes out of fear of being attacked. Some Greenwood residents and business owners were trapped by white attackers during the riots in places like nearby Rentie Grove. Some Black citizens were arrested, including journalist Andrew Smitherman, charged with inciting violence: he had been outside the courthouse when the conflict began. The newspaperman and his family fled Oklahoma.

The mobs and attacks seen in Atlanta in 1906 were along the same lines. The attacks in Greenwood have become famous, but this sort of Black-directed violence happened in many places, including Wilmington, Washington, D.C., and multiple towns in Florida. Such attacks would return to Atlanta in the form of neighborhood mobs in the 1920s through the 1950s.

This legacy of mob violence was partly a financial one. A group of white Americans took away the ability of Black Americans to live and work in the Greenwood district, thereby expropriating the hustle-bustle of a local economy. Though some property there remained in Black ownership, that energy driving local wealth would never fully return. Business owners in Greenwood would spend years battling with Tulsa over their rights to rebuild on their own property, while their customer base and community lost their strength.

The effects on generational wealth have been long term, according to research by historians Jeremy Cook and Jason Long. Writing in *The Atlantic*, Cook and Long analyzed the census records of families in the Greenwood district affected by the riots, finding in records from after the attack "a striking contrast to the rising Black prosperity of 1910s Tulsa." Between 1920 and 1930, and again between 1930 and 1940, "earnings steadily declined for Black household heads," a pattern not replicated in comparable cities at the time. "In 1920, wages of Black household heads were 9 percent higher in Tulsa than in our set of 14 control cities; by 1940, they were 7 percent *lower*. Meanwhile, white Tulsans' wages followed the same pattern as in the control cities—roughly constant from 1920 to 1930 before modestly declining from 1930 to 1940. And throughout the 20 years, white wages were *higher* in Tulsa than in the control cities."

Census records for individual families in the area also showed Black people dropping in economic status—after the Greenwood attacks, business owners and managers ended up in low-level jobs. Census records for the Rentie family over time show similar losses of wealth and status as land was lost, we found.

When the attacks in Greenwood occurred, Morris Rentie's family, located just south of Tulsa, was recovering from a tragedy. On February 12, 1920, Morris's daughter Delilah died at age thirty-four. This was Ryan Glover's great-grandmother. Delilah had two children, one of whom, Hartle Mae, would become Ryan's grandmother. Upon Delilah's death, her husband, Frederick Behn, held full custody of both her children and her land.

Like the Renties, Fred Behn had long embraced landownership. Born enslaved in Georgia in 1860, the son of the plantation owner, Behn moved to Oklahoma in 1900 as a preacher. He had started buying land there by 1903. According to his family, he owned 280 acres by 1906, and by 1925, he owned a car.

His family took pride in Fred Behn's confidence and assertiveness. He believed in equality, they said, and stood up for his family's rights. "Reverend Behn did not allow himself to be confined to the limits that society placed upon him because of his race," his descendants wrote in a family reunion guidebook, adding that "racism did not prevent him from standing up for his rights." The guidebook cited the stock market crash of 1929, after which "many Blacks were afraid to ask for their money for fear of retaliation from bankers. Not Reverend Behn! He demanded and received his money."

As we talked with Ryan Glover and studied his career, we thought about his ancestors Warrior and Morris Rentie's standing up for Black freedmen's rights to land and Warrior's starting a bank. We thought about Fred Behn's demanding his money from banks in 1929. And we wondered more about why none of this had translated into a more privileged upbringing for Ryan.

Part of the answer might lie in what happened to the land. Through a convoluted chain of records, we discovered that all of Delilah's property was sold over time to white buyers, who sold it to other white people. The overall Rentie family property had been subdivided into small suburban lots—299 parcels as of 2022. Only two of those parcels, totaling eighty acres, still belong to a person with the surname "Rentie."

In 1920, when Delilah died, Hartle Mae was three years old. Fred went on to remarry and, across three marriages, had ten children in total. He left his property to his "youngest children," which may or may not have included Ryan Glover's grandmother. By the 1940s, Hartle Mae was married to Letha Boyce Bennett, a farmer, and living in Henryetta, Oklahoma. As their daughter, Fern, recalled to us about Letha's family, "They worked from 'can to can't' all their life, from the time you could work, when the sun came up, to the time that the sun went down, as long as you could stay in the field," she added. Letha went off to fight in World War II, and Hartle Mae waited for him in Oklahoma. Upon his return, they surveyed the situation there and decided they needed to move. They ended up in housing projects just north of San Francisco, where Ryan Glover would eventually grow up.

Letha and Hartle Mae both worked and saved money to support their family, Fern told us. Regarding her family's land in Oklahoma, she told us she didn't want to dig into how her mother's family lost it, saying, "The times were so horrible way back then, I never had any desire to go back in history and look at it."

Fern's son, Ryan, however, had become interested in delving into the past. Amid his work setting up Greenwood Bank in 2020, Ryan became deeply suspicious about what had happened to the land in his mother's family. And he was preparing to go to battle for it. "I am literally in pre-litigation with a family in Oklahoma that finessed my grandparents out of land that they're drilling oil on in Tulsa," he told us. "I have the paperwork, documentation. And I am simultaneously in a battle with an institution that finessed my grandparents out of close to two hundred acres in Oklahoma."

Our in-depth research of Ryan's grandmother's property found a different storyline—the land was sold not to an institution, but to white people, decades ago. When we pressed Ryan on what institution he was referring to, he demurred, and pressed us to give him our research. (At this point, we had conducted multiple interviews with Ryan, but suddenly, his assistant pressed us to pay Ryan for spending time talking to us.)

Perhaps drawing on the determination of his relatives Warrior and Morris Rentie, Ryan had developed his eye for business and a determination to fight. He had leapt across Black wealth barriers and ended up in the Black upper crust. He had a wife who posted social media videos of herself unboxing things like Louis Vuitton purses.

After all of Ryan's ancestors' struggles to hold on to their land, to hold on to custody of their children, to fight for Black Americans' rights and build Black-owned institutions—a Black-owned bank, even—Ryan had styled himself as the modern-era version of Greenwood, Oklahoma, business owners: an entrepreneur with grand visions and deep ambition, out raising capital.

Pitching Greenwood

Alex Harris and his business partner, Drew Glover (no relation to Ryan), built their marketing services company, Fiat Growth, with a mission to help grow diversity-focused companies. "We all care deeply about financial inclusion," Harris told us. "And a democratization of wealth building."

Based in the Bay Area, Fiat was led by Black and white cofounders who had been friends for a couple of decades since college and who had worked together at a banking app start-up called Chime. In October 2020, they heard about Greenwood Bank. "It looks like we are about to reach out to a client for the first time," Harris told his cofounder. Harris saw Greenwood's mission and thought he and Drew Glover could help. But before they got a chance to call Greenwood, Greenwood called them.

Greenwood's founders were raising investor money and trying to set up a customer waiting list. They were twenty-first-century prospectors, pitching their start-up in search of new funding streams. The riches that could be found in the prairies of Oklahoma one hundred years before had been replaced in the present day by venture capital-funded start-ups. And as a mobile banking app, Greenwood had entered a hot investment space.

As important as the founders of a company are to its trajectory, an institution like Greenwood would be defined nearly as much by its investors. In the case of Greenwood Bank: Were its investors Black?

Were they committed to lifting up Black and Latino communities? What were their incentives and where would they likely push this mission-focused company?

Greenwood brought Fiat on to set up its customer waiting list. The Fiat team drew on their experience at Chime, a banking website and mobile app launched in 2014 by white entrepreneurs; Chime provided an alternative to traditional banking and relied on an FDIC-backed bank to hold its customers' deposits. Like Greenwood, Chime was in the buzzy "fintech" space, the area of technology focusing on financial services, and it had eight million account holders by February 2020. (As a point of comparison, JPMorgan Chase had twenty-five million debit card users in the 2020s.) For its customers, Chime was not focused on any one race or demographic, but many newer financial start-ups had been. There was Copper, a fintech bank for teenagers; Sigo Seguros, an insurance app focused on Spanish speakers; Fair, which focused on the Muslim population; Pomelo, for money transfers to and from the Philippines; and Daylight, for the LGBTQ+ community. The list went on. And then there would be Greenwood Bank, a platform focused on the Black and, supposedly, also Latino populations.

Fiat worked for free in the fall of 2020 and early 2021, offering a marketing plan that helped Greenwood amass sign-ups from potential customers—first thousands, then tens of thousands, then into the hundreds of thousands. In exchange for this work, Fiat's cofounders received equity and became among the earliest Greenwood investors.

It was not a given that Greenwood's long waiting list would turn into a profitable base of customers. Some people on the list might have liked Greenwood's ideas and signed up as, essentially, supporters, but when it came down to it, they might not shift their paycheck deposits, utility payments, and other ongoing transactions there, simply because of the hassle of moving such things. Still, the Fiat team was hopeful that bringing so many Black and Latino customers into one app would at least create a useful dataset—information about a bloc of consumers that could be monetized in some way and, ideally, they said, used for good.

Over time, Greenwood pitched additional investors. The demographics of the Fiat team—one white, one Black—seemed indicative of the reality of the investment and funding landscape. The scarcity of Black wealth and Black venture capitalists would make it difficult for Greenwood to get off the ground without significant white investment.

And white investors were hungry to participate. In early 2021, riding the coattails of the ongoing push for racial equity, Greenwood announced that it had raised forty million dollars. The investors included six of the seven largest banks in the country, among them JPMorgan Chase, Bank of America, Wells Fargo, and its largest investor, Truist Financial Corporation. In other words, Greenwood Bank's largest outside investor by early 2021 was a publicly traded bank with a white chief executive officer.

Perhaps these white investors simply reflected the most available pools of investment capital. Yet, besides being white-run and owned, these banks did not have great track records with Black Americans.

Truist Financial had been formed and renamed in 2019 in a merger. Before that, it was SunTrust Bank and BB&T. Like all the banks that invested in Greenwood, SunTrust and BB&T were criticized after the 2008 financial crisis for predatory lending and other mortgage issuance violations. SunTrust had been an Atlanta institution since its founding in 1891. Many of its questionable mortgage loans were in Atlanta and the broader Southeast, and many questionable loans were to Black families.

Now, with Greenwood, SunTrust had gotten a foot back into Black banking. Vanessa Vreeland, a banker who led the investment for Truist, said that the deal reflected the bank's purpose of building better communities. All the legacy banks, she said, including Truist, had trouble attracting and retaining Black and Latino customers. "We just felt like Greenwood was doing it in a very authentic way. So, we wanted to ensure that there was support for those clients, even if they weren't coming to us," she told us. "We also felt like maybe there was something we [could] learn about how to develop trusted relationships with these segments."

Another early investor was MetaBank, now called Pathward Financial. That South Dakota–based bank had a problematic history with lower-income Black Americans. The matter concerned the RushCard, a prepaid card issued in partnership with MetaBank. The card, introduced in 2003, was made famous by hip-hop artist Russell Simmons. But when the card experienced a technology glitch in 2015, customers were blocked from obtaining their money. It caused an outcry in the Black community and, eventually, a financial settlement.

As we talked with the early investors, we repeatedly heard that it was the biographies of the founders that had drawn them to support Greenwood. "They are incredibly charismatic, and they believe in the mission that they're pursuing here," said Adam Davies, another former Truist banker who worked on the Greenwood investment. "What they're trying to do is create wealth. It's not just about somewhere where you have an account. It's about creating it."

It was still early days, and though Greenwood did not yet have a mobile app—or any other product, for that matter—it already had people on its waiting list. It had love from the Black community.

For the marketing gurus at Fiat, Greenwood Bank's mission of closing racial wealth gaps made its success important not only for investors like them to get a return, but also for society. "There's some eyes on them," Harris said. If Greenwood wasn't successful, he said, "it wouldn't be fatal to the movement that they're representing, but it wouldn't be good. It'd be a step back." He added, "I really want them to be successful."

CHAPTER 5

JAMES WOODALL AND THE FEDERALLY FUNDED GAP

*The way colored people have suffered under the New Deal . . . is
a disgrace that stinks to heaven.*
—Forrester Washington, director for Negro Work, Federal
     Emergency Relief Administration, Atlanta office

JUNE 2020

In the days and nights of June 2020, Atlanta was coming apart.

Despite a 9 p.m. curfew imposed by the mayor at her press conference with Michael Render, scores of people were out night after night. Centennial Park and the CNN headquarters were common gathering points. People at the demonstrations said it was about more than the killing of George Floyd. It was also about race and money.

The inequality of daily life "is quiet like carbon dioxide, and it is killing you, but it's not like you smell it; you just start to get weak," said Carol Anderson, a professor of African American studies at Emory University and author of the book *White Rage*, as demonstrations continued. She said, "Black folks have been having the conversation for so long."

Another demonstrator, Nilaja Green, an Atlanta-based trauma specialist, said, "Yes, slavery has ended, but the prison industrial complex houses five times [the rate of] African Americans than whites. Yes, we can legally attend the same schools and vie for the same jobs, but the net worth of an African American family today falls several tiers below that of their white counterparts."

Descendants of Atlanta's Black elite pointed to a change in the city's relationship with Black Americans. "This is supposed to be our haven for Black people; it doesn't feel that way," said Isabella Jackson, a twenty-one-year-old Spelman College student and a granddaughter of Maynard Jackson, the first Black mayor of Atlanta. (Andrew Young followed Jackson as the city's second Black mayor.) "Older people may be accustomed in injustice, or they may be more compliant. Not on purpose, but out of fear," Jackson continued. "People my age say they don't mind this country burning down." Jackson said she was horrified when, on May 30, she saw a video of a Spelman classmate and a Morehouse student tased and then arrested by the Atlanta Police Department. The video showed the police dragging the couple out of their car while tasing them. Their offense? Being out after the 9 p.m. curfew.

James Woodall, the NAACP's Georgia president, stood at the center of the public debate over the demonstrations. Only eight months into his appointment, James had gained a reputation as a rising leader in Black activism and politics. He spoke for many about the Taser incident when he said, "This is the exact kind of policing behavior thousands have been protesting."

A few days later, a police officer was caught on camera violently handling a Black woman leaving a demonstration at the mall in Buckhead, the wealthy neighborhood that would soon try to secede from Atlanta. The officer pulled Amber Jackson, a local dental hygienist, to the ground two times, once pushing her forward and a second time grabbing her from behind and pulling her backward with his arm around her neck. James called for the Atlanta police chief to resign and the officer to be fired.

The demonstrations grew stronger with each beat in the story. By mid-June, James was out with demonstrators almost every day. On June 12, Rayshard Brooks was shot outside a Wendy's restaurant, and the next day, demonstrators set fire to that Wendy's. Then hundreds of demonstrators of all races walked together blocking Atlanta's main interstate. Yet there was "complete silence from the City of Atlanta," James said as the crowd linked arms to block traffic. He quoted Martin Luther King Jr.: "In the end, we will remember not the words of our enemies, but the silence of our friends." A few days later, standing determinedly, in his collared shirt and Covid-19 mask, James led hundreds of people marching on the Georgia State Capitol downtown. "We are going to take over the Capitol every single day until they do their job," he called out.

At age twenty-six, James was a wonder to many in the Black activism community. He passionately reminded people to focus on the "whos" of policies and not just the "whats." *Who* would benefit, he would prod, and was that *who* disproportionately made up of one race? Amid these provocations, James also shared his own story: He had a father in prison. He grew up watching his mother and stepfather take out payday loans. He had moved from school to school as his mother tried to keep up with rent payments. The way he told the story resonated with many "whos." He could mingle with the elite at the Aspen Ideas Festival, and he could lead young people from underserved communities in demonstrations and rallies. As Michael Curry, a longtime NAACP leader in Boston involved in the organization nationally, told us, "People *want* to hear what he has to say, and that's a critical part of being a leader."

James's ascent to leadership was more incredible, and his role more challenging, than many realized. The job to lead Georgia's state chapter for the NAACP was prestigious, but it was also unpaid. And as the summer of 2020 continued, speaking on behalf of the demonstrators grew more complicated. There were many issues motivating people—white, Black, Latino, and of all backgrounds—to take to the streets. The police killings were at the forefront, but economics and inequality were also motivating factors. The history behind the Black-white wealth gap was always present, even if not always talked about.

Beyond local actions like zoning, Jim Crow laws, and white attacks on Black business districts, the federal government worsened the Black-white wealth gap throughout the 1900s by spending huge amounts of money to support the public and, ultimately, to build a middle class. The problem, as James liked to put it, was the "who" in the recipients: who benefited, and who did not, from the federal money spigot in areas like New Deal relief, housing financing, veterans' benefits, banking rules, and most recently, student loan programs. The NAACP's rising star circa 2020 knew which side he fell on.

It Matters Where You Live

The roots of James Woodall's family in Atlanta stretch back generations to Frances Walker, his great-grandmother, who was born in 1927 to parents who *owned* their home in the city's Bankhead neighborhood. Frances's father served in World War I, then he came to the city, worked as a railyard laborer, and later at Atlanta Water Works. When he and Frances's mother became homeowners, the Bankhead area was was home to many white families. The Walker home would long provide a glimmer of hope in a family tree that was not otherwise upwardly mobile.

The picture was grimmer in rural Georgia than in Atlanta, where the man whom Frances Walker would marry, Jesse Day, James's great-grandfather, was growing up. Day's family rented farmland in rural Georgia, in a town called Broad River, northeast of Athens. The family had a long history of renting farmland: Day's father's parents and their parents had done so.

By 1930, the Day household was crowded with Jesse and his six siblings, some of whom were starting their own families; his parents; and two Black boarders, all working on the rented farmland. According to U.S. Census documents from the late 1800s, most of Jesse Day's family in earlier generations did not know how to read or write, and Day's father learned to do so only in his thirties. Day himself had a fourth-grade education, having dropped out to help on the farm. There was no radio on the property, the 1930 Census noted.

James's mother's paternal side, the Woodalls, also came from the countryside and were ensnared in the same economic cycles. His great-grandfather Ernest Woodall was born forty-five miles south of Atlanta, into a family farming rented land. Ernest's father was born to a father who also rented farmland, after he was freed from slavery. They were sharecroppers, descendants of the many formerly enslaved people who earned very small wages after paying the mostly white men who owned the land they worked, often building up debt to the landowners in the bargain. On James's father's side was James's paternal grandfather, Vester Robinson, who rented farmland east of Atlanta; and a great-grandfather, too, who rented farmland in the late 1800s. Vester had completed the sixth grade, he noted in 1940 just before he signed up to serve in World War II; his father had completed the second.

The lack of education in James's family members of the early 1900s is not surprising. When it came to schools and health care, there was a dramatic gap in what the government was providing to white families versus Black ones. Spending on Black education was pennies on the dollar compared with funding for white education back then. Schools were very much separate and *not* equal. Mississippi and Georgia were the two lowest-spending southern states in the mid-1930s, spending only $9.00 per Black child versus the average of $49.30 per white child. In a 1920 NAACP meeting held in Atlanta, the journalist and NAACP cofounder Charles Russell spoke about illiteracy being a problem in World War I and noted that eight to ten times more money was spent on white students than on Black students. According to a contemporary estimate by a charitable fund created by a co-owner of Sears, the disparity was so severe that bringing schools for Black students up to par with schools for white students would have cost $240 million nationally.

There were also far fewer medical options for Black Americans in the 1930s, and doctor's visits were costly. Services were offered differently to Black Americans than to white people. For instance, hospitals in Atlanta allowed white birthing mothers to remain under their care for three days after giving birth. Black mothers, in contrast, had to leave the hospital within twenty-four hours. The infant mortality rate for Black babies was 69 percent higher than that for white babies.

All of James Woodall's predecessors would end up in Atlanta between 1934 and 1950, in search of something better. There they would be greeted by new, unequal federal programs.

The Unequal New Deal

It was the start of the Great Depression, and news delivered via radio sets—which some of James's countryside relatives did not own—was an important way of learning about potential new benefits.

The Federal Emergency Relief Administration, established in 1933 by President Franklin Roosevelt, distributed an unprecedented amount of money to states to help residents in need. The Civil Works Administration and the Works Progress Administration soon followed. Disbursement of their funds was left up to the states, and in the South, the total giveaway from just these three programs added up to about 10.7 billion dollars.

The problem was that the local administration of funds left a lot of room for inequity, and inequity there was. In Georgia, some counties refused to give any federal relief money to Black residents, and many southern states provided rural white residents with far more relief than rural Black residents, according to Ira Katznelson's book *When Affirmative Action Was White*. That book cited a report in the 1940s that found that the relief gap between white and Black Americans came from "discrepancies in administrative practices and standards." These government units also had cases of inequitable allocations. For example, agricultural workers were not allowed to receive relief if it was harvest time, and this disproportionally affected Black families.

Forrester Washington, the director for Negro Work at the Federal Emergency Relief Administration's Atlanta office, cried foul. "The way colored people have suffered under the New Deal," he said when he resigned in 1934, "is a disgrace that stinks to heaven."

The billions of dollars in inequitable spending continued beyond the initial relief programs, with mid-1930s legislation creating Social Security benefits for the elderly, unemployment insurance, and other forms of social insurance. Again, these were not equitably distributed. Social Security excluded occupations like housekeeping and farmwork, which affected Black Americans at a higher rate than white Americans. (Social Security would be changed in the mid-1950s to allow all occupations, but by then, the exclusions had significantly contributed to the racial wealth gap.)

Charles Houston, the counsel of the NAACP, testified to Congress in 1935 that these programs were run like "a sieve with holes just big enough for the majority of Negroes to fall through." Houston also emphasized that they were disadvantageous to "Negro sharecroppers and Negro cash tenants, who are just about at the bottom of the economic scale."

This situation described the Day, Robinson, and Woodall sides of James Woodall's family: Black farmers who rented, like their parents and grandparents and their great-grandparents. Throughout the 1930s, as branches of James's family moved to Atlanta in the hope of changing their fortunes, a debate was under way about what to make of President Roosevelt's programs. Journalists and Black leaders were divided. On the one hand, they provided an influx of money to Black Americans. On the other, it was only a trickle for Black Americans while the broader sink overflowed.

A central forum for these discussions was the *Atlanta Daily World*. Founded in 1928, the *World* was located in the heart of the Sweet Auburn district, where Black-owned businesses were concentrated. Like many Black news outlets in the mid-1930s, the newspaper was ambivalent in its positions around the New Deal. Of the initial emergency relief programs, the *World* wrote that the New Deal programs put the Black American in "the same place assigned to him at the close of the Civil War." But by the mid-1930s, as Black homeowners struggled with their mortgages during the Depression, the *World* and other Black news outlets sometimes blamed Black individuals for not seeking out help, rather than questioning the government.

It was difficult to see in real time how federal funds were flowing, but in retrospect, the 1930s heralded a new period in real estate history, redlining, which built on the decades of municipal zoning discussions we described in chapter 2. In this new phase, the federal government and federal funds wove the wealth gap further into the fabric of American cities.

Redlining and the Home Owners' Loan Corporation

In 1933, Roosevelt's administration created a federal entity called the Home Owners' Loan Corporation, with the goal of stabilizing the housing and broader financial markets as the Depression wore on. The initial beneficiaries were businesses that had issued mortgages to homeowners. The HOLC, a federal entity with local field offices, bailed them out by purchasing their troubled loans and then refinancing them. Homeowners, too, stood to benefit, because the HOLC refinanced the loans on generous terms. Homeownership was not as widespread back then (in 1930, about 30 percent of all Americans owned homes), and it was more prevalent among white Americans than Black Americans. Still, the HOLC program had the potential to help homeowners of all races.

The Black community was divided on the HOLC. When there were questions about whether Black homeowners were being refinanced, the *Atlanta Daily World* criticized Black homeowners, saying they weren't seeking out the loans. "The southern Negro is a very timid creature," the newspaper wrote. "He stands back and murmurs despairingly to himself, instead of walking up to the front like a real man and asking for the things that are intended under the law." The Atlanta paper wasn't the only one that struck a positive initial note on the HOLC. In Philadelphia, the *Tribune*, a Black-owned paper, monitored the HOLC office and found that only "one in 65 or 70 persons" appearing there was Black. "This is either downright ignorance or a condition born of fool's gold," the *Tribune* wrote. "Negroes are not among those people who can afford to stand by while others walk away with the cake of something quite so valuable."

Some loan officers at the HOLC worked diligently with Black families. A review published in 2020 of HOLC's old correspondence, by historians Todd M. Michney and LaDale Winling, found that officers in Georgia's office kept the process moving quickly, especially for Black applicants. The priority, these professors found, was a high quantity of refinancings, not favoring one race over another. HOLC managers working in Georgia avoided credit reports, photographs of properties, and other things that would slow applications, especially from Black applicants. The HOLC managers pointed out that photographs might not be an option for "aged people or Negroes, generally incompetent to secure photographs and possessing no facility for photographing." The Atlanta managers at the HOLC (who were nearly all white) also made note that Black homeowners were not bad bets. "Our experience with Negro borrowers with reference to the regularity of their payments has been most satisfactory," the regional director of the HOLC in Atlanta reported. "As a general rule, a Negro will make his mortgage payments regularly as long as he is employed."

The result was that thousands of Black homeowners received HOLC refinancings and benefited from the Home Owners' Loan Corporation. While there had been instances of racism—the Memphis HOLC, at one point, said Black homeowners were "ineligible" for consideration—Black homeowners in many places were refinanced at the same or nearly the same proportion of their overall homeownership, the 2020 study found.

Still, within Atlanta, patterns tied to geography emerged. The HOLC's local office picked favored areas for Black refinancings, which contributed to the westward movement of Black families. The HOLC favored the west side of town. This contributed to an amplification of the migratory trend that would, by the 1950s, lead to the Black-led construction of Michael Render's grandparents' neighborhood in Collier Heights, but it was also creating a more segregated Atlanta. These west side neighborhoods, according to the HOLC, were the "best Negro [*sic*] area in Atlanta" with "the best type of Negro residents and highest percentage of Negro homeownership." Meantime, large pockets of Black Atlanta located more centrally in the city were areas that the HOLC did not view as favorable, and so, there were far fewer HOLC refinancings there. These neighborhoods included Summerhill and the Fourth Ward.

The Fourth Ward was a particularly notable case. Just one mile east of downtown Atlanta, it was a diverse and historic neighborhood that included the affluent Sweet Auburn district, home to Citizens Trust Bank and the *Atlanta Daily World*. It was where Dr. Martin Luther King Jr. was born in 1929 and where his father led the Ebenezer Baptist Church. Like much of Atlanta in the late 1800s and early 1900s, before zoning and white flight took hold, the Fourth Ward had been a racially mixed neighborhood, and it remained mixed even after the 1906 riots—until, in 1917, a large fire destroyed many historic homes and accelerated the push for more dividing lines. The white-run Atlanta

Real Estate Board noted that "encroachment of the races" was "harmful to the best interest of the city." Through various public programs over the next twenty years, Black residents were pushed out of adjacent areas and into the Fourth Ward. In the 1920s, the neighborhood was 61 percent inhabited by Black Americans, and that figure would increase in the following years. As the trend continued, the Fourth Ward was identified on government maps as an undesirable neighborhood. The HOLC noted that it included "one of the city's worst slums." Those words from the HOLC would have serious consequences for the people living there, including James's great-grandfather Jesse Day, who would move there from the countryside.

In the mid- to late 1930s, the HOLC set about one of its most controversial projects, creating maps for many cities that distinguished "best," "still desirable," "definitely declining," and "hazardous" neighborhoods. These maps, later known as redlining maps, would have profound and lasting negative impacts. Many historians have consequently blamed the HOLC for redlining, though other historians point out that the maps were made after the HOLC stopped refinancing mortgages and that the maps didn't exist while the HOLC made its earlier lending decisions. Whatever the case, the maps laid out a new precedent for subsequent government interaction with private lenders and encouraged lenders to avoid certain areas, often Black residential areas. The maps would lead to practices that discriminated against Black Americans, and they were central to how redlining—now known to be one of the greatest economic injustices of the twentieth century—got going in earnest.

In Atlanta's redlining map, the area labeled "D20" was the Fourth Ward. It was where Jesse Day and Frances Walker started their family, after Day moved to the city in the mid-1940s. To understand the barriers the Days would have faced if they had tried to get a mortgage, one need only look into the HOLC's commentary on the neighborhood. "Property in this area, if acquired, should be sold as quickly as possible," HOLC records noted. "Although this area is considered a good Negro rental area from an investment standpoint, it also contains one of the city's worst slum areas." The HOLC noted that the Fourth Ward consisted of 95 percent Black residents; had "many" families on relief; had residents who mainly worked as factory workers, laborers, and in domestic roles; and had typical family income between $400 to $1,200 per year. (As a point of comparison, Druid Hills, to the east of the Fourth Ward, had no Black residents and was considered a "still desirable" area by the HOLC. Residents there were described as "executives, business and professional men.") Beyond the statistics on the Fourth Ward's residents, the HOLC noted what it considered to be "detrimental influences" there: "age and dilapidated condition of many properties, difficulty of rental collections, high juvenile delinquency, infant mortality, tuberculosis incidence, death rate, and adult crime rate." It noted at the end of the list of "detrimental" factors that the area had "different racial groups." Given that by the HOLC's own admittance, the Fourth Ward was made up of 95 percent Black residents, this seems to have euphemistically meant "different from white people."

The NAACP Battles the Federal Housing Administration

Redlining, and the downgrading of the Fourth Ward, continued in earnest when the federal government introduced the Federal Housing Administration in 1934 to expand on the HOLC's rescue work. The FHA undertook a large-scale project to insure mortgages issued on homes around the country. This turned the government's housing rescue project into an ongoing, large-scale undertaking, with financial benefits to select people (generally, white Americans). It cemented discriminatory practices because it involved the federal government's pumping large amounts of money into housing subsidies for Americans.

The FHA had very particular ideas about which loans it was willing to guarantee. To create the lending rules, the agency hired leading private practitioners of valuation, including Frederick Babcock, who had been working at Prudential Insurance. In 1932, Babcock had written the main trade book, called *The Valuation of Real Estate*. His books made his views clear: "Most of the variations and differences between people are slight and value declines are, as a result, gradual," he wrote. "But, *there is one difference in people, namely race, which can result in a very rapid decline*. Usually such declines can be partially avoided by segregation and this device has always been in common usage in the South where white and Negro population have been separated."

In time, the FHA undertook a mapping project similar to the HOLC's. Its work was not transparent and at first escaped the awareness of Black social leaders. Only a tight circle of people was privy to the FHA's 1935 underwriting manual, which said, "If a neighborhood is to retain stability it is necessary that properties shall continue to be occupied by the same social and *racial classes*. A change in social or racial occupancy generally leads to instability and a reduction in values." Few knew, too, that the FHA's 1936 underwriting manual read that "the best type of residential district is one in which the values of the individual properties vary within comparatively narrow limits. . . . Such a district is characterized by **uniformity** and is much more likely to enjoy relatively great stability and permanence of desirability, utility and value." In 1938, the manual praised restrictive covenants, which were often used to block Black buyers—the manual said the covenants helped protect against "adverse influences." None of these manuals were easily obtained by the public.

By the late 1930s, anecdotes were emerging from around the country that the FHA was turning away potential homeowners because they were Black. In one example, a state senator in Ohio wrote to a resident who had been rejected for an FHA loan, saying, "I regret that you are among those whom (the FHA) does not benefit." The examples were reported in the press piecemeal and, often, to local branches of the NAACP.

The NAACP had been founded in 1909 by W. E. B. Du Bois and others in response to attacks on Black residents like the ones in Atlanta in 1906. The Atlanta branch of the organization was founded in 1917 by a group including John Hope, the president of Atlanta University; A. D. Williams (maternal grandfather of Martin Luther King Jr.); Benjamin Davis, the editor of a weekly Black newspaper; and Harry Pace, secretary-treasurer of the Standard Life Insurance Company, a rare Black-owned insurer. The branch was instrumental in the battle with the City of Atlanta to better fund schooling for Black children. As head of the Georgia NAACP in 2020, James Woodall would still be fighting similar battles more than a hundred years later.

The NAACP's record back in the 1930s is one of brave advocacy. Across the country, it was publicizing racist acts in its magazine, *The Crisis*. In 1938, the FHA caught the attention of Roy Wilkins, editor of *The Crisis*, and Thurgood Marshall, a then-rising leader of the association's legal team. A situation in New York City gave them an opening, illustrating how the NAACP oscillated between working hand in hand with the government and, when that didn't work, going public through the press and the court system. At the heart of this episode was a practice that robbed many Black Americans of the opportunity to build wealth and live where they wanted. "We received a telephone message a few days ago from a young white friend of ours in Brooklyn who said he was employed in some capacity with the Federal Housing Administration," Wilkins wrote to an official at the U.S. Housing Authority. "He advised us that unofficially the FHA is making as one of its requirements for guaranteeing mortgages that the buildings insert in the deed a clause *prohibiting sale, rental, or occupancy by persons of African descent*." The official, replying promptly on U.S. Housing Authority letterhead, said he didn't know about practices at the FHA.

As summer went on, the association collected letters from builders who said they were not able to secure bank financing to build apartment buildings for Black Americans unless they built them far away from white neighborhoods. One builder wrote to the NAACP that "it is not only extremely difficult to procure mortgages on homes where there is a mixed development, but it is impossible. There are unwritten laws by banking and lending institutions with regard to their refusal to grant loans where there is a mixed population."

Next, Wilkins wrote the head of the FHA, Stewart McDonald. "For some time now, the National Association for the Advancement of Colored People, which has 400 branches in 40 states, has been receiving complaints that the Federal Housing Administration is restricting the opportunities of Negro citizens to purchase or build homes. At the outset we felt that perhaps these complaints were merely isolated instances of local prejudice, but the complaints have increased in vol-

ume, and they come from widely separated sections of the country."
The letter concluded:

> We are unalterably opposed to any discrimination against Negroes,
> and one of our cardinal principles is opposition to residential segre-
> gation. We do not believe that the federal government, through one
> of its agencies, should use the public tax money to restrict instead of
> extend opportunities for homeownership and to enforce patterns of
> racial segregation.
>
> It is a curious and ironic circumstance that white America is wont
> to point the finger of scorn at Negro citizens for their failure to im-
> prove their living conditions. This is cited by would-be social scientists
> as "a racial characteristic." The Negro is supposed to have a natural
> racial desire to live in slums, near railroad tracks, in squalor, and to
> scorn better housing. Yet whenever colored people seek to secure
> better housing, they find all manner of obstacles placed in their path.

The Roosevelt administration was watching what was transpiring
from on high. The First Lady, Eleanor Roosevelt, had her secretary
write Wilkins a note to thank him for forwarding her the note he'd
sent to the FHA administrator.

A representative of the FHA replied to Wilkins and the NAACP,
saying, in part:

> Among the purposes for which the law established the Federal Hous-
> ing Administration was the creation of a sound mortgage market. We
> have no money to lend or grant for any purpose. Our sole function is
> to insure loans made by private mortgage lending institutions when
> such mortgages are made in accordance with the requirements in the
> law that they be economically sound.
>
> While it may be true that many Negroes and many neighborhoods
> cannot meet our required standards, it is also unfortunately true that
> the same condition exists among people of many other races and the
> neighborhoods in which they live.
>
> Also, while it may be true that some New York banks, as you say,
> refuse to lend to Negroes, it is also true that there is no power in the

National Housing Act which permits us to determine the lending policies of those institutions.

That's when the NAACP had Thurgood Marshall start writing the letters. Marshall demanded that the FHA provide its rules for underwriting loans. It did not. Soon, the NAACP obtained the FHA's manual on its own. The document—with its clear endorsement of deed restrictions around "racial occupancy"—provided proof that banks weren't acting on their own in the private market. The banks had guidelines like these written by the FHA. In particular, the document focused heavily on how important it was for officials to watch out for "adverse influences," which the agency suggested included "racial occupancy."

To draw attention, the NAACP held public forums on housing, issued press releases, and got the matter in front of Congress. But the lending practices persisted.

While this back-and-forth played out, federal funds were being used to help many white Americans purchase homes, and this would have a lasting impact on the racial wealth gap. Before the FHA, banks had not written long-term mortgages and, instead, typically loaned money on homes for only three to five years. Most bank loans had remained on the banks' balance sheets—meaning they kept the credit risk and would loan only so much money. Homeownership was thus out of reach for most middle- and lower-income families. This changed dramatically in 1938, when the federal government created the Federal National Mortgage Association (commonly known as Fannie Mae) to buy up FHA-guaranteed loans from banks and resell them as securities. All this extra money from the market poured back into banks and fueled more lending. The problem was that the FHA wasn't backing many loans to Black buyers.

In making homeownership more accessible to only some, the FHA played a central role in building America's large, and mainly white, middle class. Housing was an important wealth builder for many Americans of this era. By 1960, 66 percent of white American men who led households were owners of their homes. For Black American men with households in 1960, just under 40 percent were homeowners.

The discriminatory system can be seen in textbooks of the time. In the 1948 textbook *Principles of Urban Real Estate*, 3rd edition, cowritten by a former chief land economist of the FHA, professionals entering the field were informed that "the migration of families with certain readily distinguishable national, racial, or religious characteristics frequently stimulates the outmigration of previous residents in the area." And to be sure that students understood the point, the book gave them test questions. Here's one:

In which of the following neighborhoods would you prefer to invest?...

For example, for Neighborhood A, "The area is zoned for single-family residences. No deed restrictions are in force."

For Neighborhood B, "Deed restrictions have been established controlling the types of houses which may be built and restricting occupancy to members of the Caucasian race."

The effects of redlining were still visible across the United States as James Woodall led demonstrations in the summer of 2020. Nationally, cities that had redlining maps created in the 1930s remained far more segregated ninety years later than cities that did not have such maps, with homeownership and other economic health indicators lagging non-redlined areas. This was clear in research by Jacob Faber, an associate professor at New York University, who studies "spatial inequality." He looks at measures like the "Black isolation index," which quantifies how likely it is that a Black person living in an area will encounter only other Black people. This index and other similar ones show differences between places that were redlined in the 1930s compared to those that did not have redlining maps. As of 2020, the isolation of Black people away from white people was decreasing in many places, but the redlined places were improving more slowly than places that were not redlined.

"There's a large extent to which the segregation that was created via these programs is effectively permanent," Faber told us.

Unequal Veterans

The New Deal housing policies also created a knock-on effect for Black veterans of World War II.

Black Americans were treated unequally in the rate they were selected for the war, in how they served, and in what benefits they had upon their return home. The unequal application of the GI Bill was yet another setback for closing the Black-white wealth gap.

More than one million Black Americans served in World War II, but there were mixed messages about their participation. Especially at the beginning of the war, Black Americans who registered were less frequently called on for service than white Americans, even though the Selective Training and Service Act of 1940 barred discrimination in selecting troops.

Two of James Woodall's great-grandfathers, Ernest Woodall and Jesse Day, registered to serve in the war, but were not called up. It would have been highly unlikely that Ernest Woodall would have been called for service when he registered in 1941, because the act left it up to the armed forces and local selection boards to decide who was eligible. And when he registered as the war began, the U.S. Army had only a few "Black American" units, and the navy had none. When Black leaders pressured the government to be more inclusive, local boards still ruled many Black Americans ineligible due to medical conditions or inadequate reading skills. As pressure mounted on the military to call up Black servicemen, they were drafted but not deployed, leaving hundreds of thousands of Black Americans waiting. Many quit their jobs and became stuck in limbo with no pay.

By 1942, Black Americans were 10.7 percent of all people registered to serve in the war, but they were less than 6 percent of the deployed army. More than three hundred thousand Black Americans sat out the army backlog. The U.S. Marines were not taking Black volunteers at all.

It was 1942 when James's relatives Jesse Day and Vester Robinson registered. Day was not called to serve, but against the odds, Robinson was. He enlisted in the army in Fort Benning, Georgia, in August of that year and remained in service for four years.

By the end of the war, the military had increased the numbers, but many Black Americans served in logistical or custodial roles rather than in combat. And the discrimination went beyond the troops. The American Red Cross initially rejected blood donations from Black Americans, and when it did accept them, the blood was kept separated by race.

It was far from surprising, then, that the American public was getting mixed messages about Black Americans' participation in the war. While some white-run publications featured stories about brave troops like the Tuskegee Airmen, others featured prominent people suggesting that Black Americans wouldn't want to fight for their country. Eleanor Roosevelt, well known for her advocacy of equal rights for Black Americans, said, "The nation cannot expect colored people to feel that the United States is worth defending if the Negro continues to be treated as he is now." Black Americans shared these doubts as the war spread. As Leon Bass, a Black veteran, recalled, "I wasn't good enough in Macon, Georgia, to get a drink of water at a public water fountain. I wasn't good enough in Texas to get a meal in a restaurant. . . . I began to question my wisdom for having joined the army. What are you doing here? What are you fighting for?" Black-run newspapers featured commentary on what the war should mean for equality. The *Pittsburgh Courier* ran a letter from a Black defense worker who asked, "Should I sacrifice my life to live *half American*?" The newspaper followed that letter with a campaign aimed at demanding better rights for Black Americans, given that they had fought for the United States in the war.

At the end of the war it seemed that, for some Black Americans, better rights might finally be on the way. In the summer of 1944, the federal government created the GI Bill for veterans. The bill, officially called the Servicemen's Readjustment Act, was meant to provide benefits to veterans—*all* veterans—to aid with their schooling, health, job training, unemployment, and homeownership. Many Americans became the first in their family to attend college due to this bill. Many Americans purchased their first homes because of it. Many received unemployment or job training benefits.

The GI Bill was another big money spigot, helping form an expanding middle-class America. Among its offerings:

- Title I of the bill provided for medical benefits.
- Title II of the bill provided funds for education and training.
- Title III of the bill provided loans to purchase homes, farmland, or business property.
- Title IV of the bill provided assistance in finding employment.
- Title V of the bill covered unemployment benefits while veterans were looking for jobs.

In the peak year of the program's spending, 1950, nearly eight billion dollars went into GI programs, amounting to nearly a quarter of the entire federal budget. This was an opportunity for veterans like Vester Robinson to lift his family's fortune and trajectory. (The Woodalls and the Days would not benefit from this bill, as those great-grandparents were never called up for the war.)

In the study of the Black-white racial wealth gap, moments like these are pivotal. The wealth gap has been shaped not only by Black Americans earning less money in everyday life, but also by their exclusion from large influxes of money the government gave predominantly to white Americans. That's what happened with the GI Bill.

In Atlanta, there were about seven thousand Black veterans of the war (out of roughly one million Black servicemen overall). While the GI Bill funding was supposedly open to them, they didn't necessarily feel comfortable using it. It wasn't always so much the funding itself, but rather the places where the money could be used. In education, for instance, even schools like Georgia Tech that were open to Black students didn't seem particularly welcoming. As Joseph Albright, special assistant at the Veterans Administration, wrote in 1946, "because of established southern patterns, Negro servicemen are very reluctant even to attempt to take advantage of Georgia Tech center."

Many Black Americans didn't qualify for the GI Bill because they had not been allowed to serve in the war. Edward N. Wilson, the registrar at Morgan State College, a Black school, wrote a national war administrator in 1944, the year the GI Bill was passed, to complain that Black Americans were less likely to have been selected for the war, and, therefore, they would be deprived of the bill's benefits. It was, he said, an act of white supremacy. While it may seem counterintuitive today to complain about *not* being called to serve in a war, there was an economic cost to Black families who did not become part of the veteran community. Two of James's family lines registered for the war but were not called to serve.

Even for Black Americans who did serve, the lack of equality went on and on. For the job training benefits of the GI Bill, a common problem was that only a few job categories were open to Black veterans. In Atlanta, only six companies opened their doors to Black veterans: Davis Service Station, which welcomed porters and tire recappers; Strathmore Press, which welcomed copy boys; Greyhound Bus, which trained lubricators; C.C. Hart Plumbing Company, which trained plumbers; Harbour Quality Cleaners, for dry cleaners; and Sears Roebuck, located in the Fourth Ward, welcomed Black porters, truck helpers, and tire and battery changers. Two hundred forty other Atlanta training programs welcomed white veterans but not Black veterans.

Advocacy groups worried throughout the rollout of the GI Bill that it would not be administered fairly. Much of its administration was left up to localities, for one, and there was no anti-discrimination rule. In time, the advocacy groups' fears of discrimination were realized. The American Veterans Committee, which included former president Roosevelt's son, wrote that "Negroes are not being benefited to the extent they should be, chiefly because of the manner in which the program is administered." In practically every dimension of the GI Bill, Black veterans simply got fewer benefits than white veterans. It's not that they got nothing; Black veterans did benefit, but not as much. That is one of the essential ingredients of the wealth gap.

Perhaps the worst gap in the GI Bill was that the VA offered housing assistance but made no requirements that players in the housing market treat Black buyers equally. Title III, the part of the bill that made loans to veterans, offered wealth-building opportunities. Veterans could receive loans to purchase farms, businesses, and homes, but, before the VA would guarantee the loans, banks had to approve them.

As Kathleen J. Frydl writes in her excellent book *The GI Bill*, so many Black veterans were disqualified by the banks dispensing Title III loans that "it is more accurate simply to say that Blacks could not use this particular title. African-American veterans went to well-capitalized banks only to discover that they were viewed as poor financial risks."

By late 1946, complaints about the uneven administration of the GI Bill couldn't be ignored. President Truman created the Committee on Civil Rights to examine the matter. After extensive research, the group concluded that "When Negro veterans seek 'GI' loans in order to build homes, they are likely to find that credit from private banks . . . is less freely available to members of their race." In particular, the committee pointed to prejudices within credit ratings companies and also pointed to covenants on deeds in many neighborhoods that barred sales to Black buyers.

Missed Opportunities

We have pondered how things might have been different for James Woodall and his family if his grandparents had benefited equally during the New Deal's expanded home lending in the 1930s and the rollout of the GI Bill. What would it have meant if Frances Walker and Jesse Day could have borrowed to purchase a home in the Fourth Ward or elsewhere? Or if the Woodalls could have purchased a home there? Or what would it have meant for the Robinsons to have had more access to the GI Bill to fund education? Ultimately, if James's family had been treated more fairly, what would it have meant for James Woodall circa 2020?

Let's pause on James's paternal grandfather, Vester Robinson. He came from a family of sharecroppers before serving in World War II, and he would end up having fourteen children, including James's father. Did Vester Robinson benefit from the GI Bill? No, Yvonne Robinson, one of his daughters, said. Would it have helped his children and grandchildren if he had gone to college and bought a home with VA benefits just after the war? Yes, she said, anything would have helped. The family faced large economic challenges, sometimes going without heat. She said she is not even sure how her mother made everything work. "I mean she faced food challenges, trying to feed that many kids with no help," she said. "Pretty much no help. I'm still in awe of how she did it. It baffles me. We literally grew up with nothing, absolutely nothing."

Ebony also asked James's step-grandfather, William McKenzie, if his family had benefited from the GI Bill after his father served in the war. "No, no," McKenzie said. "You got to remember, it was still a little," he added, pausing, "segregated." Ebony pushed further to see if McKenzie's father had tried to buy a house with support from the GI Bill, and McKenzie started laughing—not happily, but as if he found the question to be ridiculous.

We talked to other people whose parents and grandparents were veterans of World War II and later conflicts, and repeatedly, we heard of a dawning realization that their families had missed out. Miriam Zinter's father served in the U.S. Navy from 1955 to 1959. After her parents got married in 1963, they tried to buy a house in New York State. Bank after bank told her father he couldn't use the government's housing loan program for veterans. The reason? Many homes for sale had deeds that prevented their being sold to Black Americans. So, she said the banks would not lend to him using a VA-backed loan. "I'm a GI," Zinter recalled her father telling her. And, she said, the bankers would reply, "That's not for you. We're not giving you a mortgage." In New York and northern New Jersey, of the 67,000 homes with mortgages backed under the GI Bill, less than 100 went to nonwhite families.

In Atlanta around the same time, another Black family found itself unable to use veterans' benefits. M. Alexis Scott, whose family long ran the *Atlanta Daily World* and who served as the paper's publisher from 1997 to 2014, had not spent much time thinking about the GI Bill until she found an old notebook from her father, a veteran of World War II. While Scott said she grew up comfortably, her family still missed out on the benefits, she learned from his diary. After serving as a sergeant in the war, her father returned to Atlanta to look for opportunities, hoping to attend Georgia Tech using GI Bill benefits. Scott told us, "And they turned him down, because he was Black." She added, "But he never said it. He never told me this."

Some descendants of Black World War II veterans would later speak out about the lost wealth from this period. As veteran Isaac Woodard was traveling home on a bus, with his discharge papers in hand, he was attacked by a South Carolina police chief, who beat him badly around his eyes and permanently damaged his corneas. Blind for the rest of his life, Woodard was not able to get the army's disability benefits or access to GI housing benefits for sixteen years, due both to loopholes in the rules and to outright discrimination. In the 1960s, after years of efforts by Civil Rights leaders—including the NAACP visiting the White House on his behalf and an eleven-verse song by Woody Guthrie—Woodard got a lump-sum payout from the government for his health benefits.

We tracked down Woodard's descendants to talk about their experience of the Black-white wealth gap. His great-niece Laura Williams told us the family missed out on wealth creation. "When he finally received the retroactive payments, that's when he purchased his first home," she told us. But prices had increased in those sixteen years, she noted, meaning lost wealth and years of unearned rental income. "I would love to know how much. It was a multi-family home."

During the New Deal and GI Bill rollout, many Black Americans saw that the Democratic-led government was spending some money on them, and that inflow helped convince a sizable number to change party affiliation, moving away from the Republican Party once led by President Lincoln. In the 1940s, Black Americans were as likely to vote Democratic as Republican, and the shift toward the Democrats would continue. But it was only with the passing of time that it has become clear that the money Black Americans received in this era was well below their share.

Indeed, federal funding for the New Deal and World War II did not raise the fortunes of James Woodall's predecessors. They rented homes just as they had rented land. And their redlined Black Atlanta neighborhoods would lag white areas of Atlanta for years in incomes, health, and education progress. The discrimination and missed opportunity under the New Deal and GI Bill programs had personal, long-lasting effects on families like James Woodall's.

Modern "Equality," Fueled by Debt

James's great-grandmother Frances sought a better life up north, but it did not work out. The year was 1959, and Frances Walker moved with her six children, ages four to eleven, to Roxbury, Massachusetts, for a year. She felt she needed to get them away from their father, Jesse Day, who struggled as World War II came and went. Day couldn't get very far in the Atlanta job market with only a fourth-grade education. Registering for the war hadn't changed things for him, and in fact, he had been investigated for a robbery in 1943, even while awaiting possible deployment. (He never deployed to the war.)

Married life had brought some hope for the Days, but the early years were difficult. Frances and Jesse's first daughter, Delores, died as a small child. They had six more children in nine years. Jesse Day worked as a day laborer and, for many years, at Safway Steel and Scaffolding. He was abusive at times, and in 1951, he had a child with another woman, after which the police charged him with bastardy. For Frances, a child of Atlanta homeowners, life with Jesse was one of deflated affluence. Frances had graduated high school, whereas Jesse's education had ended in grade school. While juggling childbearing and -raising, Frances took up work in a lingerie factory and, at times, cleaned white people's homes. Frances was young when she had her children with Jesse and carried misgivings throughout her life, family members say. As their son Frankie Day remembered it, Jesse and Frances's marital tension "goes back to the culture that was going on in Black families in particular. You have a father who got six children. He's being pulled here, very young. And it was just easy back in the day for Black men not to really stay at home. They stay out. They drink with their buddies. They don't bring their paycheck home."

And so, in 1959, Frances moved with her six children to Roxbury, Massachusetts. It was near the end of a several-decade period later known as the Great Migration, in which six million Black Americans left the South for northern or western states in search of better lives. But for Frances and her children, the move was not easy. It was hard to find work, hard to adjust to school, hard to find housing. Within a year, they had returned to Atlanta, to the home in Bankhead where Frances's mother still lived. In their move north and their return, we see a cycle of hope and disappointment that played out many times during this era. As the Civil Rights Movement gained momentum in the 1960s, the exclusionary practices of the New Deal and the GI Bill faded, but what took their place were reforms and programs that would fall short and, in some cases, cause new waves of racial economic harm. Disagreement over the role of capitalism in lifting the welfare of Black families roiled the Civil Rights Movement, as we will see in chapter 10. For now, we will see how federal policy and private enterprise influenced the fate of James Woodall's family in Bankhead.

Their home, at 643 Finley Avenue, sat just doors from a main thoroughfare and across from a factory. By the 1960s, the neighborhood had changed from how Frances experienced it as a child. No longer were white families living nearby. It was a Black neighborhood. The factory offered some jobs, but the neighborhood didn't have the sort of investment other areas of the city had. Banks were avoiding giving out mortgages there. Nearly three decades of government subsidies had skipped over this neighborhood.

The government subsidies had also skipped over Frances's family. In her nearly twenty years of marriage to Jesse, other families—mainly white families—had upgraded their education and upscaled their homes. Living with her mother again on Finley, Frances could see the gap that seemed to have grown bigger between her family and the white families whose homes she cleaned. Soon, she moved back in with Jesse for a few years. Their children were hitting their teenage years. Jesse beat them, according to police records, and he beat Frances. In 1966, Frances and Jesse divorced.

Beyond Frances's painful years with Jesse, the era was challenging for her because "segregation was really, really hard on her," as James described it to us. Since childhood, Frances had blamed the dark color of her skin for missed opportunities, family members said.

Despite having been early homeowners on Finley Avenue, Frances's family had seen their rise into the middle class stunted by the unequal policies of the middle of the century. Redlining had also corroded the property values in her family's neighborhood. But as the 1960s progressed, new opportunities were developing for Black families, including greater availability of public housing.

As she approached adulthood, Frances's daughter Charlotte (who would become James's grandmother) moved out of their home on Finley and into a brand-new public housing complex a few miles west of her family's home. Bowen Homes, a sixty-four-acre complex of orange brick duplexes, opened in 1964. One of more than fourteen public housing complexes in Atlanta, built often with federal funds beginning in the 1930s, Bowen was soon known for crime and poverty. The complexes were originally designated by race, and Bowen, like other complexes built after it, would remain a mainly Black community. It gained pop culture fame in songs by rappers like T.I., who grew up in Bankhead, and OutKast, and as the childhood residence of rapper Shawty Lo and boxer Evander Holyfield. Housing complexes like Bowen provided a needed service, but they had the effect of maintaining segregation, and public housing in general would remain a political hot potato for decades as federal agencies phased programs in and out.

As Frances and Jesse's middle child, Charlotte may not have had many options when moving into Bowen. Her parents were newly divorced and were trying to move on to new lives. Charlotte already had a daughter and not much support. Bowen, it turned out, would be a relatively short stop for her. There, around 1969, she met her first husband, Harold Woodall, a member of the military and a longtime Atlanta resident. The couple married in 1972 and welcomed their daughter, Stephana, into the world in 1974. They would not be long-term public housing residents, a point of pride for them all.

Charlotte had seen the stability that Finley Avenue had brought for decades to her grandparents' family and now had a chance of securing the same for her children: Harold and Charlotte purchased their own home just after they married. The timing of their home purchase wasn't by chance. In 1968, Congress had passed the Fair Housing Act, which prohibited housing discrimination based on race, national origin, or religion. The 1974 and 1976 Equal Credit Opportunity laws would follow, adding sex, marital status, and age to the protected categories. And in 1977, Congress would pass federal legislation aimed at ending redlining and expanding homeownership to lower- and middle-income borrowers. Called the Community Reinvestment Act, it was part of a series of laws that sought to expand access to the housing market.

These housing bills were heavily debated in Congress, which ultimately used the laws to try to reconfirm the public duty banks had to communities, given that banks are backed by the U.S. government. The senator who introduced the CRA bill, William Proxmire, a Democrat from Wisconsin, put it this way: "A public charter conveys numerous economic benefits and in return it is legitimate for public policy and regulatory practice to require some public purpose." That purpose, in the case of the lending laws, was to serve the communities where banks were chartered to do business. Federal officials made clear that the act was meant to make homeownership more accessible to Black Americans.

This series of housing and banking laws was passed during a period of debate over the best way to broaden opportunities to Black Americans. The crux of the debate was whether opportunities needed to be afforded equally to people of all races or whether Black Americans should get a special boost in the system due to the long-running discrimination and mistreatment their families had experienced.

Parallel to the housing and banking bills was an effort to open access to university education. Beyond requiring schools to admit Black Americans (and people from all races), questions persisted over what standards should be used in the admissions process. Should Black Americans have equal access to be admitted on equal terms as white Americans, or should they have an advantage? Some schools felt the boost should be hefty, and they created quotas to require more Black Americans be admitted. The quota practice, however, was quickly ruled illegal by a court in California. Most schools continued practicing this "affirmative action," to some degree boosting Black applicants and meeting mixed levels of success in adding diversity to their campuses.

Similarly, banks worked to give a boost to Black homebuyers.

Legislation can help remove the fear that businesses sometimes have of being a first mover, and this was an important part of the Community Reinvestment Act banking rule. Upon the bill's passage, federal banking regulators began examining and scoring banks on meeting their CRA obligations. This incentivized bankers to become more aggressive in reaching out to communities around their branches. The banks no longer had to worry as much about the risk of being the first and only bank to lend money in a neighborhood.

The effects of the CRA have been fiercely debated ever since, especially following the 2008 housing market collapse. The consensus view became that these policies did lead to more lending to lower- and middle-income borrowers—the question remained over how much more and whether that was good for the economy and for individuals. Similarly, more Black students entered universities. Along the way, Black families took on greater debt to pay for these new opportunities, housing and schooling. It seemed the doors had been opened more broadly, without plans to pay for it all.

James Woodall's is just one family, but they illustrate the post–World War II era, showing how, in the lives of Black Americans, the gap continued to slowly narrow, then froze into the 1990s. For James's grandmother and mother, opportunity was within reach, but it was slick as soap. With his grandmother Charlotte, homeownership turned south in 1976, when she and Harold divorced. It turned out that Harold, technically, owned the house alone, and he kept it. Charlotte took some belongings, including two portable television sets, both sets of bedroom furniture, and a 1968 Pontiac GTO, according to the divorce filing. Harold got the washer, dryer, and refrigerator. He was ordered to pay fifty dollars weekly in child support for twenty-four months and then thirty-five dollars a week until Stephana turned eighteen.

Charlotte hadn't attended college at this point, and, after the divorce, she worked several jobs at Bell South and elsewhere to support Stephana and her other daughter. She and the girls were constantly on the move. They lived in an apartment in Atlanta and a rental house in Decatur, then moved to Virginia for two years before coming back to Atlanta to live in apartments near the airport. Nine years after the divorce, she found stability when she was able to purchase a house with her next husband. The split-level home cost $82,900 and was in Riverdale, a quiet suburban neighborhood southwest of Atlanta. The purchase in 1987 meant that Stephana was able to spend her teenage years as the daughter of a homeowner.

But it was too little too late. Stephana would soon be on her own, moving through instability, as she became a teenage mother. Attending college at Georgia State University and majoring in political science and African American studies, she already had one baby in tow. In 1993, while still a student, she met Jonathan Robinson, one of fourteen children of Vester Robinson, who had died years earlier. Jonathan was ten years older than Stephana. He was hanging around the college while doing some research in the library. They hooked up, and on February 1, 1994, Stephana gave birth to their twins. One of the new babies was James Cortez Woodall.

A Childhood in Debt

As James was growing up, Stephana had scant support, and she made ends meet however she could.

Her mother's marriage had fallen apart, and Charlotte had moved in with cousins. She earned just enough as a florist to support herself, but not enough to take care of grandchildren like James. Stephana's father, Harold Woodall, was working as a cook in the employee cafeteria at Sears and says now that he wasn't aware that Stephana needed help. Whereas some of Stephana's classmates at Georgia State had parental support, Stephana juggled school, a job, pregnancy, and toddlers alone. "I was struggling to make ends meet," she told us. "You know that old-time statement: You're one paycheck from being homeless."

Just as banking laws allowed for more borrowing to fuel home purchases, access to college fueled student debt. Like many Americans in the early 1990s, Stephana took on a lot of debt at the start of adulthood. It was the early 1990s, while she was in college, that student debt across the country was taking off. In 1993, a year before James was born, the average debt load for a college graduate was $9,320. By 2000, that figure was up to $17,297 per graduate. By 2016, the debt load per graduate was $29,669.

In many ways, loans for higher education fueled the broad expansion of people attending college in the last fifty years. Virtually nonexistent before the 1960s, student loans were expanded in the 1960s and '70s with the goal of helping more people attend college. By the early 1990s, when Stephana entered college, 38 percent of public college attendees had student debt. By 2000, the share of students taking on debt was up to 60 percent. The debt helped more people go to college: 62 percent of high school graduates in 1994 attended college, according to the U.S. Bureau of Labor Statistics, up from 55 percent in 1984. In parallel to this debt expansion, universities increased their tuition dramatically, creating even more need for debt.

The intentions behind expanding student debt were good, at least in theory: There was hope that gaps in racial wealth could be lessened by greater access to higher education. It was a new chapter in American history in the sense that Black Americans were not being excluded in the ways they had been excluded during the New Deal. But they needed a lot of debt in their attempt to join the American Dream.

Over time, the student loan credit expansion has been detrimental to racial equity. As a researcher at the St. Louis Federal Reserve Bank put it, "existing racial wealth disparities and soaring higher education costs may replicate racial wealth disparities across generations by driving racial disparities in student loan debt load and repayment." Consider that the average Black college graduate in 2022 owed $25,000 more than the average white college graduate. And four years after college, average Black graduates owed 5 percent more than what they originally borrowed. In contrast, average white graduates ended up owing 27 percent less four years later than what they had borrowed.

Having student debt can change people's decisions. In 2022, one third of Latino borrowers said in a survey that student loans caused them to delay getting married. A similar proportion of Latino borrowers delayed having children. For Black Americans, the delay showed up in real estate: 46 percent of Black Americans with college debt said it had caused them to postpone purchasing a home.

Rather than delaying life, Stephana went to college on and off for fourteen years, but that came at a price. Her student debt over this period ballooned to more than one hundred thousand dollars. She eventually dropped out. As she said, "Literally, I could not finish my program because I ran out of money." Her decision to drop out was a common one among college students and has remained so. In the overall population as of 2021, 40 percent of college students were not finishing college within six years. For Black students, that figure is higher, at 59 percent. Many of the students who dropped out had student loans and weak prospects for paying them back. Some two thirds of dropouts each year came from low-income families earning less than fifty thousand dollars a year.

Degree or no degree, student debt sticks around. That would be the case for Stephana, who threw in the towel with no degree after fourteen years of attending school on and off (and piling up debt). Without familial support and affordable day care, she found over time that taking out loans to stay in school allowed her to be with her children more than if she were working full time. She thought of it all as "maintaining"—doing what she had to do. "I maintained by going to school," she said. "I took care of my kids with my loans from school. No lie. Yes, I took care of my kids." She knew other mothers doing the same thing. "It wasn't 'work at home,' like it is now [in the Covid-19 era]. It was always, 'You have to go to work, you have to go to work,' you know? But you couldn't go," she said. "So, yes, those three or four thousand dollars every couple of months, that mattered. That made a difference."

What did this look like in practice? Stephana took her children with her to school at Georgia State and found places where they could sit during her classes. For some stretches of time, when she could find babysitting help, she went off at night to work at places like a small airplane company and, for a few years, the Internal Revenue Service. She also took up hairstyling along the way, but she found that business unpredictable. She paused school when it became too much to juggle. In the end, Stephana's lenders told her she had to finish her undergraduate degree before they would give her more money, she told us. In other words, they said they would fund a graduate degree if she finished her college degree. At that point, she dropped out of school.

James was growing up during all this. He sometimes spent days with Stephana's older sister, Laree Day. Laree, who liked to go by the name "Diva Lyri," was working as a professional roller skater and self-described entrepreneur in the Atlanta area. She had no children and offered her sister free babysitting. Sometimes during this babysitting, James and his siblings would go to nearby highways and ask for money for their aunt's projects, which she told us included a public access television show about children in sports. She said this was akin to marketing, but reflecting on it, James said it was more like panhandling. "We would go to an exit ramp and ask for donations to support the work that we were doing," he said. "She taught us to do that, too. Similar to what the water boys do now," he told us, referring to teenagers who peddle cold drinks to passing cars on the side of highway exits. "Yeah, we did the exact same thing twenty years ago."

James's father, Jonathan Robinson, was rarely around. As James put it, "They were never married, so it was never like a setup through the courts. It was just kind of like, you know, he'd reach out to my mom, I guess. Sometimes you look around, and he'd say, 'Hey, I want you all to come over.' I remember he had some woman, and I spent time with their family, too. I don't remember who she was or who her kids were." As James learned to crawl and then walk, Robinson built what would become a lengthy criminal record and a contentious relationship with the Atlanta Police Department. In 1985, he had been convicted on charges of impersonating a police officer, and he was incarcerated before James was born. In 1997, the Atlanta Police arrested him for stealing police department cars, but the case was later dropped. In 1998, Robinson was accused of pointing a pistol at someone; he was acquitted. In 1999, misdemeanor charges were filed for theft, and he was found guilty. Along the way, Robinson filed numerous complaints against the police department, alleging corruption. James wouldn't have known at the time about these late-1990s charges. He was between three and five years old.

At the turn of the century, in a case that would drag on throughout James's childhood, Robinson was accused of rape. Upon his arrest, his DNA tied him to two other rape cases. Over the next seven years, Robinson, who said the sex was consensual, was held in pretrial detention while the cases played out, which made his detention one of the lengthiest in the state. In 2010, he was convicted and sentenced to two life sentences plus sixty years. Robinson said he was targeted for arrest as reprisal for what he described as whistleblowing about the police. As of the start of 2024, he was in Dooly State Prison in the middle of Georgia, and we corresponded with him via letters.

Robinson reiterated his innocence to us, and he also expressed sadness for missing so many years of his children's lives. "As a father, I can honestly tell you that I failed my kids," he wrote.

Jonathan Robinson's own childhood had not been easy, several of his siblings told us. While they were growing up, their father, Vester, was an alcoholic, two said, and money was very tight—too tight to provide fourteen children with opportunities. As Robinson described it to us in his letter from prison, his childhood community was poor and "life were often times quite challenging." Robinson's former attorney Ben Goldberg said that Robinson's rape trial was unfair. "He got totally screwed at trial," the lawyer said. "He got totally screwed on his appeal. The issues that we raised on that appeal—we should have won on. And, you know, this happens in this line of work. You know, the farther along you get in a case, the harder it is to win, and appeals are hard to win. The whole case is totally, you know—it is a miscarriage of justice."

All this was disorienting for a child to digest. Sometimes James wanted to believe sympathetic stories about his father—like that he was being targeted by the police. He wanted to believe that perhaps the interactions with women his father had had were consensual. He wanted to believe the system had unfairly imprisoned his father. But at other times, he wanted to believe the system was fair. He attended the trial, dug through court documents on the case, and looked around at the world he lived in, longing for clarity.

Meanwhile, James's family kept moving. Sometimes in the 1990s, they lived in run-down town houses next to airport hotels. These were not child-friendly places. Other times, they lived downtown. Stephana moved them every few months in some years. She found that it was easier to move somewhere new rather than settle all the pending bills. After the success that her mother and grandmother had had purchasing homes, the wave of opportunity did not seem to reach the next generation.

For Stephana, lucky breaks in housing would not involve ownership, but, rather, rental deals. She tried to rent houses, not units in big buildings. She took pride in providing for her children in houses and pointed out to people that she was not raising her kids in "the projects," as she put it, perhaps thinking of Bowen Homes. What Stephana may not have realized was that housing like Bowen would not be as available in her adult life as it had been in her mother's. In 1994, the federal government, driven by the intention to decrease segregated communities, created a program to incentivize localities to convert lower-income housing into mixed-income communities. The problem was that the reforms led to the demolition of scores of affordable housing units that did not end up getting replaced. Bowen was torn down in 2009.

Stephana's saving grace was not public housing complexes like Bowen—it was the Section 8 program. Section 8 is a rental housing program created by Congress in 1974 to provide rental assistance. At first, the program funded particular rental buildings, but after criticism that it was concentrating poor people in some neighborhoods and not others, it shifted to providing rental vouchers to individuals. Landlords were still able to decide whether to accept housing vouchers, which meant that rentals that accepted Section 8 vouchers were often clustered in neighborhoods that were poor and historically segregated from white residents.

By 2014, the program would grow to serving 3.5 million families. To qualify for Section 8 vouchers, a family's income could not be more than half the median income of their area. Most vouchers went to families that made less than 30 percent of the area's median income. These forms of assistance have remained widespread in recent years. By the 2020s, about ten million people in five million households received some form of federal rental assistance, 58 percent of them families with children. This help was needed because rents were going up—tens of millions of additional Americans who did not qualify for Section 8 assistance were spending more than half their income on rent.

Stephana got into the Section 8 program with the assistance of one of her hairstyling clients. She used her voucher to move with James and his siblings into 2480 Niskey Lake Road SW, a one-thousand-square-foot house on a quiet, tree-lined street in South-west Atlanta that seemed far removed from public assistance. Under Section 8 housing, Stephana paid just twenty-five dollars per month to live in the home. James was six at the time, but it was at least his tenth home.

While living at Niskey Lake Road, Stephana saw her financial position sink farther. In 2000, at age twenty-five, she filed for bankruptcy. The case was quickly dismissed in 2001, meaning Stephana did not get any relief from her debts.

Soon, the family moved to another Section 8 house, on University Avenue, site of the Wendy's where Rayshard Brooks would be shot in 2020. Back when Stephana and James lived there, a lot of construction was going on, and the neighborhood was becoming gentrified. When rats infested Stephana's home, she moved the family westward, to a more affordable county, Clayton. She was seeking out homes on the outskirts of Atlanta. Since the time her grandparents had lived in the Old Fourth Ward, much of the city had gotten pricier, rents included. A growing number of Black families were moving east or south of the city, to more affordable areas.

Several homes later, when her financial position had improved some, Stephana stopped using Section 8. She wanted to be sure there were vouchers available for others in need. "I was able to get on my feet through that program," she said in gratitude. When money got tight again (as it would), the idea of turning back to Section 8 remained for her a signal of personal decline.

School provided an escape for James, but even schooling was un-stable. When he was fourteen, Clayton County lost accreditation to run its public schools—the first school district in the country in nearly four decades to do so. This led to another move for James—into the home of his maternal grandmother, Charlotte. His twin sister, Char-lette, was already living there.

Partly for economic reasons, Stephana's four children often lived apart. Generally speaking, her oldest son lived with his father. Her youngest daughter lived with her. Charlette lived with Stephana's mother, and James moved around among the households. Packing up was just normal, James told us. "It was, of course, to help out economically," he recalled. "I always did activities, you know, in school. So they really didn't have to worry about me too much."

Still, James saw the contrast between his life and his twin's life when he moved in temporarily with their grandmother. Because his sister had lived there for most of her childhood, she had stability, and friends. "I didn't really have friends who could come to the house for birthdays, right?" James told us. "But my sister had all her friends at my grandmother's house, because they were all living nearby. And so, just the normal things of growing up and being able to celebrate a birthday with your friends. It took its toll on the individual."

On him.

"When you're pinching for pennies pretty regularly, the emotional tension and stress is just there," he said. "You don't know when you're going to get your next meal. You know what I mean?"

James's twin, Charlette, agreed that she had a stabler life living with their grandmother, and she made it clear that it was her choice to be there. Nonetheless, she told us, it hurt when she saw her mother spend money on James but not on her. "It was my preference to live with them more because it was stability growing up," she said of her grandparents. "Like my mother, she moved houses, and there was like—the income was very low, and low, impoverished areas and stuff like that. But it came to a point where, I remember vividly . . . only one of us could play sports." The money for sports went to James, she said. He acknowledged to us that he benefited from his mother's investment in his activities.

The peripatetic lifestyle created a steeliness in James that he carried with him. He stopped focusing on blending in and looked internally for his guideposts. The externalities of his life, after all, weren't fully his own. Even his name could be used by others—such as when his mother used it to get credit. The push and pull of opportunities available to communities without funding led to more and more debt.

Payday loans were common in his family, and on top of that, Stephana used James's identity to get credit—a workaround of America's unforgiving credit rating system. As a teenager, James had a high credit rating, if not a perfect one, so Stephana would list his name and his Social Security number instead of her own to carry out financial transactions. Other times, she turned to the black market for credit. There, she would purchase a "credit privacy number," or CPN. These numbers, an alternative to a Social Security number, can be used to get approval for apartment rentals and other purchases. They are often marketed to people who wish to hide bad credit histories. The Federal Trade Commission and other arms of the government have warned consumers against using CPNs, and they are not a good way to rebuild credit. Not to mention, it costs money to get one. Still, to Stephana, they were magical. "Everything in it will get you approved, and you'll be in the apartment," she said. "Wow."

To James, the conclusion of his mother's financial manipulations was that "she did the best she could."

This was all part of the struggle to Stephana. "You're trying to make sure you have a car, you're trying to make sure that the lights stay on," she said. "It is hard."

As James entered his high school years, the United States elected a Black president. For many people, this was a sign that the equal opportunity movement had achieved its goals. The New Deal, the GI Bill's exclusionary policies, and redlining seemed to some like the distant past. The last few decades of the century had offered Black Americans access—sometimes favorable access, even—to universities, access to more lending through banking and fair housing laws, and access to borrowing money through student loans. Black and white disparities, to some Americans, seemed to be fading.

But the shakiness of James's family's finances was common among Black Americans. The reality was that affordable housing was there until it wasn't. The borrowing access was there until someone fell behind and entered the unforgiving credit system and debt cycle. Black families were not much better off compared to white families than they had been a generation earlier. Formerly redlined neighborhoods still carried scars and inequities. Families that did not benefit from the GI Bill were behind those who had. The 2008 housing crisis and bankruptcy systems—which we will explore in the next chapters—would prove to be further setbacks for Black Americans.

In the years of the Obama presidency, James would find structure by enrolling in the military reserve. He would take on debt and go to college. He would become a minister. He would learn to speak for a broader public and address the distrust and anger in the Black community.

And as the summer of 2020 hit, he remained connected to his family. On July 1, James stepped away from the demonstrations and the press conferences for some happy and sorrowful events. His twenty-three-year-old younger sister delivered her third child, a girl. And that same day, his aunt Demorris Robinson Cody died from Covid-19. She was his father's older sister, on the side of the family that had been removed from his life while his father was in prison.

James attended the funeral in Atlanta. Family members took turns speaking, sharing stories of how Demorris had helped them with challenges like drug dealing. Midway through, James stood and walked to the front of the chapel. Many family members had never met him, and there he was before them, the president of the Georgia NAACP.

"So, I wanted to just take a moment," he said. "Many of you haven't seen me in years, but I wanted to stand here on behalf of my father, Jonathan, and to share that we are indeed praying for our family. And though he could not be here today, he is very grateful for his sister's life, and what it meant to him.

"The beautiful thing about this moment is that when family comes together and is able to stand together and to declare to the world that *we are family*," he continued. "I believe that's a beautiful thing."

He bowed and walked back to his seat in the pews.

CHAPTER 6

BROOK BACON AND THE PERCEPTION OF RISK

We just went right after them. . . . Wells Fargo mortgage had an emerging markets unit that specifically targeted Black churches, because it figured church leaders had a lot of influence and could convince congregants to take out subprime loans.

—Former senior banker at Wells Fargo

SUMMER 2020

By mid-July in Georgia, twenty-three people had been killed in 2020 by the police, including at least thirteen Black people. There would be seventeen more people shot by police in the state by the end of the year. James Woodall and his NAACP team worked to shine a light on shooting cases, including that of Rayshard Brooks, a twenty-seven-year-old Black man who had fallen asleep in his car. And James and his team focused on another non-police killing case that was drawing national attention: Ahmaud Arbery, a twenty-five-year-old Black man, who was killed while jogging by white men who said they were trying to protect their neighborhood.

In August, yet another Georgia shooting got James's attention. A sixty-year-old Black man named Julian Lewis was driving near rural

Sylvania. A white police officer followed Lewis and eventually shot and killed him after chasing his car into a ditch. Lewis was unarmed. Lewis, James wrote online, was "murdered" by a Georgia state trooper "after an alleged minor traffic offense." James called for criminal charges against the officer.

Soon, James, dressed in his yellow NAACP polo shirt, was in Lewis's hometown for the funeral. He stood behind Lewis's wife at a press conference in front of city hall and drove to the church where Lewis was buried alongside generations of family members. There, as men lay sand over Lewis's coffin, James sternly surveyed the small crowd. There, he would see Brook Bacon, the middle-aged son of the shooting victim and the member of the family who would lead a crusade for justice.

Brook, forty-one, had long ago left Georgia and moved north, eventually to New Hampshire. He graduated college. He married a white woman. He worked in finance. He had moved on from this poor rural area and, to a large degree, from his Black family and Black roots. He was barely in touch with his father.

Then his father, Julian Lewis, was shot and killed by a police officer.

Learning this violent news would set Brook Bacon's life onto a new trajectory. He would start to connect the dots between life, death, economics, and what he came to view as systemic racism. As we spent time with him on a walk aimed at publicizing his father's death, he reflected on his heritage and on the gaps between his life and that of his white wife. He talked about race and class, and especially class among Black Americans. "If you have the same wealth, then there is a base of some sorts. Given the fact that you have amassed wealth, it says, 'Oh, well, that person is of a certain character for which I do not have to feel threatened,'" he told us. "So if someone is 'wealthy and Black' versus 'poor and Black,' they will be perceived more as a threat if they are poor."

Commenting on the sanctuary he had found among a white community in New Hampshire, Brook said it was wealth *and* community that move the needle of risk for Black people. "If you can find a way into a community, they know that you've crossed the barrier of wealth," he continued, "and they don't perceive you as much as a threat."

The barrier of wealth and the perception of threat—that logic stuck with us. In Brook's family story, the financial system and the justice system were prominent players, and so was risk. There were parallels that stood out between the putative financial system and the putative justice system. In both, individuals would be heavily punished for infractions and, afterward, left to fend for themselves in an unfavorable world. They would get permanently marked as being risky. Rarely would they be offered help or recognition that they may be more *at risk* than *a risk*.

The March for Justice

We met Brook on a sixty-three-mile walk. Over the course of several days and through torrential rainstorms, Brook led his family, his lawyers, and some supporters across the eastern part of Georgia, all to draw attention to his father's death. It was three months after a grand jury had declined to indict the officer who shot his father, and Brook and his family hoped the march would lead officials to revisit the case. The issue was contentious in this small, rural town. Brook and his family were protected on this "justice walk" by security guards, who warned of local white militias.

The walk began down the dirt road where Lewis had been killed. Marking the scene was a cross and a large American flag mounted to a tree. We stood behind Brook, his aunts, his mother, and his grandmother as they spoke about Lewis. We had both recently lost loved ones, and it was difficult thinking about the way Lewis had been killed. Tears flowed down Brook's, his aunts', his grandmother's, and his mother's faces.

Brook's mother, Taneeta Bacon, spoke frankly to us. "When I left Georgia in 1989, I left looking for something else. But Georgia is everywhere. The same problems are everywhere. There is no promised land." With that, she walked off. She had framed the march: it was a march about a death, and it was a walk about all that had been taken from Black Americans.

There is no promised land. "No, there isn't," Brook agreed softly, resigned. "I mean, that's the message that has kind of been taught to me and spoken to me—that's probably been spoken to many Black men and women. That there are situations you're going to face where you're not going to be treated fairly, and you have to be prepared for that." Situations like what happened when Brook was a freshman in college at Northeastern University, in Boston. He got off the subway train at Harvard Square and saw police there stopping people—only Black people. They stopped him, walked over to a car where a white woman was sitting, and pointed to Brook. When the woman shook her head no, the police released him. No apology was given, Brook noted, and no explanation.

Brook had more examples, which we will return to, but his story is also his parents' story—and not just that of his father, but also of his mother, who lost her dream of a promised land. From their difficult northern migration to inflexible student loan policies to the 2008 financial crisis, Taneeta and her son faced a hostile system. Along the way, Brook also faced what he felt was discrimination in the workplace and discrimination by police. And in 2020, his father, who had a history of infractions with the justice system, would fall victim to an officer's bullet.

A Childhood Moving North

From the start, Brook's father was only minimally involved in his life. As several family members described him to us, Julian Lewis was "a player." He looked like the rapper Snoop Dogg, they said. Brook was given his mother's last name, "Bacon." She worked as a cameraperson for a television station in Savannah. As a young child, Brook lived with her and her father in a modest home.

In search of more opportunities, Brook and his mother moved to Memphis when he was about ten, moving in with family of Brook's mother there. They stayed a couple years before moving again, this time to Middletown, Pennsylvania, near the Three Mile Island nuclear generating station, where they lived with Brook's aunt, who rented there and worked for the Internal Revenue Service. It was a depressed area with closed-down factories and boarded-up shops. Soon they moved again, to Fall River, Massachusetts, to stay with a friend of Brook's mother. Again, they didn't stay long. Brook was only in middle school, but he had become accustomed to the peripatetic life.

The next stop was a good one, and a long one. Brook and Taneeta moved to Providence, Rhode Island, where she worked at the local television station. They were there from Brook's seventh-grade year until his sophomore year in high school. He made friends, rode his bike around the neighborhood, played ball, and got a job working for the city's parks department. It was an eighteen-dollar-an-hour job, and he found he could buy the things he wanted. That was when he started thinking about what things in life cost. He realized that the most expensive item his mother was paying for was rent, followed by food. He watched her hand a rent check to the white men who owned their apartment. Those men lived in a beautiful home with large fireplaces, pet kittens, and what Brook believed to be actual Egyptian artifacts. He noticed how different their own home was from the one they rented out. He started thinking, *This is how a homeowner's home looks.* He realized that where he and his mother lived was temporary. And that if he owned something one day, he could be a landlord and he could have other people pay *him.*

Next, he and his mother moved to Allston, a neighborhood in Boston. Taneeta wanted her son to have the best shot he could in high school, and the week they moved to town, the school for which he was zoned was the site of a stabbing between students who were arguing over a jacket, Brook told us. So, Taneeta faked an address to qualify Brook for the nearby prestigious public high school, Cambridge Rindge and Latin School. Brook did well enough at Cambridge Rindge to be admitted to Northeastern University. He was good at math and science, so he signed up for the engineering program, which included an internship for on-the-job experience. He thought he was on a track for success and worked hard in his first trimester.

But then, the financial aid office called him in for a visit. There was a problem. He needed to pay more money, and they would not grant him more loans without a cosigner. Because Taneeta was saddled with her own debt as she tried to earn a college degree, she could not cosign.

Brook called anyone he could: his uncles, for instance. (He demurred when we asked him if he had called his father.) Ultimately, no one said yes, because no one had sufficient collateral to back the loans.

And so, he left Northeastern. Without a cosigner, Brook was apparently too risky for the institution. But without a college degree, he would be at risk economically. The roughly $12,000 in loans that the school had granted him his first trimester (with no cosigner) remained with Brook for years to come. It was his debt to deal with on his own, with no help from Northeastern. He upped his hours at the ice-cream shop where he worked, and put his college dreams on hold.

As we talked with Brook while on the march for justice, we paused our conversation every so often. Brook and the other demonstrators had tributes to make. At each mile, the lawyers held up signs of other Black people who had been shot by police. "Rayshard Brooks. Say his name!" they yelled. "Michael Brown. Say his name!"

A Tale of Two Families

Julian Lewis, say his name, Julian Lewis.

He was born June 16, 1960, into a family that had been in Georgia since at least 1820. To study his family tree is to understand the path that brought Brook all the way to Northeastern University but then failed to provide him with a cosigner for his student loans. And to compare Brook's ancestors to those of his wife, Shalagh, is to see in stark, personal relief the differences in white and Black family histories.

Brook's father's family had two main sides: Julian's father, Roosevelt Lewis, and his mother, Lindsay Milton. Lindsay's parents and grandparents have no signs of homeownership in the U.S. censuses. Her family was marked by early deaths of the men and service jobs performed by the women. Her grandmother on her father's side was a widow by age thirty-five, with eight children to care for and rent to pay. The Lewis family side first appears in public records in 1867, when Julian's great-great-grandfather Jerry registered to vote. Born in 1820 in Georgia, Jerry Lewis appeared in the 1870 Census listed as a farm laborer. At the time, he was fifty, and he and his wife, Cilla, had six children at home, including Jerry Jr., whose son would be Julian's grandfather. The family lived in Screven County, Georgia, where, 150 years later, Julian would be killed. There was an early history of landownership going back to the family of Jerry Lewis, whose name appeared in Georgia property tax records in the 1880s. In the 1900 Census, Jerry Jr. was listed as the owner of his home, but his grandson was a renter throughout most of his life, acquiring land only in his fifties. Though the Lewis family had land in several generations, and Julian's father acquired some land, Julian's childhood and lineage were not shaped by significant opportunity or education.

Brook's mother, Taneeta, on the other hand, came from a family that had benefited from World War II service and that prized education. Her father, Martin, served in the U.S. Navy. He then was able to graduate from Paine College and earn a certificate from Teachers College in New York City and a master's degree at the Tuskegee Institute in Alabama. This lifted Martin out of the renting-farmer's life of his upbringing in the nearby rural town of Daisy. Martin served as principal of the local elementary school for twenty-one years and, in 2007, in one of the proudest moments of his life, was the grand marshal for a local Martin Luther King Jr. parade.

In between the Lewis branches and the Bacon branches of this family came Brook. The fact that he was raised primarily on the Bacon side, where education was prized, likely led to his upward mobility. It was Principal Martin Bacon's home, down the road from the Lewis family, where Taneeta and Brook had lived when he was a child. Taneeta's father's commitment to education and her own regret that she had not gone to college fueled her mission to get Brook into college one day.

These family trees stand in contrast to those of Brook's wife.

Shalagh Kelly was born on April 23, 1982, three years after Brook. The two met in 2005, when Shalagh and Brook worked at the Barnes and Noble store at Brandeis University. She was twenty-three and already a college graduate. Brook, age twenty-six, was still working to become one.

Shalagh's parents, born in the 1950s, both graduated from college. (Brook's parents did not.) Education and property ran in her father's family, going back generations. In our research of Shalagh's family tree, we found that her father's mother's family can be traced in the United States as far back as the 1760s. These relatives originally came from Germany, but by 1766, they were in Pennsylvania. The family migrated to Ohio in the early 1800s, after the state was formed in 1803. Federal land acts at the start of the 1800s provided credit to farmers—mainly white farmers—to purchase land there. When many of them ran into trouble making their interest payments, Congress passed relief acts in 1820 and 1821, extending the terms of the loans and making other concessions to help the (almost entirely white) farmers hold on to their land. The Ohio Territory was one among large swaths of the current-day United States forcibly purchased from Native Americans in the 1800s and given to white Americans on highly favorable terms. As covered in chapter 4, these sorts of land grants occurred in many places throughout the 1800s and mainly benefited white Americans. The land grants, even if they no longer remain in those families' hands, provided a foundation for white wealth growth.

And so it was that some of Shalagh's ancestors were settled, with land, in the 1800s. While there are not many other records shedding light on their lives back then, one record seems to indicate that Shalagh had a relative in college by 1854. These are advantages not present in Brook's ancestors' records.

A comparison of Shalagh's relatives with Brook's using 1870 Census documents—the first year that Black households were recorded by the Census—is informative. The 1870 Census for Jerry Lewis Sr. shows him as a farm laborer. "Cannot Read?" and "Cannot Write?" the census asks. "Yes" he cannot read. "Yes" he cannot write. In the 1870 Census for Michael Oldfather, Shalagh's ancestor, he is *not* recorded as "cannot" read or "cannot" write. Michael Oldfather, age forty-four, is listed as a farmer; Jerry Lewis, age fifty, is listed as a "farm laborer." In the history of our country, there has always been a difference between a farmer and a farm *laborer*.

In 1870, the government's census asked both Black and white Americans about "personal estate value." Jerry Lewis listed his estate value as $200; Michael Oldfather listed his as $2,700. In addition, the government asked Oldfather for his real estate value, which he listed as $9,000. Lewis listed nothing for real estate value. We bring you these numbers from only one biracial couple's family tree, but they are emblematic. The wealth gap between Shalagh's ancestor (Michael Oldfather) and Brook's ancestor (Jerry Lewis) was 58.5 to 1. For the nation, just after the Civil War, the white-Black wealth gap was nearly 60 to 1.

Shalagh's family continued to stay ahead. Michael Oldfather's son John—Shalagh's great-great-grandfather—briefly rented a home in his twenties in 1900, but by the 1910 Census onward, he was listed as owning his home, free and clear without a mortgage. No one in Brook's lineage is recorded as owning a home during this time.

The 1930 and 1940 Census records also list education levels. Lining up both Shalagh's and Brook's great-grandparents, comparable generations where we could find records, we found that two of Brook's great-grandmothers made it to the seventh grade, but the other four great-grandparents that we could track stopped school between the third and fifth grade. In Shalagh's family, a great-grandparent was educated in four-year colleges, both grandfathers went to college, and homeownership was more common.

Few family portraits are entirely shaded in one direction. Shalagh had a great-grandfather who was a school principal. Brook had a grandfather who was a principal. This sounds level on its face, but when you fill in enough of the picture, it becomes clear that while Shalagh's family was never considered extremely wealthy for white Americans, some branches of her family were more bountiful than Brook's. Consider her father's career path: A trained engineer, he decided to start his own business in New Hampshire. As an entrepreneur, he was plowing savings back into his business, and as a white entrepreneur, he was more likely to get loans than a Black entrepreneur. When Shalagh reached high school, she attended Phillips Exeter, one of the most prestigious private high schools in the country. Her parents didn't have the free cash to pay tuition, so they took on debt for her to attend. Her parents paid off the debt, not Shalagh. This is the sort of unevenness in her marriage that Shalagh was thinking about more in the summer of

2020, after the murder of George Floyd. She had had some student loans in college, but they were paid off by then. Brook's, however, were not. Shalagh had once made the same amount of money as he did, but by 2020, her earnings had doubled, and he was unemployed that summer. She had become the primary breadwinner.

Shalagh was not on the justice walk. No one from her family or Brook's mainly white social circle in New Hampshire was there. There were some safety risks, to be sure, but as Brook opened up, he shared that he had misgivings about their absence. His white mother-in-law, named Karen, and his father-in-law, Bob, had urged him to talk with them about his father's death even though they did not join the march. Bob told us they were doing their best to be supportive, but being in a biracial family was new terrain to them.

Still, Brook was hurt by the absence. "It's like, 'Okay, well, do you want to march? Here's your opportunity if you want to do something. Here it is, right in front of you.' And you know, no one bit on that," he said. "Sharing information for the sake of sharing, it doesn't do anything for me—at this point, here is something that was actionable."

Brook also closely watched the sign-ups on his family's petition to charge the officer who killed his father. He noticed that there were far more financial donations on Facebook to his family's legal battle (to seek justice for his father) than there were public signatures to the petition. Though grateful for the funds, he wondered where the names were. Something was off-kilter about money with no names.

Weeks after the march, in the fall of 2021, Shalagh spoke to us about how she had been viewing the situation. She rolled the story back to June 2020. It was the first time in her biracial marriage that she had reflected on racism. George Floyd was killed, and that lit something in her. She felt angry, and ashamed that she hadn't delved into the topic before, connecting it to injustice nationally or on a personal level. She realized that she had been lumping Brook into her own privilege. "I would say that on the spectrum of privilege—because there is a spectrum of privilege—Brook is in the middle," she said. "Especially, I think, being in a relationship with me and having opportunities that my family has afforded to him, has wrapped him in a bit of privilege himself."

Shalagh had begun reckoning with how their upbringings differed, how they had been afforded different things, and how society looked at them differently. "And especially him being a Black man—being deemed a threat," she said.

Shalagh hadn't known Julian Lewis very well. She met him briefly during a visit to Georgia while she and Brook were dating, and again at their wedding in Hilton Head. Their children had never met him. Brook did not know his father well, either, he said. When we asked if Julian, a carpenter, had gone to technical school, Brook said, "Good question."

The spring of 2020 wasn't the easiest time to fit in long-distance family relations. With the Covid-19 pandemic, the Bacons were locked down in their 2,300-square-foot house. Brook was freshly unemployed as the pandemic hit, and he and his wife created a homeschool routine for their two children. Sometimes, their four-year-old son put on his backpack even though he was sitting at home doing worksheets. Ice cream by the firepit was a treat. Brook sent his father a few photos of the children as the summer passed. The kids sat for a photo holding hands in front of a hand-drawn rainbow; perfect for their mom to share on Instagram: "Hello Friends," they wrote. Another day, the kids undertook a memorable photo project to imitate the famous cherubs in Raphael's *Sistine Madonna*, circa 1513. The resemblance was striking. And they participated in the "teacher parade" in April 2020: As their teachers drove by, waving from their cars, Brook's daughter, six years old, stood outside in a blue puffy coat and a pink hat with a pom-pom topper, holding up two homemade signs reading "I Miss You" and "YAY for Our Broad Street Teachers."

Aside from Brook's family, the people who lined the streets to salute their teachers were white. In Nashua, the population was less than 4 percent Black, and the Bacons were one of the few biracial families there. Race went unremarked upon, except for rare occasions—like when a neighbor called Brook the N-word. The latest incident of race intimidation had occurred on July 11, 2020. The Bacons had placed a Black Lives Matter sign in their yard. They woke up that morning and found that it was missing. "Presumably stolen," Shalagh said at the time. She was infuriated.

The Bacons promptly put up another sign and started looking into security cameras. Shalagh felt over this period in the summer of 2020 that she was growing closer to Brook, even as she saw the differences.

A month later, Julian Lewis was driving home late at night when a police car began to tail him. Lewis did not pull over. The officer, who would report that Lewis had a broken taillight, began to chase him around winding country roads. They ended up on a dirt road, where the officer blocked Lewis from driving farther. Before Lewis got out of the car, the officer shot him.

Brook learned of his father's death hours after it occurred. His aunt called him, but he was making his son oatmeal and missed the call. Shalagh was out with her cousins and her daughter, getting their nails done and shopping. Brook's mother, Taneeta, called her and told her the news. Shalagh's reaction was "Are you kidding?" Having spent the prior two months diving into issues of race for the first time and overcoming guilt over not having done so before, she was now facing the fact that her Black father-in-law had been fatally shot by police. Around the same time, Brook called his mom. "There was a calmness in my mom to deliver the news to me," he said. "I don't know if you've ever been angry enough where you can't really hear? The blood starts to rush at such a rate that all you can hear is that rushing through your temples, that's it. Your eardrums are just swollen with that. That rush. So, as she was telling me, at first, I didn't understand it at first. . . . I thought, *Oh, you know, something happened. There was some argument or some disagreement or some altercation or something like that. And he was just injured.* And so, she continued to explain it, and she told me that he was shot in the face and, uh, and that was it."

The news of Julian Lewis's death turned the Bacons' world upside down—as if it weren't already upside down enough. Brook was unemployed, covering his earnings through the Covid-related federal stimulus package. The pair had long ago paid off Shalagh's college debt, but they were still working to pay off Brook's. They had refinanced their house. Staring at their financial statements, they saw the reality of their inequality more clearly than ever: whereas they had been earning at equal levels when they purchased the home in 2012, eight years later, Shalagh earned two times as much as Brook had most recently made. They talked throughout that summer about the racism they felt Brook had experienced in his last job. They discussed how he had been promoted less often in jobs over the years compared to Shalagh. He worked in finance but was still in entry-level jobs in his forties.

Now, with Brook's father having been killed, Shalagh was rethinking their past decisions. In addition to Brook's day jobs, he had worked seasonal shifts at FedEx to earn Christmas present money. But that temporary job was the overnight shift. It meant he was out driving late at night, and he was pulled over by police three times. Shalagh felt guilty. Why had she let him work overnight shifts? Why, she asked herself, had she not realized how *at risk* her husband was?

The thoughts kept racing through Shalagh's mind: Why hadn't she realized until Julian's death that she, too, was at risk from the system and the upbringing Brook had had? Even financially: Her earnings now were helping to pay off his student loans. "I never considered, entering into an interracial marriage, that by doing so, I would be assuming systemic racist debt," she said. She said she wouldn't change anything based on that realization, but she now understood she was tied to Black Americans in a way that many white Americans were not. "I have more skin in the game. Because now it's my family. It's my problem. It's my money," she said.

She also thought a lot about the lengths to which Taneeta had gone—raising Brook as a single mom, in Julian's absence—for Brook's mobility and success. "She had his interests entirely in mind," Shalagh said admiringly. "Taneeta was literally doing it all for him."

An Unequal Financial Crisis

It was after her son had left home, in fact, that Taneeta Bacon's finances reached their greatest point of crisis. She had joined scores of other Black Americans in becoming a first-time homeowner, even as the American financial system welcomed her with a mortgage that put her at risk. And she was far from alone.

Taneeta was still in the Boston area in 2005, as Brook moved toward one of their top goals: he would soon graduate college. He had earned a degree in economics from Brandeis University. It had been a long climb. After leaving Northeastern—carrying about $12,000 in student debt but no degree—he had worked a few months at the ice-cream shop and then had managed to get into the customer call center at BankBoston. The entry-level position in finance changed his trajectory. He quickly did well, and he spent several years at a number of banks, including State Street. He moved from customer calls, to sales, to trading, and pulled in a good salary—but without a college degree, he found his progress stymied. He eventually enrolled in a program at Brandeis that focused on older students attending college. And now he was about to graduate.

Taneeta, too, was moving toward a life goal. She would purchase her own home—a first. No more couches or rentals. It seemed the move north was finally paying off.

Taneeta's new home was a two-bedroom condominium in the Hyde Park neighborhood of Boston, an area that seemed on the rise, though there was still drag racing outside at the traffic stop each night. Built in the 1960s, the condo was only 780 square feet, but it was home. The purchase price was $173,000, and she funded that fully with a mortgage, putting zero dollars down.

The last time Taneeta's condo had changed hands, in 1992, it had sold for $39,250. As in most of the country, Boston property prices were on a rapid rise in the early 2000s. Low interest rates and aggressive lending from banks had allowed more people to purchase homes, including first-time homebuyers like Taneeta. Building on decades of expanded lending dating to the Community Reinvestment Act in the 1970s, the early 2000s housing boom expanded homeownership among Black and Latino Americans and other minority groups. On its face, this seemed like a good thing, because more people could pursue the American Dream of owning a home. The problem was that many of the loans given out in this period were predatory and presented borrowers with unrealistic payment plans. The fall of 2005, it would turn out, would be the Boston area's peak for housing prices. The city headed into a falling market before some other parts of the country.

The 2008 financial crisis, sparked by the cratering housing market, had different effects on people in different racial groups. This was not a topic widely covered in real time in 2008, perhaps in part because of a lack of racial diversity among the financial reporters at major news outlets. But by 2020, it had become clear that Black Americans did not recover as much as white Americans. We were reminded of the remark by a local Harlem reverend back when a Black bank there failed in the early 1990s: "When downtown catches a cold, Harlem gets pneumonia." People with access to wealth have financial resilience. When troubles come their way, people in families or social settings with wealth can lean into their family's reserves to help them emerge less harmed. Because many Black families—and Latino families—have less access to wealth, setbacks can hit them harder and last longer. When the American public catches a cold, Black Americans get pneumonia.

The effects of the 2008 crisis stretched beyond home foreclosures. The recession tied to the housing bust led to many jobs lost in particular segments of the economy—like construction, which employed many minority workers. The peak Black unemployment rate after the 2008 housing bust reached 16.8 percent in 2010, just as it would in 2020, during the pandemic, but the white unemployment rate from the 2008 crisis peaked at 9.2 percent. As we interviewed hundreds of Black Americans for this project, we asked whether their families had been affected by the 2008 crisis. Many people pointed beyond foreclosures to spillover effects like evictions (when their landlords faced foreclosure and evicted them). To understand the ways people were affected, we designed and ran a national Harris Poll. In it, we found that Latino and Black Americans were slightly more likely than white Americans to say their family had experienced a home foreclosure or short sale in that period and were more likely to say that their families had needed to move to less expensive homes. White Americans were more likely to say they lost money in the stock market. We also asked people how their personal wealth in 2008 compared with their wealth in 2022. Asian and white Americans were most likely to say their wealth was better by 2022 than it was in 2008. Black Americans were more likely to say their wealth in 2022 was about the same as it was back then.

These findings match other economic research, which has found that between 2007 and 2010, Hispanic and Black families lost a greater share of their wealth than white families, on average. For Hispanic families, the drop was 40 percent. For Black families, it was 31 percent. For white families, it was 11 percent.

Often, people do not know why their friends and family members move. People we interviewed recalled people they knew moving from 2006 through 2010, but they didn't know if that was because of a foreclosure or an eviction. People don't always tell even their closest family members their circumstances. Money is personal, a private matter, and sometimes the lack of it is embarrassing.

When we initially asked Brook on the justice walk whether anyone in his family had experienced foreclosure, he said, "Not that I know of." Later, we found out, it was a topic that his mother was not eager to discuss.

Brook was originally proud of Taneeta's condo. When he graduated from Brandeis, he stayed with her there for a few months before moving in with his wife-to-be. By then, Taneeta was working at Brandeis as a coordinator for the intercultural center, focusing on diversity issues. She continued rising through a variety of campus administration roles. She was the one to whom students would send housing forms. She was the one who got involved when there were campus policing issues. She was there as a shoulder to lean on for students sorting through problems. The university recognized her with several staff awards. "Taneeta was basically the welcoming face when you would walk into the intercultural center," said Amanda Dryer-Koloski, a Brandeis alumnus. "No matter what kind of day you were having . . . or if you were disappointed with a grade or a boyfriend, she was that old soul in the front being like, 'All right, you're a warrior woman. We're going to get it together.'"

Taneeta outwardly seemed to have finally landed on firm footing, financially and otherwise. Her past years of struggle helped her advise students, a former colleague told us. "Sometimes, when we would deal with difficult situations with students or parents," said Timothy Touchette, assistant dean of student affairs at Brandeis, "she would always reference the fact that some people's view or sense of reality is pretty warped, because they think what they're going through is traumatic or hard, but they don't take the time to look around and maybe give other people a little bit of empathy or sympathy to understand what they may have gone through. Those were the types of conversations that we would have that would reference her struggle and, you know, how difficult it was for her to make ends meet and to make sure that she was supporting her family."

By 2006, new problems were stirring. It was around this time that Brook moved out of his mother's condo to live with his future wife. Taneeta fell behind in paying the $2,995 she owed in association fees. In June, her building's association filed a legal complaint seeking those fees. That October, the trustee on her mortgage filed a foreclosure notice.

Longtime critics of government banking regulations like the Community Reinvestment Act from the 1970s seized the moment of the 2008 crisis to blame those laws, saying that they had caused banks to lend too liberally. But was the lending really so liberal when it was tied to such onerous, predatory terms? Was Taneeta *a risk* to the financial system, or was she *at risk*? Identifying the victim and the villain in the 2008 crisis became television fodder. Bankers blamed the homeowners for being greedy, and homeowners blamed the bankers for their greed. Whatever the case, there were not many bankers losing their homes and watching their personal credit ratings take a nosedive.

Taneeta's banker—her mortgage issuer—was New Century, the second-largest subprime mortgage issuer. The Irvine, California-based company was one of the most aggressive lenders in the years leading up to the crisis, and the loans it issued to homebuyers were bundled into mortgage bonds by the likes of Bear Stearns, Merrill Lynch, and Lehman Brothers. By the time Taneeta got her mortgage in 2005, lax home lending had become very common. The "no money down" loan (like Taneeta's) helped fuel the financial crisis, as did NINJA loans ("no income, no job, no assets" required) and IO, or interest-only loans (for which the borrower paid only interest and not any principal).

Beyond New Century, there were the Wall Street banks bundling up the loans that New Century issued. In many instances, the bankers there knew there were problems with the loans. As Morgan Stanley employees wrote around the time of Taneeta's condo journey, the New Century loans were "a bunch of scaaaaaarrryyyy loans" and they were "crap" and "like a trash novel." In January 2006, months after Taneeta bought her condo, a Morgan Stanley trading executive wrote New Century to ask, "What is going on with these loans?" To which a New Century executive wrote back, "You mean besides borrowers who apparently don't have the money to make their mortgage payments? (Sorry to be flip. . . .)"

Data in numerous lawsuits since the financial crisis have shown that mortgage companies like New Century routinely issued more of the "scary" loans to Black Americans than they did proportionally within the white population. Granting someone a no-money-down loan was not necessarily doing them a favor. Such a loan often carried a high interest rate or, possibly, an adjustable rate that could balloon up sky-high. These rates did not have the feel of community reinvestment. They seemed more like community exploitation.

Even before the 2008 crisis, it was well known to the banking industry and to the U.S. government that "subprime" loans, which ultimately had more onerous terms for consumers than "prime" loans, often targeted Black Americans. Prime loans are those made to people whom bankers consider to be low-risk and are, thus, given lower interest rates. The problem has long been that the people "considering" which borrowers are lower risk often have bias clouding their consideration. This was not a new problem leading into the 2008 housing crisis. As far back as 1998, the Department of Housing and Urban Development found that subprime loans were three times more likely to be issued in low-income neighborhoods than in wealthy ones. And they were *five* times more likely when the neighborhood was predominantly Black versus white. This meant that 51 percent of home loans in Black neighborhoods at that time were subprime. Subprime loans were prominent even in high-income Black neighborhoods: about 39 percent of the loans in high-income Black neighborhoods were subprime, while only 6 percent of loans in white wealthy neighborhoods were subprime. Wealthy Black neighborhoods even had more subprime loans than poor white neighborhoods, where just 18 percent of borrowers had subprime loans.

The Black-white mortgage gap is not all that different from the wealth gap in its patterns. With the wealth gap, even white people with lower levels of education have more wealth than highly educated Black Americans. With mortgages, even white people in low-income neighborhoods are granted better mortgages than Black people in wealthy neighborhoods. So, who here is *a risk* versus who is *at risk*? HUD concluded in its 1998 report that much more should be done by the financial industry and the government to expand access to the higher-quality prime loans in Black communities and to protect Black borrowers from predatory lending that unfairly steered them into subprime loans. However, unfortunately, there were not significant reforms after this late 1990s report. And the Black-white mortgage gap continued.

At the peak of the 2006 housing boom, Black and Latino families were 2.4 times more likely to receive high-cost, subprime loans than white families. Even Black and Latino families earning more than two hundred thousand dollars a year were more likely to get subprime loans than lower-income white families.

It was in this context that Taneeta got a subprime loan. Exactly how the decision was made for her, we do not know, but typically, when mortgage brokers look at loan options, they review factors like the prospective borrower's credit rating and then offer options for loans based on the risk they think the borrower represents. A lower credit rating, which may be tied to past trouble paying bills or loans, will mean a higher interest rate on the loan. It is easy to see how this makes sense for investors and banks seeking to be compensated for the risk of the borrower's defaulting. But as a society that has made wealth creation (and daily life) more difficult for generations of Black Americans, this is one of the ways in which the financialization of our system is "market first" rather than "citizen first." Are we trying to help Black Americans get ahead or punish them for the challenges that have brought them to where they are today?

Purchasing the condo in Hyde Park was likely a financial stretch for Taneeta, and we don't know what other loans she was offered or whether she would have qualified for a prime loan. What we do know is that in 2005, she earned about $34,000 working at Brandeis. She had to make interest payments on $5,000 in student loans from when she took some college courses, as well as payments on furniture loans and on debt on her minivan. And she lived in the Boston area, where housing costs were high compared to incomes. By 2005, 40 percent of homeowners there were paying more than 30 percent of their income for housing, up from a quarter of homeowners who paid that much in 2000. Renting would not have been much better—more than half of renters paid more than 30 percent of their income on rent. In just five years, the number of communities in the Boston area considered affordable had fallen from 101 to 19.

Taneeta's mortgage statement showed that in the first three years, she would owe about $1,280 per month on the condo, or 45 percent of her 2005 monthly income. After three years, her interest rate would float at a premium above the LIBOR benchmark, a reference used to determine interest rates for financial instruments. Cleverly, the mortgage lender had asked Taneeta to sign on to the terms under a line that sounded like consumer protection. Under the header "Limits on Interest Rate Charges," it said: "My interest rate will never be greater than 15.3% or less than 8.3%." To Taneeta, this could have sounded like a safeguard, given that it said what would "never" happen. But it was actually a weight around her ankles: she was locked into high interest rates . . . and high payments. For Taneeta, this meant paying something between $15,000 and $27,000 or so per year. Taneeta was earning $34,000 per year. Nonetheless, she signed on.

Taneeta was not the only Black American anchored to weighty mortgage terms. In the years before the financial crisis, only 6 percent of white Americans with a 660 or higher credit score were put into high-interest loans, but 21 percent of Black Americans with the same credit scores or higher were steered into loans like Taneeta's. As a former Wells Fargo employee testified in a lawsuit brought by the City of Baltimore, Wells Fargo had a unit set up explicitly to push high-interest loans for refinancing of Black customers' debt. That suit became infamous for testimonies in which a former Wells Fargo employee said colleagues sometimes referred to Black Americans as "mud people."

Following the housing collapse, the median Black household had its wealth drop by 53 percent, while the median white household's net worth dropped 16 percent. This drop captured deflated wealth of all types, including savings, which people tend to use when they lose their jobs. The drops in housing wealth, which measures the total value of property owned, were more closely matched: from 2005 to 2011, while white Americans lost 32 percent of their housing wealth, Black Americans lost 36 percent.

The Black-white gap in homeownership increased after 2008 only because of what came next in the housing market. The next stage of the housing market is a topic for later in the book, when we turn back to real estate in Atlanta. For Taneeta, what came next was financial rock bottom. Three months after getting the foreclosure notice, she filed for bankruptcy. In doing so, she entered another labyrinth within our unequal financial system, one we will explore in the next chapter. But first, let's turn to another kind of crisis.

Race, Money, and the Justice System

Midway through the four-day justice walk in September 2021, we peeled away to do some additional reporting. We drove along Highway 17, where we had walked two days earlier, passing fields of cotton. We drove down a long driveway of a large rural plot, passing a small café run out of somebody's home. Dream Burger, it was called. Farther back was Brook's father's home, a small orange building with a red roof that Julian Lewis had built himself years ago. We walked up to knock and saw that, at hip height, the door was pocked with a bullet hole. We quickly left.

Our next stop was the Rev. James Brown's church, where we heard about Julian Lewis's childhood and his most recent stay in prison. Brown's family had long known the Lewises—Brown's father drove the school bus Lewis took to school, and their parents were longtime friends. Their mothers worked together in the local textile factory.

Brown, sixty at the time we met him, said he had seen the area change in his lifetime—downtown Sylvania used to be composed almost entirely of white residents and was now mixed. But he noted that even in his memory, the old plantations in the county, which stretches up to the South Carolina border, were a big presence, and families still farmed there. He listed off the factories that had closed in recent decades and then noted that the one that employed him—a glass factory that had supplied material for the Twin Towers in New York—had announced just that day that it would be closing, too.

Brown and Lewis attended the local elementary school together when it was still segregated and then went through high school together. After graduation, around the time Brook was born, Lewis moved to Atlanta to become an electrician and learn other trades. Brown joined the military. "I think when we all got out of high school, we all thought, *This is it. We're never coming back to school, and we're never gonna move back here*," Brown recalled. "*There's nothing here.*"

But Brown and Lewis both ended up back in Screven County. Brown used to see Lewis around town starting in the mid-1990s, and he would give him rides home. Because of prior infractions, Lewis tried to avoid driving, Brown said. The 2008 crisis hit Lewis's construction business hard—people did not install new decks after the housing market sputtered. Twelve years later, the pandemic was also not an easy time for locals, Brown said. Businesses ground to a halt; Brown himself was furloughed. The trickle-down effect meant that business sputtered for Lewis, too. In other parts of the country, people were rushing to build indoor-outdoor living spaces and were buying up country houses to escape the pandemic; in Lewis's town, there was not a lot of wealth sitting around to do that. "The pandemic has caused everybody to struggle," he said. "Myself and Julian, we don't let it be outwardly seen that we're worrying. We don't want the families to be stressed. We are wondering, *How are we going to feed our family?* We are wondering whether we can get unemployment. We are wondering different things, because as men, we were raised up to just survive, to do what we got to do to survive. And I think anytime you get to a point like that, depression does set in on a lot of people. Depression does set in."

One moment with Lewis stood out in Brown's mind. In his role as a part-time reverend, Brown visited state prisons. One day around 2018, there was his friend, Julian Lewis. "Now, you don't belong here," Brown told him. Lewis was quick to tell Brown he had big dreams for when he got out. "And, I said, 'Okay, I believe, I always believe,'" Brown recalled. "He was always one of those types of people that he would—he was a go-getter."

As we listened to Brown, we looked at each other wearily. In the course of our reporting, the more interviews we held, the more a common thread emerged: Many of our interview subjects' fathers had been caught up in the criminal justice system. We had not gone out seeking people whose fathers had been in prison. We had looked for young Black people whose careers and families seemed on the rise. But reaching up the economic ladder was not all these individuals had in common, and we had to accept that this other shared experience— the U.S. justice system—was also an important part of understanding them . . . and the Black-white wealth gap.

The disproportionate effect of the criminal justice system on Black Americans is intertwined with the wealth gap, historically and in modern times, in myriad ways. Beyond Brook Bacon's father's records, James Woodall's father was in prison for a rape conviction, and as we looked back over generations, we found other serious offenses, like a murder conviction of Jesse Day tied to a domestic dispute. (The incident occurred years after he had been divorced from James Woodall's great-grandmother Frances Walker and involved someone not related to James.) Sorting through how to view these incidents, and especially how to view the impact these infractions had on loved ones and descendants, was tricky. As we researched the ancestors of people discussed in this book, we found past arrests that seemed dubious. One relative was arrested on a charge of fornication in 1944. Another was arrested for participating in the lottery. Scores of these sorts of arrests can be found online now in convict registers from states like Alabama and Georgia. The arrests, sometimes, were for breaking laws that applied only to Black people. There were so many such state laws on the books in the early 1900s that scholar Pauli Murray's book collecting them, *States' Laws on Race and Color*, is just over two inches thick.

Beyond these, laws for all people were unequally applied, and charges were often simply made up.

False accusations against Black men and boys led to many of the gruesome lynchings that scar America's history. There were more than four thousand lynchings in southern states and hundreds in northern and midwestern states. These were often justified after minor social infractions by or baseless allegations against Black individuals. In many towns, practically the entire white population would turn out to watch the lynching. The Equal Justice Initiative, which tracks lynchings, has found that they were often used to "enforce Jim Crow laws and racial segregation—a tactic for maintaining racial control by victimizing the entire African American community, not merely punishment of an alleged perpetrator for a crime."

Some Black Americans who were accused of crimes during the Jim Crow era were thrown into work camps while in prison. There they labored decades after slavery had been abolished. People in convict work camps in Atlanta are known to have helped construct buildings that still exist today, like the federal penitentiary and homes in the upscale neighborhood Inman Park. That legacy in Atlanta is tied to a former mayor from the 1880s, James W. English. He owned the Chattahoochee Brick factory, among other businesses, and according to a book by the journalist Douglas Blackmon, English's companies managed 1,206 of Georgia's 2,881 convict laborers, who made bricks, among other manual jobs. English's "great personal wealth was inextricably linked to the enslavement of thousands of men" decades after slavery had been outlawed, Blackmon wrote. In addition to the convict-staffed brick factory, English owned a bank that merged into Wachovia, which is now part of Wells Fargo. From these businesses, his descendants had money and opportunities to build more wealth: a great-grandson, James D. Robinson III, went on to serve for twenty years as the chief executive of American Express, and then he had wealth and connections to help his son, James IV, found a venture capital firm in 1994. That firm, RRE Ventures, became one of the most successful and lucrative venture capital firms in the world. Robinson III referred our question about the era of convict leasing to a relative by marriage, who told us, "It was a black mark, and history is messy."

This book is not long enough to include all of the examples from history of crime allegations against Black Americans that seem ridiculous today. But one egregious example was the case of Callie House. Formerly enslaved, House became a well-known advocate for pensions to be paid to Black Americans who had been enslaved. In 1915, she formed an association that sued the U.S. government for $68 million, the amount of money the U.S. Treasury had received from the sale of cotton confiscated during the Civil War. In 1916, the nation's postmaster indicted House for falsely claiming that reparations were coming to her association's members. She was jailed for nine months in 1917.

The financial repercussions that came to Black families when their loved ones were accused of crimes in the late 1800s and throughout the 1900s trickled down just as surely as the compounding wealth of James W. English. These individuals and their families were viewed as *a risk*, but in retrospect, they were *at risk*.

Financial discrimination is still common for those caught up in the justice system. Most people were not making much money before being incarcerated. While they are in prison, there are fees and fines, sometimes exorbitant fees, even to make phone calls. When these individuals come out of prison, those fees and fines can be taken directly out of their wages. And while they are in prison, debts they owed beforehand continue to rack up interest. That includes credit card debt and loans, but often also child support payments. So, once they leave prison and get a job, their wages may be garnished for years for all this prison and pre-prison debt.

That is, if they can get a job at all. In a longitudinal study of 740 incarcerated people who were released between 2002 and 2005, researchers at the Urban Institute found that only 31 percent were in jobs two months after their release—this was despite most of them making their job search a priority. Eventually, many former prisoners find jobs, but a permanent gap remained. In mid-2008, for instance, the former prison population (of all races) had an unemployment rate of 27.3 percent. At that time, the general population had an unemployment rate of 5.8 percent. And these statistics are even starker when disaggregated by race. White men who had been incarcerated had an unemployment rate of 18.4 percent, while Black men who had been incarcerated had an unemployment rate of 35.2 percent. For Black women who were incarcerated, the unemployment rate was 43.6 percent—far higher than the unemployment rate of 23.2 percent for formerly incarcerated white women.

As these data points show, it's not just incarceration that affects job prospects. It's race. In the early 2000s, the sociologist Devah Pager ran experiments in New York City and Milwaukee to see if white and Black applicants with felony convictions had equal likelihoods of landing job interviews. Not only did white male job applicants with a felony record get more calls back than Black applicants with felony records, she also found that white felony offenders were more likely to be called for interviews than Black men who had *no* criminal record.

There's also inequity in access to training while in prison. Educational and job training opportunities are more often awarded to white prisoners. The reason? The programs often use education and family background information to determine who gets to participate, a 2023 report about Massachusetts facilities found. In effect, this exclusion of Black and Latino prisoners contributes to a reentry gap and, ultimately, to the Black-white and Latino-white wealth gaps.

It's also difficult for the formerly incarcerated to borrow money after prison. Either they have bad credit scores from debts that mounted while they were behind bars or they have no credit history at all if they went to prison at a young age. Often, former prisoners need to find someone to cosign for loans, such as to purchase a car to get to work. In addition, landlords often run background checks, and it can be difficult for people with a criminal record to rent an apartment.

In recent decades, these issues have hit more Black families than white families because Black people have been imprisoned at a higher rate. The statistics for this are striking. As Michelle Alexander noted in her powerful book *The New Jim Crow*, as the U.S. prison population expanded from three hundred thousand to two million over the last three decades of the twentieth century, permanent records were created for many people in Black communities. By 2010, up to 80 percent of young Black men in major cities had criminal records. Alexander attributed much of the overall increase in the prison population to the drug war, which she described as "the literal war that has been waged against our communities" creating a population of people who will experience "legalized discrimination" their entire lives. By 2021, Black Americans were in prison at nearly five times the rate of white Americans. This meant the prison population was 38.4 percent Black Americans while Black Americans were only 13.6 percent of the U.S. population. Alexander described people who have been in the prison system as having "second-class status." She noted they would be punished for years to come—and that's in part because of the financial repercussions of being incarcerated.

Prison "is either a pathway to poverty or it is an entrenchment of impoverished conditions that a family is already in," Gina Clayton-Johnson, executive director of Essie Justice Group, which supports women who have incarcerated loved ones, told us.

All this contributed to the Black-white wealth gap—and still does. One interview we did with an Atlanta-based judge stuck with us. Asha Jackson was the chief judge of the Superior Court in DeKalb County, which includes the east side of Atlanta. Jackson had a personal passion for finding new ways to help break the cycle of repeat convictions. Coming out of commercial litigation to become a judge, she was surprised by the numbers. "I looked out, and I saw a sea of young people who were charged as first-time felons," she told us. "And I thought, *There's got to be some other way*, because if they take a plea, they've impacted their ability to earn and be valuable citizens because of this, now, stain on their record." Jackson set up her own program, funded through corporate donations, to help some defendants in her court avoid prison by going through a self-improvement program.

The people we feature in this book mentioned repeatedly that they were well aware of the toll of the U.S. criminal justice system. They often cited statistics. James Woodall noted that as of 2021, Black Americans were about 30 percent of Georgia's population but about 60 percent of the state's prison occupants. And he noted that there were more Black men in prison, jail, or on parole or probation in 2021 than were enslaved in 1850. James also told us that he spent some of his teenage years attending his father's rape trial and wondering if his father was fully to blame or if he was facing retaliation for having pointed out flaws in the Atlanta police force. He still has his doubts, and while we are not taking a position on what occurred with Jonathan Robinson, what's interesting to us is that people like the head of Georgia's NAACP told us they have reason to believe false claims have been made in cases against their loved ones. This level of distrust of the system is common among Black families.

The topic of policing was frequent as we walked alongside Brook Bacon during the justice march. Asked about his father's past with the justice system, Brook said the infractions were racing, gambling, and probably possession of substances, but never anything violent. Julian Lewis's court records provided more detail. They showed that when Reverend Brown visited Lewis in prison in 2018, he was there for driving while impaired and fleeing the police three years prior. He had been sentenced to five years in prison, but he ended up getting out early. In 2005, he was charged with possession of cocaine. In 1994, he was convicted for driving under the influence and for domestic violence. This was when Brook was around fifteen and living in Rhode Island with his mother, who was raising him on her own.

At the time of Lewis's release in September 2018, he was placed on parole until August 27, 2020. Because of these violations, the police who thought that his taillight was out might have been more inclined to pull him over if they looked up his car's license plate number. It was early August 2020 when they pulled him over, so Julian was still on parole.

But an officer's right to pull a car over does not equate to permission to carry out a roadside shooting. Lewis's lawyer, Francys Johnson, insisted as much when he told us he could not confirm details of Lewis's criminal record, because he had not researched it. It was "not relevant," he said. "It was not known to the officer at the time of the incident and played no factor in the officer's decisions," he said.

The criminal justice system played a role in Julian Lewis's limited financial means and limited wherewithal to support his family. To Brook, his son, the biggest cost of his father's criminal record was "the opportunity cost": "Your time being locked up, you can't be productive," Brook said. "There is nothing you can really do. I mean, there's no library in that place. You can't read. I mean, if you really want to, I'm sure you could get a hold of a book. But I mean that that's not what people are thinking about when they're in there, probably especially in a county jail."

We asked Brook if he had personally escaped the risks his father experienced as a Black man. No, he said. "The idea that my father was shot . . . [It] could just as easily have been me." Brook had examples to back this up. There was his experience getting stopped while exiting the subway in Boston. And when he was nineteen, he told us, he was coming home from the gym, walking along the Charles River in Cambridge, when he stopped for a drink of water. It was summer, but it was late enough to be dark. A police officer came over and asked what he was reaching for in his bag. Brook was flip and said, "Very bad things." That got him in trouble. The citation was for trespassing, but it was a public park, so the matter was thrown out when Brook appeared in court, he said.

More recently, as a father of two, Brook had incidents with police in New Hampshire. As we mentioned earlier, he worked a second job with a late shift to make extra money to buy Christmas presents. On his drives home, he was pulled over multiple times. In none of those incidents was he accused of having committed a traffic infraction; he was pulled over because he was out driving at night.

Brook's wife, Shalagh, told us she now agonizes over protecting him. She recalled that a few years ago, when a neighbor used the N-word with Brook, the Bacons called the police. The police handled the situation respectfully, but after 2020, she began to wonder if that was because of her "whiteness." She told us that if this occurred now, she would *not* advise Brook to call the police. Then there were all the times that Brook was pulled over while driving at night. "The chances of something like a misunderstanding happening—in snap judgments being made—are so high," she said. After what she'd learned through the story of Brook's father, she had become "ultra vigilant." In her view, her husband's skin meant he was *at risk*.

As time passed after his father's death, Brook told us he could not escape from feeling guilty. Guilty he hadn't protested the killing of

George Floyd. Guilty he hadn't seen his father since his wedding to Shalagh several years before. Guilty he hadn't gotten involved in fighting injustice before it came so close to home. Guilty he had not fully connected with his Black roots.

Now he lived with all of that, and it was a struggle.

CHAPTER 7

THE BANKRUPTCY GAP

Once in debt, it is no easy matter for a whole race to emerge.
—W. E. B. Du Bois, *The Souls of Black Folk*

Michael Render's financial crisis came in 2011.

The rapper had just put out his fourth studio album, called *PL3DGE*. On the album, he addressed rich celebrities, including Oprah, Bill Cosby, and Sean "P. Diddy" Combs, warning them, "Don't forget your color, brother, we still muthafuckin' slaves." In it, he drew on the class divide that occurs within Black communities as some Black families break through to wealth while most stay behind. ("We know that house got air conditioning and the sweetest lemonade," he rapped about the Black people who have made it.) He also pointed out that it's a rarity to have a Black person become a billionaire: "Think about it, what's a rapper standing next to Warren Buffett?"

Explaining the lyrics, Michael said he was concerned that breakthroughs by a few Black Americans made it look like the problems of the past were gone. "I will never allow media to fool me to somehow think that, just because a Black kid from Marcy Projects becomes a billionaire," he said at the time, referring to Jay-Z and that rapper's childhood home in the projects in Brooklyn, that "the tables are fair when he's standing next to a man who's worth $56 billion." Michael continued: "[Warren Buffett] can give away his money, and the next year make more money and plus $10 billion. Jay-Z has had to fight, bleed, kill and die for every dollar he's ever got."

Michael knew about fighting *for every dollar*. Even as he was becoming more famous in the music industry, he was in a personal crisis. He would soon be bankrupt.

Four people featured in this book have filed for bankruptcy: Taneeta Bacon; Michael Render; Stephana Woodall Campbell, who filed twice; and James Lovelace (whose case will be covered later in the book). In these filings, we see people with diverse economic and financial histories converge on the same equation: net worth = zero dollars (or, often, less than zero). Michael, who would become an outsize success; Taneeta, a onetime homeowner; and Stephana, the perennial debtor and fake credit score user—they all went through the same legal gauntlet. Their bankruptcy cases shine a light on the challenges Black Americans face beyond the criminal justice system, when they go to civil court, where racial patterns contribute further to the Black-white wealth gap.

These cases document a moment in each individual's financial life and provide evidence of why many Americans are looking for something different in the financial system beyond traditional banking and beyond the government-run programs that rarely seem to land in a Black person's favor.

A Rocky Road

As a teenager, Michael Render became so close with Andrew Young's family that the former mayor chipped in to help pay his freshman year tuition at Morehouse College, a Historically Black College. The year did not go well. Michael became a young father, dropped out, and then spent some time dealing crack.

He wanted to be a rap musician. His father, a police officer, made a point of telling him, "They call it a 'starving artist' for a reason." Still, he started hanging out in Atlanta's music scene, specifically in the home basement space known as "the Dungeon," where OutKast and Goodie Mob recorded their music. Michael worked his way in to become a featured artist on OutKast's *Stankonia* album and eventually on a Jay-Z album. He was a guest performer in the 2001 OutKast song "The Whole World," which won a Grammy, and he traveled around the world singing his part. The experience made him want *more*. He looked beyond Collier Heights, beyond Atlanta, beyond the South, and saw a whole world. "That song showed me everything I could have on my own if I worked my ass off," he said. But secondhand fame was not enough. That song, he said, "it wasn't *mine*. I wanted *mine*."

Michael began recording albums on his own, but he didn't have much luck. "Killer Mike" wasn't resonating broadly with people. Working as a rapper is entrepreneurial, and it didn't generate much cash. Within a few years, he had mounting financial problems. He was now separated from the mother of his children. The two had financial disputes.

In March 2011, a sheriff in Atlanta showed up at 2615 Collier Drive NW, Michael's childhood home—the home where his grandmother Bettie Clonts had served him biscuits, history, and Black Power, all the while she was tracking down his father for child support. Only Michael's grandmother was home when the sheriff arrived. The summons was for a claim that Michael wasn't paying all the child support for his two children, who lived right around the corner. Their home was on Baker Road, just a few doors down from the home where Jewell Stewart lived briefly in the 1950s, before the white mob forced him to move away.

A few months after the sheriff's summons, Michael filed for bankruptcy. He had $2,550 in assets and $78,008 in debt. In addition to the child support issue, he owed tens of thousands of dollars in income taxes on past earnings. Michael never publicly discussed his bankruptcy in detail, though he would say, "I went broke, I failed, I was on my ass." In the song "Ju$t," on his 2020 album, he rapped, "I get broke too many times," shortly before rapping that "the Thirteenth Amendment says that slavery's abolished (shit)."

The rapper's period of personal financial struggles would inform his views on what Black banking should do for Black Americans and what, ultimately, he hoped Greenwood Bank would do. He knew what it was like to go bankrupt, to be underbanked, to rely on check-cashing shops, and to work for minimum wage at AutoZone. He wouldn't forget.

Many Americans are, in reality, broke. They have negative net worth, meaning their debts are bigger than their assets. Big debts pull net worths under zero. In modern times, the 2008 housing crisis made it more common for people to owe more on their homes than their homes were worth, and the student loan crisis made it common for young professional workers to owe more in loans than they had in savings. This translates for many into negative net worth.

But it's a special kind of "broke" that leads people into bankruptcy court. That's the broke that has no hope. That's the broke that can't see how any amount of earnings will soon pay off those debts. It's a broke felt at times by people of all races, and bankruptcy exists as a rare example of mercy in the American system. But if people of one race have an easier time obtaining that mercy than people of another race, that can contribute to wealth gaps. An unequal bankruptcy system contributes to the Black-white wealth gap simply by being a benefit (like New Deal–era FHA loans or historic land grants) that is more easily obtained by white people.

The United States' unequal financial system often pushes Black people into turmoil. Many Black Americans pay higher interest rates on debt than white Americans, making those debt payments more difficult to cover. And Black Americans, even wealthy Black Americans, are more likely to be put into subprime loans. There is a perverse morality to a financial system that claims there's fairness in the debt rates and the other financial terms Black people receive when it is that same system that created the inequitable treatment of Black Americans that tarnished their credit histories and financial prospects. It's simply not a system where all people get what they deserve.

With the historical and present-day hurdles Black Americans face, one might predict a bankruptcy *filing* gap, with Black Americans filing more than white Americans. In fact, Black Americans have been represented among bankruptcy filers in roughly the same proportion as they are represented in the U.S. population. A survey from 2006 to 2010 put Black Americans' incidence of filing at 11 to 15 percent of the population, a range close to their portion of the population. The gap appears instead in the *outcomes* of the cases: Black Americans are less than half as likely as white Americans to have their debts reorganized or relieved. This outcome difference has severe effects on Black wealth over time—specifically for the 19 percent of Black families in 2019 that had negative wealth, versus the 8 percent of white families. All those families with negative wealth would be prospects for bankruptcy . . . but, as we'll see, they would enter an unequal relief system.

Each bankruptcy seeker faces choices over how to file. Most important, they must decide whether to file a case under Chapter 7 or Chapter 13. The consequences of that choice are stark: Chapter 7 wipes away debt, whereas Chapter 13 reorganizes debt and puts individuals on multiyear repayment plans. Under Chapter 7, individuals must give up assets like cars and houses; under Chapter 13, they can keep them.

In 2011, Michael Render was among the people with negative wealth navigating the bankruptcy system. Shortly after the sheriff went looking for him at his grandmother's, he filed a Chapter 13 case in Fulton County, Georgia. For his assets, he listed a $200 pair of Nike sneakers, $300 worth of leather coats, $250 worth of blue jeans, and a $300 shotgun. He had owned a 2007 Chevrolet Tahoe truck, but documents in the case noted that it had been repossessed. Michael also had some money in the bank: $1,200 in accounts at Chase Bank, a white-run conglomerate. He did not own a home, according to the filing, and he listed his grandmother's Collier Heights property as his address.

Michael's debts were substantial. He owed $47,032 to state and federal tax authorities for unpaid taxes on income from 2006 through 2010. He owed $17,716 on his old car note. And he listed the $13,260 he owed in child support.

In all, Michael owed $75,458 more than he could pay off, the filing said.

Bankruptcy filings also include income and expense information, so the court can work out reasonable debt payment plans. Michael's 2011 income was $2,200 a month, paid by his music manager, supplemented by $1,000 per month in unemployment benefits from his wife, whom he had married in 2006. Their monthly expenses were $1,648.45, including $860 in rent, $200 for transportation, $329 for food, and $119 for clothing.

These figures look orderly on the page, but bankruptcy filings tend to come from complex personal stories. For Michael, the story revolved around child support. Like his own parents, he became a parent at a young age. The filings and a related case in the local court system make clear that he wanted to be an involved father. In one of the cases in 2004, Michael filed for the right to see his children more often and to share in their custody. The agreement in that case outlined the child support payments he would make, but by 2011, he had fallen behind on them.

In the end, Michael was not able to get assistance from the bankruptcy court. Within two months of his filing, the trustee on the case filed an objection to the repayment plan being created. The trustee pointed out that some of Michael's obligations (like child support) were not fully reflected in the plan and that the plan was therefore not workable. The trustee raised questions about potential future sources of income like voice-overs and future albums, which Michael had not mentioned in his filing; the trustee also said that Michael had failed to make a required court payment. And the trustee said the case should be dismissed because Michael had not included his nicknames— "Killer Mike" and "Mike Bigga"—in the filing. Two months later, the judge dismissed Michael's case, and no debt reorganization or relief was granted.

Taneeta Bacon, Brook's mother, at first had a similarly disappointing experience up in Boston. In 2006, just after she was notified of a pending foreclosure on her home, she filed for bankruptcy. She had $191,761 in assets and $197,784 in debt. Beyond her mortgage, she owed money to a utility company, for a furniture loan, on student loans, and for her cell phone. Her negative wealth: $6,023.

Whereas Michael Render's bankruptcy case was quick to end, Taneeta's fight to obtain relief dragged on. She did not want to lose her condo, her version of the American Dream. As she said at the time, "the real estate I own is my home where I live with my fiancé. We believe it is worth holding on to." When her first bankruptcy case was dismissed because she had "failed" to complete credit counseling, she started over and filed a new case. By then it was 2007, and the debt on her condo was mounting; more than $5,000 in unpaid mortgage payments and fees had built up. But Taneeta had taken on a second job, her fiancé also worked, and she believed they would be able to meet the expectations of a reorganization plan if given the chance.

Taneeta's case was assigned to the same trustee who had gotten her case dismissed the prior year, and the trustee again moved for dismissal. But this time, Taneeta had everything in order. She fulfilled what the trustee was looking for, the dismissal motion was dropped, and a payment plan was worked out. For five years, Taneeta would pay $551 per month, and that would resolve her debts. She could stay in her home.

The system, it seemed, had worked. Except that $551 per month was a large expense to carry for five years on top of her ongoing future expenses. And the value of Taneeta's condo was declining. One month after the payment plan was set, Taneeta filed a motion to have her case dismissed, and the motion was granted. That meant she would get no debt reductions but also no payment obligations. Her $173,000 condo was sold that month for $155,000. Taneeta moved onto a farming compound outside Boston as the property's caretaker.

Some may view Taneeta's walking away from the eventual bankruptcy relief as a sign that it was her choice—and not the system—that deprived her of relief. Financial lives are always a combination of choices and opportunities (or lack thereof). The reality is that in terms of wealth building, Black Americans often do not have the steadiness in jobs and financial savings to *choose to* hold on to assets during a downturn. Holding on while prices dropped in Boston may have required more savings than Taneeta had, even with the bankruptcy settlement. The lack of savings and wealth can mean it is harder for Black Americans like her to choose to stay put in their homes and benefit years later when prices increase. Had she been able and inclined to stay in her condo, she might eventually have profited. Over a decade later, in 2019, the Hyde Park condo she had sold for $155,000 was resold for $247,000.

The results of the bankruptcy system echo the experience we have seen in this chapter—for whatever reason, Black Americans are less likely to end up with debt relief. While the bankruptcy system helps many Americans of all races, it helps white Americans more. The system "is designed to give relief to people who fit a certain profile," Mechele Dickerson, a professor at the University of Texas at Austin School of Law and a leading researcher on race and bankruptcy, has said. The people who benefit the most from the system, she said, are "not going to be, in most instances, Black people."

Research has shown that Chapter 13 filings in particular have a rocky road to success. Chapter 13 cases are dismissed if the judge does not find the information provided to be credible or if the individual filing does not manage to follow all the terms of the repayment plan. In Chapter 13, debt is restructured with some amount of it paid back over time, and the remaining debt is relieved only if the payment plan is completed. (Judges and trustees determine how much of the debt should be paid back over time and how much should be forgiven.) When someone drops out of a Chapter 13 payment plan, as Taneeta did, all the original debt is left in place. Foreclosures then close in, homes are lost, loans mount, and legal fees are still owed from that failed bankruptcy.

Roughly two thirds of people who file for Chapter 13 do not end up completing their repayment plans, according to research by Sara S. Greene of Duke University, Parina Patel of Georgetown University, and Katie Porter of the University of California, Irvine. In their study of data from the 2007 Consumer Bankruptcy Project, they found that race is highly predictive of whether a person will succeed in obtaining bankruptcy relief. It is more of a determining factor than the amount of the debt, having a job, or having had prior bankruptcies. Simply put, if a bankruptcy filer is Black, they are less likely to make it through the system and get relief from their debt. *When white Americans get the common cold, Black Americans get pneumonia.*

Why is this? One factor, tracked by scholars at Brigham Young University, the University of Pennsylvania, and the Massachusetts Institute of Technology, is the subjectivity in the decisions by bankruptcy judges and the recommendations from Chapter 13 trustees. These people must answer questions like: Did this person stop payments for the Chapter 13 payment plan because of setbacks that were out of their control? Was their list of assets or debts incorrect due to a mistake or to fraud? And is this person realistically able to make the payments the court is setting? In Michael Render's case, the trustee raised questions in several areas, like Michael's car and voice-over work. Was Michael lying that his car had been repossessed? (The trustee later claimed that actually it had been sold.) Was he trying to dodge something by not declaring income from voice-overs? (The trustee researched Michael on Wikipedia and got suspicious when he read that Michael had made money from voice-over work.) And what was up with his delayed tax statements from Turner Broadcasting? (Michael provided notes from his accountant explaining that Turner simply wasn't providing the documents.) In each case, the bankruptcy trustee pointed to these open questions when he objected to Michael's plan for relief.

The trustee assigned to Taneeta Bacon similarly raised many doubts about her case, leading to the initial dismissal of her claim. Were those doubts reasonable? It might depend on whether Taneeta was viewed as a risk or as someone who needed help. In looking at trustees, a model devised by the Brigham Young University, University of Pennsylvania, and MIT scholars painted a disturbing picture. The scholars compared the race of bankruptcy trustees, the race of filers, and then the outcome of the cases. They found that for Chapter 13 bankruptcies, Black people assigned to white trustees were far more likely to have their cases dismissed. They also found that the vast majority of bankruptcy trustees were white.

In both Michael Render's and Taneeta Bacon's cases, the trustees were white. So were the judges. Adam Goodman, the white trustee on Michael's case, declined to comment to us in an on-the-record way that we could print in this book. Carolyn Bankowski, the white trustee on Taneeta's case, dismissed race as a factor. "I honestly haven't seen any differences based on race—on how there's any different outcome—in any of our bankruptcy cases," she said.

In Atlanta as of 2023, no Chapter 13 trustees were Black. In 2021, the director of the U.S. Trustee Program, Clifford J. White III, acknowledged the lack of diversity among bankruptcy trustees. "I think that all of us who have attended professional bankruptcy conferences . . . can agree that the lack of diversity is apparent," he said.

Given that Chapter 13 creates so many ways that cases can fail, it's reasonable to ask why anyone files under it at all. There are good reasons—mainly, that Chapter 13 can enable people to keep their homes, whereas Chapter 7 does not. However, research has also shown that very few people filing Chapter 13 actually end up with their homes in the end. The weight of the process combined with the fragility of these people's financial lives stacks the odds against them. The nonprofit news outlet *ProPublica* and *The Atlantic* co-published an investigation in 2017 about why Black Americans were so much more likely to file Chapter 13 cases rather than Chapter 7. They placed part of the blame on bankruptcy attorneys who steer their clients in that direction. Fees in bankruptcy are higher in Chapter 13 cases, because the cases are often longer term, but the fees aren't paid until the end. To people fighting for every dollar, Chapter 7, with its immediate fees, can be out of reach, and so they turn to Chapter 13, where fees are included in the gradual repayment plans. The problem was, these journalists found, that filers in Chapter 13 were 50 percent more likely to have their cases dismissed than those in Chapter 7.

Fixing all this would be difficult. Bankowski, Taneeta's trustee, said that roughly 80 percent of people using Chapter 13 in the year after the 2008 financial crisis did so to try to keep their homes. She expressed concern that some people criticize Chapter 13 without thinking enough about how meaningful it can be for people to keep their homes and be able to negotiate lower interest rates on their debt (a feature not available in Chapter 7).

Researchers have found that choices around bankruptcy can involve practical considerations that may affect Black people differently from white people—like commuting. One study in 2020 found that bankruptcy filers wanted to keep their cars. When the scholars compared Black Americans to white Americans with commutes of the same length, there wasn't a difference in the Chapter 13 filings. But Black Americans often have longer commutes than white Americans. *Bloomberg News* has written that some people also use Chapter 13 to try to force car lenders to give them lower interest rates; by filing for bankruptcy, they end up in a position to renegotiate their future debt payments as well as any arrears. But when you consider that Black

Americans statistically get less reasonable rates on car loans and unfair treatment in the banking system, this use of bankruptcy is not surprising. And then there's housing. In Georgia, the volume of Chapter 13 filings goes up just ahead of regular monthly foreclosure sales. As we have seen, foreclosure disproportionately affects Black homeowners.

All in all, Black Americans may be in greater need of some of the features of the Chapter 13 system. But that system will then often fail to provide them relief, will bring new fees, and may lead to the loss of the very things they hoped to keep.

Michael Render likely found Chapter 13 appealing for another reason. Congress has said that child support debt cannot be forgiven in bankruptcy; it's too important. That means that in a Chapter 7 process, which plays out quickly, sometimes in a matter of weeks, there's no option to restructure child support debt. A parent simply must pay immediately or face jail time. With Chapter 13, child support arrears can be paid over time in the repayment plan, helping the filer avoid jail or further penalties, and so that may make Chapter 13 appealing to some people. There is not complete national data on how often people are put in jail for not paying child support, but surveys have found that one in seven fathers with child support debt has gone to jail for not paying it. And a South Carolina survey found that one in eight inmates were incarcerated for not paying it. Often, these individuals simply do not have the funds to make the payments. In one Georgia Supreme Court case about a father who had only one dollar in his bank account but was jailed for owing four thousand dollars in child support, the father would say, "I feel like it's more unfair to the kids, because now not only do the kids not get any money, nor do they even get to spend time with their fathers once they get locked up."

Owing child support is even a reason someone might decide not to pull over for a police traffic stop—in 2015, Walter Scott tried to elude a police officer in South Carolina because, his family surmised, he feared that he would go back to jail for his child support debt (and while in jail, would continue to build up even more debt). That officer shot and killed Scott.

Michael Render talked with us about child support and the justice system when we asked about his bankruptcy case. "I don't like the way child support is weaponized against any man . . . and especially Black men," he said. When his bankruptcy case was dismissed, that meant there was no restructuring of any of his debts, child support payments included.

Stephana Campbell, the mother of James Woodall of the NAACP, learned about the failure rate of Chapter 13 the hard way. Back in 2000, when James was six years old and they were living in a Section 8 house, Stephana filed for bankruptcy under Chapter 13. The case dragged on for four months, as she created a repayment plan, but then her case was dismissed after the judge agreed with the trustee's objections. The trustee with the objections was Adam Goodman, the *same* white trustee who would, eleven years later, raise objections in Michael's case. The judge was Margaret Murphy, also white. She was also the judge who would later dismiss Michael Render's case.

Eventually, in 2016, James's mother was bankrupt once again. This time she filed for bankruptcy using a Chapter 7 filing, and this time she was successful. Some of her debts were forgiven.

Calculating the Value of Life

Bankruptcy court is just one corner of the courthouse. Wealth gaps are made and expanded in criminal court, housing court, and civil court, too. When there's bias in how legal matters are handled, it can have impacts not unlike banks have when they systemically refuse to loan money in a certain neighborhood or to a certain group of people.

To further explore Michael Render's courtroom experiences, we called up his lawyer from one of his cases, Nathaniel Blackmon, who is also Michael's distant cousin. There is racial inequity, Blackmon said, in both the criminal and civil court. "If you ask a lot of Black men what they fear the most as far as being stopped in the middle of the night by two white cops, they'll say the legal system, and not just the criminal side, [but also] the civil side, because they feel like they're taken advantage of . . . They feel that they don't have a fair shot," he said. "They don't want to face a white judge . . . You're going to come up on the wrong side of the law."

The lack of senior Black professionals in the judicial system is part of the problem, Blackmon said, noting that the courts need officials who can relate to the public they serve. And, he said, when you think about closing the Black-white wealth gap, that's also connected to a lack of Black Americans serving in these lucrative judicial jobs.

Beyond representation, Blackmon continued, the inequity pervades the way the tort system establishes the value of a life. Traditionally, wrongful death cases provide damages to survivors' families based on calculations around how much money that person would have earned in the future and how long they would have lived. This can mean that families compensated after, for example, police shootings would be awarded less if the victim worked in a low-paying job. Built into these calculations are historic inequities that have created racial disparities in projected life expectancies and earnings alike. By the 2020s, some states, notably California, had begun to outlaw the use of race and gender in calculating damages, but the system remained pervasive in most other places. It's a system that also affected the way the government has paid out damages in cases involving the victims of the September 11, 2001, terrorist attacks and other cases. Black victims of the September 11 attacks were more likely in lower-paying jobs like cafeteria, janitorial, or administrative roles, while white victims were most likely to be in white-collar jobs. That meant the Black workers' families typically got less money for their deaths. We discussed the September 11 fund with Blackmon, and he became visibly irritated, saying, "You have a janitor that works in the building, and you have a banker who works in the building. Both of them are going to get hit and get blown up. I think they should get the same compensation."

Blackmon paused and then told us that his family—Michael Render's family—also experienced being in a victims' compensation fund. Primus Blackmon, born in 1872, was Michael's great-great-grandfather. In the 1930s, he was living in Tuskegee when he was rounded up by the government as a test subject in a now-infamous study of syphilis, in which the participants' informed consent was never obtained and men who already had syphilis were denied penicillin. Decades later, the federal government compensated families of the people in the study, but the money was scant. Nathaniel Blackmon held up the final check his family had received, to show us: it was for just $21.11. "I wanted the original check so I could show my kids," he said. "This is what they think of us, this is what they do to us, this is how they experiment on us. And this is the check that they paid." Blackmon mused on how it might have affected his family's wealth trajectory had they been properly compensated for what happened to Primus Blackmon in Tuskegee. He said he doesn't have much hope that the legal system will change. "I don't think this is a system where equality is the torch that we carry and really, really stand behind," he said. "This is the way it is, the reality Black families live with. It's always in the back of your head that even if you're doing good, the inequities are there every single day. We don't complain about them all the time. But do you know what? The majority, we just know it's how it is, and we're just trying to keep it moving."

Keeping moving is difficult when you're broke. But one thing that can give people hope is the prospect of joining something that might change their lives, might change the system, might even the playing field for Black Americans. That's the hope Greenwood Bank would give to its customers when it debuted in the year 2020.

CHAPTER 8

TANDREIA DIXON AND THE GENERATIONAL WEALTH HUSTLE

I want to say to every Negro woman present, don't sit down and wait for the opportunities to come. . . . Get up and make them.
—Madam C. J. Walker, entrepreneur and businesswoman

MAY 26, 2020

Tandreia Dixon woke up in the room she was renting in her cousin's home on the outskirts of Atlanta. She had just returned after a few months back home in rural North Carolina. Her childhood home, Trenton, was a one-stoplight town, she liked to point out, not a place where she believed she could accumulate wealth. Her mother was counting on her for a better life. Tandreia had promised her that she would deliver.

But Atlanta? Yes . . . it's the Black Mecca.

Being Black was a point of pride for Tandreia—she admired Black entrepreneurs and followed them closely on social media and in podcasts, books, and films. Tandreia spent her graduate school years volunteering as the treasurer for the Black Graduate Student Association. She was the first generation of her family not to have spent her childhood picking cotton.

By many measures, Tandreia had made it. At thirty-one, she was earning one hundred thousand dollars a year working for a large national consulting company. In her free time, she and some colleagues had started an online financial education firm, Hack the Markets. Tandreia had big ambitions. Before getting going that morning, she took out her diary and wrote: "I will be a multimillionaire. I will be a multimillionaire. I will be a multimillionaire." Over and over, she filled an entire page with those same five words in hopeful cursive: "I will be a multimillionaire. I will be a multimillionaire. I will be a multimillionaire."

She signed it at 9:08 a.m.: "TAN."

It was the day after Memorial Day, and a morning when many Americans were waking up to racial horror. Tandreia looked online and saw two trending videos in her social feeds: First, a nearly ten-minute video of a Black man in Minneapolis named George Floyd being killed by a white police officer. The officer held his knee on Floyd's neck minute after minute. "I can't breathe," Floyd said twenty-seven times before he died. Next, Tandreia watched a video of a white woman in New York City named Amy Cooper walking her dog in Central Park. The woman's dog was off leash and, when a Black man carrying Swarovski binoculars stopped to ask her to leash her dog, she went ballistic. That man, Christian Cooper (no relation to Amy), calmly videotaped her as she called the police. Shaking, she told the police multiple times, "An African American man is threatening my life." The woman in Central Park, then an investment professional at Franklin Templeton, quickly became known as another "Karen," a meme referring to white women of privilege who engage in verbal attacks and can't keep it together when things don't go their way. Tandreia watched both videos and posted her reaction on Instagram: "Imagine everything that isn't caught on video . . . #numb."

Soon, her family and friends were attending demonstrations and texting her photos of themselves and their signs. One cousin in Washington, D.C., carried a blown-up photograph of Black Americans protesting police violence in 1965. In it, protestors held up a sign reading "Stop Police Killings." In bold letters on top of that old image, her cousin's sign said "This Photo Is 55 Years Old."

Tandreia stayed home and listened to inspirational music to cleanse herself of the weight of it all. She was terrified of what might happen to her at the demonstrations. Instead of being out there, she spent her time reading more about the Black-white wealth gap, entrepreneurship, and Black-owned businesses. She resolved that her children would be financially literate and that she'd leave them "generational wealth," which to her meant both the money and the legacy of leaving wealth. She followed Black influencers online like Michael Render, whose rap music and business savvy she admired. She liked his many dimensions and his commitment to helping the Atlanta community. As she put it to us, Killer Mike "takes the cake."

By October 2020, Andrew Young, Michael Render, and Ryan Glover were all over the news for launching Greenwood Bank. They had raised three million dollars in seed funding, announced their product, and started a waiting list that they said had drawn tens of thousands of people within days. They said they'd become operational in January. They talked about issuing mortgages, small business loans, and investment products. The founders—a Civil Rights leader, celebrity rapper, and TV mogul—had grand reputations and grand plans. As one Medium writer put it in a post featuring Ryan Glover, "This Black King Has Plans to Help Repair Centuries of Racist Banking with His New Startup."

Tandreia Dixon also had grand plans. She wanted to own a home by the end of 2021. She wanted to start her own company and see it soar. She wanted to use her family's farmland for something that would last beyond her. And perhaps most important, she wanted to secure her mother's financial future. She was starry-eyed when talking about Greenwood Bank and how it might help her reach all these goals. She eagerly added her name to Greenwood's customer waiting list. She "hearted" and "liked" its marketing on social media. She rushed online to Greenwood's virtual community events.

"These community events are like an education, right?" Tandreia told us after attending one. "I take that stuff seriously just because I know that there was one point in time where a lot of this information wasn't that accessible. Again, coming from me: I come from a one-stoplight town. Yeah, like a rural place. My father had a tenth-grade education. I'm not saying it's like a 'woe is me' situation. But I just really take *every* opportunity, you know, *seriously*."

She wasn't the only one. Within months, the Greenwood Bank customer waiting list would boast more than five hundred thousand names, and the new banking product would come to mean a lot to Tandreia and the other prospective customers. Greenwood was a promise of a better financial life. Its stated mission—to close the Black-white wealth gap—was also exactly in line with Tandreia's personal mission to close the gap between her family and typical white families.

Tandreia's journey as a customer and observer of Greenwood would reveal a lot about how difficult and confusing it is for someone to jump over that gap. In the years Greenwood was getting started, Tandreia oscillated between trying to make it as an entrepreneur on her own and working professional jobs at large white-run companies. She dabbled in crypto investing, and she saved up to try to buy a house in order to build wealth. She knew the history of her family and how one side had possessed land and the other side had not. She knew what that gap had meant for wealth and stability in the past, and she was looking for the modern-day equivalent. She wanted to give her family assets, power, and freedom.

Growing Up with Land

While growing up in rural eastern North Carolina, Tandreia would prick up her ears whenever her aunts and grandmothers discussed family history. As her Washington-based cousin Charles Everett told us, "She's going to be like the encyclopedia for the entire family."

When it comes to money and resources, both sides of Tandreia's family were at more or less similar points back in 1900. On her father's side, multiple branches of the family owned substantial tracts of land and even funded the local funeral home and a local grocery store. On her mother's side, land was also plentiful, providing several generations room to roam and work in the fields picking cotton. Having space to pick cotton back then was in and of itself an asset.

The dividing line in her family was in what happened to the land. By the mid-1900s, her father's family had lost theirs. Her mother's family, in contrast, still owned the land they had farmed as sharecroppers and then purchased. Tandreia grew up surrounded by the warm blanket of this land—a safety blanket, a dream maker. It was the land she wanted to use for entrepreneurship one day. She was considering a wind farm. It was this land that had kept her mother and aunts rooted in their small town of Trenton. It was this land that had brought Tandreia back. She saw the differences it had meant for her mother's family, in contrast to her father's upbringing and life.

Though the federal government failed in the post–Civil War promise to give formerly enslaved people forty acres and a mule, and despite all the bias against Black people in both antebellum and postbellum land allocation, some Black Americans were able to amass land in the late 1800s. This was partly because when the U.S. government rolled out the Homestead Act of 1862, word came back east about the riches of the West, and white residents of eastern areas moved west to take advantage of the Homestead Act land grants. Though Black Americans generally did not have the resources to move west for the new land (and, as we saw in chapter 4, the Homestead Act was hardly intended for them), the white exodus left them with the opportunity to purchase land more easily right where they were. The land they bought on the East Coast was separate from the land granted to Black Americans who were affiliated with the Native tribes. The Black-owned land on the East Coast was purchased, and the purchases came with a great deal of pride.

By 1890, as many as 264,288 Black heads of household owned their own homes and farms. That represented 19 percent of the then 1.4 million Black heads of families. The growth in Black farm ownership continued up until the 1920s. In Durham County, North Carolina—not too far from Tandreia's family—9 percent of Black farmers owned their land in 1900, and that figure climbed to 26 percent in 1920. Farmland did not lead to high profit margins in this era, but it gave Black residents something that was theirs. Like Michael Render one hundred years later, searching to make his name on his own after his breakthrough with OutKast, this would be a recurring theme for Black Americans. There was value in having something *that was mine.*

By 1910, Black Americans owned on the order of sixteen million acres, historians have estimated. Not coincidentally, this was the period in history that saw the fastest shrinking of the Black-white wealth gap: the gap decreased as Black landownership grew. Landownership and the Black-white wealth gap were intertwined. As W. E. B. Du Bois wrote in 1901, "Perhaps there could be found no other single index of the results of the struggle of the freedman upward so significant as the ownership of land."

The Black-owned land included farmland, but it was also composed of thriving downtowns. With mounting Black resources, North Carolina towns like Wilmington and Durham featured Black business districts, and Black-led financial institutions like Mechanics and Farmers Bank became successful. This rise in Black wealth made some white Americans uncomfortable. Scholars say the desire to seize Black-owned land motivated violent attacks in the late 1800s and early 1900s.

The subsequent loss of millions of acres of land in the 1900s came at great cost to Black Americans. *Loss* is a broad term—some was sold, some was given up in other ways. Often, the former landowners did not receive great deals, and often they did not give up their land by choice. Much of the land went to white Americans. Sometimes Black Americans or even family members played a role. In many instances, structural features in the economy, which we will detail, made it difficult for Black property owners to hold on to their land.

The loss of land is one more item in the long list of economic crimes endured by Black Americans. Following the trauma of slavery itself, the reneged forty acres and a mule, the biased Homestead Act grants, the collapse of Freedman's Bank, the inequity of sharecropping arrangements, convict leasing, inequitable pricing in insurance policies, and the start of Jim Crow laws—after all this, the disappointment of losing land was wrenching for many Black Americans.

There's a name for what happened to Black communities over time: "post traumatic slave syndrome," in the words of Joy DeGruy, an author and scholar of the intersection of slavery and trauma. DeGruy has written that "post traumatic slave syndrome is a condition that exists when a population has experienced multigenerational trauma resulting from centuries of slavery and continues to experience oppression and institutionalized racism today. Added to this condition is a belief (real or imagined) that the benefits of the society in which they live are not accessible to them."

So traumatic was the loss of land for Robert Epps in the late 1800s that he was committed to a mental asylum. Epps, a great-grandfather of Andrew Young, lost four properties in Atlanta in less than a decade. The properties were situated in the Summerhill community, one of the areas where formerly enslaved people first settled after the Civil War. Epps's land had a storied pedigree. One plot had been owned by the family of William Jennings, who founded the Summerhill community just after the Civil War. And another property had been owned by Edward Rawson, a white banker and politician in Atlanta who was among a group of prominent city leaders that negotiated the surrender of Atlanta to General Sherman. Epps, a preacher and, later, a janitor, became owner of the properties through inheritance and intrafamily sales. He lost some of his property to the county and sold some of it after borrowing against it. It's unclear exactly why he gave up the properties, but it was clearly a stressful situation. As an Atlanta newspaper wrote in 1902, "In the court of ordinary yesterday, Robert Epps, colored, was declared insane and will be sent to the state asylum. It was claimed that *the loss of property caused him to become demented.*" Epps was confined in a tower at the Georgia State Sanitarium and died just shy of three weeks after arriving.

For Tandreia's family, the stories of lost land and trauma were openly known. And for Tandreia, the fact that the land losses were on her father's side explained a lot about wealth and opportunity. The differences she saw in her mother's family, which had managed to hold on to their land for more than one hundred years, compared to her father's family had played a formative role in creating her personal obsession with closing her own Black-white wealth gap.

Tandreia would always wonder how things might have been different for her father had two different branches of his family not lost their land. The tales still stung.

The first tale of lost land was by way of Smithy Davis, Tandreia's great-great-grandmother (that is, her father's mother's grandmother). Smithy and her husband, John Clark, managed to amass wealth and land. Smithy never trusted banks, given that most of them were white-owned. To avoid the banking system, she wore a money belt under her petticoat and kept all her money there. Also, the couple held a good deal of their net worth in the land they bought. Smithy had applied for life insurance with several institutions in the late 1800s, but was turned down. Eventually she got a policy with a small payout (enough for a burial) from North Carolina Mutual Life Insurance, a Black-owned company. With their money, the couple funded the establishment of a local funeral home that survived even into the 2020s.

Driven by a fear of being taken advantage of, they kept careful track of their spending. Smithy liked to tell her grandchildren stories of the time an organ seller tried to repossess her instrument. A musician who could not only play pipe organ, but also banjo and guitar, Smithy had purchased the organ outright. But the seller (a white man, she'd note to her grandchildren) nonetheless showed up at her house and tried to take the organ back so he could sell it to someone else. Smithy reached under her petticoat, into her money belt, and pulled out the receipt.

Smithy's husband, John, worked in bootlegging during Prohibition. He died mysteriously, as did some of the other wealthy Black men in their rural town. Family lore has it that he was poisoned because of his wealth. That's unprovable, however, family members told us. With John Clark's death, Smithy's wealth and land went away—the land, the wealth, the assets, all gone, and the family does not really understand why. That's the story of Tandreia's father's mother's side and the financial footing they once had.

The second tale of lost land, on her father's father's side, featured Ephram Dixon, a farmer born around the mid-1850s. He and his wife had at least five children. The couple scraped together enough money to purchase the land in 1891. It was a small plot, one sixth of an acre, but it was theirs. By 1901, they had saved enough to buy a forty-acre lot. The land was lucrative—in 1907, they were able to sell off the timber on it. As his sons grew older, Ephram sold them small portions of the forty-acre plot. Despite the lack of education when Ephram was a child, he learned to read (though not to write). As of 1920, the couple still owned their home, mortgage free.

Over the next decade, though, the Dixons needed to borrow money. The area they lived in was heavily Black, but the lenders were white. The couple borrowed money against their forty-acre plot at least three times. When they defaulted on one of those loans, in 1932, their land was sold by the lender at auction. The buyer was a white woman who paid a little less than what the Dixons had paid for the land in 1901. Ephram, soon a widower, spent his final years as a boarder in someone else's home.

It's unclear why the Dixons could not afford their land, but there are plenty of structural reasons why Black Americans have lost land over time. One long-running issue has been the value of Black-owned properties being overappraised by tax assessors. When Black owners could not afford the inflated taxes, the county would seize and resell their property. Andrew Kahrl, a University of Virginia professor, has written about Black homeowners in the 1920s and '30s who sued their city governments for relief from overly high tax assessments. The town of Edwards, Mississippi, deliberately overassessed Black homeowners' property in the 1960s to punish Blacks who had boycotted businesses and protested Jim Crow, Kahrl told us. Other historians have traced this pattern through the 1960s and '70s, even as minority groups mounted legal challenges to the practice. In the 1990s, the NAACP accused a town in South Carolina of pushing up taxes in an effort to push out Black families as developers came in. The problem of inequitable taxation continued into the twenty-first century and played a role in the financial crisis of 2008. In Detroit, more than one hundred thousand properties, or about 25 percent of the houses in the city, had been foreclosed upon between 2011 and 2019 after property taxes were not paid. Bernadette Atuahene, a University of Wisconsin Law School professor, and Christopher Berry of the University of Chicago have written that Detroit's overassessments of taxes displaced many Black Americans in the community.

Nationwide, Black and Hispanic residents faced a 10 to 13 percent higher property tax burden than white Americans, a 2021 study found. The authors of the study—Carlos Avenancio-León of the University of California at San Diego and Troup Howard of the University of Utah—looked at data tied to 118 million homes from 2003 to 2016. They found that the overassessment of minority homeowners was due to appraisals not factoring in the condition of the surrounding neighborhood. And they found that minority homeowners were less likely and less able to challenge tax assessments compared to white homeowners.

A second way that Black Americans have lost property over the years has been through sales to developers. In many cases, Black families received mediocre prices for their land and, in some cases, did not even want to sell. Tandreia's home state of North Carolina has been one of many places with forced sales, known as partition actions. In these cases, when one family member chooses to sell land that has been passed down through generations, all family members are required to go along. It's been common in Black families to pass land via what's called an heir transfer, in which the deed does not change. In these cases, partition sales are required when one family member wants to sell. These sorts of sales are a large part of what freed up land in places like Hilton Head to create lucrative tourist destinations. Hilton Head is where Brook Bacon and his wife, Shalagh, were married and where they vacationed annually. The ground they walked on, from some people's point of view, was stolen.

When partition occurs, *someone* in the family is trying to sell. "You need to have some willing participation from Black families—driven by the desire to profit off their land holdings," Kahrl, the University of Virginia professor, told *ProPublica* for an article on partition sales. "But it does boil down to greed and abuse of power and the way in which America's history of racial inequality can be used to the advantage of developers." Why is it that laws allow these forced sales when it's Black families that mainly lose out and white developers who benefit?

A third way land was lost was through plain, old fraud—as in the case of Evelina Jenkins. A lifelong resident of coastal land in South Carolina, Jenkins could not read or write, and she trusted a white neighbor to turn in her property taxes each year for the island she owned. In the late 1960s, Jenkins took her fifteen dollars in taxes to her neighbor, but this time, he told her that the land and a nearby island were no longer hers and that it hadn't been for a while. He had long owned it, and she had been paying him rent. Then he told her that he had just sold the land, and Jenkins lost it all. Houses on Jenkins's old island now sell for four or five hundred thousand dollars apiece.

Additionally, there has been plain, old intimidation of Black Americans, causing them to flee their land. In 1912, William Bagley was a farmer who owned on the order of sixty acres in Forsyth County, which is northeast of Atlanta. That year, there was a week of racial violence there after a white woman was found dead in the woods. Not only was one of the accused Black men lynched, but a group of white people also began setting fire to numerous Black homes in the area. Bagley was not accused in the woman's murder, but he felt he had to move his family immediately and left his land. He opened a grocery store in what would become modern-day Buckhead, a rich neighborhood in Atlanta, but then he would later lose his home and business there due to the threat of eminent domain. These stories of lost land lived on within families for generations. Bagley's granddaughter, Elon Osby, grew up hearing the stories, and they became tangible to her, she told us, when she went to visit Forsyth County. There, she saw there were rows of homes on her family's old land. The homes cost four or five hundred thousand dollars, she said. Then it clicked. She started thinking over and over, "This could have been yours. Should have been yours."

Whatever the reason for Ephram Dixon's "losing" his land, the result was that his children and grandchildren didn't have the wealth the land might have given them. His descendants would end up in public housing; some would spend time in prison. Ephram's son Samuel had a son, Samuel Jr. *His* son, Samuel III, ended up with Christine Clark (granddaughter of the money belt–wearing grandmother), and the couple had children, including a fourth-generation Samuel. The couple split up, and it was at that juncture that Christine Clark moved the children to Kinston, a small urban area half an hour north of the rural area where Tandreia would be born. Clark was a single mother and had no choice but to move her family into public housing. It was a blow to her pride. "She always knew that wasn't her; it should not have been her trajectory," her daughter told us.

This downward path, however, became the trajectory of Clark's son Samuel. He dropped out of high school at sixteen, and by the time he was nineteen, he was incarcerated for theft and breaking and entering, a felony. He didn't go to college. After prison and a few transitional jobs, he ended up working at the William Barnet and Son textile factory in Kinston. There, in 1987, he met Allie Dixon, another young employee. The two were smitten. As Allie and Samuel got serious, their families compared notes to make sure they were not from the same line of Dixons. They weren't. Another concern to Allie's mother were the rumors she had heard about Samuel, and she pulled Allie aside one day to warn her that she had heard he was using drugs. Allie, deeply in love, put together her own money to pay for the wedding. Her father told her just beforehand, "You make your bed and you will have to lie in it." The words stung, and they stayed in Allie's head for the rest of her life. "Anytime I think about my life," she told us, "I think: Had I only listened to my daddy. Mm-hmm."

Allie proceeded to marry Samuel, but out of caution, she kept her money separate from his; she also kept the modest home she had bought just around the corner from her family's land in her own name. This turned out to be a good move. It was Allie's earnings that paid for her two children's needs, that put food on the table. There were times when her husband made money, but she said those funds often went back out the door to buy drugs. Allie was on her own most of the time. She had to make most of the decisions and most of the money. As her daughter, Tandreia, told us, "My mom was stability for my dad, but he still had one foot in the street." From a young age, Tandreia said, she and her younger brother resolved with each other that they weren't going to follow their father's path.

And so, technically, Tandreia was not raised by a single mother, though sometimes it felt like that, at least to Allie. She tried to climb the career ladder at the Barnet textile factory. First, Allie was a "creeler," affixing yarn onto the "creel" of the knitting machine. This gave her tendinitis, so she applied to be a "cutter," cutting yarn with scissors once it was in the machine. This only made her wrists worse. In the early 1990s, a job opened up in the quality control department, which had higher pay and would be easier on her body.

A test was required. Allie took it and excelled, she said. But the job went to someone else, a woman she believed had a lower score. The woman was white, Allie told us, and had some family members working there. "I was two points over her. I made the most, but," Allie said, "she got the job." Eventually, Allie got into the quality control department, but soon afterward, the company downgraded the ranking of that job and lowered its pay. It suddenly paid the same as her old jobs.

In the early 2000s, the factory began asking people who had been working full time to work part time. The Dixon family had to get by with far less pay, but they made ends meet. Allie refinanced their mortgage, extending the timeline of their thirty-year mortgage, which had been well on its way to being paid off. The new mortgage was one of the pre–housing crisis loans with payments that would balloon. And the promise of owning the home free and clear by 2017 was long gone. It didn't help that Tandreia's father was convicted for drug possession in 2006. Along the way, Tandreia tried to stay focused on school. She contributed to family funds by working at her uncle's local junk-collecting facility. Whereas her mother had grown up picking cotton, Tandreia sorted junk and metal scraps. In 2009, the family's financial problems got rapidly worse. Tandreia's father failed a random drug test at the factory and was fired, losing what had also been his long-term source of employment. And then Allie was laid off from her job. She had worked at the factory for twenty-eight years.

The economy in rural Trenton had been struggling due to the national recession that followed the 2008 crisis. Allie couldn't pay the mortgage on her home—"their" home at this point, because she'd added her husband's name to the deed in the late 1990s, in a brief period in which he seemed to be committed to shared goals and improving himself. She called Tandreia, who was in college, and told her the house was about to be foreclosed upon. Desperate to keep a place to live and knowing that the financial crisis had turned off the lending spigot, Allie took a large share of savings out of her 401(k) and paid down the loan so she could refinance it. They had almost lost their home.

During all this, Tandreia was away at college at the North Carolina Agricultural and Technical State University, three hours west of Trenton. It was while she was in college that the accident occurred. Out of work for two years, making some money with a self-run catering business, Tandreia's father had been offered a temporary position back at the Barnet textile factory. After several months as a temp, he was told he'd be moved on to the staff. As that time approached, Samuel was standing near a forklift when the driver forgot to put on the safety latch and the fork fell onto Samuel's foot. His bones shattered. Work was over for him. He received what the family said was a small amount of money and would need nursing the rest of his life, as diabetes and, ultimately, kidney failure took hold.

The rest of the money in Allie's 401(k) did not last very long. In 2012, when Tandreia was twenty-two, she was admitted to Purdue University, in Indiana. She wanted to get a master's degree in industrial technology. Her mother didn't hesitate to offer to help, but she also told her daughter that *this was it*. Not because she wanted to stop helping her, but because it was actually the last of Allie's money. Tandreia reassured her mom, "You can bet on me, bet on me."

Tandreia and her mother pulled up to Bank of America together and held hands in the parking lot, crying, knowing the gravity of what Allie was about to do. *This was it*. Allie walked into the bank and emptied her bank account. She was investing in Tandreia.

"I will get you a return," her daughter told her. "I will get you a return."

A Starry-Eyed Customer

Nine years later, one evening in mid-April 2021, Tandreia logged in to a Greenwood banking event.

The trial of former Minneapolis police officer Derek Chauvin for the killing of George Floyd was in the news at the time. In Atlanta, the commissioners of Fulton County were joining a growing list of local officials setting up a task force to study the Black-white wealth gap and to explore whether reparations should be paid to Black people to even the playing field. All these conversations were providing momentum for the new virtual banking platform founded by Michael Render, Andrew Young, and Ryan Glover. Greenwood had just raised forty million dollars more in investor funding.

As its customer waiting list grew longer, with Greenwood now three months over its original estimated launch date, the founders were kicking off a program of virtual events featuring Black celebrities talking about money. Tandreia listened in while she was out exercising on a public track in Marietta, Georgia, just twenty miles northwest of Atlanta. The thirty-one-year-old aspiring entrepreneur had quit her job a few weeks earlier and was in the process of looking for something better. She wanted to do something closer to finance, something that would help her learn ways to lift the fortune of her family back in North Carolina. In her free time, she was reading everything she could find on investing, banking, entrepreneurship, and cryptocurrencies. She had already invested $1,500 in Dogecoin. ("Don't judge me!" she told us.)

Tandreia stopped on the track as Pinky Cole, the thirty-three-year-old pink-haired, vivacious owner of the Atlanta-based restaurant chain Slutty Vegan, started to speak. Cole was living "the American Dream," in Tandreia's view, and was one of her heroes. It's hard to aspire to be what you can't see, Tandreia told us, but when you see someone like you, and they're doing it, it makes it relevant. Cole was a Black female, only a year older than Tandreia, and like Tandreia, she hadn't come from privilege. Like Tandreia's father, Cole's father had spent time in prison—the first twenty years of Cole's life. "I watched my mother literally work four jobs and come home, and we were the sacrificial lambs because she literally helped everybody," Cole said on the Greenwood virtual gathering.

For Cole, getting through college, starting an acting career, and then moving into the restaurant business hadn't been easy, but she had pulled it off. Now the owner of a successful restaurant chain, she said she wanted to help others. She and a friend had recently paid off the student debt of thirty graduating seniors from her alma mater, Clark Atlanta University. "I went from having a five hundred credit score to now having an almost perfect credit score because of being responsible, right," Cole said. "But my car had to get repo'd to do it. I had to get evicted out of my apartment to do it. I literally had to go through so many things and fall on my face along the way. And I do think there's an easier way, and *I do believe that Greenwood is one of those ways that can make it easier for families and for people.*"

Tandreia started to take notes on her phone; exercise could wait. This Greenwood event had become educational, as talk turned to accounting and other financial matters. Tandreia took these opportunities seriously. She knew there was a time when this kind of information hadn't been accessible, but that she could now be a part of the conversation simply by joining a virtual gathering. She often reminded herself that her father had a tenth-grade education. She reminded herself that her mother used to pick cotton on her family's land.

"Greed trumps race," she wrote down. The idea was articulated by Tanya Sam, the host of the gathering, who was interviewing Pinky Cole. As Tandreia understood it, the message was that it didn't matter what your race was—if a person or entity saw that they could make money from your business, then the color of your skin went away. She liked it. *Greed trumps race.*

Tandreia was one of several hundred people on the Greenwood online hangout, listening and chatting with one another in the comments area. Darrielle Poole joined from Durham, North Carolina. A thirty-one-year-old aspiring health and wellness entrepreneur and the mother of six children, Poole leaned in as Cole spoke about wanting to pass knowledge on to her children one day. "I'm going to make sure that my children understand about credit cards, they understand LLCs, they understand how to open up bank accounts and paying their bills on time, because those things are important," Cole said. Poole's children—ages one to twelve—ran in and out of her living room as she watched on her laptop. Her eleven-year-old daughter stopped and looked at the screen, intrigued by Cole's pink hair, which the restaurateur wore naturally—without straightening it—just like the young girl did.

Poole was excited to see other listeners posting comments. "This is why I want to be part of Greenwood!!!" wrote a person watching the event from St. Louis. "It's this amalgamation of reinvestment, community build-ing, solidarity, and seeing everybody succeed.... Love, love, love seeing every-body's success!"

"Right!" Poole responded.

The chat room was almost over-the-top ecstatic, and Greenwood customers-to-be started swapping LinkedIn accounts. "Love how you are sharing the highs and lows of the entrepreneurial journey," one wrote as Cole continued to talk. "Sis is preaching! I love it!!" another said. "Lift as you climb," said another.

Cole began talking about her recent purchase of a day care center. It was a way to give back to the community and develop the neigh-borhood where she does business, she said. The people in the chat room loved this. "That's what I'm talking about," another customer-to-be, John McCullough, replied in the comments. "The whole vil-lage MUST eat." McCullough was a fifty-five-year-old technology solutions architect from just east of Atlanta. He wanted to open an account with Greenwood because he wanted his money recirculat-ing among Black Americans, he told us. Plus, he was distrustful of large, white-controlled banks. Three years ago, Wells Fargo closed his son's account due to what they said was suspicious activity. But there were transactions that his son didn't make, according to Mc-Cullough, and then, to make matters worse, McCullough's own ac-count faced questions from the bank. His son closed his account, and McCullough resolved to do the same. It came to light soon afterward that Wells Fargo had a widespread internal issue with accounts being opened in other people's names, but McCullough was still unsure what had happened and why. "I was wondering: Did the [Wells Fargo representative] treat me like that because I was Black?" he told us.

This question—the race question—came up with nearly every Greenwood customer we spoke to: Is it because I'm Black? Have I faced different questions and doubts at white-run banks simply be-cause I'm Black?

As Poole, the mother of six, said, "I know people think we Black Americans have this all in our head, like a paranoia, but this is a real thing. We never know: Did we get a bad deal because we are Black?

At Greenwood, that factor will be removed. I can get the information, and maybe it's bad news or good news, but I can receive it without the doubt."

Greenwood's customers-to-be had signed up to join the bank for many reasons, and their economic diversity was apparent in the chat room, where they were meeting one another even as Cole continued to speak. There was Verna Dottin-Maitland, a fifty-year-old New Yorker who had worked in retail banking all her life. (As of 2021, she worked at Chase.) She told us she was mainly curious to see how Greenwood would handle things differently and whether the bank would help Black Americans build more lasting wealth. "We don't have generational wealth," she said. And there was Rashaanne Lewis, age forty-six, who had records of her family going back seven generations and had studied the financial challenges her grandparents faced with redlining in Texas. And then there was Kela Lester, a twenty-eight-year-old creative director in Washington, D.C., whose family lost their home in 2008. The experience had left them with a distaste for white-run banks.

Another Greenwood customer-to-be, Clive Davis, had made wealth activism a cause. A former corporate attorney based near Atlanta, Davis ran the African American Multifamily Investor Network on Facebook, where about eight hundred people were helping support Black-owned businesses. "I'm just very much supportive of every, *every* initiative that is designed to improve the financial well-being of the Black community," he told us. "It's critical. I think it's important for the Black community, obviously, but I also think it's important for America."

As Cole wrapped up the hangout, she closed by paraphrasing advice she had taken away from the Eminem track "Lose Yourself": "I've got this one shot," Cole said. "It only comes once in a lifetime." She added: "Everybody don't get exposure like this. This one shot is really going to change the lives of all the people around me."

Tandreia returned to her exercise, all alone on the track. She opened Spotify on her phone and pulled up the white rapper's top songs about having *one shot*. There it was: "Lose Yourself." She walked with a skip in her step and sang along about owning the moment and not losing her one shot . . .

"This opportunity comes once in a lifetime."

Excitement Among Black Professionals

Greenwood was not a brick-and-mortar bank, and customers like Tandreia liked that. She wouldn't have been as interested, she told us, if it were doing things "the old way." She already had a budding interest in banking disruption and in neobanking, a rising subindustry of technology companies that offer banking services. She closely followed famous stock pickers and had started wondering how she herself might get a job in fintech.

She wasn't the only Black professional excited by fintech. As Greenwood Bank got going, its job listings attracted top talent, including Aparicio Giddins Jr., one of Greenwood's first hires. As president and chief technology officer, Giddins would be the primary leader responsible for Greenwood's technology—a planned mobile app and website. He came to Greenwood in August 2020, after more than twenty years of banking experience, including as a product development leader at Bank of America and TD Bank. It was a change for Giddins to leave such large companies in favor of a start-up, but Greenwood seemed like a positive step he could take to help Black Americans.

Giddins, forty-two, and his wife had spent the summer of 2020 discussing issues around race with their daughters at their relatively new home near Charlotte, North Carolina. The couple spent some of their free time during the Covid-19 pandemic making a joint podcast about their lives as parents. They dedicated an episode to the killing of George Floyd and race in America. In that episode, Giddins shared that his mother was a police officer, yet he remained nervous whenever he was pulled over by the police. Giddins added that police often doubted that his nice car belonged to him even after he showed the officers documentation. His wife, Kasha, described the long shadow of history in the daily life of Black Americans. "Our families were broke up from the very beginning, and people don't think there's a consequence from that, like, from the time we've been here, we were purchased and bought and drug over here against our will," she said. "They tore up our families, and they just kept doing all those types of things, and they kept us uneducated, and that stuff was as recent as the

Civil Rights era. And you thought for a second that we were making progress, and to be faced with an incident like this again lets you very much know that there is no progress."

Giddins looked around at the white-run banks that had employed him and decided to make the move to a Black-run bank. "I'll just be honest with you, I don't feel comfortable, you know, banking out of Wells Fargo, but it's a necessary evil," he told us. "Whether it's, I mean, insert the name, Citibank, JPMorgan, Wells Fargo—you name it. The history is not great." Giddins was hopeful that Greenwood would address the prevalence of Black Americans who did not have a bank. Some 40 percent of the Black population, he noted, still didn't have a bank account, or they used alternative banking solutions, such as payday loans. "You can't build wealth without a checking account," he said.

Giddins and Greenwood's founders also recognized the opportunity inherent in hiring Black people to be on Greenwood's team. Professional workplaces have an important role to play in narrowing the Black-white wealth gap. Professional jobs tend to be well-paying and stable. They offer retirement plans, health care, and other benefits. Black Americans in professional jobs have opportunities to lift their families' fortunes. By building résumés at brand-name companies, they create strong reputations that would be helpful if they decided to raise money and go out on their own as entrepreneurs, another path to building wealth.

Companies often say they want to hire more diverse teams, but as the data make clear, as of 2020, most companies had dismal records in terms of hiring and promoting Black Americans. At Google, only 4.4 percent of workers were Black as of 2021. At Goldman Sachs, only 6.8 percent of its U.S. workers were Black, and that figure was lower at the higher-ranking jobs, where only 3 percent of the firm's top 1,548 people were Black. The same pattern existed in the federal government, in the U.S. Treasury Department. There, in 2019, of the top officials, only 6 percent were Black. In contrast, 45 percent of the lowest-ranking jobs were held by Black Americans. (Those Treasury jobs were mostly IRS call center jobs.) Latino Americans were also not well represented in top jobs at any of these employers. In the U.S. Treasury, Latino Americans were only 2 percent of the people in senior roles. This pattern carries across many industries. In real estate, for instance, only 6 percent of agents and brokers were Black as of 2023. And those that were Black made on average one third as much money as white brokers. This is not just a financial sector problem—there have long been far too few Black and Latino Americans in U.S. newsrooms, for instance.

Black Americans, who were 13.6 percent of the population in 2021, and Latino Americans, 19 percent, were concentrated in many non-professional jobs that typically paid less money. According to the Bureau of Labor Statistics, Latino Americans were overrepresented as painters and paperhangers (where 51 percent were Latinos), housekeeping (46 percent), and construction laborers (46 percent). Black Americans were overrepresented as home health aides (37 percent), transit and intercity bus drivers (37 percent), nursing assistants (35 percent), correctional officers and jailers (33 percent), and security guards and gaming surveillance officers (31 percent). This overrepresentation of Latino and Black Americans in lower-paying industries in the 2020s was a key reason their median weekly income was lower than the median income for white Americans.

At every education level, white workers in the early 2020s made more pay than Black and Latino workers. Even within the *same* industries, and within the *same* jobs, there were pay disparities, according to federal data. Some samples of weekly pay levels in comparable jobs:

- In management, business, and financial operations, white Americans earned $1,482 per week, and Black Americans earned $1,211 per week.
- In computer and mathematical occupations, white Americans earned $1,589 per week, and Black Americans earned $1,352 per week.
- In education, white Americans earned $1,100 per week, and Black Americans earned $1,017.
- For health care practitioners and technical occupations (not including health care support), white Americans earned $1,236 per week, and Black Americans earned $1,030.
- For food preparation jobs, white Americans earned $533 per week, and Black Americans earned $497.

- In construction and extraction activities, white Americans earned $915 per week, and Black Americans earned $740.

The list goes on and on, and the pattern remains the same. Latino Americans, also, consistently earn less than white Americans.

Why have Black professionals been underrepresented and under-paid in these industries? There are many reasons, ranging from educa-tion to people's personal networks. In our reporting, we heard about the reality on the ground from dozens of professionals, who all said it was simply harder to be a Black professional in a white-dominant workplace. Brook Bacon, who worked his way from an entry-level call center job at BankBoston onto the trading floor and then worked for State Street Bank, all while saving up enough to be able to go back to college, repeatedly saw that other people—white people—moved up faster than he did, despite their not producing better work results. "You see other people that seem to be fast-tracked," he said. "They're just kind of cruising along, and you're like, 'Well, why have I been in this position for two years now? They left this position at nine months.'"

Tandreia's career seemed to be flourishing just before the pandemic. She worked for Manhattan Associates, doing supply chain consult-ing for some of the biggest brand-name consumer goods companies. She was hired to visit warehouses and figure out what was working and what wasn't. One day, she would be engaging with on-the-ground minimum-wage workers not unlike her parents in the textile factory; the next day, she would be talking to the company's management. "What's going on, on the floor?" executives would ask her. It was an important role, and Manhattan Associates was able to bill her services out to clients at $250 an hour. Tandreia herself was paid a lofty sum— $100,000 a year.

However, she didn't feel important. She felt worthless. The execu-tives at many companies she interacted with treated her like she was "nothing," she recalled to us. Was it because of her race? That was always the unanswered question. Tandreia worked ten- to eleven-hour days, traveling constantly, trying to bring up her family's fortune and never forgetting that she had an obligation to her mother. But she said she wasn't treated like a professional. It got so bad that one day, in

December 2019, she fainted on the warehouse floor. "It was one of the darkest times of my life," she told us. She felt uncomfortable going to the hospital, so she just went back to her hotel room and rested. She lay in bed thinking, *I gotta find a way for economic freedom.* She was stuck in the wealth gap in a no-man's-land between the warehouse floor and the executive offices. She was determined to figure out how to jump to the other side of the gap, whether it would be through professional jobs or something else, like entrepreneurism or investing.

Tandreia admired Greenwood Bank's focus on Black founders and Black workers. For Greenwood, it would be important to hire Black *and* Latino leaders and employees, given that the company said it would be selling products to people in both groups. According to the Greenwood employees we interviewed, however, Greenwood prioritized hiring Black Americans over Latino Americans. At first, the company featured both Black and Latino speakers in the educational videos and virtual gatherings it was organizing. Over time, however, the emphasis seemed to be mainly Black Americans, and how much to focus on Latino Americans, Greenwood employees told us, became a topic of internal dispute.

Still, for Black employees, Greenwood stood out as committed to hiring Black workers. For Ryan Rowland, Greenwood would be the most diverse place he had ever worked. Rowland had spent much of his career at television companies like Viacom. At Country Music Television, he was the only Black designer in the marketing department. Arriving at Greenwood, he told us, felt like arriving in Wakanda, the fictional East African country featured in Marvel Comics and, later, the movie with Chadwick Boseman.

Rowland started at Greenwood as a freelance art designer, helping to create the look and feel of the company's marketing; he later joined the staff as the creative director. The mission felt personal to him. As he watched his parents age, he was thinking more about estate planning and other personal finance matters that had not previously been big conversations in his family. At a company off-site, Rowland made a point of telling Greenwood's leaders how meaningful the job was to him. "I want our culture to get better," he said, talking about Black American communities. "I want us to be educated about financial planning, estate planning, that kind of thing." Working at Greenwood, he told them, "this is personal for me."

In 2021, as Greenwood's waiting list kept growing, the workplace was full of excitement. One promise Rowland cared about was money recirculation. He had been a fan of Michael Render's political and economic commentary, and he highlighted "really insightful" points the rapper had made "about, you know, how the Black dollar doesn't stay in our community long . . . After eighteen hours, it's gone into other communities." The goal of keeping Black dollars in Black communities, Rowland said, was a big part of what had brought him to Greenwood. He said, "That was fueling my decision [to work] there."

Recirculating Money

Tandreia had made numerous attempts to strike it rich. She and her friends founded Hack the Markets, but she split from the team before they gained much traction. She invested in cryptocurrency. And in the summer of 2020, she had decided to become a consumer goods entrepreneur. Her idea was to sell individual packets of sanitary equipment. Disposable toilet covers, hand wipes, and masks in to-go bags. She called her company Dixon Brands and launched a social media campaign to spread the word. "I'm Tandreia Dixon, the visionary and founder of the Dixon Brands No Contact Kit," she narrated in one video accompanied by Maasai music. "It's essential hygiene and toiletry items to help you keep safe."

The product itself was basic—as Tandreia explained, "one of the first ones is an extra-large toilet seat cover. The toilet seat cover covers all sides of the toilet, so when you pull your undergarments down, right, you don't have to worry about anything gross or nasty from the porcelain getting on your clothes."

But her ambitions were big. She created a logo, "DXN BRNDS," and T-shirts and company colors. Her pride and hope showed on her sleeves. She wanted to make it big like Pinky Cole had with her restaurant chain, Slutty Vegan. Tandreia also had mounting misgivings about always working for other people. Fainting on the warehouse floor at her most recent job had been a wake-up call. "I have worked hours and hours and hours, working for somebody else, for someone else's legacy," she said at the time. "Granted, what I received in return has helped me. But I want to do something to incorporate my family as well as to be able to leave a legacy for my children and my children's children." Her hopes were tied in part to what her father had always told her: "Dream big." She had tattooed the phrase on her arm after his death, a reminder not to miss her *one shot*.

Becoming an entrepreneur can help close the gap. Successful Black entrepreneurs, data show, are closer in wealth to white entrepreneurs than the overall Black-white wealth gap would predict. Still, it is more difficult for aspiring Black entrepreneurs to get their businesses started. Part of this is attributable to a lack of wealthy personal networks: Black Americans have fewer contacts who can help form business partnerships and invest. And part of it is getting a business loan: Numerous studies have shown that Black business borrowers have not been treated equally. Black Americans are not offered as many credit options as white borrowers, and even when Black Americans become entrepreneurs, they sometimes struggle to get capital to support their operations. A 2019 study by the Congressional Black Caucus Foundation found that nearly 30 percent of Black entrepreneurs said they had lower profits because they had difficulty obtaining capital—nearly three times the rate of white Americans who said that. (About 17 percent of Latino Americans said lack of access to capital curtailed their profits, and 14 percent of Asian Americans reported the same.)

As one veteran banker of twenty years told us, "My Black clients had done everything that they could to get to the place where they did deserve a higher level of service. But their loans were being scrutinized." That banker, Toni Goins-Brockman, was so "angry," as she put it, about the inequities she saw at a national white-run bank that she left her job in 2020 to work for a Black-owned bank in Kansas City, Missouri.

Michael Render put a somewhat comedic spotlight on the challenges of Black-owned business borrowing in his 2019 Netflix tongue-in-cheek docuseries *Trigger Warning*. Michael and members of a gang called the Crips tried to start a business. One gang member proposed taking on the zipper industry, but they settled on making a rival soft drink to Coca-Cola. At the bank, a loan officer asked what kind of businesses the Crips had engaged in and how they had documented their past income. In the episode, the gang members ended up not being approved for a one-hundred-thousand-dollar business loan because they did not have tax returns and other financial documents.

"Without any history in the financial system, the Crips would never get support from the establishment," Michael said. Funding a soda brand by a Black gang might seem risky to some people, but Michael made the point that the Hells Angels, which he called a white gang, sell T-shirts. This was all part of a broader point the rapper made throughout the series: that it's tough for Black businesses to thrive. In another episode, Michael attempted to consume only Black-produced products. Quickly, he found there was nothing in his fridge he could eat, no vehicles he could drive, and not even weed he could smoke.

Buying Black was central to Greenwood's marketing. It was part of a broader proposition that banking with Greenwood would help recirculate money within the Black community, as employees like Ryan Rowland hoped. Greenwood was about more than the services it would provide to its customers. It was about calling on consumers to be part of a movement: to Bank Black.

The movement was one Michael had been championing for years. In 2014, after Michael Brown was shot by a white police officer in Ferguson, Missouri, and the Black Lives Matter hashtag gained momentum, people were looking for actions that might make a difference. "Take one hundred dollars and put it in a bank," Michael declared at a Bank Black event in Miami in 2017, with a cheering crowd in the background. "Then people call and say, 'What do we do next?' Take another one hundred dollars and put it in the bank. And the following month, take another one hundred dollars. Because you ain't saving the bank. You are teaching yourself to save. You are teaching yourself basic economics." Beyond addressing Black Americans, Michael called out "young white progressives" and said, "If you're not banking Black, me and you can't have a conversation."

By 2020, Michael would be more than an evangelist for Black banks. He'd be the owner of one. He negotiated for a larger stake with the other Greenwood founders, he told us proudly, and they gave him a bit more.

Banking with Greenwood would not be just a one-step action of buying Black, Michael and the other founders promised; it would be more akin to dropping a pebble in a pond and watching the ripples flow outward, paying it forward to other Black Americans. The idea became a key proposition. Greenwood stated on its website that the very reason it exists is because "our communities suffer from a lack of wealth, *money circulation in the Black community* and generational transfer."

The pitch resonated with Tandreia, who was ready to leave Chase Bank for Greenwood as soon as she moved up on the waiting list. "Chase is fine," she told us. "But just looking at the grand scheme of things and what is meaningful to my community and possibly what will be meaningful to my children, it's really important that my money is being circulated back into my community. So people who look like me can thrive." Her entrepreneurial dreams seemed increasingly connected to Greenwood's banking goals. She saw the logic of helping Greenwood help the Black-owned part of the economy in order, in turn, to help herself.

As Greenwood refined its pitch around the ripple effects of buying and banking Black, however, the two of us began to see problems and, potentially, false marketing. The business school teachers in us knew well that money is fungible and cannot easily be tracked. The journalists in us knew, too, that ideas and claims can take on a life of their own as numbers get cited around the internet with little or no fact-checking.

So, we fact-checked. Greenwood's three major claims about recirculation were that:

1. Money spent in the Greenwood business district of Tulsa, Oklahoma, in the 1910s circulated "within the neighborhood's Black-owned businesses at least 36 times" before leaving the community.
2. As of 2021, "money circulates one time in the African American community, six times in the Latino community,

and nine times in the Asian community. In white neighborhoods, money circulates nearly an unlimited number of times. In part, this explains the wealth gap for Black communities."

3. The operations of Greenwood Bank would be a solution to this problem and play a significant role in increasing recirculation of money within the Black community.

Let's follow the trail for the first claim about the historic Greenwood district in Tulsa. Greenwood Bank linked to an article from 2017 on JSTOR Daily, a website featuring scholarly articles by university professors. That article said that money circulated in Greenwood "36 to 100 times," citing figures from a 2014 article in the *Atlanta Black Star*. That earlier article cited the numbers from a 2011 story in the *San Francisco Bay View National Black Newspaper*. Precisely, the *Bay View* story said, "The dollar circulated 36 to 100 times, sometimes taking a year for currency to leave the community. Now a dollar leaves the Black community in 15 minutes." The *Bay View* piece gives no sources for those figures, but the article was provided to the site by the Ujamaa Network, an advertising email subscription business run by Mike House, who is based in Chicago.

We called House to ask where he got the data, and he said it was simply online: "You can even google 'Black Wall Street.' You'll see that information. This is general knowledge."

Greenwood Bank was not the only party to republish these unsourced figures. In 2020, CNBC published them, cited a "historian," and linked to the JSTOR piece (which led back to the Ujamaa Network). So did the *Boston Globe*, and the *New York Times DealBook*.

Despite the lack of sourcing for the "36 times" recirculation figure for Black money in Tulsa's Greenwood district, let's take it as a given and say the figure is accurate, or at least directionally correct, for the sake of following the argument through. It is logical that back then, around 1920, money would not leave a community as quickly as it does today. It was a time of segregation, after all, which meant that Black workers and business owners were not as likely to take their earnings far afield. And there was no internet back then. Going shopping meant physically going somewhere, and without widespread car use or bus service, that place needed to be nearby.

A lot has changed since the 1920s, however, and those changes may mean it's more difficult today to create strong recirculation of currency within a given community. All kinds of local businesses battle national chains and internet shopping. Some localities have created their own currency to help keep money circulating locally, and that has helped to some degree. This approach offers insights into how recirculation does, and does not, work in practice.

The idea of creating a local currency has precedent: during the early years of the Great Depression, Yale economist Irving Fisher brought an idea used in Germany and Austria to dozens of towns in the States, introducing local "scrip" that governments agreed to convert back into U.S. currency later on. Fisher was helping towns battle a shortage in currency while creating rules that required people to purchase stamps every week to validate their "scrip." This meant that whoever had the scrip at the end of the week had to pay for the stamps; this incentivized people to spend their local notes. As a writer at the Cleveland Federal Reserve Bank described the system in 2008, "Money became a hot potato, with individuals passing it quickly to avoid having to pay for the next stamp." A locale that embraced scrip at the time was Mason City, Iowa, where several companies paid their employees partially in scrip and where numerous merchants agreed to accept scrip in exchange for goods. The currency enabled the city to employ more workers, build a road, and keep money circulating around town. By definition, with scrip, money would not leave town because no other towns accepted that town's currency. The scrip programs were wound down in the mid-1930s, amid concern by the U.S. Treasury that the federal government would lose control of money.

More recently, community currencies have been used in international development so that government or nongovernmental organization cash infusions were more likely to circulate within a given community, rather than being spent elsewhere. In the United States, local business advocates have created local currencies to keep money in their regions. In this model, people can purchase the currency and use it in local stores instead of credit cards or U.S. dollars. In 1991, an individual in Ithaca, New York, created Ithaca Hours, which were used there until the 2010s. Another effort, BerkShares, was introduced in the Berkshire Mountain area of Western Massachusetts in 2006, and by 2022, there was ten million dollars in BerkShares in circulation, according to the local nonprofit that administers the currency. That spring, the nonprofit created a new version of BerkShares: cryptocurrency BerkShares.

Greenwood Bank, however, was not talking about using a community currency. The dollars that would flow in and out of Greenwood Bank's platform would easily be spent on anything in the economy—including, as would often be the case, goods from white-owned businesses. Greenwood Bank was also not formed within a particular geography, which distinguished it from the Greenwood district of Tulsa, Oklahoma, and from the Berkshires and Ithaca communities. It was difficult for us to see how Greenwood, as a national bank using dollars that could be circulated anywhere, would ensure that Black dollars, so to speak, were spent in Black businesses.

Greenwood Bank's second claim was about how many times money circulated in different racial communities. On its website, Greenwood said that dollars circulate for six hours in Black communities, compared to twenty days in Jewish communities and thirty days in Asian communities. Michael Render has cited similar figures, telling CNN in 2020, when Greenwood was announced, that "a dollar circulates for 20 days in the white community, but only six hours in the Black community."

Greenwood sourced this data from the Selig Center for Economic Growth, a department at the University of Georgia. But the director of the Selig Center has publicly denied backing the recirculation data. "The statistics you cited do not come from the Selig Center for Economic Growth," the director told us. "The Selig Center has never produced any estimates on money circulation. I do not know the source of those statistics."

The Selig Center director also disowned the statistics to a Howard University reporter in 2015. It was the Howard reporter, writing for a campus publication called *Truth Be Told*, who did the most fact-checking of these data points. The reporter found that the recirculation figures by race and religion (specifically Jewish communities) originally came from a book from the mid-1990s called *Talking Dollars and Making Sense: A Wealth-Building Guide for African-Americans*. We called the author of that book, Brooke Stephens, to ask about the recirculation figures. She told us they came from two businessmen she met at a conference in the early 1990s and that they had done the recirculation study in Washington, D.C., in the 1970s. That's all the information she had on them. When we asked her if recirculating Black money is possible today, she said, "Right now, there's limited opportunities for that."

Part of the issue with the recirculation numbers is they cited Jewish recirculation, but the government doesn't track that sort of data. William Spriggs, a former economist and Labor Department official in the Obama administration, pointed this out to the Howard reporter and called the figures "urban myth." "What makes me suspicious is that it has economic data based on religion when the federal government doesn't collect any information by religion," Spriggs said. "Where would you get that from?"

Even if we set aside the details of these old datasets and whether the recirculation idea has any veracity, there's one more claim that Greenwood Bank makes about recirculation, and it's by far the most important. The new bank's value proposition was rooted in the idea that people who invested their money with Greenwood would be helping currency recirculate in Black communities. This bears asking: How would Greenwood Bank do this? The company's website stated that *the* "solution" to circulating more money in Black communities was the establishment of Black-owned banks "like Greenwood." Its copy went on:

There is heated debate over how to solve the problem of low-dollar circulation in Black communities. While reinvesting money by shopping in Black businesses can help, it may not be enough. Many Black businesses source their products from White-owned or foreign-owned companies. *An emerging solution for reinvesting in Black communities is Black-owned banks. Banks like Greenwood help to circulate wealth within Black communities.*

Greenwood's website was light on specifics for how that recirculation would occur, but beneath its claim that it would help with recirculation, Greenwood stated that it would give monthly grants of up to ten thousand dollars to Black or Latino businesses and provide five meals to poor families for each new customer who signed up for a Greenwood account.

Greenwood also created what it called a GreenBook on its website, which lists businesses owned by Black individuals. We were curious to see whether those businesses would see a benefit from these listings and hopeful that they would. But even if Greenwood convinced its customers to use their Greenwood debit cards only in Black-owned businesses, we reflected, it would not be the case that all that money would actually go to Black Americans. Those Black-owned businesses would have suppliers that could be white-owned. The landlords of those businesses could be white. Some employees might also be white. In a sense, the impact of spending with a Black-owned business would be in the profit margin to the Black owner and the pay to any Black employees. These individuals, in turn, might or might not spend their money in Black-focused companies. The "recirculation" might or might not occur.

Greenwood Bank itself would need to have its own suppliers. The manufacturer of its debit cards, for instance, might end up being white-owned. The building Greenwood rented for its office in Atlanta could be owned by a large, publicly traded company with a white chief executive and a nearly all-white board.

As Greenwood Bank put together its marketing and launch plans in 2020, the reality was coming through in mainstream rap music. In August of that year, Jay-Z rapped about the soda brand that Michael Render had helped create with the Crips. The lyrics point out that Black Americans had been creating content that subsidized Twitter (now called X) and then reminded Black Americans that even behind Black businesses like Crip-a-Cola, there would be white money involved . . . unless the entire supply chain became Black through vertical integration.

"Black Twitter, what's that? When Jack gets paid, do you?" Jay-Z rapped, referring to Jack Dorsey, the cofounder of Twitter. "For every one Gucci," he continued, support "Crip-a-Cola." (The same month the song came out, Michael Render announced that Jay-Z was becoming a partner in the Crip-a-Cola company.)

Lest it seem that our view of Greenwood Bank had turned entirely skeptical, we want to make it clear that we approached Greenwood's marketing claims with open minds, and we were continuing to make a strong effort to remain open-minded. Listening to Greenwood gatherings like the one Tandreia Dixon joined still made us hopeful that Greenwood would be the real deal. Amid our fact-checking, we came up with one main way that Greenwood might be able to help with recirculation in the Black community: lending money to Black Americans.

Lending may seem obvious for a company that marketed itself as a banking platform, but as time passed, we noticed that it wasn't something Greenwood or its founders talked about publicly. Michael Render told us that part of his participation in the bank was based on a promise from the other founders that there would eventually be lending, but months passed with no signs of an introduction of loans to the bank's menu of products and services.

Tandreia, ranked at 536,537 on the waiting list for a Greenwood customer account, told us she was looking forward to the day she could borrow from Greenwood. After Greenwood's virtual gathering, she said, "I aspire to be an entrepreneur, and when the time is right and I'm positioned, I would be able to go to Greenwood and get a business loan."

CHAPTER 9

THE SO-CALLED BLACK DOLLAR

We as a nation must undergo a radical revolution of values. We must rapidly begin in the shift from a "thing-oriented" society to a "person-oriented" society. . . . True compassion is more than flinging a coin to a beggar; it is not haphazard and superficial. It comes to see that an edifice which produces beggars needs restructuring. A true revolution of values will soon look uneasily on the glaring contrast of poverty and wealth.

—Martin Luther King Jr., 1967

At the heart of Greenwood and its founders' claims about money recirculation was a pervasive and controversial idea about wealth and race: the power of the illusive Black dollar.

In June 2020, Michael Render posted on social media that he was reading *The Myth and Propaganda of Black Buying Power* by Jared Ball, a professor at Morgan State University, alongside the book *Race and Economics: How Much Can Be Blamed on Discrimination?* by economist Walter Williams. "If u don't study all the perspectives u don't really wanna know," Michael wrote in a post featuring the book jackets and the authors' photos. "U just wanna be agreed with."

Sitting in his Maryland home—which, because of the pandemic, he'd barely left, save for a few outings, like a Black Lives Matter protest—Ball got his back up when he saw the post. First of all, he didn't think he should be associated in any way with Walter Williams, a conservative economist. And second, he was unsure whether the rapper knew what he was talking about when it came to economics. The expression "Black buying power" was often used to refer to the more than $1.6 trillion that Black Americans supposedly had at their disposal to use for consumption or for change, if they wanted to. To Ball, it was a myth that there was a bloc of money that could bring real change. It was that myth, according to him, and it allowed businesses to skirt blame for the Black-white wealth gap.

On Instagram, in real time, Michael was responding rapid-fire to the comments people had written in response to his post. He told a student of Ball's that the economist had "very interesting perspectives." Another person in the comments criticized Michael for the post, saying he was laughing out loud at the word *perspectives*. "Dr. Ball delivering straight facts," the person posted. "So-called 'Black buying power' is a myth that is debunked in his book. Framing it as merely a 'perspective' is kinda disingenuous."

At the heart of this exchange is a debate over the business world's framing of Black Americans. On the one hand, they have been called a "hidden gold mine" by advertising executives dating back to the 1930s. On the other hand, Black Americans hold fifteen cents on the dollar, compared to white families, hardly enough to be a gold mine. "Black buying power" has been framed as a concept of empowerment, but it can lead to forms of exploitation when Black Americans are viewed mainly as a resource to be tapped by white America. It's a concept that has often been used by white-owned businesses who want more Black customers, though sometimes it's used by Black-owned businesses to make a point about how much Black-controlled money there is to recirculate in the Black community. Whatever the case, Black buying power is a concept that can distract the business world and broader public from the severe economic inequality between racial groups.

By the 2020s, Jared Ball was one of the leading critics of this concept. He argued that it is misleading to look at the income earned by Black Americans as being a sort of "power" they could use. That supposed power belies the reality of the gaping disparity in Black and white wealth. And it allows companies to think that all they need to do to help with change is market their products to minorities.

Ball's views of the Black-white wealth gap were in part shaped by his experience standing right in the middle of that gap, with his mother's white family on one side and his father's Black family on the other. Both his white uncle and his Black father fought for the United States in the 1940s. "Post–World War II was that moment where the break really occurred," Ball told us, referring to the growth of the middle class that benefited many white families but left much of Black America behind. "My [Black] father," he said, "did not have access to the GI Bill. My [white] uncle did, and he ended up being able to use the VA to buy a home in Long Island for—I don't know—thirty thousand dollars. And I remember, after he passed and his widow had passed, they sold the house for over five hundred thousand dollars." Ball's father had purchased a more modest home without the support of the GI Bill, which, upon his death, sold for a fraction of the price of Ball's uncle's home. Ball received five thousand dollars in inheritance from the sale.

Ball and Michael would continue to interact online—with Ball criticizing Greenwood's assertion that it could change the Black-white wealth gap—until, one day in the spring of 2021, Michael called Ball on his cell phone. "Where would you suggest I go to get different information?" he asked, according to Ball, who replied that he would recommend a few sources in line with his book. Michael said he would study them and that he hoped to keep in touch. (Aside from a few text messages, they haven't talked since.)

Central to Ball's thinking is a critique of companies that create content. His views extended to all news and entertainment companies, but especially to content companies targeting Black consumers, like Bounce TV, which Ryan Glover founded in 2011 with Andrew Young and Martin Luther King III. As the *New York Times* wrote at the time, "Bounce TV . . . is indicative of the multiplying media choices for multicultural consumers like African Americans and Hispanics, whose increasing numbers and buying power make them attractive audiences for marketers."

The impact of the media on Black Americans' wealth is multifaceted. A story in the *New York Times* or the *Wall Street Journal* can help companies get funding and sell their products; if more white-owned businesses get featured, there are implications for racial wealth gaps. By the same token, getting quoted as an expert in news articles can help a person's career, and journalists select whom they call and quote in stories. The business sides of news companies, meanwhile, contribute to the framing of Black Americans as marketing targets, according to Ball. "For the segment of the Black bourgeoisie involved in media, journalism, or advertising," he wrote in his book, "to 'capture' meant delivering a newly created Black market packaged in a mythic economic strength, labeled buying power, to white corporate ad buyers."

The idea that Black entertainment and news exist, in part, to help large corporations sell their products to Black Americans has a relatively modern history. And in some ways, the idea has been at odds with movements for progress in closing the Black-white wealth gap. Still, it is an idea that continued to fuel new Black-owned media companies in 2020 and beyond.

Capital *B*

The Black News Channel was launched just before George Floyd was killed in 2020. By that summer, the network was four months old and gaining steam. The fact that it was largely Black-run at that point was an important recruiting factor. For new hires, it seemed to offer the promise of lifting up Black voices and perspectives in ways the mainstream media had often failed to do. For Charlotte Wheeler, forty-six, joining the Black News Channel felt like "a natural shift to actually go to a network that focused on underrepresented communities and sharing stories that impacted me."

Wheeler had felt marginalized and, sometimes, ignored at Court TV, where she was working as a booker when Ahmaud Arbery was killed while jogging in rural Georgia. She said that Court TV was waiting to report the story after CNN. A reporter there also wanted to dig into Arbery's background on the first day of reporting, instead of investigating the people who had killed him, she said. "I was just like, 'You know what? When you go over to BNC, you're probably not going to have to fight those fights,'" Wheeler told us.

In Atlanta, as the summer of 2020 progressed, the local bureau of the Black News Channel was still operating mainly with contractors. Tamara Banks was one of them. At sixty, she had worked for many of the large television networks before joining BNC and had reported from Uganda, Haiti, and across the United States. She and her colleagues at the new network often talked about why a Black-led press was needed. As she would tell us, "The white mainstream media will say, 'Well, you know, we cover the protests in George Floyd behind the scenes and all that.' But they didn't do it from the perspective of 'We live in that neighborhood.'"

Banks noted that, when she worked at mainstream news outlets, she often saw "man" used for Black teenagers and "boy" used for white teenagers of the same age. "Often, I'm at a desk inevitably run by a white person," she continued. When gun violence occurred, she said they would say: "That's just gang members shooting each other." Banks had her reply ready, "Well, first of all, you don't even know that they are gang members. Secondly, those are still people. And thirdly, why would you even say that? Those kids . . . they're somebody's son or daughter."

Even as Banks and her colleagues were getting going at BNC's Atlanta bureau, they encountered skepticism over the network. At one point, Steven Bacon [no relation to Brook Bacon], who was running the Atlanta bureau, was talking with a white freelancer who said that just having the word *Black* in the name of the network would eliminate its chance of success. The freelancer told Bacon that the network wouldn't last more than three years and would eventually be sold for pennies on the dollar. "American people expect stuff that says 'Black' to not be successful," Bacon said.

Separate news outlets by and for Black Americans have a long history in American media. The challenges and opportunities that Black media have faced over the years have much to say about how the broader business world perceives of "the Black consumer" and to what extent journalism and commerce can coexist. Many Black media outlets have grappled with what it means for any business to be by and for Black Americans.

One of the earliest Black news outlets was *Freedom's Journal*, a newspaper established in New York in 1827, the year that state ended slavery. *Freedom's Journal* lasted only two years, but it generated interest among other Black Americans to start newspapers across the country. In 1847, Frederick Douglass began publishing the *North Star*, a weekly newspaper that dedicated its first page to abolition efforts. By the Civil War, about forty Black-owned newspapers had been established. Many of these early papers were weekly or monthly, but the Black press became more influential as it transitioned to publishing daily. Atlanta's *Daily World* became the forty-sixth Black-owned daily in 1932, and more were established over the next few decades. But surviving wasn't easy. The roughly sixty Black dailies that have existed have lasted an average of 4.5 years, Howard University and Lincoln University historians found. As these news outlets have come and gone, Black journalists have also faced barriers in the broader white-run news industry.

In 1968, the Kerner Commission carried out a seminal assessment of the media's relationship with Black Americans. Set up by President Lyndon B. Johnson, the commission (officially called the National Advisory Commission on Civil Disorders, but known by the name of its chairman, Illinois governor Otto Kerner Jr.) researched the causes of demonstrations by Black Americans across the country. At that time, the commission found, less than 1 percent of working journalists were Black. The commission strongly criticized the white-led mainstream press for its coverage. Specifically, it wrote, magazines, newspapers, and television programs were not including Black Americans in a representative way.

The absence of Negro faces and activities from the media has an effect on white audiences as well as Black. If what the white American reads in the newspapers or sees on television conditions his expectation of what is ordinary and normal in the larger society, he will neither understand nor accept the Black American. By failing to portray the Negro as a matter of routine and in the context of the total society, the news media have, we believe, contributed to the Black-white schism in this country. When the white press does refer to Negroes and Negro problems it frequently does so as if Negroes were not a part of the audience. This is perhaps understandable in a system where whites edit and, to a large extent, write news. But such attitudes, in an area as sensitive and inflammatory as this, feed Negro alienation and intensify white prejudices.

—National Advisory Commission on Civil Disorders,
better known as "The Kerner Commission," 1968

The report created some pressure to diversify newsrooms, but even decades later, in the early 2000s, Black journalists would hold only around 5 percent of newsroom jobs.

The lack of diversity in major newsrooms resurfaced as a hot-button topic in the summer of 2020, as demonstrations once again rocked the country. Journalists working at newsrooms including the *Los Angeles Times*, the *New York Times*, the *Wall Street Journal*, the *Philadelphia Inquirer*, and the *Washington Post* circulated petitions and memos and called for meetings with management to share concerns about internal staffing and coverage of race. At the *Washington Post*, the newsroom's union called on management to follow eleven suggested changes aimed at resolving inequities in the pay, training, retention, and hiring of minority employees. At the *Los Angeles Times*, editor in chief Norman Pearlstine responded to similar concerns with a memo acknowledging that the *Times* had not addressed "concerns of people of color in the newsroom" and that it had focused "on a white subscriber base even as the city became majority nonwhite."

The *New York Times* kicked off an internal review that would culminate in a lengthy report that read in part, "We have arrived at a stark conclusion: the *Times* is a difficult environment for many of our colleagues, from a wide range of backgrounds. . . . This is true across many types of difference: race, gender identity, sexual orientation, ability, socioeconomic background, ideological viewpoints and more. But it is particularly true for people of color, many of whom described unsettling and sometimes painful day-to-day workplace experiences."

Behind the scenes in the weeks after George Floyd was killed, editors at many publications debated what might seem like a small matter—namely, whether to use an uppercase *B* when describing Black Americans. Black-focused publications—like *Essence* and *Ebony*—had been using the uppercase for years, and now the question had moved to the broader press.

In the 1920s, the NAACP urged publications to capitalize *Negro* to show more respect to Black Americans. When the *New York Times* did so, its editorial board wrote that it was "not merely a typographical change. . . . It is an act of recognition of racial self-respect for those who have been for generations in the 'lower case.'" A survey of the Black press over time, *A History of the Black Press*, documented continual discussions over the proper term since the 1830s, but loosely speaking, there was a trend in the late 1800s and early 1900s from *Colored* to *Negro*. By the 1960s, *Black* became more in vogue in the Black press, and by the 1990s, in part due to advocacy from Jesse Jackson, *African American* led the way. That last term receded from favor in the 2020s because it did not include non-American citizens nor did it contemplate the cultural connections among Black people around the world.

Debates around style and wording can be emblematic of wider stances. By 2020, the choice of *black* over *Black* had been debated for years at the Associated Press—a wire service whose standards set the writing rules for many news outlets. The logic of advocates for an uppercase *B* was that the names for other groups with a shared identity and history—like *Asian, Latino, African American,* and *Native American*—were capitalized. But their proposal hadn't gained traction, former AP staffers said, in part because it was largely being promoted by Black journalists, and there was a tendency inside the AP to suggest that Black journalists were not a neutral party to decide such a matter. As a reporter for the AP, Errin Haines said she saw a similar pattern in other debates around language. She had argued that remarks by President Trump should have been called racist. "I have colleagues who were using some of these euphemisms for racism—'racially charged' being my least favorite possible euphemism," she said. "I was kind of quietly reaching out to people to say, 'Do you know why? Why did you use the phrase? What is it that you meant to say?'"

For Haines, a Black woman from Atlanta, it was about how the media was contributing to the current conversation and also how coverage would be looked at by future historians. It was also about the culture of her workplace. "It was not just about coverage, it was about trying to change the culture of the organization as it pertains to race," she said. Black journalists, like Black professionals trying to change practices in any white-dominated industry, have to confront the question of whether they receive more credibility on issues of their race because they are Black, or are they discouraged from speaking up in that area? Haines left the AP in early 2020 to be a senior editor at a new publication, the *19th*, which focuses on news for women and minorities.

If the media—the fourth estate, tasked with representing society to itself—couldn't change its own culture, language, and perception, then who could? If the media, funded by businesses and by generally upper-income, mainly white people (via subscriptions), didn't *want* to change, what did that mean?

As the summer of 2020 passed, journalism leaders like Sarah Glover, a recent president of the National Association of Black Journalists, called on the news industry to capitalize the *B* in *Black*, calling it "a good first step to affirm the significance of being Black in America." She continued: "It's to bring humanity to a group of people who have experienced forms of oppression and discrimination since they first came to the United States 401 years ago as enslaved people. I ask for this change in honor of the Black Press, which already capitalizes the 'B' in Black." After two years of discussions, the AP made the change. Soon most other large news outlets did so as well.

Semantics and capitalizations tie into broader questions around race and business. How much does it make sense for any business to speak directly to a particular racial group? There has been a growing push for news outlets to reach out to audiences of different races, and the same is true for consumer goods companies. This leads to more questions: *How* should companies target particular racial groups? And how much nuance and variety must be recognized within racial groups when they are targeted? For Greenwood Bank, given the many economic levels among Black Americans, *which* Black Americans to focus on would become a point of discussion.

Black news outlets wrestled with how to speak to, if not for, their readership long before mainstream (white) culture wrestled with it.

Were they producing news for the subset of Black Americans who were becoming middle class? Or were they doing it for more marginalized Black Americans? The answers changed over time. Until the mid-1900s, much of the Black press was advocacy-oriented, including publications started by the NAACP in 1910 (*The Crisis*, seen in the redlining battles in chapter 5) and by the Black Panther Party in the 1960s. Many Black-led publications, even ones branded as independent news operations, spent the early and mid-1900s advocating for Civil Rights and social change as part of their coverage. But, as the Civil Rights Movement passed major milestones in the 1960s and '70s, some veterans within the Black press said it was becoming less advocacy-oriented. One prominent editor captured the changing tides in 1977 in a piece he wrote for an industry trade publication. "The disturbing question that keeps bubbling to the surface of my mind is that the Black press lost its sense of mission in the last decade," wrote Enoc Waters, who had been the editor of the *Chicago Defender*, a prominent Black newspaper. "In my days—1925 to 1965—as I recall them, the total commitment was to advancing the cause that called forth the birth of the Negro press. We are not only Black newsmen but we regarded ourselves as a specialized division of a vast Black Civil Rights crusade."

Part of what Waters was speaking to was also an increasing commercialization of Black Americans as "consumers." In the late 1800s, most major consumer goods companies ignored the Black press and didn't advertise in it. At the same time, Black thought leaders questioned whether they should emphasize Black entrepreneurship or that Black Americans were valuable consumers. How much should Black Americans buy into the white economy and how much should they try to keep dollars in the Black community, with a focus on Black-owned businesses? By the early 1900s, Black leaders like Marcus Garvey were using the word *power* to describe Black shoppers, and the term spread to white marketers. In the early 1930s, William Ziff, a white advertising executive in Chicago, helped portray Black consumers to marketers as a "hidden gold mine" and published two advertising industry books about the buying "power" of Black consumers. Ziff was popularizing this idea of Black buying power at the same moment that the government was excluding Black Americans from benefiting from many New Deal wealth-building programs.

The concept of Black buying power spread over the years from advertising and the media into a broader framing of the Black population for the entire business community. It remained commonly cited in the 2020s, by both white and Black executives.

Black-Focused or Black-Owned?

The Black News Channel was ready to meet the moment. A modern, news-centric effort at creating Black content developed with the help of former Republican congressman J. C. Watts, the network seemed to have all the right ingredients to bring together commercial success with impactful, Black-focused news as it launched in 2020.

There was just one problem: It wasn't Black-owned. Though Watts was a Black American, he was not the majority owner when BNC was launched. At the time, the network described itself as "minority-owned," a nod to its majority shareholder, Shad Khan, a Pakistani billionaire. It launched with a white CEO, Bob Brillante, a longtime Florida television executive. Brillante told us the network tried to raise money from Black investors and couldn't.

Just how important it is for Black Americans to own the companies that Black people patronize has been a long-running question in racial wealth gap history. Black company ownership has been a point of pride in many communities, dating back to the Greenwood district in Tulsa, Oklahoma, among other places, as we have seen. There has also long been a public good argument that Black-owned firms can better serve the needs of Black consumers. This movement works in opposition to joining the white-run economy—the more Black Americans who own, work at, and patronize Black-owned companies, the fewer Black workers and Black shoppers exist for white firms. Individuals like Tandreia who have been trying to bring up their families' wealth face a constant battle over whether to start their own businesses, where they can enjoy the upside, or try the professional route working in well-resourced, white-run firms. While most start-ups (for people of all races) have low odds of becoming major businesses, the companies that do break through can provide steady wealth to their founders. It may sound obvious, but in a capitalistic society, the people who hold the capital (i.e., the ownership) often come out ahead. If Black Americans are merely the faces of businesses catering to minority groups, that leaves those Black professionals out of ownership and wealth growth.

The Black News Channel's top programming executive, who was Black, was strikingly candid when talking about the network's ownership gap. "How many people of color own the channels versus others?" that executive, Gary Wordlaw, said. "How many managers do you have in broadcast versus the [faces] you see in front of the camera? So, yes, we may gain in front of the camera, but our struggle is still station management and station ownership! It's still a fight. We may progress, but there's still progress to be made."

Another wealth gap could be seen within the Black News Channel, one between high-ranking Black executives like Wordlaw and lower-ranking Black employees. One of the entry-level employees at BNC was Vynessah Dasher, a production assistant trying to find a path out of poverty. On launch day for the network, she got dressed up in a brand-new bright yellow Calvin Klein dress, she recalled to us. She kept telling herself, "This is historic, I'm part of something historic." Celebrities flooded in for a ribbon cutting in the control room. Dasher, age twenty-two, started posting photos and videos on Snap. *This is something special*, she remembered thinking.

Dasher was making fifteen dollars an hour. Even as she bought the yellow dress, she was crossing her fingers that she could pay off the back rent on her apartment. She was in her final year of college, and her landlord was in the process of evicting her. At work, she helped in a variety of tasks, including writing stories on topics such as how "the Black dollar" could be a defense against "systemic oppression."

The image of Black Americans was a priority at the network. Wordlaw, the programming executive, said that he was motivated by wanting to show Black people at their best. "I want the world to watch us and catch Black people doing good things. Because now we're, unfortunately, too often being seen on TV as criminals and that sort of things! So, to help me fulfill this mission, I have a staff of beautiful African

American people dedicated to telling these positive stories as well as what's going on all over the world." He said he recognized that there is variety within Black audiences. "We are as diverse as any other people," he told us. A common thread for all the channel's programming, he said, would be that "you don't have to explain what being Black is to a Black person. No matter what our experience in life is, we all know what that feels like."

One person featured on the Black News Channel in its first couple of years was James Woodall, increasingly well known for his NAACP work. The network also featured *New York Times* opinion columnist Charles Blow, who had moved from Brooklyn to Atlanta in early 2020. Georgia, Blow wrote the next year, was "on the cusp of transformational change," having voted for a Democrat for president for the first time since 1992 and having elected the state's first Black senator in history, Raphael Warnock, a pastor at Ebenezer Baptist Church in Atlanta, where Martin Luther King Jr.'s father had been pastor. The way Blow saw it, the timing was perfect for Black Americans to reverse the Great Migration—when so many Black people left the South for the North—and move back to the South. "In effect," he wrote in a *Times* column, "Black people could colonize the states they would have controlled if they had not fled them."

This was not the gospel of Black buying power. This was a vision of power in larger terms.

Given its prominent Black founders, Greenwood Bank might have seemed insulated from debates over the essence of Black ownership and empowerment. But this was not the case within the banking industry. Among legacy players in Black banking, Greenwood was becoming a flash point for controversy.

CHAPTER 10

BLACK BANKING AND CIVIL RIGHTS

Hopefully the day will arrive when Black Americans will no longer have to suffer from such great unemployment; when the vast majority of them will have the degree of education necessary to enter the mainstream of American economic life; and when their path will not be covered with the thorns of prejudice. When that day comes, there will be no Black or white banks, just banks; and everyone in this country will be judged according to his individual worth, and not according to the color of his skin. When that day comes, that is when there will be no further need for Black banks.
—Samuel Pierce Jr., general counsel, U.S. Treasury Department, and a cofounder of Freedom National Bank, 1971

In December 2020, an anonymous filmmaker who calls himself the "Poor Black Man" published a video on YouTube questioning how "Black" Greenwood Bank really was.

He pointed out that Greenwood had posted a notice in small text at the bottom of its website saying that it was not FDIC-insured by the federal government and that it would be partnering with another bank. In other words, the debit card accounts that Greenwood would provide its customers would be supplied by another bank. "Greenwood is the middleman," the Poor Black Man said. He added that as of December 2020, it appeared that Greenwood did not have a Black-owned bank to work with.

He put the bank on notice: "Greenwood, we are mid- to early December. You are scheduled to launch February 2021, so you have from now until then to partner with some Black banks, and if you can't find a Black bank, the FDIC has a list of Black banks."

From the inception of Greenwood, dating back to Ryan Glover's safari birthday party, the idea was to be a "neobank." That's an entity that offers banking services in new ways but, often, is not technically a bank. This was a critical point: Greenwood was not licensed as a bank and did not have Federal Deposit Insurance Corporation backing, meaning it had to partner with an actual bank for its depositors' money to be protected in case of bank failure. This is what the "Poor Black Man" on YouTube meant when he called Greenwood a middleman. It was a "banking platform" set up to sit between the customer and an actual bank.

In Greenwood's case, that bank was Coastal Community Bank. Based in the small city of Everett, Washington, Coastal had become one of the hottest community banks in the country. The bank's parent, Coastal Financial Corporation, had an initial public offering on the Nasdaq in 2018 as the bank set about a new strategy to offer "banking as a service." In addition to its local business as a bank to the Washington public, Coastal was a popular bank behind the scenes for fintech companies. As of 2021, it would have sixteen fintech partners and seven more coming on board. The amount of money deposited with Coastal via fintech partners grew from $607 million in September 2021 to $1.2 billion over the following year.

Pause and think about this for a moment. More than a billion dollars had flowed into a bank in the northwest corner of the United States that few Americans had ever heard of. Even many of the people putting their money into this bank might not have recognized its name on a billboard, because they primarily thought of their banking relationship as being with a partner company like Greenwood.

Greenwood employees who had joined to be part of a Black banking company started having internal debates. The problem to them was not so much that Greenwood wasn't actually a bank. The problem was that Coastal was a white bank. Of Coastal's top ten executives, all were white.

While some of Greenwood's employees complained about Coastal, Ryan Rowland, Greenwood's creative director, had become resigned to what he saw as the reality of banking in America. "Our financial system is already set in stone," he said in a matter-of-fact tone. "It's been Caucasian-owned." Greenwood's leadership had educated Rowland and others about how fintech worked, he said, and the only way they thought it worked was in partnerships with banks like Coastal.

Greenwood leaders explained it in similar terms. Bo Young told us, "The reality is that, I mean, there's services within the space [where] there are no Black companies who would do it."

Eric Sprink, the chief executive of Coastal Bank, agreed, telling us there were no Black banks that he knew of that had the infrastructure to provide the banking services that Coastal provided for Greenwood and other fintechs. "The bar is very high" for this kind of service, he has said. In large part due to Coastal's fintech business, Sprink had become one of the highest-paid community bank CEOs in the country.

Others in the Black-banking world were shaking their heads. The fact that Greenwood Bank wasn't a bank, and that it used the white bank Coastal to take deposits, was tantamount to false advertising, some felt. Michael Render used to support actual Black banks, they noted, where the companies were banks themselves, not banking intermediaries like Greenwood. His "Bank Black" campaigns had benefited numerous Black banks, including OneUnited Bank, one of the largest Black-owned banks in the country. Did the rapper's role in Greenwood mean he wouldn't support actual Black banks anymore?

And then, to top it off, there was the name itself: "Greenwood." In November 2020, Greenwood's leadership initiated a trademark application for the name. This seemed presumptuous to some people in the Black community. Like, how could one company own the name "Greenwood"?

OneUnited filed an opposition to the trademark claim, attempting to block it. As Teri Williams, the president of OneUnited, told us, people within Black banking were incredulous, like, *really*? "We think that the name 'Greenwood' should be one—like 'Black Wall Street'—that isn't owned by anyone, including us," she said, adding that if Greenwood Bank were eventually purchased, then its new owner would control the name "Greenwood." And that owner, she said, might be white. "They're going to own *our* history, and you just don't want that," she said. "I don't think that anyone should be able to own 'Greenwood,' given that it's *our* history."

Williams is one of the most influential Black bankers in the country. Her bank, OneUnited, was formed fifty years before Greenwood Bank came along. It began in Boston as Unity Bank and Trust, and then its founders merged with numerous Black-owned banks around the country, including institutions in Los Angeles and Boston. As of 2020, OneUnited was one of the rare Black-owned banks. In 2021, there were only sixteen Black-owned banks in the United States. That was out of a total of just over four thousand banks.

Behind these institutions' responses to Greenwood is the story of the triumphs and challenges of Black banking across American history. We saw the beginning of that story in chapter 3, with the fall of the government-created Freedman's Bank in the years after the Civil War. In 1907, when W. E. B. Du Bois compiled a list of Black-owned banks in the country, there were forty-one of them, including the Black-owned Creek Citizens Bank, set up in Oklahoma by one of Ryan Glover's ancestors.

There were many more chapters in Black banking between those old banks and 2020 and more debates to wage about what a Black bank should do, and be. Much of that history would play out in the Civil Rights era as Andrew Young ascended as a leader, pushing relentlessly for change while also believing in the power of capitalism.

A Celebrity-Led Black Bank, Capitalism, and Civil Rights

Long before becoming a Greenwood founder, Andrew Young had seen the rise and fall of Black banks. After growing up in New Orleans in a mostly white neighborhood, Andrew graduated from Howard University and then divinity school in Hartford, Connecticut; he then worked for a few years as a pastor in Georgia and in Alabama. It was in Alabama he met Martin Luther King Jr., in 1957, when the two men shared the stage at a fraternity program at Talladega College, a Historically Black College there. That same year, Andrew moved to New York City to work for the National Council of Churches.

While living in New York City, Andrew would get to know Black leaders involved in the creation of Freedom National Bank. The brainchild of a businessman closely associated with Dr. King and the Civil Rights Movement, Freedom was an example of what capitalism could, or couldn't, do to close the Black-white wealth gap. It would also become a final chapter in the life of Jackie Robinson, the baseball star and another close associate of King and Andrew.

To understand the ties of Freedom Bank to the Civil Rights Movement, it is informative to pause on September 20, 1958, when a woman stabbed Martin Luther King Jr. while he was signing copies of his book at a Harlem department store. A handful of his closest associates—NAACP, union, and ministry leaders—gathered in the hospital with him as a surgeon operated to keep King alive. Among them was a businessman, Dunbar McLaurin.

Dunbar McLaurin came from a prominent Civil Rights family in Oklahoma. His parents, George and Penninah McLaurin, lifelong advocates of education, fought a twenty-five-year battle to open education in the state to Black Americans. Their success in the U.S. Supreme Court helped pave the way for the landmark Supreme Court ruling in *Brown v. Board of Education* against segregation in public schools. Dunbar, for his part, had graduated high school at age twelve and then left Oklahoma to pursue higher education. By age twenty-one, he had a doctorate. After serving in World War II in the Philippines, he set up a business in Manila selling used military vehicles. By age twenty-seven, he was a millionaire, according to *Ebony* magazine, which called him a "business wizard."

McLaurin had a strong interest in race and economics and the role the private sector could play in changing things. In 1958, he attended an economics conference in Washington and met another economist planning to start a Black-focused bank in Houston that would be called Riverside National Bank. Soon, McLaurin woke up in the middle of the night and told his wife, "I'm going to start a bank in Harlem."

There had been banking efforts in Harlem before. Chelsea Exchange Bank, a white-owned bank with branches around the city, had opened a branch in 1912 in Harlem and advertised heavily to Black depositors. Another Black-focused bank in Harlem, Dunbar National Bank, was founded out of charity by John Rockefeller Jr. It was staffed and run by Black Americans, notable at the time, but its funder considered it an experiment and closed it down after a decade in 1938.

There have not been many banks focused on Harlem's community, so these efforts filled a void for several decades. But they also enabled exploitative patterns we've seen elsewhere in this book. As a teller at the Harlem branch of Chelsea Bank said in the 1930s, the bank accepted Black residents' deposits, and then "all of this money is transferred downtown to the home office where it is loaned to white customers." Both these banks ended up leaving distrust in the minds of Harlem residents.

As McLaurin got going in 1964, trust was on his mind. To bring in more community involvement, he decided that Freedom Bank would sell ownership shares to local residents. He began walking up and down 125th Street and Lenox Avenue, day after day, selling bank stock out of his briefcase.

This early focus on the importance of Black ownership—not just Black depositors—set Freedom apart. McLaurin was an expert on what came to be called "ghetto economics," which also led him to focus on the bank's role in lending money to the Black community and on supporting other Black businesses, which wasn't always easy. When Freedom wanted its office built by a Black-owned construction firm, but couldn't find one locally, the bank helped obtain bond financing for a Black-owned construction firm that then helped build its office.

In search of star power, McLaurin reached out to perhaps the most famous Black businessman he knew: Jackie Robinson, the baseball player who had gone on to work as an executive at the coffee company Chock full o'Nuts. McLaurin invited Robinson to join Freedom Bank. Robinson had "become increasingly persuaded that there were two keys to the advancement of Blacks in America—the ballot and the buck," as he would write in his autobiography. He joined Freedom

Bank because he felt that "if we organized our political and economic strength, we would have a much easier fight on our hands."

As they got going with Freedom Bank, Robinson and McLaurin talked about how white-owned banks were not doing much "to fulfill the needs of Harlem people," as Robinson put it. "By and large, in the banking business, Blacks were considered bad credit risks, not only because of their median low income as compared to that of whites, but because of the stereotype which had existed for many years that they were not to be trusted," he said.

Robinson was an active Civil Rights leader. He had been at Martin Luther King Jr.'s side as a speaker at events, including the 1962 meeting of the Southern Christian Leadership Conference (the Civil Rights group founded by King) in Birmingham, Alabama; at fundraising events to rebuild Black churches destroyed by arson in Georgia; and onstage at the March on Washington for Jobs and Freedom in 1963. Standing alongside his wife and three children at the Lincoln Memorial that day, Robinson said, "I know all of us are going to go away feeling . . . we cannot turn back." Some 250,000 people chanted in response, "Freedom! Freedom! Freedom!"

A few weeks after that, Robinson held a jazz concert at his home in Connecticut to raise money for Civil Rights leaders who needed bail when jailed in the South. A longtime fund-raiser for the NAACP, Robinson had long fought segregation, notably as far back as 1944, when he was a lieutenant at Camp Hood and was court-martialed for refusing to move to the back of a bus. He faced threats, like in 1949, when his Brooklyn Dodgers were coming to Atlanta and a member of the Ku Klux Klan threatened to shoot Robinson on the field. During that visit, Robinson stayed with King, who told him, "Don't worry about these threats. You carry on just as you've been doing. That's the greatest thing for our country." As King would say of Robinson, he "was a sit-inner before sit-ins, a freedom rider before freedom rides." King also said in a televised interview that "the founder of the Civil-Rights movement was Jackie Robinson."

Jackie Robinson was able to elevate Freedom National Bank both in popular culture and in activist circles. In 1965, the year after King won the Nobel Peace Prize, he started a nonviolence foundation and set up an account for it at Freedom National Bank using his prize funds. It was, a bank leader would recall, great "public relations."

The mid-1960s to mid-'70s, Freedom National Bank's first decade in business, was a period of significant debate over how to help Black Americans economically. Even among the leaders of the Civil Rights Movement, disagreements were emerging. The relationship between Martin Luther King Jr. and Andrew Young embodied this tension. Both men were raised by prominent parents who provided comfortable lives and supported their sons' college education, but King focused on poverty as early as in a 1950 college paper in which he wrote about "the inseparable twin of racial injustice and economic injustice." His upbringing was also shaped by his father's role as a well-known Baptist preacher, which included a strong focus on the poor. He would write, "Although I came from a home of economic security and relative comfort, I could never get out of my mind the economic insecurity of many of my playmates and the tragic poverty of those living around me." Seeing people in breadlines contributed to King's "anti-capitalistic feelings."

Andrew, for his part, firmly believed in capitalism and working with businesspeople. His father was a dentist, and he emphasized to his son the toll of Blackness. When Andrew was around ten, his father showed him a bar of soap. "See this Ivory soap bar? One hundred percent pure," he said. "That's pretty clean, pretty good. That's not good enough for you. You're Black." Andrew needed to be more than 100 percent pure, his father was saying. "You cannot cut corners. Period." Andrew kept this advice in mind as he took after his grandfather, New Orleans insurance impresario Frank Smith Young, in developing an interest in business.

Andrew enjoyed making deals and representing King and other Civil Rights leaders to local businesspeople. Such overtures were needed during demonstrations in places like Birmingham, Alabama. There, in 1963, he took advantage of white contacts he had from his work in a national church organization and persuaded them to support the demonstrators, paving the way for King and other leaders to declare victory. Andrew "met with the business leaders who said, 'I need my customers back,'" John Hope Bryant, a close friend of Andrew's, told us. (Bryant is an Atlanta-based businessman who also runs a nonprofit focused on teaching personal finance.) "Majority of these customers in these neighborhoods, these small towns are Black. And it got to a point where the business owners were like, 'I don't give a damn whether they come to the front door, the back door, the side door, I need the green to come back,'" Bryant told us. Andrew leveraged this sentiment to get WHITES ONLY signs taken down. "His job was to take the overalls off, put on a business suit, and go in quietly and cut a deal that left everybody with their dignity, including Black people, but also his white so-called adversaries," Bryant said. "That was a unique skill that Andrew Young had."

As Andrew described it to us, "I made the argument in Birmingham that, 'Look, the pie gets bigger—and you get a bigger piece of the pie—when you let other people into the pie.'" Throughout his career, later in Congress and as mayor of Atlanta, Andrew would seek to get Black Americans into the pie while making the pie bigger all at once. But who exactly did he mean when he said *you* get a bigger piece of the pie when *you* let people in? This would become a running conversation we had with him over the course of our research.

Andrew earned his Civil Rights stripes in demonstrations—notably in Selma in 1965, when the police used tear gas and other violent tactics against him, King, and about six hundred other people. In the 2020s, he still featured a photo on his office wall that captured that moment: police officers violently attacking him and others as the demonstrators pushed for progress.

Even with their different views on capitalism, King and Andrew were getting traction on the local and national level. Within Black advocacy, they were charting relatively new territory in leading mass movements involving large numbers of people demonstrating and speaking out. This was different from the NAACP, which had functioned primarily through the legal system. King, Andrew, and others were also basing their movement in the South, whereas much of the NAACP's strength had been in the North.

As the Civil Rights Movement achieved victories for voting rights, King shifted his focus to poverty. It wasn't a total departure—the March on Washington, after all, was officially called the March on

Washington for Jobs and Freedom. Several leaders then worked on what became known as "The Freedom Budget for All Americans." It called for job creation through national programs to build more high-quality affordable housing units, create better water and power supplies, and build classrooms and hospitals. The text of the budget declared that anyone who could work should be able to find a job, and those who weren't able to find a job should be provided with an "adequate income." The budget, written by Black labor officials, was distributed in Black neighborhoods. King wrote a cover letter endorsing it, saying, "The Freedom Budget is essential if the Negro people are to make further progress. It is essential if we are to maintain social peace. It is a political necessity. It is a moral commitment to the fundamental principles on which this nation was founded."

King spoke increasingly about a guaranteed income. In his final book, *Where Do We Go From Here: Chaos or Community?*, published in 1967, King argued that Americans should be given a minimum income and that it should be set to the median level of American families. "To guarantee an income at the floor would simply perpetuate welfare standards and freeze into the society poverty conditions," he wrote. That same year, King preached about what he positioned as Black Americans' entitlement to more American wealth, due to the role slavery had played in creating a robust American economy. "It is the Black man who to a large extent produced the wealth of this nation," he said at a Baptist church in Chicago. "The Black man made America wealthy."

Throughout these years, Andrew Young had a standard role in conversations. "It almost always fell to my lot to express the conservative view," he said. King's view of Andrew's economic stance would become more clear in conversations at the end of King's life. At a final meeting of the Southern Christian Leadership Conference in 1967, King spoke about pushing the Civil Rights Movement in a new direction—to focus on a more radical redistribution of money and power. "Something is wrong with capitalism as it now stands in the United States," he said. Two months later, in January 1968, King announced what he called the Poor People's Campaign. The plan was to recruit thousands of people from urban areas to meet in Washington and hold demonstrations until Congress created a guaranteed income or new jobs programs.

In March, with Poor People's Campaign planning under way, King and Andrew had a friendly clash as they dined in New York City at the home of Civil Rights activist and singer Harry Belafonte. King had been with the poet Amiri Baraka in Newark that day and had spoken with young Black Americans there who were advocating for violence to achieve change—a value in opposition to King's nonviolent approaches. As Belafonte recounted in his book *My Song*, King said, "I feel their frustration. It's the system that's the problem, and it's choking the breath out of our lives."

Andrew retorted, "I don't know, Martin. It's not the entire system. It's only part of it, and I think we can fix that."

"I don't need to hear from you, Andy," King replied. "You're a capitalist, and I'm not."

That line—"You're a capitalist, and I'm not"—embodied a growing tension in the movement. Whereas activists pursuing voting rights all agreed on the goal, Civil Rights leaders pursuing economic equality often did not see the desired outcome the same way. Were they trying to integrate Black Americans into the white system, or were they trying to change the system?

A week after the conversation at Belafonte's, King gave his final speech, in Memphis, Tennessee. He was there to support the local sanitation union, underscoring his interest in advocating for higher income for both poor white and Black Americans. The speech has been most remembered for his concluding passage: "I've seen the promised land. I may not get there with you. But I want you to know tonight, that we, as a people, will get to the promised land." But midway through the speech, he also talked about harnessing Black buying power to convince companies to change:

> Go out and tell your neighbors not to buy Coca-Cola in Memphis. Go by and tell them not to buy Sealtest milk. Tell them not to buy—what is the other bread? Wonder Bread. And what is the other bread company, Jesse? Tell them not to buy Hart's bread. As Jesse Jackson has said, up to now, only the garbage men have been feeling pain; now

we must kind of redistribute the pain. We are choosing these companies because they haven't been fair in their hiring policies; and we are choosing them because they can begin the process of saying they are going to support the needs and the rights of these men who are on strike. And then they can move on downtown and tell Mayor Loeb to do what is right.

But not only that, we've got to strengthen Black institutions. I call upon you to take your money out of the banks downtown and deposit your money in Tri-State Bank, [a Black-owned bank]. We want a "bank-in" movement in Memphis. So go by the savings and loan association. I'm not asking you something that we don't do ourselves at SCLC. Judge [Benjamin] Hooks and others will tell you that we have an account here in the savings and loan association from the Southern Christian Leadership Conference. We're telling you to follow what we're doing. Put your money there. You have six or seven Black insurance companies here in the city of Memphis. Take out your insurance there. We want to have an "insurance-in."

King's views about capitalism have been debated ever since that speech. On the one hand, he bought into capitalism: he held boycotts and framed Black Americans as consumers who had buying power. But on the other hand, he doubted capitalism's capacities: In his final visit with Harry Belafonte, King shared with him and Andrew his increasing sense that "we live in a failed system. Capitalism does not permit an even flow of economic resources. With this system, a small privileged few are rich beyond conscience and almost all others are doomed to be poor at some level."

After King's death, a group of scholars attempted to keep his anti-capitalistic views alive in a think tank called the Institute of the Black World. The institute lost support from the King family, one of its scholars said, because some King heirs decided to "support the myth of Black capitalism as a means to 'save humanity.'" It likewise fell out of favor with the King Memorial Center, run by the King family, according to a 2021 book by scholars Andrew Douglas and Jared Loggins, because it "unsettled the center's philanthropic backing." Belafonte, one of the executors of King's estate, expressed lasting regret in his memoir that the King Center had focused so heavily on funding. As an early board member, Belafonte says he proposed support for grassroots campaigns in areas that King had championed, but he was told by other board members, "We can't offend the funders!" Belafonte also noted that Coretta Scott King, King's widow, chose to honor King's birthday with corporate dinners featuring the leaders of Ford, even though that auto company was working with South Africa's apartheid government.

(To understand the King family's steps after King's passing, Andrew told us it was important to know that they had very little money. For all King's fame, he died without much money, and in fact, while King was still alive, Belafonte had tried to get life insurance for him, but had been repeatedly turned down by insurance companies. Eventually, Belafonte helped King get a policy, but it would pay out only one hundred thousand dollars, Andrew told us. The insurers were not willing to put a higher value on King's life. Insurance payouts are typically based on what someone earns, and King did not earn much money.)

When King was fatally shot in Memphis on April 4, 1968, Andrew Young was there. Both men were staying at the Lorraine Motel. King had been in a light mood, pillow fighting with people in the room. Andrew came in from the courthouse, where he had been testifying against a restraining order blocking their planned demonstration. King asked where he'd been, and Andrew said, "I was on the witness stand trying to get you the right to march and keep you out of jail." King replied, "Oh, you're getting smart with me," and threw a pillow at Andrew.

"He was in a more playful mood than I had seen him in years, I mean, acting like a child. I threw the pillow back and then everybody else picked up pillows and started beating me up. It was like a bunch of twelve-year-olds," Andrew recalled.

A few minutes later, when King slumped over on the balcony, Andrew at first thought he was "still clowning."

That May, Andrew helped carry out the Poor People's March in Washington. He joined Coretta King and other Civil Rights leaders in building a temporary tent city on the Mall, where many camped out for a month. On June 24, their park permit expired, and the Department of the Interior forced them to leave. The U.S. government made a lackluster response, offering food distribution in two hundred counties and promising to create some jobs.

Andrew himself was torn over the effort. As Harry Belafonte wrote, "Andy was ambivalent about the Poor People's Campaign. All the other goals that we had set for ourselves up to this moment were tangible. Almost all of them were focused on justice. But when it came to economics, the goals were more complicated, the lines more blurred. Andy didn't believe that all the victims came from the same level of experience. He felt that there was a critical difference between poor whites and Hispanics, on one hand, and poor Blacks on the other." Andrew, as Belafonte put it, saw a distinction with Black Americans and a special need to focus on them. His views on this would shift some over the next sixty years.

For the Civil Rights Movement, the focus on poverty sputtered with King's passing, Andrew acknowledged to us.

After the march, Andrew moved into politics. He became a U.S. congressman, then the U.S. ambassador to the United Nations, and then, in 1981, the mayor of Atlanta. Decades later, he spoke about his Civil Rights work humbly. He made it clear that he was but one member of a broader team. And he described his focus during the movement as creating opportunity within capitalism—and within Black business ownership. As he put it, "The work that we did in the Civil Rights Movement wasn't just about being able to sit at the counter. It was also about being able to own the restaurant."

King was not the only one who had different economic views from Andrew Young. Malcolm X, who had drawn many hearts and minds toward his more aggressive approach to activism and Black Power, had been a fierce opponent of capitalism. As he said a couple months before his death in 1965, "You show me a capitalist, I'll show you a bloodsucker. He cannot be anything but a bloodsucker if he's going to be a capitalist." In line with these remarks, scholars and activists debated whether it was the entire concept of capitalism that blocked Black progress or more the ways Black Americans had been discriminated against within American capitalism. In the meantime, Black

Power groups continued to protest, and politicians became concerned about what they viewed as street violence.

When Richard Nixon ran for president in 1968, the year King was killed, he wanted to stem the tide of protest, and he looked to the idea of Black capitalism. Black Americans wanted "a piece of the action," Nixon said. Now it wasn't just Black Americans fitting into capitalism, it was "Black capitalism." The idea of focusing on owning the restaurant, not just being allowed into it, was popular with many policymakers and large business interests who hoped it would ease the pressure on them to make more systemic changes. After the election, the Nixon administration set up the Office of Minority Business Enterprise, first, to study minority-owned businesses and, later, to offer grants to organizations that helped minority-owned businesses with administrative tasks.

Critics of Black capitalism ranged in their focus. Scholars like Robert L. Allen, author of the 1969 book *Black Awakening in Capitalist America*, suggested that the benefits of the OMBE might accrue to only a few Black Americans. "Simple transference of business ownership into Black hands, either individually or collectively, is in itself no guarantee that this will benefit the total community. Blacks are capable of exploiting one another just as easily as whites." Was it enough for social progress to create Black business owners, many asked, or were existing businesses supposed to put in place redistributive and equitable practices that, realistically, might go beyond what would be expected of a white-owned company?

This was a concern raised during Freedom National Bank's early years. In 1966, the bank's president took the podium at the end of a church sermon and urged congregants to deposit their money into Freedom Bank, so that the bank would be able to issue a mortgage to their church. It seemed, to some, that the bank was treating the church unfairly. "To many Negroes, refusal of the church mortgage until the bank has picked up extra depositors is a clear case of exploitation," wrote the *Harvard Crimson*. "To the skeptics, the Freedom National Bank is simply an example of middle-class Negroes taking advantage of race sympathy for their own personal gain." Here, in this prescient college newspaper story, we see an early focus on class within race. The paper went on to argue that elevating some Black businesspeople was not necessarily a step toward broad equity:

> [Freedom Bank], like the other 10 white-run banks in Harlem, is one more part of the power structure, one more reason why Harlem is an economic colony of New York City. They feel that Negro bankers who live outside Harlem—as do almost all of Freedom National's 50 employees— can drain money out of Harlem just as effectively as the white businessmen who own almost all of Harlem's stores. Black bankers do not help Harlemites, they maintain, they help themselves.

In other words, the *Harvard Crimson* was opposed to Freedom Bank's behaving in the profit-first manner that tends to be standard at white-run banks.

On top of the concern that a bank like Freedom didn't help its poor Black customers, Black leaders worried about segregating business. Andrew Brimmer, for instance, an economist and member of the Board of Governors of the Federal Reserve and a Black American himself, did not agree with the separatist idea, arguing in numerous essays that separating Black business from the rest of industry would not succeed. He noted that Black consumers were not all that likely to be able or interested in sustaining those businesses and that a focus on Black-led business formation was a distraction from creating a more integrated economy. Brimmer was up against the strong school of thought in the Black community (supported by Nixon's minority business office) that Black dollars would be best earned and spent at Black-owned businesses. The idea of recirculation of funds was omnipresent even though its actual existence was unproven. As Civil Rights leaders and much of society pushed to end the segregation of schools, restaurants, and other facilities, the idea of segregating money had strong supporters across racial lines.

Black banking became a key area of discussion among the Nixon administration officials who were debating the right approach for Black capitalism: segregation of money or its integration? And Freedom National Bank became Exhibit A in that dispute.

By then, Jackie Robinson's bank had been through several presidents and turns in its fortune. Its original founder, Dunbar McLaurin, had resigned after he and Robinson didn't see eye to eye about the makeup of the bank's shareholders, some of whom were white. Since then, McLaurin had continued to attract national attention as an economist with what he called the GHEDIPLAN (for Ghetto Economic Development and Industrialization Plan), a proposal to develop poor neighborhoods using methods typically used in developing countries.

As chairman of Freedom Bank's board of directors, Robinson had brought in leaders, including a former principal in Carver Federal Savings Bank, a Black-led bank founded in 1948 and considered successful. But by 1968, the baseball player turned banker was being warned that his team was struggling. There was too much generosity in the lending at Freedom National Bank, some advisers said. "If you want to save Freedom National Bank, the only way you are going to be able to do it is to take it over and clean house," a leading Wall Street banker told Robinson that year. "You are in serious trouble."

Federal Reserve governor Brimmer ran a study in 1970 that compared the twenty-two Black-owned or Black-controlled banks in the United States with all other banks and found that the Black banks were not faring well. He concluded that they weren't accomplishing much for the economy or for the well-being of Black Americans. "Black banks might be viewed primarily as ornaments—that is, as a mark of distinction or a badge of honor which provides a visible symbol of accomplishment," he found. But, he added, they would not "become vital instruments of economic development." This conclusion went against the grain at a time when the Nixon administration was planning to deposit one hundred million dollars into minority banks.

McLaurin, the founder of Freedom Bank, immediately criticized Brimmer's study. He argued that the Federal Reserve leader had been inaccurate in comparing Black banks to all banks in existence and that the comparison should have been only to banks predominantly owned by white Americans. McLaurin also pointed out that the age of banks had not been factored into Brimmer's conclusions and that newer banks may tend to be less stable than older ones. McLaurin also went on ad hominem: "The most important thing about Brimmer," he said, "is that he is Black." He noted that a Black man coming out against putting Blacks into business made waves, and he invited the Fed governor to Harlem to see that "there is indeed a role for the Black entrepreneur to play just as there is a role for Brimmer himself to play at the pinnacle of the white financial world."

It was a bit of a cheap shot. Brimmer was not arguing that Black Americans should not be in business. He was making the case for something more nuanced: he suggested that the U.S. government create a new form of company in which white-run banks could invest that would lend money in underserved neighborhoods. It was a suggestion aimed at working within the system rather than setting up a separate system. But the general counsel of Nixon's Treasury Department, Samuel Pierce Jr., attacked Brimmer's proposal: "One of the major themes of the Black movement is for Black men to own or control their own businesses, and for the Black community to have substantial influence over the nature and direction of the economic development of their areas. Under the proposal, banks, through the proposed corporations, could set up businesses in ghetto communities and this would just be a means of continuing what has gone on in the past, namely, the white ownership of businesses in the ghetto communities. In short, such a measure would not ensure the Black man of getting a 'piece of the action.'"

Pierce was also one of the founders of Freedom National Bank, and he spoke to its influence: "I have had many Black businessmen tell me they were able to expand and improve their businesses because of loans Freedom Bank had granted them," he said. "I also know that since Freedom National Bank was founded, major banks have liberalized their lending policies in predominantly Black areas in New York City."

Pierce's argument that Freedom was creating new credit opportunities was shared by many in the Harlem community. As another local leader, Clarence Funnye, put it, "Before Freedom National, you went into the white bank with the distinct impression you went with what you had in your hand, begging the powers that be and generally you were turned down. With Freedom, the community looks less like a colony, less like an area for exploitation."

Unfortunately, as Jackie Robinson wrote in his 1972 memoir, it was also "becoming obvious in the latter part of the sixties that we were not being cautious enough with the processing of loan applications." The warnings Robinson had received from a Wall Street banker were accurate. "We were not doing enough research on applicants, and . . . we had a tendency to favor friends on the basis that one can trust one's friends in business—an utterly risky philosophy." Robinson noticed large amounts of bad loans being written off. He began working with the board to find a new president, all the while acutely aware that the bank was in a delicate position.

"On the one hand," Robinson wrote, "we did not want the white banking community to coddle us, to overlook mistakes we made because we were a Black bank. The more they had patted us on the back where we were wrong, the deeper we had become involved in our problems." Yet, he wrote, "there are some ways that we had to be different because we were a Black bank. Without being loose in policies, we had to be a lot less rigid than white banks have been under similar circumstances. A delicate balance had to be struck."

The same year his book was published, Jackie Robinson died of a heart attack at age fifty-three. His death removed the bank's most famous supporter. Not long after, in 1973, Dunbar McLaurin took his own life. He had been forced out of his role at Freedom and, afterward, had tried to build the first Black bank on Wall Street, an effort that met with frustration. McLaurin told students at Harvard Business School in a 1971 speech not to bother trying to help other people as they made their way upward. The "first obligation is to be successful. To go back and help others is just massaging your ego." At the time of McLaurin's death, his wife said he was despondent and struck by the challenges of building a Black business.

By 1974, Freedom had a new president, Hughlyn Fierce, who had been given a sabbatical leave by the white-run conglomerate Chase to try to save the Black bank. Fierce had worked at Citizens Trust in Atlanta very early in his career. He had studied Black banking for his master's degree in 1967, writing his thesis about Freedom National and Citizens Trust. One of Fierce's principles was for the banks to work with the minority businesses, but also, when appropriate, "constructively discourage them" from going into business.

Fierce prioritized raising capital for Freedom. This would mean significantly diluting the original stock owners, many of them Harlem residents who had purchased stock out of Dunbar McLaurin's briefcase. In 1975, Freedom raised $2.2 million from eleven of the nation's largest banks and borrowed $1 million from the Ford Foundation. Freedom offered its prior shareholders the chance to pay more money to purchase up to $1 million in stock. Freedom National Bank's Black ownership decreased. The new investors were given board seats, and by the 1980s, half the board of Freedom National was white.

The bank was making a sizable profit each year by the time an outside investor, Travers Bell Jr., who led the only Black-owned member firm of the New York Stock Exchange, launched a proxy fight for it. As the 1980s rolled on, Bell pushed for higher profits and growing assets. Freedom Bank began investing in projects outside New York, including a loan to an oil refinery in Arizona, some of which did not pan out. The mission of Freedom Bank was to hold money for depositors, lend money to the community, and in the interim, grow the funds through smart investments—but those investments were becoming less Harlem-based. Freedom Bank was not alone in taking on poor investments: This was the era of the savings and loan crisis, when more than 360 banks would fail. Seven of those banks would be minority banks. In 1988, Bell, the man who tried to push Freedom to be bigger and bolder, died of a heart attack at age forty-six. As the crisis became more apparent, regulators were asking many banks to tighten their belts. Funding slowed, and Freedom Bank was losing money.

In November 1990, Freedom Bank was closed by the federal bank regulator, the Office of the Comptroller of the Currency. The bank had 22,000 depositors at the time, and many different owners, thanks to the individual stock ownership program once peddled from McLaurin's suitcase.

To the Black community in Harlem and beyond, Freedom was not just any bank. "Symbolically, it's a terrible blow," Charles Rangel, who represented Harlem in the U.S. Congress, told the *New York Times*. In the same article, Abiodun, a poet and a depositor with the bank, told the *Times*, "It's a step backward for the empowerment of Black people."

Another bank depositor, real estate broker Emily Ricks, told the

Times that it made her feel sick. "I've had money in Freedom from the beginning, and we have mortgages with it. I lose and Harlem loses," she said.

In congressional hearings held in Harlem, legislators asked how this bank could have been allowed to fail. FDIC officials explained that they had tried to find a buyer—they had invited more than sixty interested parties to offer bids on taking over the bank and had reached out to other minority-owned banks as well. Only four parties showed up at the bid meeting, and only one performed on-site due diligence. In the end, no bids came in. No one wanted to purchase Freedom Bank. People at the hearing were quick to list the white-owned banks the U.S. government had recently saved, like the Bank of New England, where the OCC deposited $1 billion; and the National Bank of Washington, where uninsured depositors were given ten days to withdraw their money and foreign depositors were paid out to avoid investment flight. Continental Illinois Bank, considered "too big to fail," was also saved.

"The FDIC's unfortunate and destructive action is a classical action of institutional racism. It is apparent that the FDIC operates using a dual standard: one for the so-called rich and powerful, and one for the so-called poor," Grace Harewood, executive director of the Fort Greene Senior Citizens Council, which had deposits in Freedom, said at the hearing.

Freedom Bank had funded affordable housing, small businesses, church projects, and other community projects that no one else in Harlem had been willing to fund. Muriel Siebert, who ran a successful women-owned financial firm, served as New York State's superintendent of banks, and was the first woman to own a seat on the New York Stock Exchange, testified that regulators had failed to look at the big picture. Freedom National Bank, she said, could have and should have been saved. "I think the FDIC was quite insensitive to the unique position that Freedom National had in the community," Siebert said.

Even Andrew Brimmer, the former Federal Reserve governor who used to tussle with Freedom National Bank's founders over the value and merits of Black banks, said the bank could have been saved. "Freedom National Bank took on far more risk in both its fundraising and lending activities than did the average Black-owned bank," Brimmer testified. "Yet, in the end, the narrow and insensitive approach of federal bank supervisors terminated its life."

The loss of Freedom Bank as an institution was long remembered. Black leaders would say for years that the bank's demise during the savings and loan crisis was a metaphor for Black Americans in the U.S. economy. Anytime there has been a downturn, Black Americans have not rebounded to the degree that white Americans have. This was the case with Freedom Bank, and it would be the case, years later, for Black Americans after the 2008 housing crisis. As Wyatt Tee Walker, a local reverend and a board member for Freedom National Bank, put it when Freedom collapsed, "When downtown catches a cold, Harlem gets pneumonia."

Black Banking Is Difficult

A lot has changed since Freedom National Bank collapsed, but some things have not. As of the 2020s, there were still very few large Black banks. When he took the job at Freedom in 1988, George Russell Jr., the final chief executive of the bank, recalled to us, he fantasized about building the first "billion-dollar, Black-owned bank in this country." By 2022, there were only two Black-owned banks that had more than a billion dollars in assets, and their assets were only a bit over the one-billion mark. Black-owned banks had dwindled in number overall, from forty-one in 2001 to just seventeen in 2022.

Russell still had his hand in banking, on a part-time basis. He was a board member for OneUnited, the Black-owned bank opposing Greenwood Bank's attempt to trademark the name "Greenwood." He said he hoped to see tech-focused companies like Greenwood partner with Black banks to help on technology.

Greenwood focused from day one on convenience and technology, building a mobile app to put banking directly into its customers' hands. But banking is about many things beyond convenience: it's also about keeping people's savings safe, helping them with financial transactions, and providing credit. There is a connection among these functions, in that one customer's deposits fund the loan to another person. From a broad societal standpoint, it's important to inquire of any bank's owners, "What was the motivation of the people to get into banking," said Tim Todd, a historian at the Federal Reserve Bank of Kansas City and author of a book on Black banking. Because, Todd pointed out, the owners' motivations will play a role in what they do with depositors' money. "When you deposit money," Todd noted, "*whose* opportunity is being financed with that savings?"

We heard from numerous Greenwood customers that one reason they had opened accounts with the bank was so that their deposits would be loaned to other Black Americans. As time passed in 2021 and 2022, and more people opened Greenwood accounts, we kept waiting to hear that the bank was starting a loan program, but no such news came.

Setting up a new lending program takes time. And lending comes with the requirements of the federal Community Reinvestment Act, the law from the 1970s that had helped push banks to lend more to people of varied economic levels in their communities. Under the CRA, banks issue public reports with statistics about their loans, showing the variation in income level in their borrowers.

But because Greenwood was not created as an actual bank, it enjoyed a loophole in that it did not have any CRA requirements. Coastal Bank, the actual holder of Greenwood accounts, had CRA requirements for the money deposited directly with it. And Coastal had CRA requirements on the money it held for Greenwood and other fintechs. But those rules were broad and not directly tied to the Black community. There is no requirement regarding race in the CRA, only income. There was therefore little assurance that money deposited in Greenwood would be used to increase opportunities for Black borrowers. And in terms of geography, CRA rules simply required that Coastal lend money in the areas where the depositors from the overall group of fintechs lived. If many of those depositors were in the middle- and upper-income bracket—as Greenwood's were turning out to be—they might live in wealthy areas.

The vagaries of the CRA laws made it downright impossible to trace lending to a particular racial group. The best way for Greenwood to get its depositors' money loaned to Black Americans would be for it to start a lending program aimed at that group.

Black Americans' lack of access to lending has been a major factor in reinforcing the wealth gap. To build wealth, people need loaned money—capital—and banks can lend out money only in proportion to their deposits. The more deposits that people make to Black banks, the more those banks can lend out, noted Fred Cummings, an investor whose firm, Elizabeth Park Capital, invests in Black-owned banks. On Greenwood, Cummings said that if it didn't lend money to its Black customers, it was not going to make a dent in the Black-white wealth gap. "It's not going to help create wealth," he said, "because in order to create wealth, you've got to lend to small businesses and individuals."

Besides establishing a loan program, Greenwood could choose to increase the deposit pool of Black-owned banks by partnering with a Black-owned bank. So, we asked, did it have any plans to work with Black institutions that were actually banks? Ryan Glover told us in 2021 that Greenwood had planned a digital banking program that allowed Black banks to partner with Greenwood for a co-branded debit card, with the partner bank and Greenwood sharing the merchant fees. In that program, Greenwood would send its customers to those Black banks for loans. Using its long customer waiting list, Greenwood, he explained, would be the "customer acquisition engine" for those Black banks. This program, though, would have to overcome whatever setbacks Greenwood originally saw with Black banks, when Greenwood chose to start its business with the white-run Coastal Bank.

We asked several prominent Black banks if they were considering partnering with Greenwood. First up, Citizens Trust, the Black-owned bank in Atlanta where Michael Render and his grandmother Bettie had accounts when he was a child. Was it true that Citizens would not have the capacity to partner with Greenwood like Coastal did? "I'm not going to go down that road," said Frederick Daniels Jr., the bank's chief credit officer. "Citizens Trust focuses on Citizens Trust and our customers and our impact on the community. You know, Greenwood has a different model. And so, you know, we hope that they have success with that model, and I'll leave it at that." We asked if individuals like those featured in this book were likely to get help building wealth from Greenwood. "On Greenwood," Daniels said, "I have some definite opinions, but those will stay with me."

Teri Williams, the president of Black-owned bank OneUnited, told us that there was risk involved holding deposits for fintech companies like Greenwood. "That used to be called 'renting a charter,'" Williams said. "It actually was precluded and frowned upon by regulators. Because it was really important for a bank to know who their customers are." She noted that typically in these arrangements, the fintech has the relationship with the customer. It combines the deposits of all its customers and deposits them into a bank in one account. In such an arrangement, she noted, the partner bank—for example, Coastal, in the case of Greenwood—would not have the relationship with the actual customer. Regulators, she said, do not like that.

We were talking with Williams in March 2023, at the same time that Silicon Valley Bank was on the brink of collapsing. Soon, Signature Bank, Credit Suisse, and First Republic Bank would run into their own troubles. Silvergate Bank, which serviced cryptocurrency companies, had just been closed.

"There is a concern that at some point the regulators are going to clamp down on this whole area of fintechs, similar to how they're clamping down on crypto right now," Williams said. At the same time, she emphasized how important it was for OneUnited to have deposits, so it could lend that money out within the Black community. She said that 85 percent of its deposits were from Black people, but that 15 percent came from non-Black companies that deposited with OneUnited so that their funds would be loaned to the Black community.

Several people told us that fintechs may prove to be a setback for Black banking. "I kind of hate to hear that you took money out of a Black bank to put it into a majority-white-owned bank with no connections to the community other than being the holding bank for Greenwood," said Jay Bailey, a former member of the advisory board for a Black-owned bank in Atlanta, in a clear reference to Coastal Bank holding Greenwood's customer funds.

Another shortfall of Greenwood and other fintechs, in the eyes of many in Black banking, is their distance from the communities they serve. Throughout history, banks in Black communities have played important roles beyond holding deposits and lending money, according to Todd, the historian at Kansas City Federal Reserve Bank. As an example, Todd pointed to the 1920s Chicago banker Jesse Binga, who helped residents of the South Side neighborhood who were shut off from the world by having food brought in to them. In Memphis in the 1960s, Todd noted, Black-owned banks provided meeting space for Civil Rights organizers—even those arguing against the very premise of capitalism. In 2005, after Hurricane Katrina hit, Liberty Bank and Trust Company, a Black-owned bank, allowed residents to withdraw money during the flooding, without even having the systems running enough to know the exact balances on their accounts, he noted. "These are not purely financial institutions," Todd said. "They're really community institutions, and they're sort of serving that higher purpose."

Greenwood's customer relationships would not be made face-to-face, and its owners would not be community members who purchased shares out of a suitcase or otherwise. And in important ways, Greenwood would not be in charge of its customers' money. It would be a step removed from the real business of banking, something its customers may or may not have realized.

"If you ask many people, they would say that Greenwood is a Black-owned bank, and [with] some really young heavy hitters in Atlanta, they're changing the game," Bailey said. "But you know, they're . . . a marketing company. And they've done an incredible job in reaching a population that's been crying out for something different. And very quickly, they've amassed an incredible following."

He continued, arguing for transparency. "But if I pull my money out of Citizens Trust and deposit it with Greenwood," he said, "I'm depositing it into a white-owned community bank that we've never heard of in my community that has never stood up and defended or supported or invested in us.

"So," he said to Greenwood, "kudos to them."

CHAPTER 11

PUSHING FOR CHANGE, FROM THE INSIDE

What's the world for if you can't make it up the way you want it?

—Toni Morrison, *Jazz*

His star still rising, James Woodall was welcomed into a Georgia Chamber of Commerce meeting with quite the introduction. The host said that James was being described by respected politicians as "the most exciting Civil Rights leader I've seen in a generation."

James smiled in acknowledgment. He was there to answer questions from business leaders, and he proceeded to do so with ministerial patience. One question: What do you say to "white business leaders about how to engage and how to make a difference," especially if those leaders are "nervous . . . to say the wrong thing or say it the wrong way?"

"I would suggest two things," James replied. "One is: be genuine, be organic. Do not try to pander or say what feels right or respectable, because that's not necessary. Just be yourself. We are all human beings first. And I often say: 'If I can see the humanity in a person, I think God smiles down on that and is happy.' Because that is the goal of humanity—it's to be one with each other. That's community. 'Com—unity.'

"The second part I would suggest is," he continued, "if you have senior leadership, and the only African American you have, or the only person of color you have [in your organization] is the diversity and inclusion officer, then that's not diversity and inclusion, right? We want to have an inclusive environment across the board, from the lowest-level worker to senior executives."

At the time, the summer of 2020, companies across the nation were, by many accounts, working to develop environments that were more inclusive. That year and the following one saw a historic deluge of corporate pledges to diversity—likely even beating out the 1960s, when there were fewer international companies and when professional workforces were even less diverse.

The tide did not swell in a vacuum. Companies in all industries were experiencing immense pressure from their workforces, especially younger generations, to respond to calls for more racial equality at work. If the corporate pledges turned into real action, they could genuinely impact racial wealth gaps, given the important role that people's careers play in their ability to earn money and build wealth. "Diversity, equity, and inclusion," or DEI, was discussed not only as a matter of human rights, but also as an economic imperative. A Citigroup report that fall said that in the first twenty years of the 2000s, discriminatory practices against Black Americans had cost the U.S. gross domestic product $16 trillion, an amount nearly the size of the economy at that time. The report said that fixing the discrimination—in areas like access to loans and education—would create $5 trillion in new economic value within the next five years.

James Woodall, with his NAACP prominence and his youth, was viewed as a natural leader to speak about race and business. He was reform-minded, pushing the NAACP, a venerable but legacy organization, to evolve to meet the changed expectations about compensation and the empowerment of young workers—and pushing the corporate world, which was giving money to his branch of the NAACP as well as to the organization's national office, to diversify their teams. The moment of racial reckoning was one the NAACP and James Woodall did not want to miss. It was a chance to influence both the public and private sector nationally and to lead demonstrators in the streets. He was eager to bring his idealism to the organization and to the larger fights it was waging.

But by the summer of 2021, James had fallen out with the NAACP and resigned.

Corporate Pledges

James's journey with the NAACP began around 2013, when he was in college at Georgia Southern University in Statesboro, which was in an area near where Brook Bacon would begin his sixty-three-mile march for justice eight years later. James was nineteen and was continuing his service as an intelligence analyst with the U.S. Army Reserve. He was drawn by the prospect of organization building at the NAACP; the chapter at his school had not been active, and he rebuilt it. The day they held a gathering to restart the chapter, about one hundred students showed up, James told us. It was a day he'd never forget.

In 2015, James became president of the entire set of youth and college NAACP chapters in Georgia. By 2019, the state NAACP was in the midst of change after a series of short-term leaders, and James decided to run for president of the entire state organization. It was a bold move, as most leaders were decades older than he, and it was rare that a recent college graduate would even run. Still, he managed to get enough support by busing in college students to vote at the state conference. And at twenty-five, he became the youngest person ever elected to lead Georgia's NAACP. His opponent in the election, eighty-four-year-old Deane Bonner, a longtime leader in the state, told us she was excited by the outcome. "That's a smart young man," she said. "And when we talk about the future of the NAACP, he is the kind of person that should be leading." Bonner compared James Woodall to Kweisi Mfume, a charismatic politician who was the leader of the national NAACP from 1996 to 2004. "Put a mic in front of Kweisi, and he could talk and articulate and make us proud," she said. "That's how Woodall would be."

James immediately set about trying to change the way the state NAACP did business. First, he looked into how to professionalize the work. Outside the national office, the NAACP was run largely by unpaid officers. The entire annual budget for Georgia's chapter was sixty thousand dollars, he told us. State president roles—though they can demand full-time focus, especially in years like 2020—were unpaid volunteer roles. James felt people should be paid for their work, not only out of principle, but also out of necessity: they needed to eat. Otherwise, it might be difficult for people without strong economic means to become leaders in the NAACP. For an organization that was supposed to speak for Black Americans of all income levels, economic diversity in its leadership seemed important.

Moreover, James told us, being able to pay professional workers was the only way to attract the talent needed to "create a political machine that could actually get results for our communities." Others, like Deane Bonner, told us they agreed with him. And younger leaders, especially those who were not from elite backgrounds, agreed—working for free while pushing for a more equal world just didn't feel right. As Leslie Redmond, the Minneapolis branch president in 2020, told us, "I don't want to get money based on Black people being murdered. But, on the other side, I do have to pay my rent. I do have to live." She added that people who saw how much she worked in 2020 were "shocked" to know she worked for free. "White people were like, 'I cannot believe that you were working like that,'" she said. "I was funding myself. I would quit jobs in order to work for community—to work for the NAACP for free. That was costly."

As James began looking for ways to increase the state budget, a terrible killing took place in Georgia. Ahmaud Arbery was jogging in a neighborhood on the east coast of Georgia when three white men in the neighborhood chased him down, two of them armed. While the third filmed the encounter, one of the other two shot him. James soon became something of a national spokesperson on the Arbery case, calling it a racial injustice on television and radio and at demonstrations. Three months after that, George Floyd was killed.

Those deaths and the public outcry over them opened up conversations inside many workplaces. Employees—especially younger employees—began asking their bosses where the diversity was and whether the paths to the highest-paying jobs at their companies were inclusive. Workers questioned why so much diversity-focused work in their companies was being handled on a volunteer basis, upped the pressure on their bosses to remove leaders who had mishandled racial inclusion, and urged their companies to take a public stand for inclusivity and racial equity.

Black business leaders like Kenneth Frazier, the chief executive of Merck Pharmaceuticals, and Kenneth Chenault, the former chief executive of American Express, called for a modern-day Civil Rights overhaul of corporate policy. Those two men as well as Ginni Rometty, the white former chief executive of IBM, and several other business leaders pledged to create one million corporate jobs for Black Americans who had not gone to college. They backed a start-up called OneTen to create the jobs and were joined in the initiative by thirty-four other senior executives who helped fund it with one hundred million dollars. It was, they said, the best way for companies to respond to the killing of George Floyd. "Where corporate America can actually create value in this area or help the most is hiring," Frazier said. "We are the creators of wealth in this country." In addition to corporate America hiring more Black workers, there was a resurgent call for Black ownership of companies. It was in this climate that hundreds of thousands of people added their names to Greenwood's customer waiting list and that Ryan Glover and his team were able to go out and raise millions of dollars in funding to build Greenwood's platform.

The discussions in corporate America moved from hiring to politics and social change. When Georgia passed a new voting rights act to protect against what Republicans saw as a risk of voter fraud, Frazier, Chenault, and other Black executives rallied business leaders to speak out against it. "Corporations have to stand up. There is no middle ground," Chenault said. "This is about all Americans having the right to vote, but we need to recognize the special history of the denial of the right to vote for Black Americans, and we will not be silent."

For many decades, companies had tried to stay apolitical on policies that weren't directly tied to business, but that seemed to be changing. As Barron Witherspoon, a Black former executive at Procter and Gamble, told us, "Companies have political action committees because they want to advocate for issues that they feel are relevant to their business. A lot of times it's in tax policy. I think because there's already that precedent for those kinds of policy interventions and policy action, it's clearly an option for companies to think about doing that with respect to social policies." Specifically, Witherspoon said, "areas like education, access to education, employment, wealth generation—are areas where there is sound logic that corporations should get involved. The consumer is demanding change, yesterday. And the younger that customer base is, the least its tolerance is for inaction."

As Frazier of Merck said, business executives and corporations are "the creators of wealth in this country." Not only do corporations hire the vast majority of American workers, having a large impact on the public's well-being through their wage, work, and benefit policies, but publicly traded corporations themselves are also huge lockboxes of wealth.

And so, beyond the way that large companies affect the wealth gap through their workforces, they also affect the wealth gap through their ownership—specifically, the racial makeup in public stock holdings. The Black-white wealth gap is highly visible in the ownership of public companies. The entire U.S. stock market was worth about forty trillion dollars in the early 2020s. That's the stock market value of all companies that were publicly traded, and most of that value was owned by white Americans. While 60 percent of white households own stocks, only 31 percent of Black households do.

The lack of progress of the Black-white wealth gap following the 1980s, Princeton economist Ellora Derenoncourt and her team found, has been caused in part by the difference in stock investments by white Americans as compared to Black Americans. The stock market's major rise from the 1980s into the 2000s benefited people who owned stock in that period, and the Black-white stock ownership gap meant Black Americans missed out. In aggregate, as of the fall of 2019, white people (albeit, a small group of white people) owned 92.1 percent of public corporate holdings. Only 1.5 percent were owned by Black Americans. In dollar figures, this meant that white Americans owned $23.11 trillion in public companies while Black Americans owned just $0.38 trillion. These figures make it clear why so many people were enthusiastic about Greenwood and other Black founders starting companies in 2020. The hope was that companies like Greenwood would be public one day. Maybe companies like Greenwood would remain Black-owned and start to make a dent in the Black-white stock gap.

The gap in stock ownership also played a role in the uneven recovery of white and Black Americans from the 2008 financial crisis. Just five years later, in 2013, people in the top 10 percent of wealth in this country had higher amounts of wealth than they did in 2003. But for people in the bottom 90 percent, their net worth was lower in 2013 than it was in 2003. This was because the wealthiest households were more likely to have owned large stock portfolios, so they benefited as the stock market recovered. People with lower levels of wealth were not as likely to have stock to increase that wealth.

Further widening the gap, companies are treated differently from people in our legal system, benefiting from so-called corporate loopholes. Because white people own a greater value in the stock of companies than Black Americans, white Americans benefit more from these corporate loopholes. One example of corporate preference (and thus, white wealth preference) has been the ability of companies to isolate liabilities by setting up legal structures that separate some parts of the business from others. This practice serves an economic purpose, allowing a broader company to survive even as one unit runs into trouble. But because stock owners are on average more likely to be white, this can play a role in the wealth gap. That's especially so if the people who lose out from the troubled business unit are disproportionately nonwhite.

Another example where white Americans disproportionately benefit from stock ownership is the federal government's treatment of capital gains tax. That's the tax paid on income from stock appreciation or other assets that appreciate. These profits are taxed at a lower percentage than the income tax paid by high earners, allowing some wealthy people who make money largely through owning things to avoid paying much in taxes. In 2023, the U.S. Treasury Department published research showing the racial disparity in the use of the capital gains tax. The paper said that across all income levels, racial gaps "are particularly stark for the preferential rates for capital gains and dividends. White families generally are more likely to benefit from these preferential rates across the income distribution."

In general, the use of corporate structures to separate people from the actions of the companies they own benefits the rich more than the poor. This is common in real estate disputes where property owners hold property in LLCs. By running a real estate business through an LLC, the property owner is shielded from personal liability in any given dispute, such as injury on the property—whereas the average tenant or homebuyer is not hidden behind an LLC. This practice can be carried out by Black or white property owners and is more common among people with money. In one LLC example beyond real estate, Paul Judge, a Greenwood board member, set up a corporate structure, called Judge Holdings, to hire people to provide personal services. When a woman Judge had hired to help prepare tax returns finished the work, she asked for the payment as outlined in an email she had received from Judge's fiancée. Judge and his fiancée didn't pay her, she claimed. She sued them, and in the court reply, the couple said that *they* hadn't hired her. Judge Holdings had. This left the payment nebulously with the LLC, removed from the people involved. Judge is the Greenwood board member who likes the saying "Greed trumps race."

People who have studied the Black-white wealth gap have sometimes seized on stock ownership as a way to close the gap. One idea has been to give stock in companies in a major stock index to Black Americans as a form of reparations. Though this has not happened, many companies have made efforts to spread earnings through minority contracting programs, for example, purchasing products from companies owned by women or by nonwhite people. In the period of racial reckoning in 2020 and 2021, many companies increased their commitments to minority contracting.

Despite the inequities embedded in corporate America, reform seemed truly in the air the year after George Floyd was killed. This was evident in the hiring practices at large companies: in 2021, 94 percent of all people hired at eighty-eight of the nation's largest companies were people of color. It was the heyday of DEI programs—and it was likely the strongest opportunity in modern times to reform legacy organizations to be more inclusive.

As companies began changing their hiring, they also made donations to diversity-focused organizations. And during this time, one of the beneficiaries of these corporate pledges was the NAACP.

The NAACP Rakes It In

In 2020 and 2021, the NAACP, a nonprofit that subsists on donations and membership dues, was having strong fund-raising success. Some of the money was raised at the state level. For James Woodall, landing these funds in Georgia became the path to creating an organization that could effect the change he felt was needed in the state. The NAACP, as he saw it, was there not only for statements about justice, not only for demonstrations, but also to push for economic fairness and equal access to opportunities. The work was on the streets and in communities, but also in the halls of state and city governments, where he faced well-funded policy opponents. "We went to corporates, corporate sponsors," he said. "We used coalitions. We also had just peer-to-peer fund-raising. I mean, I think at one point we had reached ten thousand or eleven thousand individual donors. And that was because I was always in the media, I was always . . ." He paused. "I literally pimped myself for the NAACP," he said. "Let's just put it that way."

The money kept rolling in—the utility company Southern Company, the Sapelo Foundation, the Annie E. Casey Foundation. All told, $5 million was pledged to the Georgia NAACP, James told us (a lot more than the $60,000 annual budget he had inherited). That was a large share of the $29 million James said had been raised nationally by the NAACP empowerment programs in the aftermath of the killing of George Floyd and a fraction of the $50 *billion* that companies trying to prove their commitment to diversity and equality pledged to causes nationwide after Floyd's murder.

With all those new funds, James saw the opportunity to address problems he saw on the ground. One problem, he felt, was that many people at the NAACP were not paid; that included him. To make ends meet while volunteering full time for the NAACP back in 2020, James moved in with his grandparents and tried to spend very little money. With the unpredictability of racial justice demonstrations and of issues arising in court or in the statehouse, James felt he couldn't commit to another full-time job. He cobbled together some work as a consultant and speaker. The lack of income meant that during the summer of 2020, even as he marched for economic fairness for other people, James had negative net worth. He had about $1,200 in cash and about $68,000 in debt from student loans and medical costs. The total: -$66,800.

James's concerns over fair pay were similar to concerns within companies, where workers who pitched in on their company's diversity initiatives were not being compensated for doing so. Often, those workers were women or nonwhite people. As diversity discussions continued at companies, those workers were saying they should be paid for that labor, not only because it would be fairer to them, but also because it would demonstrate that the companies valued diversity.

James felt that the NAACP, of all organizations, should be a role model in compensating the people doing diversity work. That was the only way he could see its being able to hire talented people who didn't come from family money. He felt that the organization's leadership should itself include economic diversity.

Soon, new funds in hand, he had hired a small staff. He moved the organization out of a six-hundred-square-foot office and into one that was nineteen hundred square feet.

By the one-year anniversary of the killing of George Floyd, lots of money had come into the NAACP. James felt that too much of the money was being held nationally and not being deployed on the ground, where grassroots work could happen. He said of the tens of millions raised by the NAACP, he didn't see it coming to Georgia. Where did it go? "You tell me," James said.

The NAACP's national office, he said, was not an organization "of the people."

"Being the state president, I've gotten to see the beast from the inside out," he said. "When it came time for the cameras and all that kind of stuff, national officials were there. But when it came time to support these families, organize these communities, and actually build capacity and infrastructure, they were more of a barrier than a benefit."

James found that other state leaders shared some of his concerns.

In late 2020, he rallied presidents of several other states to sign a letter protesting the way the money was flowing. Their letter criticized numerous aspects of the national operation, including its implementation of new software systems. Most controversial was what he and the other state leaders said about the money. More money, they urged, should go to the local units. "The National Office has benefited from the summer of uprisings that have led to millions of dollars in investment in racial equity work, while the units on the ground who are the foundation of the NAACP's ability to fulfill that work should be supported in very real ways," their letter said, noting the lack of new funding opportunities for the local units who mobilized members regularly and whose presence had helped lead to the recent flood of donations.

"National," James told us in 2021, "is not doing its due diligence, nor is it being, you know, fair in the decision it makes when it comes to financial resources."

It was a bold move to send a letter like that to the national organization. Derrick Johnson, the NAACP's national president, called an emergency meeting with the presidents who wrote the letter and expressed displeasure, James told us. Danielle Sydnor, the former Cleveland chapter president, was also in attendance at that meeting and said it was "contentious" in part because it was younger leaders questioning the older generation. She said James's role in pushing the letter forward made him seem like a troublemaker. "It ruffled feathers," she said. "Anytime you have a group of people that kind of speak up against whatever the power structure is, people don't like that."

Tensions were rising between the national NAACP and local leaders like James. And then, those tensions seemed to be increasingly focusing specifically on James. We began hearing about them from people like Deane Bonner, James's former competitor in the race to be state chapter president. She did not want to get into internal NAACP business with us. Bonner simply said there were people in the organization who felt threatened by James's quick rise and the reforms he urged. "This pettiness," she told us.

The word was the tensions had to do with the multiple hats James wore as he represented the NAACP in the state capitol, but details were sparse. For James, all kinds of childhood memories were coming back—memories about justice, deliberation, fairness. He called his mentors in the organization and complained that there had been no investigation and no hearing. The allegations against him, he said, "weren't proven; nor were they true."

Feeling betrayed, James took matters into his own hands. He simply resigned. He had been a volunteer, after all, and he had not been suspended. "I told them, 'I'm going to just leave, and I dare you to try to suspend me. See what happens. Okay?'" he said. "So I forced their hand, and I knew I had public support."

It was May 2021, a year and a half since he became one of the youngest and most prominent leaders of the organization. "Serving as the state president of the Georgia NAACP has truly been the greatest honor of my life," James wrote in his resignation letter. "This is not a goodbye, as I am still forever a Gold-Life member of the NAACP," he added. "I still remain on the battlefield."

We asked the NAACP why it did not compensate local leaders like James Woodall for their labor, and the organization's communications officer said the NAACP "is a volunteer organization that relies on the dedication and commitment of members and advocates to advance our mission." The spokeswoman noted that units across the country operate independently and that it is up to a state's executive board whether to pay its leaders.

Often, many NAACP leaders told us, the decision was no pay. This approach raised questions about whether the organization was for the full Black community or more for the Black elite. Leslie Redmond, the NAACP leader in Minneapolis, said the stance on not paying local leaders was "disheartening." She said she loved the organization— "Anybody who's done anything great for Black liberation in America has passed the NAACP at one point or another," she noted—but she said that the organization was not thinking enough about leadership by non-elites. She noted that she and James were two of the younger leaders at the NAACP. They were both Millennials, she said, "but we're not Black *elite* Millennials. There are a lot of young Black Millennials that you see . . . they've been groomed for this."

Redmond said she knew that what she was saying was "controversial." Ultimately, she had quit her leadership role in the fall of 2020 because of the stress and the lack of pay. "It just was too much. It was like too much labor. I don't believe in free labor," she said.

A Rare Payout

One of the cases James Woodall worked on for the NAACP in 2020 was the police killing of Julian Lewis. James stood at the press conference beside Lewis's widow and at the burial alongside Lewis's son, Brook Bacon.

Something came from all this work. In March 2022, the Lewis family was awarded $4.8 million in damages from the state of Georgia. It was a "historic" amount in Georgia—the highest tort settlement ever paid by that state. The settlement amounted to an acknowledgment that a wrongful death had occurred. It was covered in the *New York Times*. "We will not rest until his killer is behind bars," Brook said at the time.

Life kept moving around Brook, and economic realities remained. Nearly a year after the settlement, he would be laid off from his job as a financial analyst. It had been a good job, one where he'd felt welcomed and supported while dealing with his father's death. He had been the only Black person in the small finance department there. But then the job was gone—again. It was his third time being laid off within a decade.

But this time, the layoff would feel different. He had money now, albeit money from a tragedy. Still, this meant he could take his time to decide whether to look for a new job or go back to school for an MBA. If he decided to pursue a business degree, he could do so *without taking on debt*. This was a far cry from the college freshman who was turned away at Northeastern University because he didn't have anyone to co-sign his loans.

After the multimillion-dollar settlement, Brook was openly saying that, even with a job loss, he was fortunate. Not only did he have the influx of money and a wife with a steady job, but he had broken away from his father's financial standing. Brook appreciated that he could collect unemployment benefits. That, in and of itself, was fortunate.

People like his father, who at the time of his death was self-employed as a contractor, weren't considered "unemployed" when there was a downturn—they simply didn't have any business. Only people who work enough hours and on an ongoing basis for employers that pay unemployment insurance can collect the benefits. In addition, among the people who receive unemployment, the payouts are paid in part based on past income—so Brook would get more per week than other low-paid workers.

He said he didn't think it should be this way and asked why the rising tide of government support couldn't "lift all boats" more equally. "You have to set a new high-water mark for everybody to, you know, kind of subsist at that point," he said. "I know there are people who are receiving a tenth, a fifth of what I'm getting. And that's systematic. That's all based on income."

Brook's newfound wealth was not infinite, but he felt it gave him a layer of protection. The first thing he did upon getting the settlement was give money to his grandmother and his two aunts; he also reimbursed his grandfather for his father's funeral expenses and gave a nest egg to his mother, Taneeta, who was now farming in Georgia.

Brook and his wife did not plan to move; their home was good enough, they felt. Pointing around his basement home office in a conversation with us, Brook showed us one improvement they had made with the money: they had fixed the ceiling to protect it from leaks.

Brook went on to hire a financial planner at Ameriprise Financial and create an estate plan. Asked about Black banking, he said maybe now was the time he could start depositing money in Black banks to support lending to Black families.

He set up his estate so that money would be passed to his two children. It meant they would have options when they were older, he said. "It's enough in order to make an impact on their lives on a go-forward basis. If they decide they want to do art or something in education, where it's underfunded, they can entertain that without thinking, *Oh, if I do that, I'm going to need three roommates.*"

Brook now had generational wealth, money that he and his children could carry with them.

CHAPTER 12

THE BLACK WALL

Is it not right and fair that we should make payment for the slaves?

—President Abraham Lincoln

As a child, Michael Render went on field trips to Georgia's state capitol. Those trips developed his "love affair with [Georgia's] political history and the political process." In 2017, he visited the capitol building to be honored by the senate for his work advocating for improvements to Atlanta's water system. "I don't ever want to cry for Atlanta like I've cried for places like Flint," he said. "Water is a right that people deserve. This is an equitable distribution of water."

While there, Michael took his wife to see a painting of a member of his family: Crawford W. Long.

It is difficult for many Black Americans to trace their ancestries. Enslaved people were not regularly listed in public records until the so-called slave schedules of 1850 and 1860, and at that time, they usually did not have a surname recorded. When records showed their surnames over the following decade, they were sometimes those of their former enslavers and sometimes not. Property records and marriage and death records often spelled names in multiple ways. In some places, the records have been lost. We talked with Michael about the challenges of knowing who your ancestors were. He said he often thought about novelist James Baldwin describing "how intertwined Americans are," and yet, he said, "we like to treat ourselves separately . . . There is a regular family out there that owned us." He paused to emphasize his point, then he added firmly, "I *do* know the provenance on my dad's mom's side. Crawford Long's family owned them. They are the Longs. My grandmother was Mary Vatie Long."

Crawford Long was famous for being the first doctor to administer ether to his patients before surgery, a procedure credited as the first form of modern anesthesia. He became one of two residents of Georgia depicted in the U.S. Capitol's Statuary Hall. And if the lore in Michael's family is true, the famous doctor's family tree may have a Black descendant branch that led all the way to the famous rapper.

Enslaved People and High Finance

The Michael Render who founded Greenwood Bank in 2020 was shaped by his family's long backstory tied to slavery. Likewise, the financial system he hoped to disrupt was shaped by the economics and mores of slavery, in ways that have far outlasted abolition.

Thus far in this book, we have followed the wealth gap beginning after the Civil War, because so many ways of telling the story begin then—with the large-scale postbellum decisions on how to recognize Black Americans as citizens; how to apportion property, credit, and all the monetary assets available to citizens under capitalism; and with that era marking the beginning of more reliable records for Black businesses, families, and individuals. Many accounts of what it means to be Black in this country begin with the condition of being enslaved. Yet, as foundational as that condition was, this orthodoxy in the historical narrative can lend itself to reductive understandings of the Black-white wealth gap, in which slavery is the only great sin to be rectified, rather than the first atrocity in a national history of exploitation, exclusion, and expropriation of Black Americans in all manner of contexts. This first atrocity went on for generations, and as it continued, much of the nation's financial culture, mores, and terms became established. Many of these mores remained etched in America long after abolition.

To trace these persistent financial mores and themes, you have to look at how the early American economy was yoked to race and money. It was a system built with economic return in mind, as England and other European colonizers came to the North American land to make a return. The colonies went to war with England in part because the settlers felt they were being asked to pay too much money in taxes; they felt they were being exploited. At the same time, the settlers wanted to expropriate more land from Native Americans, and Britain was blocking that. The colonists wanted England to extract less from them and to allow them to extract more from the Native Americans.

In 1776, Adam Smith, a Scottish economist, published *The Wealth of Nations*. In the book, Smith described "the invisible hand" that helps fuel economic growth and capitalism. The idea was that individuals' self-interest and desires to advance within the economy spurred people to make business choices that were good for the economy overall. The invisible hand would remain one of the most influential metaphors in economic history, but it ignored the externalities that can be created by people pursuing profit without regard to human rights. As Jonathan Levy wrote in his 2021 book *Ages of American Capitalism: A History of the United States*, beyond the invisible hand, the early American colonies depended on enslaved people and "rode their backs to commercial prosperity."

The Royal African Company, set up in 1672 by the rising king of England, fueled and ran much of the slave trade from West Africa to the British colonies. And so, the very American institution of slavery was also a very British institution. About 2.6 million Africans were brought to the American colonies by the British and enslaved. By the mid-eighteenth century, 80 percent of U.S. exports to Britain had been produced by enslaved people of African origin. "If commerce was a 'kind of warfare,'" Levy wrote, Britain's decision to pursue it "was tantamount to an act of continuous warfare against African and Afrodescendant people."

Black hands, or at least the fruits of Black labor, were far from invisible. In 1840, the labor of enslaved people fueled cotton that was worth 59 percent of the country's exports, as author Ta-Nehisi Coates has written. As of 1860, the eve of the Civil War, there were four million enslaved people in the United States. They had an estimated value of one thousand dollars per person, meaning they were "worth" four billion dollars. David Blight, a historian at Yale University, has said that enslaved people in the United States were "worth more than all [U.S.] railroads, more than all manufacturing, all other assets combined."

Slavery was becoming essential to the colonial economy just as landownership and the enclosure movement gained momentum in England. In that movement, the common land that communities had used for grazing animals was shifted to private ownership. Slavery and land economics had an idea in common: both were about creating assets that could be traded. The development of these tradeable assets, both land and people, was critical to the large-scale system of wealth building that would spread throughout the Western world. The ethics of treating human beings as commodities was embraced not only because of the free labor but also because trading people helped create broader markets and growth economies.

As the United States was formed, the Constitution further subordinated personhood to profit by declaring that people who were not free—the word *slave* was not used—should be counted as only three fifths of a person. This was intended for determining how much representation states would receive in Congress, but it may also have played a role establishing cultural norms for Black people that spread to business: financial products providers, like insurers, would long after count Black Americans as being less valuable than white people. On top of the partial recognition in the Constitution, enslaved people had no right to vote; only property-owning white males could do that.

And so it was that enslaved people were owned and traded and borrowed against. They were financial assets. Before the Civil War, Lloyd's of London was central in beginning the practice of pricing enslaved people's lives. As captured and sold Africans were carried across the Atlantic Ocean, shipmasters and maritime investors worried about losing their "cargo." They purchased insurance on enslaved people's lives from Lloyd's and other companies. (It wasn't the slaves' families who were paid upon a death, but rather the white "owners" of those enslaved people or the owner of the boat.) One concept invented during this period was "insurrection coverage." In addition to "mortality coverage," in case an enslaved person died from disease or an accident, white investors behind slave-shipping voyages could get coverage in case the enslaved people revolted. "Insurrection coverage," wrote Benjamin Wiggins in his insightful book *Calculating Race*, "recognized a different aspect of enslaved persons' humanity: their agency."

The pairing of mortality and also agency, baked into insurance, shows that from the start, white Europeans and white Americans viewed Black people as being both "at risk" and "a risk" themselves. This concept, as we describe it in chapter 6, would carry through to present day in both the justice system and the financial system.

Finance based on slavery expanded from the insurance industry to the banking sector in the 1800s. Many banks, including Citizens Bank and Canal Bank of Louisiana (both of which later merged into J.P. Morgan); Brown Brothers Harriman; the Bank of Charleston (now part of Wells Fargo); and the First Bank of the United States (the early fiscal bank for the federal government) regularly loaned money to Southerners, with enslaved people pledged as "collateral." The banks could seize these people if the plantation owners didn't pay back their loans. Banks liked enslaved people as collateral because, in the pre–Civil War economy, they were treated as assets that were easy to resell and move. (In recent years, JPMorgan Chase has acknowledged that its predecessors loaned money using at least 13,000 enslaved people as collateral.)

Bank loans based on enslaved people became one of the strong ties between the North and the South in fueling and prolonging slavery. Not unlike the thousands of subprime mortgages bundled and rebundled leading up to the financial crisis of 2008, enslaved people's lives were the collateral for loans that were bundled and rebundled and sold to the North and to Europe. *Securitization, leverage, hypothecation, collateral, collateralization*—these terms gained prominence leading up to the 2008 financial crisis, but they were also being thrown around in the 1830s, tied to loans backed by slavery.

An entire network of bankers and middlemen participated in the global slave trade, and they stood out as some of the wealthier people of the time. They were based in the North, the South, and overseas. West of Georgia, in Natchez, Mississippi, for instance, banker

Stephen Duncan connected large plantation owners like the Surget Shields family to New York banker Charles Leverich of the Bank of New York, Barings Bank in London, and the Rothschild family of London. Using Duncan's banking connections to borrow money from around the world, the Surget Shields family increased the number of enslaved people on their multiple plantations to 2,200, historian Edward Baptist has written. By 1860, when the government ran a census of enslaved people, Duncan himself would be recorded as one of the largest enslavers in the country, having purchased many of those enslaved people with debt (or been awarded them when borrowers did not repay money he loaned them).

These slavery-banking families are remembered in oral histories provided late in their lives by the people those families once enslaved as part of a Works Progress Administration project in the 1930s. As Charlie Davenport, a former enslaved person of the Surget Shields family, put it, his enslavers were "pretty devilish; for all dey was de riches' fam'ly in de lan'. Dey was de out-fightin'es', out-cussin'es', fastes' ridin', hardes' drinkin', out-spendin'es' folks I ever seen."

To consolidate borrowing, Duncan adopted a model created in Louisiana by the Consolidated Association of the Planters of Louisiana. That model was soon used in other states, including Arkansas and Florida. These systems of slave-based lending and slave-based securities became central to the new fortune of none other than the original Lehman Brothers in Alabama.

These lending systems weren't just private matters. Slavery-based loans contributed to booms and busts in early American history, with public funding consequences. In Florida, John Gamble of Union Bank worked through a northern broker to bundle slave-based loans into bonds and sell them to investors in London, including Barings Bank. When the 1837 cotton market panic hit and turned into a transatlantic financial crisis, plantation owners defaulted on their payments to Union Bank, and the collateral for those loans was often enslaved people. The bankers' bravado during this period sounds familiar to the sales pitches of the early 2000s, when bankers securitized mortgage loans into bonds and sold them to investors in the United States and Europe. The subprime loans, pushed in particular to Black American homeowners, were a favorite input to those bonds. In the 1830s, Gamble spoke about the Florida loans with hyperbole. "So great are her advantages of soil and climate," he said, "that the query is not 'what can Florida produce' but 'what production will yield the greatest profit with the least labor.'" The labor of course was carried out by enslaved people. This was an early example of bankers making risky bets and, in some cases, using Black Americans as the pawns.

The banking system was also important to James Render, who as of 1850 owned 1,900 acres of land in Meriwether County, Georgia, and enslaved seventy-six people. After the Civil War, forty-two of them stayed at the plantation and worked as contract laborers. We know the banking system mattered to the slave-owning Render because we found an original mortgage statement tied to the sale of one of his enslaved people. In other words, he was able to sell that person in a transaction in part because the sale was facilitated by a mortgage for which that enslaved person was collateral.

Michael Render's great-great-grandparents Dollie and Jim Render were still living near James Render's plantation in a rental house as late as 1900. That palatial plantation—along with a cook's house, a children's playhouse, guest quarters, and a jail—was sold in 2022 on a portion of the original land for $1.1 million.

During the 2020 demonstrations, Michael Render publicly called out the insurer Lloyd's of London. "Dear Lloyd's of London," a social media post he reposted read. "You've built your $56 billion empire on the backs of our ancestors."

"I stand in solidarity," he wrote.

Compensated Emancipation

The Black-white wealth gap was created in a time with strong sentiments among white people about the economics of slavery and the economics of ending it.

Let's go back to 1833, the year Crawford Long turned eighteen. That was also the year that Britain moved to outlaw slavery and the idea of "compensated emancipation" gained traction. This idea held that the people who owned slaves (rather than the enslaved people) should be compensated. When Britain outlawed slavery, the government compensated the former enslavers, taking on debt from the Rothschild family to do so; the British public paid this money back in installments up until 2015. Eight years earlier, in 1825, France had required Haiti to pay a hefty fine to former French enslavers as part of a deal for Haiti to gain independence. Haiti also borrowed money to pay this money back, and it took until 1947 for that nation to pay off the debt.

The logic behind compensated emancipation was that the owners should be made whole for losing "their property." It was thought to be enough for the formerly enslaved people to receive their freedom. This perversion drew on long-standing laws and on financial practices that labeled enslaved people as property and assets. With insurance, it had been the owners of enslaved people who got paid out when an enslaved person passed away. There was a through line in the laws and in the business world that informed the idea of compensated emancipation. Ideas beget ideas and persist in the culture of an economy.

In the United States, compensated emancipation had backers as prominent as President Abraham Lincoln. When Lincoln was a congressman in 1849, he created a plan for Congress to offer enslavers in Washington, D.C., a buyout of their enslaved people. The plan did not go through, but Lincoln pursued the idea again as president. In 1862, he got his way—Congress passed a law authorizing payouts to enslavers in the District of Columbia who freed the people they had enslaved. (Nearly one million dollars were paid out, or three hundred dollars per enslaved person. That money would be worth far more in today's values.)

Abolitionists before the Civil War warned about the troubling precedent that would be set with such compensation. "If compensation is to be given at all," the abolitionist William Lloyd Garrison said in 1833, "it should be given to the outraged and guiltless slaves, and not to those who have plundered and abused them."

Even ideas that are considered but not carried out can be integrated into economic culture. Did anyone stop to think who would pay if compensated emancipation occurred nationally? Would the United

States have been, like Britain, taking on debt to pay former enslavers, with American taxpayers (white and Black alike) paying that tax bill for generations? Think of the continued wealth transfer that would have occurred between future Black families and the enslavers' families. Think about how this *did* occur in Great Britain. Compensated emancipation embodied the flawed financialization of ethics.

Nonetheless, as the Civil War carried on, Lincoln continued to suggest payouts to enslavers. He offered them to Confederate states in an 1865 meeting with Alexander Stephens, the vice president of the Confederate States. It seemed to him a way to help end the war, inequity notwithstanding. Stephens declined the offer to compensate enslavers, and the South continued to fight.

Generations later, when Michael Render invoked history, he sometimes brought up Alexander Stephens. In his televised speech with Atlanta's mayor just after George Floyd was killed, Michael talked about one of Stephens's speeches:

> As I sit here in Georgia—home of Stephens—former vice president of the Confederacy—white men said that law, fundamental law, stated that whites were naturally the superior race. And the Confederacy was built on a cornerstone—it's called "The Cornerstone Speech"; look it up. The Cornerstone Speech [says] that Blacks would always be subordinate.

The Confederate leader had been Crawford Long's friend and former roommate at the University of Georgia. Stephens was also the other figure from Georgia, alongside Long, depicted in the U.S. Capitol's Statuary Hall. And so, given Michael's family's believed ties to Crawford Long, his references to Stephens are poignant references to a close friend of an ancestor.

Long, for his part, had his own views about enslavement. Like President Lincoln, Crawford Long supported compensated emancipation. He wrote that "the great body of slaves should gradually be emancipated under regulations that would be beneficial to them and equitable to their owners." He did not expand on that much in his writings, and so it is unclear why he felt that the owners who enslaved people needed to be treated fairly. But this early version of money-over-morals thinking would repeat itself throughout history, including when residents in places like the Bankhead neighborhood of Atlanta suggested that Black people shouldn't move in, for fear of its inflicting harm on their property values. The very essence of compensating enslavers bought into the idea that enslavers had rightful property in human beings and that human beings were in fact property. If one rejects the notion that people can be property, then one cannot agree to compensate someone for taking away property that never rightfully existed.

But Crawford Long tended to blend in with his surroundings and follow the norms. Historical papers show that he "considered slavery as God's method of civilizing the African, and felt deeply the responsibility of having slaves to control and influence." Long enslaved people as domestic help and regarded them with benevolence. One Long letter showed that he had concern for one of his enslaved people who was sick while he was traveling. Long, however, was not necessarily simply altruistic when he showed concern for an enslaved person who was sick. When people were viewed as property, money was often on the minds of their "owners."

Michael's possible ties to the famous Dr. Long trace back generations through a man named John Henry Long. His father's mother's family has stories passed down to them about their great-grandfather being enslaved by Dr. Long. At the time John Henry Long was born, in 1860, nearly half the residents of the county containing Athens, Georgia, were enslaved people. The 1860 slave schedule—a federal population document that listed enslaved people by sex and age but not by name—showed that Crawford Long enslaved sixteen people, including nine children and seven adults. Of those, six were women between the ages of sixteen and thirty-seven. One of those women could have been John's mother, Carolina Baldwin, but it's unclear. John's 1951 death record listed his mother, but no father.

A film made today about Crawford Long would have to contemplate how it could be that his family tree included only white children. Was the family lore among Michael Render's relatives wrong? Or was it that Crawford Long's children chose not to acknowledge the relationship with half-siblings who had been enslaved?

When Crawford Long died in 1878, he left behind his wife and several children. He had "financial success" in his life, a book written for his descendants noted: he had inherited property and had been able to recover from Civil War–related financial losses through his profitable drug business. These funds would become generational wealth for Long's *white* children, though they lived on for only one more generation. Just one of Crawford Long's white children went on to have children, and that line of the Longs died out in the 1950s.

John Henry Long, Crawford's possible "mulatto" son, eventually moved to North Carolina and lived to around one hundred. At the end of his life, he worked as a janitor in a white church.

"Please Let My Family Know"

We drove from Atlanta to Jefferson to meet Michael Render's relatives at the Crawford W. Long Museum. Though many Black Americans have not grown up with generational wealth, they have grown up with an inheritance of family stories. These narratives have not always been well represented in mainstream texts. For some, it's an important point of validation to have their stories heard.

Michael's great-aunt Jennifer Long Bridges and her daughter, Nikki, listened as the director of the museum filled them in on Dr. Long's official history. They passed by Long's original medical bag. They passed a prototype of the statue of Long that sits in the U.S. Capitol's Statuary Hall. And then they started talking about descendants. "We have tried to find descendants to invite them," said the museum director, Vicki Starnes, who is white, motioning to a family tree on a display board. "Like if you look over here. He had twelve children and out of the twelve—"

"Well," Long Bridges interjected. "He had more than twelve children, but he had twelve that was acknowledged."

Starnes quickly replied, "Yes, from Mary Caroline," referring to Crawford Long's white wife. "We've never been able to find a direct descendant of Crawford Long," Starnes added.

Long Bridges, standing over by a picture of Crawford Long, held up a photo of herself next to it, comparing the two and thinking of her great-grandfather, John Henry. "That is John Henry," she said of Crawford. "That's John Henry right there; it's his twin." She started to cry. "Something I'm feeling, honey, it won't let me go, it's moving in my spirit."

As the group passed by 1940 postage stamps featuring Crawford Long, Long Bridges shared a memory. She was a child, curled up on her grandfather Will's lap on the front porch of his Georgia country home. He was swaying, and the two were laughing, and she looked up at him, at his big blue eyes, and said, "You're not Black."

And her grandfather said, "Yes, I am a Black man."

Even on Long Bridges's father's deathbed, she added, he was still talking about the connection to the famous Dr. Long. "My dad would tell you that my great-great-granddad was Dr. Crawford W. Long," she said. "We were so proud of him being the first man to operate with ether."

Upstairs in a conference room, the group reviewed Crawford Long's slave schedule. There were women of childbearing age in the doctor's household when Long Bridges's great-grandfather John Henry was born. And they read through a chronology of all the places John Henry Long had lived that overlapped with Crawford Long. They looked at John Henry Long's death certificate and records in which he was described as "mulatto" with blue eyes. These were all the records that were available. The Long Bridges didn't have diaries or written records; what they had was oral history and their self-tested DNA, which showed Irish blood. (Crawford Long had Irish ancestors.)

The museum director had not heard of the "Black wall," so Long Bridges's daughter, Nikki, described to her the barriers in ancestry research that Black Americans hit when they try to go earlier than 1860. When people were enslaved, they were property, and they weren't often recorded with names. "When you hit [the Black wall], you hit it hard," Nikki said. It's something that had saddened her mother for years. Long Bridges started crying again. "Bless your heart. You deserve to cry," Nikki said.

Long Bridges stopped crying to make a point about sex and slavery. "You know, in the eighteen hundreds, slave owners were having sex with the women, so that's how that came about. When Crawford

Long had sex with her," she said, referring to Carolina Baldwin, "he wasn't going to tell. You just don't go around telling that back in the eighteen hundreds."

The museum director agreed. "It was a fact of life back then," she said.

It was time for Starnes, the museum director, to share. She opened a file folder and brought out emails and records for three other Black families who thought they were descendants of Crawford Long. None of the claims had been proved, she added, but perhaps the Long Bridges would like to reach out to them? One woman had emailed only a year earlier.

The words in the email from this possible relative were almost the same as the words from Long Bridges. "I'd like to meet my family from his side," the woman wrote in her email about Crawford Long. "Please let my family know."

CHAPTER 13

TWO ATLANTAS

[Politics is] really about who divides the money and whether or not you get your share.
—Atlanta mayor Andrew Young, commencement speech, Alabama State University, 1984

After her father died, Tandreia Dixon needed a fresh start. She wanted something more than rural North Carolina.

Atlanta was her answer. "Just to be able to be in a neighborhood where I could tell my kids, 'Yeah, your neighbor is a doctor or a pilot, and they're Black.' That's why I feel a purpose to be here," she told us. "To be able to go in a Hallmark store and not be followed."

The Black American Dream had strong ties to Atlanta. But for many people, it was more a dream than reality.

Until now, we've followed people in the Black middle class and above—upwardly mobile young professionals like Tandreia and Brook and the already wealthy founders of Greenwood Bank. James Woodall, though his debt burden placed him below the poverty line, was a college-educated public figure who moved in socially and financially elite circles. All were a generation (or less) removed from profound financial struggle, and the ground beneath them remained unstable, but as of 2020, they were not in the demographic most held back by the Black-white wealth gap and its consequences.

James Lovelace was.

Lovelace had the same dream as Tandreia, the same dream of so many Americans seeking security, stability, and the promise of generational wealth: homeownership. Up and down the income ladder, many Black residents in the Atlanta area wanted to own homes. Lovelace bought the same home in Southwest Atlanta two different times. He kept doubling down on a dream to make that house a place of his own. It wasn't so easy for him, we'd learn as we stood with him at the edge of a gas station parking lot, listening to blaring rap music while he cooked sausages and ribs on a giant smoker. Lovelace's earnings were under ten thousand dollars some years. He had been in and out of jail, was burdened with student loan debt for unfinished technical training, and was in a rent-to-own deal to gain the title to his home. In his early forties, he had a young daughter the same age as one of Louise's sons. He had hopes for the future.

Though Tandreia Dixon earned close to ten times Lovelace's income, stepping into homeownership was a struggle for her, too. The day we first met her in person, in 2021, she was just kicking off her housing search and lining up a meeting with an agent. Chatting over enchiladas at a Tex-Mex restaurant north of the city, Tandreia described living in her cousin's basement and pinching every penny to buy a place of her own. She was clear in her plan: buy a condo or a town house, get a thirty-year mortgage from Greenwood Bank, pay the loan off while living in the home, then move out and rent the place to provide a stream of income. A former colleague of hers had just purchased a place to rent out on Airbnb. "I'm saving right now, and I'm taking notes," Tandreia told us. "I'm willing to do the work and take my time and save and be disciplined, so that I can get that extra stream."

In both Tandreia and Lovelace, we saw steely determination to do what it would take to leap over the gap. In both, we also saw the constant struggle of trying to figure out exactly what would work for them to make that leap.

Atlanta was long ago anointed the Black Mecca for a reason: a strong middle and upper class of Black Americans had emerged there. But many felt that the middle was being squeezed, and the path to mobility was narrowing, as Atlanta became a city of two populations even within racial groups. While Tandreia and Lovelace scrambled to gain ground, Buckhead, the richest part of the city and home to both the Black and white elite, was attempting to split off and form its own separate government.

It was the "Atlanta Way" for the elite to work together regardless of race—or, as Greenwood Bank leaders liked to say, Atlanta was a place where greed trumps race. At first blush, "greed trumps race" seemed to mean that capitalism and a desire for economic growth could bring people together and that it could do so across racial lines. But to us, as we spent time in and around Atlanta from 2020 to 2023, the expression also seemed to have an additional, darker meaning. If money trumped race, did that mean that it trumped racial allegiances? Did money also trump morals? Did this sort of greed inevitably lead to divisions within racial groups? Was Atlanta the mecca for all Black residents or just for the people who had made it to the top? Data provided a partial answer—Black and white incomes had gotten closer for top earners by the 2020s, but this convergence had not occurred for middle- and lower-income levels. Did convergence at the top mean some people felt the problem was over? Were people forgetting that convergence of income is different from convergence of wealth?

We asked all these questions as we thought about Greenwood Bank and its stated mission to help close the Black-white wealth gap. Greenwood Bank's founders lived luxurious lives, some of them with large homes in Buckhead. Its customer base, we would find, was shaping up to resemble Tandreia Dixon and Brook Bacon: college-educated Black professionals. But a large part of the Black population in Atlanta was like James Lovelace, at the lowest end of the Black wealth spectrum—and these people were underbanked and under siege.

A Civil Rights Leader and Ambassador Turned Mayor

After four years as a U.S. congressman and two years as the U.S. ambassador to the United Nations, Andrew Young was elected Atlanta's mayor in 1981. Looking back on Andrew's term as mayor, his friend

John Hope Bryant, a business and nonprofit leader, framed it as a continuation of the Civil Rights Movement. "Really, the only sustainable growth example of the Civil Rights Movement in a capitalist world is Atlanta, and he made it," he told us. "So, the only real embodiment beyond the Civil Rights legislation where you have a commitment of morals *and* money—not morals *or* money—is Atlanta. And it was built by the only mayor trained by Dr. Martin Luther King Jr. So, I think that is a business plan for the nation and a model for the world: Atlanta."

What was that business plan? For Andrew, it was twofold: to grow the economic pie in Atlanta and to give Black Americans a bigger share.

One of the most important battles fought by Mayor Young and his predecessor, Maynard Jackson Jr., centered on city contracting. This effort was important for building the wealth of local Black businesspeople. It was kicked off by Jackson, who found when he took office in 1974 that only one tenth of 1 percent of city contracts were awarded to Black-owned businesses. Jackson prioritized awarding more to Black businesses, and that figure jumped to 38 percent by 1978. Many in the Atlanta business community were not comfortable with the shift. As Prentiss Yancey Jr., a Black lawyer, recalled, "This change at City Hall had a gut-wrenching effect on the business community. There was a tremendous amount of resentment early on." Some white businesspeople felt giving contracts to Black businesses was a form of discrimination against white people.

Companies were reluctant to provide the city with information on the race and gender of their employees, but Jackson set up an office of contract compliance and insisted on pertinent data. As we have seen through history, it's important to get a full picture of any company that says it is Black-owned or Black-led. Does it employ Black people? Does it pay those people fairly? Does it purchase its supplies from Black-owned companies? When data on these aspects of a business are not provided, it is difficult to assess the impact of that company on Black communities.

In Atlanta, construction of a new international airport became a prime opportunity to shift more business to Black-led firms, as did construction of the Underground Atlanta, a large shopping mall downtown. There was also money to be made in municipal bond issuance, which picked up nationwide in the 1970s and '80s, as cities took on more debt. A law partner of Jackson's, Bernard Parks, became the first Black lawyer listed in the national municipal bond book. When the city sent the bond paperwork for Parks to sign, he initially refused, because he felt that he was being asked for his signature with token involvement, rather than real involvement. Parks's son, Bernard Jr., explained to us that "he made them teach him the bond business, and he had to do some of the bond business, in order to sign. And that's how he was able to go to other municipalities and do bond work."

When Andrew Young took office as mayor in 1982, he kept a strong focus on minority contracting, viewing it as a policy to redress "past discrimination." In other words, the city's efforts to steer business to Black Americans was a form of reparations or, to look at it another way, of the same sort of favoritism that had long existed for other races. "African-American mayors did in Atlanta what Boston and New York City mayors did for the Irish," explained Michael Lomax, the long-time chief executive of the United Negro College Fund, which funds scholarships for Black students at Historically Black Colleges and Universities and other schools.

Andrew was fierce when a state court ruled that an Atlanta minority contracting program was not legal. He responded by halting all city contracts while pushing for the program to be reinstated. He didn't want Black firms to miss out on any opportunities. He also led the city to commission a 1,100-page study on public and private contracts to document that government intervention and quotas were needed. Otherwise, he thought, Black Americans would not get their share of business. "Discrimination in Atlanta's business sector is deeply rooted in the city's history," the report said. "The evidence for this conclusion is both qualitative and anecdotal."

In our conversations with Andrew, he highlighted minority contracting as one of the bright lights of his time as mayor. He talked about meeting with white businesspeople to convince them of the importance of including Black businesses in their dealings. "The thing that I understood about capitalism is," he said, "the pie gets bigger, and you get a bigger piece of the pie, when you let other people into the pie."

He said many people in business today still don't get that concept. "It really pains me that there are so many people in the business community who—how do I put it? They don't understand capitalism," he told us. "They think that in order for them to have more, the poor have to have less."

Andrew's message to us was one he had been delivering for years. As he left his mayoral office, he had said in a speech that "the most significant impact we've had in Atlanta is probably to get the business community to realize that white people can't be the only ones making money."

Andrew had a global vision of the money that could come to Atlanta's business community. Known for his tennis matches with the international dignitaries who visited him at the United Nations in the 1970s, he worked his ambassadorial network to bring business to Atlanta from around the world. With federal funding for cities cut in the 1980s, the mayor had extra impetus to find other ways to bring money into the city, and he has been credited with helping Atlanta become the leading city of the South. "I made this pitch about Atlanta—that it could only make it as an international city, right?" he told us. "There's not enough money in Washington. And there is money overseas, and I'd been at the UN, so I knew where the money was."

Andrew's salesmanship and international prowess brought in tens of billions of dollars, by some counts. And he was critical in helping Atlanta become the host of the Democratic National Convention in 1988 and, then, the 1996 Summer Olympics. Within Atlanta, Andrew was well liked by the white business community—in contrast to his predecessor, Jackson, who had not been as diplomatic or open to partnering with white business leaders as Andrew would be. Dating back to his congressional runs, Andrew had long had the support of prominent white families in Buckhead, like the Mims Cook family and the Loudermilk family, and he had the reputation for his strong white alliances. As another Civil Rights leader, Hosea Williams, once said about him, "Andy Young can do more with white people than an elephant can do with a peanut."

But as Andrew's tenure as mayor ended, the local white-run newspaper and many others in town concluded that, despite his success at bringing businesses to town, many Black Atlantans were not sharing enough of the buck. The *Atlanta Journal-Constitution*'s editorial board wrote that "During eight years as mayor, Andrew Young has been that rare commodity—an eternal optimist who delivers. He set audacious goals and achieved most of them." The article listed international investment, building the Underground Atlanta mall, and creating new jobs as examples. But, the piece said, "Mayor Young's critics don't dispute his accomplishments; they simply say they were purchased at too high a price. . . . The loudest criticism Mayor Young has heard concerns his alleged neglect of the needs of the city's poor."

Indeed, in 1989, Atlanta's poverty rate was the second highest in the country, and unemployment in many Black neighborhoods was three times as high as the citywide average. An editorial in the *Atlanta Journal-Constitution* said that many of the jobs created that decade were low paying. Williams, a Civil Rights leader with King in the 1960s and an Atlanta councilman in the 1980s, harshly criticized Andrew's record with poor Atlantans, saying the mayor focused more on good relations with white business leaders than on the city's poor people. "Mayor Young represents the middle class establishment, which is dominated by the rich white establishment," Williams said in 1988. On the city contracts awarded to Black businesses, Williams pointed out that a large share of the money in those contracts went only to a handful of firms—a point confirmed by the city's contracting office.

The pie was not helping enough people.

Andrew has reflected on all this since he was mayor. In a book he cowrote about Atlanta's economy, he argued that local public policy could do only so much to reduce poverty. He said that unemployment in Atlanta during his tenure was mainly driven by nationwide recessions. And he said that Atlanta's economic success attracted "poor people to Atlanta who had limited job skills." In interviews while he was mayor, Andrew blamed the federal government for cutting back national poverty programs.

Something that public policy might have addressed was housing inequity. While Andrew was mayor, redlining still existed in Atlanta, due to bank discrimination. In 1988, the *Atlanta Journal-Constitution* found in an investigation that Black residents were only one fifth as likely as white residents of the same income to receive mortgages to purchase homes. Income and home values did not explain the discrepancy: A white person with the same income as a Black person had a better chance at obtaining a mortgage. To make the injustice all the more galling, the newspaper's editorial board pointed out that Black people in Atlanta had their savings deposited with some of the very same banks that were not lending to them. "Dollars flow into banks in the form of deposits; and dollars flow back to the depositors in the form of wealth-creating loans," the editorial board wrote. "In white communities, the flow-back is $13 for every $100 deposited. In Black communities, it's just $9. Black communities are not asking for something for nothing when they ask banks to treat them equitably; they're asking only for fair reinvestment of the $765 million they have invested in the banks."

In the 1930s, the bank tellers at the Harlem branch of Chelsea Bank talked about how they accepted Black residents' deposits and then transferred all the money "downtown to the home office where it is loaned to white customers." As the Atlanta newspaper found, this was still happening in 1988.

Several leaders at the NAACP called for a boycott of Atlanta's banks. They also urged the city to withdraw its municipal deposits from banks that were not lending fairly to Black Americans. "If lending policies and practices do not change substantially," said Earl Shinhoster, the southeast regional director of the NAACP, then "economic withdrawal makes sense."

Wearing his mayoral hat, Andrew Young said the newspaper investigation had made a strong case that there was a problem and that banks would "probably" give a strong response. But he also said he thought banks were simply risk-averse about Atlanta as a whole and not just Black areas. After a real estate crash in the 1970s, "the banks lost a lot of their bullishness on Atlanta," Andrew said. "But they've made money hand over fist being conservative. The city's grown—almost despite them."

Still, the *Journal-Constitution*'s data compared Black Atlantans with white Atlantans and did find a gap. "I would hate to think we've slipped," Andrew told the newspaper. "It's the kind of thing you want to hope we've moved beyond. If there is serious redlining, it's not good for the city. It poisons the whole city."

Homeownership, of course, was only a part of the challenge. The city also needed affordable rentals. In the 1980s, Atlanta focused more on development of offices and hotels than on providing affordable housing. It didn't help that Andrew Young's housing chief, Robert Sumbry, had to step down when he was convicted of wrongdoing as a landlord. (Sumbry had forced low-income renters to pay extra rent, and he lied about it in government documents. He was sentenced to five years in prison.) When federal housing subsidies fell, cities like Chicago aggressively sought out other funding, but not Atlanta. This was particularly notable given that the mayor was well known for international fund-raising, which could have helped with the funding gap, but he did not do enough when it came to housing. This meant that Atlanta's homeless shelters were overflowing. City residents who did have rentals commonly lived in units that were dilapidated or without plumbing. The city estimated that 21,000 of Atlanta's 118,000 renter-occupied homes were in substandard condition. And the rent was expensive—many people in Atlanta paid more than 30 percent of their income for rent.

On the way out of office in 1989, Andrew admitted that housing was a problem. Early in his tenure, he had initiated a few programs to lend money to Black homeowners and had pushed other plans, including one to build thousands of units aimed at attracting white people to move to downtown Atlanta. But the City Council by and large did not pass his housing proposals. "I resent people saying that I haven't put any effort in it," he said. "The failure is not the failure of cities and states, it's the abandonment of a problem by the federal government."

In his final city address as mayor, Andrew was candid. "One of the areas where we've struggled—valiantly, I think, but nevertheless struggled—is in housing," he said. "We have to find affordable housing for all of our citizens."

By 2005, he said, roughly seventy thousand new units would be needed to house Atlanta's citizens.

"I Am Atlanta, Georgia"

In 2005, James Lovelace was walking through the Bankhead neighborhood in Northwest Atlanta when he saw a house for sale.

Lovelace had grown up visiting these streets: Chappell Road, Blyss Avenue, and Elbridge Drive. Bankhead was once a mainly white neighborhood that had changed to being mainly Black in the 1930s and '40s. Lovelace's mother and aunts had lived here as children, and his aunts and an uncle remained in two houses there throughout his childhood.

Now Lovelace was back in the neighborhood because he was seeing a woman who happened to live there. Tall, fit, and confident, it seemed he was emerging from a rocky period and several run-ins with the law. He wanted the stability that homeownership could seemingly bring. He remembered this neighborhood as a stable place, where someone could raise a family.

He didn't have the money to purchase the house outright and rejected the idea of going to a bank. Would a bank lend to someone who had been convicted of felonies? Someone charged with the intention of cocaine dealing, possession of marijuana, and domestic violence? Someone with student loans and no degree? Someone who had dropped out of high school in tenth grade? Someone without a stable job history or a good credit score? The system was not a system for him, he understood. With this home, though, the seller said that Lovelace could "rent to own." The seller would be the lender, and the title would not move hands, but Lovelace's rent would be considered payments on a loan to purchase the home. He signed on, becoming the owner of 547 Chappell Road NW.

The house, built in 1925, had four fireplaces, a den, and a living room. It sat up on a hill, behind a little stone wall, set off with a white front porch featuring three regal columns and a black gabled roof. From the porch, you could look down the hill at the rest of the block and feel a sense of space. Lovelace felt he had arrived.

"Renting to own" has come in and out of common practice in real estate, and it has generally been abusive to Black Americans and other people who are not well-off. It encourages people to believe they are buyers, while their loan paperwork does not provide them the same legal protections as ordinary homebuyers. If they miss a loan payment, the person who holds the title to the property often ends up acting like a landlord and evicting them, and anything the "buyer" has "invested" in their new home evaporates. In the 1960s, this practice was rampant in Chicago and led to mass organizing of Black homeowners seeking fairer deals. In recent times, it became popular in Detroit, where the number of homes sold in this way sometimes exceeded the number sold with traditional mortgages.

What Lovelace didn't know was that Paul Fleischer, the seller of his new home, also had a mortgage on the property. Each month that Lovelace made his rent-to-own payment, Fleischer was making a mortgage payment on it to a bank. Lovelace had been paying for about three years when he heard that Fleischer had stopped paying the mortgage. Lovelace was paying, but the bank wasn't being paid, and the bank initiated a foreclosure.

Lovelace didn't think he would be able to win a battle for the house. Never mind that as a standard provision of a rent-to-own contract, he was supposed to have an option to purchase it and that the bank would have a responsibility to honor that. Lovelace simply gave up all the money he had paid into the house and watched as the house he adored, the house he had been paying for, went through foreclosure. He moved to a rental around the corner to stay nearby.

It was 2007, and Atlanta was barreling toward the financial crisis that would come the next year. The city had gentrified rapidly during the economic boom of the 1990s and beyond. Lower-income housing had cratered with the demolition of about around forty public housing complexes, and whole neighborhoods were removed to make space for Olympics infrastructure and other development. In 1996, before the Olympics, the local county offered homeless people one-way bus tickets out of town if they promised not to come back.

Overall, city leaders were pushing to change who lived in Atlanta, following on Andrew Young's initiative from the 1980s to get more white people to live downtown. As consultants at McKinsey wrote in a report, the goal was to "get more middle-income people into the city." Georgia State University professor Dan Immergluck observed in his smart 2022 book, *Red Hot City*, that these efforts "focused strongly on attracting middle class in-movers and not on supporting and improving the lives, livelihoods, and economic mobility of existing, lower-income residents."

Lovelace was an existing lower-income resident, and descendant of longtime Atlanta families. As the house he had purchased went into foreclosure, he discovered plumbing and electrical problems in his nearby rental, so he then rented a room at another, nearby house, where an aunt of his had once lived. As a child Lovelace had constantly moved homes and apartments with his mother, a hotel cook. Stability for him had come in the form of visiting his grandmother and aunts, and he liked being back in their neighborhood.

The economic fallout from the 2008 financial crisis hit Atlanta hard. About 248,000 jobs—one in ten—were lost, and there were more than 250,000 foreclosures. Black Americans were hit harder than white Americans, once again. While the unemployment rate for white Americans rose to 9.2 percent in reaction to the crisis, the Black unemployment rate peaked at 16.8 percent. Again, we witnessed that, as a nation, when white Americans got a cold, Black Americans got pneumonia. Or, as Andrew Young said about the 2008 crisis, "We don't recover as well because we can't—we don't have access to capital." Not having access to capital in 2008 meant that many Black homeowners did not have the wealth or savings to ride out the price drops and wait for a turnaround. And when the economy was so weak and people were out of work, it was not often that Black families or Black-owned companies had the wealth to buy distressed properties and benefit as prices went up. Unemployment and job losses were highest among minority men who did not go to college. Lovelace had left high school in the tenth grade.

Through Taneeta Bacon's story in Boston, we saw the implosion of the housing market. But just as important to the wealth gap was what happened next, which involved a corporate takeover of much of the housing market. This could be seen clearly in James Lovelace's neighborhood, just northwest of the center of Atlanta.

On Lovelace's block in 2008, distressed buyers were popping up all over, ready to make a buck. Soon enough, a For Sale sign appeared outside Lovelace's old house. After being in foreclosure, the house had sold for $5,576 to a company called Stonecrest Investments, LLC, which was offering it as rent-to-own. Lovelace called the number on the For Sale sign.

By February 2009, he was once again the owner of 547 Chappell Road. Or was he? The title was held by Stonecrest Investments, a limited liability company. LLCs mask the identity of the owner and relieve the owner of liability. They are often used in high-end real estate purchases, and after the 2008 financial crisis, investment firms increasingly used LLCs to make purchases on the low end, turning inexpensive housing into a Wall Street bet. Atlanta was ground zero for this tactic, though it was common across the country.

The federal government also played a role. When banks closed during the financial crisis, the Federal Deposit Insurance Corporation often took over their loan books. These loans were highly concentrated in areas hit hardest by the housing collapse, areas with many minority homeowners. Across the country, the FDIC sold off foreclosed homes in bulk. In just a few days in 2009, for instance, the FDIC sold hundreds of homes in Atlanta to investment firms at low prices. These mass sales changed the character of many neighborhoods. "The city of Atlanta could have bought all of those properties," a resident told the *Atlanta Journal-Constitution* at the time, expressing a common concern that the sales were happening without local community groups being given the opportunity to purchase the homes. Instead they were sold to investors who planned to use many as rent-to-own properties.

The FDIC was not the only arm of the government selling off homes en masse. Fannie Mae and Freddie Mac sold many delinquent loans, putting the choice to foreclose into the hands of investors. In addition, scores of mortgage-backed securities—complex financial instruments that ballooned in use leading into the financial crisis—also sold off foreclosed homes.

In 2009, Lovelace's home was just one of many investments Stonecrest made. Bank of America also sold the firm a bundle of 150 homes it had foreclosed on in low-income neighborhoods. Based in San Jose, California, and in business since 1986, Stonecrest operated across the country. "There are huge opportunities out there for those who have cash and guts and foresight," Jon Freeman, Stonecrest's chief executive officer, said at the time.

From Lovelace's perspective, Stonecrest was a good partner. They worked with him, he said, when he couldn't make full payments, and treated him with respect, calling him "Mr. Lovelace," he noted. The firm's business model was making loans to people who were struggling. On its website, Stonecrest described these as "hard money loans," which they said were "for borrowers with less than traditional bank qualifications." When the firm listed homes for sale, it often offered financing to potential buyers. There had been foreclosure disputes between Stonecrest and some homeowners, but Lovelace was satisfied with the arrangement he had.

But we had questions. Given what came next in Lovelace's story, we wondered why Stonecrest put Lovelace in a sales deal in which Stonecrest's name remained on the title. The purchase agreement was issued with Lovelace's stepfather as the signer, standing in for Lovelace (though Lovelace was the occupant and the payer). If Stonecrest was selling the home to Lovelace or his stepfather, as the contract indicated, why didn't it transfer the title? Stonecrest was in business with many low-income people with limited financial opportunities, and the company allowed Lovelace to believe he owned a home without putting his name on it. The purchase contract said that the title of the property would be transferred down the line after "probationary" payments. According to Lovelace's legal filings, loan statements were regularly sent to him in his name, as he kept paying.

We also wondered how Stonecrest came up with the price for the house: $27,113.19. Lovelace and his stepfather agreed to purchase the house for that amount, but were they made aware that Stonecrest had just purchased it for $5,576? And how did Stonecrest determine that a 9 percent interest rate was appropriate? That was nearly two times the typical mortgage rate from that period for people who had good credit.

To Lovelace, his actions were that of an owner, not a renter. He put $500 down on the house and stepped in to pay the $610.83 in delinquent property taxes, as an owner would. His mortgage was set at $325 per month. Settling in, he invested in his house because he believed he owned it. He changed the windows, took out the carpeting, and rewired the whole place. "I loved the house," he told us. He loved it enough to purchase it twice.

Rocky times persisted. Between 2009 and 2011, Lovelace was arrested several times for offenses including battery and cocaine possession, with a few days in jail per arrest. In 2012, he was arrested for assault, battery, and false imprisonment and was incarcerated for a longer period, this time closer to nine months. While away, he allowed his younger sister and her boyfriend to use his home in exchange for making his loan payments, but they made only some of them.

As Lovelace was being released, a neighbor called to tell him the place was a mess: a broken window, problems with the electrical wiring. When he arrived at the house, he found even more damage: someone had stripped the wires of their copper, a valuable commodity in his neighborhood. Many Americans don't worry about someone breaking into their basement or attic to pull all the wires out, but those in low-income neighborhoods do. The power was gone, too. Lovelace called his electrician for help. The electrician felt bad for him and gave him a discount. Still, Lovelace, just recently incarcerated, where he had had no ability to earn money, had to pony up four thousand dollars. He was purchasing wires for a home he had already rewired in 2009. He did it again and again because this was his house.

Life improved from there. Lovelace largely stayed out of trouble with the police. In 2017, another child was born. Job prospects were slim due to his criminal record, but Lovelace started an ice-cream company out of a van he had purchased. The van was featured on a documentary to be shown on the BET Network. Lovelace felt proud. He painted some rooms in his house. He kept paying off his loan to Stonecrest—the money he was paying brought him closer each month to having full title to the home.

Around Lovelace's neighborhood, houses were flipping. The LLC trend in Atlanta was continuing with vigor. In many transactions, these buyers could bid and close a deal faster than individuals, because they came in with smooth discovery operations and all-cash offers. As the years passed, investment firms would end up purchasing a large amount of homes coming on the market in the Atlanta area, especially in Black communities. Even Lovelace's relatives' old homes became part of the trend. The home his great-aunt used to own on Elbridge would go through six LLC owners between 2006 and 2021.

Perhaps not surprisingly, in 2018, Lovelace heard from Stonecrest that they had sold his loan to another LLC. Wealth Creating Investments, a representative from Stonecrest told him, would keep the same terms on the loan, Lovelace told us.

With all the homes in his neighborhood thrown around like hot potatoes, Lovelace didn't worry about the sale at first. He had been told he'd have the same terms on what he viewed as a loan. But therein lay the problem: he believed he owned the house and that these corporate parties were his lenders, but these corporate parties actually held the title to the house. Was Lovelace a risky borrower or was he at risk of having his house stolen?

Wealth Creating Investments paid just $7,000 for the house. In retrospect, the whole thing was ludicrous. Lovelace had already invested on the order of $8,000 just for wiring the home twice. Then there were the new windows, the floors, the newly painted walls. His improvements went back to his first go-around with the house, such that from 2004 to 2018, he had both invested substantially in the house, and he had paid some of his loan back to Stonecrest. Yet no one was passing the title to him.

Upon the sale in 2018, it remained unclear whether Wealth Creating Investments owned 547 Chappell or if they owned the rights to a loan made to Lovelace. We called Stonecrest's CEO, Jon Freeman, to ask which one, and he said "both." "The contract is being sold, and yes, the property is being sold, too, but it goes along with the contract," Freeman said. "We were on the title of the property, so we sold the property, and along with the property came a land contract." Freeman seemed unruffled by most of our questions.

Why didn't Stonecrest allow Lovelace to purchase the home, instead of selling it to Wealth Creating Investments? Freeman's answer: Lovelace could have purchased the home any time under the terms of the contract.

Why did Stonecrest charge Lovelace high interest and put him into a rent-to-own contract? "At that time, there was no financing from the banks anymore; it was shut down," Freeman said, indicating that a rent-to-own deal was perhaps the only type of financing Lovelace could get in 2009.

And why would Stonecrest charge Lovelace on the order of $27,113 just weeks after paying $5,576 for the house itself? His answer: Stonecrest purchased Lovelace's house in a large batch of one hundred houses or so, and it had had only seventy-two hours to do due diligence. It took the risk that many of the houses were in bad condition, and in fact, many were, he said. Their low prices were due to the bulk purchase.

In all property sales, Freeman said, Stonecrest passed over "the whole file" to purchasers like Wealth Creating Investments. "They'd have to live up to the contract," he said.

As months passed, Lovelace's house kept getting new "owners," as numerous deed-related filings were made with the county. The filings were made by several companies, including I Buy Everything LLC and CSB Logistics LLC, and featured various statements of debt among the companies.

These real estate filings were far removed from Lovelace's day-to-day life. He had gotten a call that there were yet again new lenders, but he told us he wasn't given names for people behind the companies and started wondering if it was all legit. Then a man claiming to be the owner of Lovelace's home called and told him to start paying rent.

Lovelace, who believed that *he himself* was the owner, was taken aback. He replied that he wanted to see some proof of ownership, he told us. He paused his payments when nothing came. "At that point," he told us, "there wasn't nobody to pay."

Atlanta demographics, by this time, had shifted. At first blush, it seemed that economic conditions had improved for people in the city: The poverty rate had dropped from 24.7 percent in 1990 to 15.5 percent in 2019. But a closer look, as presented by Immergluck in his book *Red Hot City*, showed that the drop wasn't because life got better for the people who were living there in 1990. It was because the people living in Atlanta had changed. Gentrification had continued, especially after the recession during which longtime Black homeowners struggled to hold on to their homes. Atlanta went from being two-thirds Black in 1990 to a bit less than half Black in 2019. The goal, begun in Andrew Young's tenure, of getting more white people to live in the city had become a reality. As white people moved into Atlanta and Black people moved out, the percentage of residents with college degrees increased and the ratio of income levels of in-city residents compared to suburban residents increased. More Black Americans were living in areas far from downtown. These trends, Immergluck wrote, accelerated from 2012 to 2019, at least in part because of the turnover of homes—foreclosed homes went to new types of buyers. Atlanta had become a case study in change through demographics rather than in a lifting up of existing residents.

In 2019, though, Lovelace was still there. In comparison to people moving in around him, he was low-income. In 2018, according to his bankruptcy filing, he earned $5,000 the entire year. In 2019, he was earning about $1,680 a month, which put him on track to earn around $20,000 that year. For the state of Georgia at that time, the median income was $47,953 per year.

Then Covid-19 hit. In the spring of 2020, Lovelace was an essential worker, out amid the virus, delivering tires and other large items for Amazon. As with most of his past employment—given his arrest record—he worked as an independent contractor rather than on staff. He took the heaviest deliveries. He also took a job building a mask-making facility, exposing himself to Covid-19 for the sake of making Covid-19 masks. One day in between all these work shifts, while many Americans were sitting safely at home, he went to the top of a skyscraper downtown during work and took a selfie to post to Instagram. "I am Atlanta, Georgia," he wrote.

One of Lovelace's longtime passions was barbecue. He bought a huge smoker—it was the biggest either of us had ever seen. He wheeled it a block from his driveway, to a vacant lot next to the Exxon station on the corner. He quit Amazon and started his own business. BBQ Shawty, he called it. He bragged to us that he could make more on his smoker than he did at Amazon. When we reviewed his finances, the numbers did look good, as if this could be a real financial path forward for him. By 2022, he would earn $13,445.51 in profit over four months, putting him on track to earn $40,336 that year. Feeling more confident, he printed his last name, "Lovelace," in an art deco style on a pair of Converse sneakers and showed them off to friends.

Lovelace's life was most calm when he was with his daughter, who was five when we met him in 2021. He played with Spirit pony toys and colored with her. He showed her his old Spider-Man comic book collection he had kept since he was a child. "She is me," he said of his daughter. He arranged a good babysitting situation for her with the woman next door. "I'm trying," he wrote in one post with a photo of his daughter. In the photo, she sits tall in the pink toy car she rode around the neighborhood. "The Queen of Chappell Road," he called her.

There was, however, ongoing confusion about who was the king of 547 Chappell. It had been sixteen years since Lovelace first moved into the house, and he was in a fierce battle to stay there. The man who had called him claiming to own the house and demanding rent had not let up. That man, named Don Jacobs, took Lovelace to housing court and initiated eviction proceedings. Jacobs was treating him like a renter, and Lovelace was furious, his neck still tensing when he recounted the incident to us months later. "Like, I'm a tenant, and he the landlord, and I'm not paying rent," Lovelace said. "Right!"

The hearings ran high in tension between the two men, Lovelace said. Lovelace recalled to us that at one point he was so frustrated at a hearing that he yelled out to Jacobs, "Bro, you're playing with my life, and you ain't even right."

Lovelace started researching Jacobs. A former basketball player who subbed for a few teams, Jacobs had gone into real estate after he left the basketball court. The company he had built was called HouseJerk. On its website, HouseJerk explains that the company name "is not describing a type of 'person.' Instead it's actually referring to the accelerated action of learning to 'jerk,'" by which it means to "quickly buy and sell real estate with little or no money down." In the case of 547 Chappell Road, LLCs connected to Jacobs and his business partner had taken out short-term mortgages on the house: first for $70,897 and, later, for $101,000. Another LLC connected to Jacobs was approved for a $13,750 Paycheck Protection Program loan from the federal government in 2021.

"I'm always trying to figure out what makes money, man," Jacobs said on a podcast in 2015. "You know, what really makes the money." In 2007 and 2009, Jacobs had been arrested for identity fraud and deposit account fraud.

When we called him to talk about real estate and Lovelace, Jacobs was happy to pontificate. The pandemic and the summer of 2020, he said, were an opportunity to make some quick money. "Some people take advantage of it—devastation—and they win, and some people fold and crumble. And for the people that see devastation as opportunities, that's the best time to strike," he said.

By the summer of 2020, Lovelace and Jacobs were embroiled in multiple court proceedings. First was the eviction case that Jacobs had filed in housing court, claiming that Lovelace was only a tenant and not an owner. Then there was a Chapter 13 bankruptcy case in which Lovelace asserted that *he* was the owner of the house. Lovelace's pro bono lawyer had advised him to file for bankruptcy as a tactic to keep his house secure. By stating in bankruptcy court that he owned the house, he would protect it for the time being as his case played out. Lovelace had few options other than the bankruptcy process to try to keep his home.

It was an exhausting process. At one point, Lovelace got so fed up that he offered to walk away. "Give me thirty days, I'll find another house," he declared to his lawyer. Recounting this to us one morning before heading to his barbecue stand, he was so upset that he swayed back and forth, his nostrils flared, and the veins in his neck popped. Some of his front teeth were silver. A tattoo on the top of his chest glimmered in the sun. If he had decided to walk away, all his payments would have been lost, we noted.

"Everything," he agreed. "It would have been a disaster."

Meanwhile, property values in Bankhead were soaring. Microsoft announced that it would open a building there, a few minutes' walk from Lovelace's house. That would bring jobs, jobs would bring housing needs, and all the nearby property owners stood to make strong profits. Developers came in nearby with plans for high-end townhomes, some to be listed at seven hundred thousand dollars apiece.

In a court filing, Jacobs's business partner and the LLCs involved in the case said that it had not been disclosed to them that Lovelace had an interest in the home. In other words, they said Stonecrest did not share that information. In a phone call with us, Jacobs, in turn, insisted that he had been duped when he bought the property. "I had no idea that they had a land contract. . . . There's nothing recorded in court records."

We looked at every public property filing on 547 Chappell and did not see the rent-to-own agreement filed there while Stonecrest owned the property (it was filed later, in 2020, by Lovelace's lawyer, when Lovelace was battling for ownership). Still, it's often the case that rent-to-own contracts are not filed in public records. A key paper trail would be the private paper trail between Stonecrest and Wealth Creating Investments (the company that purchased the house), which we did not have access to. Freeman, Stonecrest's CEO, told us that his firm "disclosed everything we had on every property we sold." Freeman added that the party that bought 547 Chappell and claimed they didn't know about the rent-to-own deal seemed like they were just "trying to blame others."

For Lovelace, the gap between his financial situation and Jacobs's rubbed him the wrong way. He was particularly outraged, he told us, when Jacobs, who is also Black, called him "broke." Lovelace's perception was that Jacobs himself "had millions."

By the fall of 2021, we checked in with Lovelace's lawyer about the case. The lawyer, who got on the case while working at Atlanta Legal Aid, which provided free legal services, believed his client had a good case and that the LLC owners would not prevail. "They're going to lose," Darrius Woods, the lawyer, told us. "But we can never be one hundred percent confident with it. That's what I tell Mr. Lovelace."

In the meantime, Lovelace tried to keep a smile on while at his meat smoker. His customers arrived in vehicles as beaten up as his own thirty-year-old car. They sometimes bought meat for themselves, but often they were DoorDash drivers taking his food to another part of town. Lovelace worked most days from 1 p.m. to 3 a.m., standing next to the Exxon across the street from his house and five minutes from a park that was shut during the pandemic following the shooting of a seventeen-year-old by the public pool. When he went home, he spent time with his daughter. He also took care of an elderly homeless man who had been wandering the neighborhood, first making a couch available on his front porch and, later, moving the man into his home.

Standing with him at the smoker, we listened as he talked about how he was doing his best in life . . . and his best to hold out hope. "Darrius called me, letting me know that the judge is going to recognize my house," he said, mentioning his lawyer. But he also expressed his own doubts and fears. "I'm going through the Twilight Zone."

Rich Atlanta, Poor Atlanta

Seven miles north, a group of wealthy, mostly white residents of the richest part of Atlanta were getting together in meetings and parties to talk about breaking away from the city.

Warren and Kimberly Jolly held one such party at their historic home in Buckhead, known as the Arden house. Designed by a famous local architect, the house was built in 1917 by the son of an insurance executive who bought up four hundred surrounding acres and attracted others to the area. He was considered the creator of modern Buckhead. It was fitting, perhaps, that the Arden house was the setting for a meeting about the identity of their neighborhood. A ten-thousand-square-foot home with eight two-story-high columns guarding the grand façade, it sat across the street from the governor's mansion. Driving east past the Arden house, the first road you intersect is where Andrew Young's son, Bo, lived.

At the well-attended fund-raiser, which the group said raised $450,000, the man who would become the face of the secession movement, Bill White, said that the city was failing Buckhead. As he summed it up on Instagram, "the city of Atlanta has failed and exploited the residents and businesses of Buckhead for decades. It's over. We are official[ly] filing for divorce."

The history of what's inside and what's outside Atlanta goes back decades. Buckhead once was outside Atlanta's boundaries—until the public of Atlanta and of Buckhead voted to bring it within the city's limits in 1952. That vote came after years of efforts by the white mayor, William Hartsfield, to add more white voters into the city. As Hartsfield wrote in a private letter, it was about race. "The most important thing to remember, cannot be publicized in the press," he wrote. "Our Negro population is growing by leaps and bounds. They stay right in the city limits and grow by taking more white territory inside Atlanta. Our migration is good, white, home-owning citizens. With the Federal government insisting on political recognition of Negroes in local affairs, the time is not far distant when they will become a potent political force in Atlanta if our white citizens are just going to move out and give it to them." But to make the case to Buckhead residents, Hartsfield also made it about money. School taxes, sewer fixture taxes, private garbage, and water rates would all come down for them, he said. "The outside areas of Buckhead," he wrote, "will pay practically nothing to come in but in many cases make substantial savings."

Decades later, in 2008, a movement to leave Atlanta surfaced in the area but gained little traction. Then, Buckhead's connection to Atlanta came back into question in 2020. A group of residents began talking about forming a separatist movement, saying they were concerned about crime and safety. They hosted a secretive and anonymous Zoom gathering in early 2021, in which their cameras were turned off and their names were not provided. They asked attendees to give between $10,000 and $15,000 apiece to a "Buckhead City" exploration study.

Soon, a few of the members of the group, including local real estate agent Sam Lenaeus, were identified as backers, and a political operative was brought in to front the effort. That was White, who had recently moved to Buckhead. Previously, he had been president of the Intrepid Museum in New York City and years ago had been implicated in a pay-to-play scandal with one of New York State's public pension funds, though he was not criminally charged. Most of the backers of the secession effort and the money behind it would remain masked, however, especially to people who were not Buckhead insiders. We got a glimpse of the people behind the movement by examining fund-raising party photos to decipher name tags and by driving around Buckhead to find the occasional signs in people's yards and then researching who owned those homes.

In an interview with the *Atlanta Journal-Constitution* as the effort got going, White said the group planned to raise at least $1.5 million and use it on lobbyists to promote secession to state lawmakers and Buckhead residents. The goal was for the state to pass legislation allowing Buckhead residents to vote on whether to remain in Atlanta or create a new city of Buckhead. Given his backers, he said he had no worries about obtaining the lobbying funds. "I've been told many times by a lot of our significant donors who are 100 percent behind us that no matter what, we're gonna have all the money we need."

By that May, others in Buckhead were growing concerned that the group was gaining traction. Republican state lawmakers had introduced legislation to create the separate city, and White was making headlines and rolling in funding. Several businesses and local residents joined together to create the Committee for a United Atlanta, a Buckhead group working to block secession. Linda Klein, a white lawyer at Baker Donelson, formed the group because she felt it was important "to keep Atlanta united," she told us.

There were 90,000 residents in Buckhead, only 18 percent of the city's 496,000 residents. But Buckhead's businesses and residents occupied twenty-four square acres so valuable that its taxes represented 40 percent of Atlanta's property taxes. "Think about this: You're a bondholder for City of Atlanta debt, which is a lot. And forty percent of your collateral just marched out the door," Klein said. "What if you're a City of Atlanta pensioner, and nobody has thought through any of this? We're just told, 'Don't worry about it. We've got it covered.' Have we?"

Klein also pointed to the racial connotations of a secession movement in a majority-white enclave in what has long been a majority-Black city. "Buckhead," she added, "is seventy-eight percent white, and that should concern everyone. And it did certainly concern me."

James Woodall was blunter. "It's racist," he said of the secession movement.

The fact that 18 percent of Atlanta's residents (and the businesses around them) were paying 40 percent of the city's taxes was the wealth gap on display. The elite living in Buckhead included some Black residents, like Bo Young and Greenwood Bank cofounder Ryan Glover, and its proportion of Black residents was higher than in other wealthy neighborhoods in the United States—testament to the presence of an upper class of Black Americans in Atlanta. But that upper class, the Atlanta of Bo Young, Ryan, and their white neighbors, was far removed from the Atlanta of James Lovelace.

Bill White and his nameless Buckhead backers were determined to further separate the two Atlantas. In the fall of 2021, the two of us met with White to learn why some Buckhead residents wanted to leave. In an hour-long meeting outside a Starbucks in a Buckhead strip mall, White said that violence in Buckhead was out of control and that the police weren't doing their jobs. "Violent crime is through the roof here," he said, occasionally interrupting our conversation to direct people to move away from his car, parked nearby. There had been shootings at strip malls just like the one we were in, right there in Buckhead, he told us. Quickly pointing to a lump in his pants pocket, he added, as if we needed reassurance, "I have a gun in my pocket." Asked if he was serious, White, a showman and a marketer, nodded slowly. "You're safe here because of me," he told us. "Not because of you."

As much as White talked about the violence in Buckhead—and it was true that crime there had increased that year—we noticed that the conversation also kept coming back to something else: zoning. White said that people's fears of zoning changes was what actually had brought his initiative the most support. After the city released a plan that would allow for more condensed housing in parts of Buckhead, "there was an explosion." The outcry was broad-based, he said.

"This was by some very—just some normal, not-activist-side-either-way people, who are listening to both sides and are well respected," he said. "They were crazy against this because, I mean, just for somebody who owns a piece of property: you wouldn't redevelop your property and put two houses there, but the person across the street could. And what would that do to your property value? It would decimate it. Especially with what a developer could do. So, you might build, you know, two cute little houses, and you could get two cute little families, and you would still be maintaining a certain level of your property valuation. But if a developer comes in, it's rental units. They could get an abatement for low-income housing, and you can have a completely different demographic. Not saying anything about what's good about that. It's just about the property value—it would go in the toilet."

You can have a completely different demographic. It's just about the property value. In the early history of zoning in Atlanta, white neighborhoods had voted to keep Black Americans out. White owners had said decades ago that they didn't *mind* Black people per se; they just didn't want to lose money on their property. This money-over-morals thinking never seemed to go away in the United States. That very morning, we had been with James Lovelace, hearing about his rent-to-own struggles. Now the head of the Buckhead separatist movement was explaining to us how a group of wealthy people felt exploited by Atlanta.

After coffee with White and his gun, we went to the Whole Foods across the street. While shopping, Louise got sick in the middle of the store. Ebony quickly came to help her, and people in the store seemed confused. "Do you know her?" they asked. "She's my friend," Ebony said.

We weren't the only people feeling queasy after talking with Bill White. One Buckhead family had met with him early on and told him that his movement struck against the core values of Atlanta. Rodney Mims Cook Jr.'s family had been in Atlanta for generations. His wife's family dated back to a postbellum mayor of Atlanta, James W. English. And Mims Cook Jr.'s father, of the same name, was a business and political leader in the mid-1900s who ran for Congress (and lost to Andrew Young, who would become a lifelong friend). Mims Cook Jr.'s father stood out among white leaders when he introduced a resolution for the Peyton Wall to be torn down. That wall—more a wooden barrier across a road in Southwest Atlanta—erected by white mayor Ivan Allen Jr., was meant to dissuade Black Americans from moving into white neighborhoods after a Black doctor's move upset white residents there (who then threatened to burn down his house). The year was 1962. After months of demonstrations against the wall, a judge ordered the barrier torn down.

Mims Cook Jr. was a child at the time, but he would always remember the bombing and kidnapping threats his family received after his father spoke against the wall, he told us. But his father was not deterred. He was driven by an epiphany he had had as a soldier during World War II that he needed to return home and work to "fix race relations," his son said, and "make America post-racial."

In 2021, Mims Cook Jr. and his wife had a large property in Buckhead. The roughly 8.4-acre farm features a lavish, classical design, Mims Cook's signature style. Mims Cook had also redeveloped a nearby Buckhead property in the style of a European castle. Bill White came to see Mims Cook early in the secession movement, acting as if he would be a shoo-in to go along with the movement. "He thought I would be a rollover for his garbage," Mims Cook told us. "And it's bad for the city. It's bad for everything we stand for. It is not us. It is not the Atlanta Way."

The Atlanta Way circa the 1960s and '70s was a partnership between Black political leaders and generally white business leaders. That partnership, to some degree, was one between white Buckhead and the Black neighborhoods downtown and on the west side of Atlanta. And so, a secession of Buckhead would be symbolic as well as financial.

Buckhead wasn't the only place circa 2021 that had a secession movement under way. Elsewhere in the country, wealthy enclaves were trying to leave economically diverse cities. In Louisiana, Baton Rouge has been at risk of losing a wealthy neighborhood. In California, some residents of San Bernardino County were trying to split off to form a new state. Just in the Atlanta area, residents of three other majority-white areas—East Cobb, Vinings, and Lost Mountain—were trying to create new cities. In a twist, as some white communities have been incorporating their own cities (taking county tax revenue with them), some nearby Black communities have pushed to form their own cities. Some formed in recent years were Stonecrest and South Fulton, and one effort under way in 2021 was a majority-Black area, called Mableton.

Calls to leave Atlanta had initially surfaced in Buckhead in 2008, three years after a nearby area in the county created a new city called Sandy Springs. In the years following the creation of Sandy Springs, some half-dozen other neighborhoods in the nearby counties—DeKalb, Gwinnett, and Fulton—split off and made their own cities. This meant they pulled out some of the money they had been contributing to local budgets. In Fulton County, this amounted to an annual drop in revenue of $38 million by 2012. The new cities "have become mostly white islands of safety and affluence," wrote the *Atlanta Journal-Constitution* in 2015. "What's remaining is heavily Black [and] less well-off."

The mayor who led the push to annex Buckhead in 1952 had wanted to slow the growing prominence of Black voters. Sandy Springs was in the county at that time, and Atlanta's mayor also attempted to bring it into the city in the 1960s, but he was met with racist resistance. (Spokesmen for the Sandy Springs neighborhood said in the 1960s that they would "build up a city separate from Atlanta and your Negroes and forbid any Negroes to buy, or own, or live within our limits.") Sandy Springs remained in the county, but did not join the city of Atlanta.

The dollars and cents on secession are complicated. First, there is the precarious nature of municipal bond ratings, as cities like Atlanta depend not only on tax revenues but also on debt issued in the public markets. If something major were to happen to Atlanta's budget, like the secession of Buckhead, that would impair Atlanta's ability to pay off its outstanding bonds and would likely increase the rate of interest the city had to pay on its debt. For the Atlanta school system, secession could mean a funding drop of two hundred million dollars or more.

Buckhead residents might also face higher costs, at least in the short term, because of the transition to buy out their parks from Atlanta, to shift the setups of their water and sewage systems, and to create new departments, like the police. A plan from the movement showed it intended to pay its new chief of police one of the highest salaries in the country. It was also unclear whether Buckhead would face reasonable debt costs in the public bond market.

And to focus on crime: it was hard to know whether secession would lead to a drop in crime. It's not as if Buckhead would be transported farther away. It would still border the rest of Atlanta. Opponents of Buckhead's secession noted that crime was up in places like Sandy Springs, which had been made a new city in 2005. And, they noted, if Buckhead remained in Fulton County, crime in the new city would still be handled by the same "backlogged" county court system. A Buckhead separation "will disproportionately harm Black residents within the City of Atlanta and will not lead to improved public safety," James Woodall was telling people in the fall of 2021. "Violence doesn't recognize political boundaries."

In January 2022, the secession movement brought out supporters to speak at a press conference. "A thriving Buckhead is a thriving Atlanta," a woman named Leila Laniado said. "All we want is for our families to be safe—we spend all our time and energy just caring for your families."

Phillip Blow, a business owner, said, "The citizens here that call it home should have a right to protect it and have a right to voice their opinion and stand up for what's right." And a woman identified as Shanna Gikonyo-Waweru said, "Not only do we need to be able to vote on these things, but our voices are very important."

Blow and Gikonyo-Waweru were Black. In promotional videos on the movement's website, several Black people were shown flanking Bill White, and some appeared at pro-secession fund-raisers. One was a young former mayoral candidate named Devonta Sullivan. Sullivan was in his early twenties, and public records showed that his addresses were in South and West Atlanta. Another Black American promoting secession was a man named Myron Fountain. A new resident of Atlanta, Fountain ran a nonprofit aimed at helping at-risk youth. The Buckhead secession movement was a large funder of his nonprofit.

We called all these supporters of Buckhead's secession, and a few returned our calls. We found that some no longer supported secession (yet they were still featured on the movement's website). Blow told us he had changed his mind and that "to annex from the city of Atlanta is not the answer. I think the answer is to fix what is happening [with crime], to hire more police officers to be actively involved in that area." Blow, who is a developer, said the whole debate had made him realize how much of the nicest development had been centered in Buckhead. "In the city of Atlanta, downtown and south side of Atlanta, all the major malls and restaurants have been shut down. Like . . . Shannon Mall doesn't exist anymore. What's the closest mall from the south side to the north side? It's Lenox [Square]," he said, referring to the mall in Buckhead. "And so, now you have this part of the city that is like the mecca, and you have another part of the city that is deteriorating. . . . There's no hospital on the south side of Atlanta." The answer, in Blow's mind, was to redevelop neglected areas—and keep sharing the tax revenues with broader Atlanta. "Although I live in Buckhead, we are still part of the city of Atlanta," he said.

By February 2022, the secession movement had raised two million dollars in donations. Facing concerns that he himself was getting rich off the effort, White paused his consulting business and announced that he would be working for the movement entirely for free.

We wanted to see whether Bo Young's neighbors were supporting secession. In the summer of 2022, we drove around his neighborhood, known as Tuxedo Park. It was formed on land carved off over time from the Arden house property. It's an area of lavish homes. Driving around in it, it was hard not to think of Tom Wolfe's novel *A Man in Full*, whose fictitious neighborhood is based on Buckhead. The lawns there "rose up from the street like big green breasts," Wolfe wrote. One house down the street had its name written on a sign: "Nirvana."

There was no pro-secession sign in Bo Young's yard, though there was one for Raphael Warnock, who was up for reelection to the U.S. Senate. But three nearby neighbors prominently displayed pro-secession signs. One sign supporting secession was at a home owned by Lisa Loudermilk DeGolian, the daughter of a prominent business leader in Buckhead. Her father, Charlie Loudermilk, was a major supporter of Andrew Young's campaigns and a civic leader in Atlanta. DeGolian did not return our calls for comment. Her brother, Robin, was active in Buckhead business councils and had spoken out against secession.

Bo Young told us that Bill White was trying to drive "divisiveness" and "fears." It was something happening all over the country, he said: fearmongering over racial and sexual minorities' gaining more influence. "People are very gullible," Bo said, "and they're very afraid of all the change that's happening in the country and in the world. And they feel for some reason that they're losing their grip on dominance."

When Ebony spoke with Rodney Mims Cook Jr., it was two days before the secession effort was to be voted on in the state legislature, and it seemed as if it might have enough votes to pass. Mims Cook expressed disappointment with the state of racial progress in Atlanta and elsewhere. When talking about his lifelong friendship with Bo Young's family, he described living in the Plaza Hotel in New York City at the same time the Youngs lived in the Waldorf Astoria (when Andrew Young was the U.S. ambassador to the United Nations). Mims Cook said he still liked to tease Bo about their housing arrangements. "He and my daughter, both children of Atlanta, Georgia," he said, "both of these kids, one Black and one white, grew up in the two best hotels in Manhattan. And that to me is, I mean, that's not only the Atlanta Way. That's . . . that's . . . the American Way. And I think we're losing it, honestly. I think we're going backward and—" Mims Cook Jr. started to cry. "I feel we were so close to being post-racial, and we really were, and I don't know what happened. Something happened."

What had happened was that some Black Americans had moved up the wealth and income curves to some degree. People saw the break-through lifestyles of Black people like Bo Young and thought the problem had gone away, that we had reached a post-racial America. In some people's eyes, the *opportunity* for Black Americans to become wealthy had come to stand for the finish line in the quest for equality. The fact that there were wealthy Black people living in Buckhead (like Bo Young and Ryan Glover) was proof to some white residents there that all the past problems had been solved. Yet, the economic data clearly continued to show that the Black-white wealth gap had not closed and is not closed, at any income level.

At the same time as the secession movement, another group of Atlantans who believed that past inequities had not been adequately redressed was pushing for reparations. So, while the pro-secessionists were meeting in mansions in Buckhead, this other group of Atlanta residents was working to convince the commissioners of Fulton County to examine reparations for Black Americans. Among the people they felt might merit a payout were Black Americans who used to live in Buckhead and also descendants of people who had been forced to participate in convict work camps.

Karcheik Sims-Alvarado, the chair of the county's task force on reparations, told us the argument for reparations was, in the simplest terms, about governments at the local and federal level granting restitution to atone and help society move forward. "You've been damaged," she said about Black Americans. "You've been damaged. You need to be made whole."

The first case study for the Fulton County Reparations Task Force centered on the convict work camps used over a hundred years ago at the Chattahoochee Brick Company, on the northwest side of Atlanta.

The brick factory had forced jailed people, mostly Black, to undertake brutal labor. Many of these people subjected to "convict leasing" had been arrested on phony charges. It was Mims Cook Jr.'s in-laws' ancestor, an early mayor of Atlanta, who carried this out, building up a fortune that would benefit his descendants.

The second case study that the task force examined was set in Buckhead, in a neighborhood formerly known as Bagley Park. That case revolved around William Bagley, a farmer with sixty acres in Forsyth County who had fled his land when Black families were being attacked there. Bagley had moved to what would become Buckhead and set up shop as a grocer. It was a thriving Black community. Hundreds of Black people lived there by the early 1930s. However, white residents were moving closer. The Ku Klux Klan started coming to intimidate Black residents. Some white people in a nearby subdivision called Garden Hills didn't want to be near a Black community. In the 1930s, white residents and civic groups asked the county to do something about the "Negro section," referring to Bagley Park. The commissioners agreed to look into the situation. The next year, a civic group asked for the Black area to be condemned, pointing to shack-style homes and garbage. After numerous meetings, in 1944, the commission passed a measure to create a park in place of the neighborhood homes. It allocated fifty thousand dollars to compensate Black residents, who would need to move. That priced properties at far below market value. The Bagley family and other exiled Black Americans moved away. In an odd gesture, the county ended up naming the new park built over their community "Bagley Park."

This second case study about Bagley Park had a sad ending in the 1980s, when William Bagley's daughter and granddaughter were driving past the area and they saw that the Bagley Park sign was gone. The park had been renamed "Frankie Allen Park," after a local baseball umpire. The Bagley family was now fully erased from their old neighborhood. Bagley's daughter started to cry. No one had warned the family about the name change. "My mother was so upset, I thought she was going to die," said Elon Osby, the granddaughter of the grocer William Bagley. "She was just devastated," Osby told us. Her mother's tears would become evidence of wrongdoing for the Fulton County

Reparations Task Force when Elon Osby joined the task force's advisory board.

And so it was in Buckhead in 2021: some white residents saw the future of their city in creating new divisions through secession, while some Black Atlantans saw the future in healing old wounds. Two movements at the same time, secession and reparations, with neither side in dialogue with the other. As some Americans tried to remove themselves and their companies and neighborhoods from a more inclusive future, other Americans became more interested in reparations payments and efforts to lift up historically underserved communities.

These two movements on a national scale would increasingly pull apart coworkers, friends, and even families.

Leaving Atlanta

Tandreia wanted her own place more than anything, but she couldn't afford to move out of her cousin's home. Purchased for $350,000 in 2019, the redbrick house sat proudly in a comfortable suburban development located in Marietta, a town northwest of Atlanta, in a neighborhood that featured "Yard of the Month" awards and trivia nights. Though the neighborhood was near a former cotton factory, the Gone with the Wind Museum, and a Civil War Heritage Trail, it felt friendly to people of all races. A sign in front of one neighbor's house read "Racism Has No Home Here." Black children played in their driveways.

Tandreia moved in soon after her cousin purchased the home. She paid seven hundred dollars per month in rent to live in the basement, and she washed her clothes at a nearby coin laundry. She didn't have a comfortable place of her own to cook, so she ate carryout, often pushing her budget. "Please don't judge me," she said to us at the time, "but I'm spending a hundred fifty dollars some weeks on food. I know it's a lot."

It was all worth it to be in the Atlanta area, though. She met Pinky Cole at the Atlanta branch of Cole's restaurant, Slutty Vegan. She went to technology start-up talks held at TechSquare Labs, the tech incubator founded by Black venture capitalist Paul Judge (the Green-wood Bank board member and one of the attendees at Ryan Glover's safari birthday party). She saw the power and promise of being in the Black Mecca. And, important to her, she saw these Black leaders working—"I was able to see them grinding. This is not just TV. This is right here in Atlanta and they're hustling," she told us in the summer of 2021. "I feel a purpose to be here right now."

However, her timing was not ideal. She was trying to find her path to homeownership in Atlanta in arguably one of the worst periods. The huge inventory of houses purchased by investors after the 2008 finan-cial crisis remained in the hands of those investors, and many of those houses had been turned into rentals. This simply meant there was less housing available to purchase. As the *Atlanta Journal-Constitution* put it, Atlanta had come to offer the "American Dream for Rent."

The investor acquisition trend had, if anything, accelerated. By 2022, according to the *Journal-Constitution*'s excellent investigation, investors purchasing large batches owned close to 10 percent of single-family homes in the lower half of income levels in Atlanta neighborhoods. In nine census tracts, they owned 20 percent of all single-family homes. These investors were two times as likely to go after homes in Black neighborhoods, the *Journal-Constitution* found, than in white areas. They avoided wealthy areas. Who were these investors? Some were af-filiated with some of the largest players on Wall Street, like Blackstone, a publicly traded private equity firm. Other real estate investment firms were created in the years after the 2008 financial crisis occurred. One Goldman Sachs executive named Donald Mullen—who had been in-volved in shorting the housing market to help Goldman profit—left that bank and raised money to create a large fund to purchase homes whose values had collapsed in that crisis. Then his company, Pretium Partner's Progress Residential unit, became a large landlord, renting out homes.

Investment firms were sometimes subsidized by the U.S. govern-ment because government funds like Freddie Mac offered loans for bulk home purchasing at lower interest rates than those a typical indi-vidual homeowner could obtain.

What these years of investor-owned property added up to for people like Tandreia was a missed opportunity. Brian An, a professor at Georgia Tech University who has studied the Atlanta housing market, said that the influx of investors into the Atlanta market had deprived families of four billion dollars. That was wealth that families there could have accrued in the housing market if they, and not investors, had owned the homes. Instead, he said, the investment firms got that wealth. "When they have investor meetings, the CFOs brag 'our rate of return has really increased,'" An said. "So where does that money come from? That comes from those who have lost their homes, or those who cannot move in, and even those who have moved in as renters." Or, as the *Journal-Constitution* put it, "investment firms are extracting wealth where families normally build it: the single-family home."

This was particularly hitting first-time homebuyers, like Tandreia. And it was especially hitting Black Americans, leading to a 4.2 percent decline in Black homeownership from 2007 to 2016, according to the study at Georgia Tech. (Across all races in that period, the drop was just 1.4 percent.)

"Whether or not it is an intentional redlining that's occurring, it is disproportionately affecting Black and brown communities," Lorraine Cochran-Johnson, a commissioner in DeKalb County, told the *Journal-Constitution*. "There's just no denying it."

Tandreia looked around with a real estate agent in the summer of 2021. The prices kept climbing, and properties sold quickly. Feeling like she was wasting money renting, she made the tough decision to go back home and wait for when the market was better. "I'm just focusing on saving and working," she said, as she settled back into her childhood bedroom in rural North Carolina.

Outside her bedroom was the highway that led to the one stoplight in town. Cars covered the grass next to her mother's house, stored there by her uncle, who ran a local junk business. When an ambulance passed by, her mother would call their family members—so many lived nearby—to make sure everyone was all right. Tandreia couldn't hang out with her friends from high school; they did things she didn't approve of, she said.

Tandreia set up her computer in her mother's small living room, surrounded by houseplants. She checked her email for updates from

Greenwood Bank. She still wanted to get a mortgage from Greenwood, when the time was right. She was starting to get impatient. "I think they stand a chance of losing a lot of business," she said. "Especially with mortgages, now's the time.

"Now is the time."

CHAPTER 14

A WHOLE LOT OF MONEY

A life is not important except in the impact it has on other lives.
—Jackie Robinson, chairman, Freedom National Bank

As the fall of 2021 came, Greenwood Bank had around six hundred thousand people on its customer waiting list, but no actual products. "I'm one of those people," Ebony told Ryan Glover, the founder most involved in the company's ongoing operations. She noted that some customers were getting tired of waiting.

"Yeah, yeah," Ryan responded, chuckling. "Right now, since I met you and you're a friend-friend, I'm a move you up the waiting list."

The exchange was a friendly moment in the relationship we had built with the founders over more than two years as we followed their work and researched their lives and their ancestries. By the summer of 2021, as Greenwood's customers grew impatient, the founders continued to talk about their big mission. As Ryan told us in that conversation, he saw Michael Render, Andrew Young, and himself as "freedom fighters." As Ryan put it, "Our goal is to even the playing field to close the wealth gap in America through deploying capital."

Part of what he was doing while his team ran Greenwood's products was getting to know their customer base, he said, referring to the waiting list. He mentioned Pinky Cole, the fast-food restaurateur. "People will say, 'Oh, she's an amazing Black female CEO.' No, she is an amazing freaking CEO who happens to be a female and a minority," he told us. "Pinky Cole is somebody who I want to help turn into the next Ray Kroc."

Exactly how Greenwood Bank would help Cole, let alone undiscovered future entrepreneurs, seemed unclear, as did the bank's plans to serve regular people who just needed a decent place to deposit their paychecks and borrow money. Ryan's claims were sweeping. As he told us: "I want to help people have access to capital personally and professionally to reach their goals in their dreams. That's really what Greenwood is really all about, is playing Robin Hood for deserving people of color and allies to grow their dreams personally and professionally."

Pressed for specifics on *how* they would create financial equality, Ryan said, "We will have full-service banking in your hand. Apple and Android pay. Global ATM networks, two-day early pay, peer-to-peer transfers." With the fall of 2021 approaching, he promised that "we are launching a product this year—debit, spending, savings product—and will go into credit and lending and then investment in lifestyle products as well. It will be a full-service bank."

Generally speaking, the odds have been against success in start-ups. Financial websites estimate that 80 to 90 percent of all start-ups fail, typically between their second and fifth years. Some of the common reasons: the wrong team was running the start-up; the product didn't meet actual customer need or didn't have a path to making a profit; the start-up faced too much competition or did too little marketing; or the founders secured too little funding to get off the ground. With Greenwood Bank, initial customer interest was not a problem, nor was investor money. The other factors—customer follow-through, customers' ability to pay (thus developing a path to profit for Greenwood), competition from other financial platforms, and leadership—remained uncertain. Also unclear was whether the founders' definition of success was the same as their marketed goal, to change the world.

As we waited for Greenwood's products to be released, we researched some of the founders' past dealings to learn about their approach to business. One past investment that several worked on together was Bounce TV, a free, over-the-air broadcast network focused on programming for Black Americans. As the clock ticked and customers waited, we looked for patterns.

This Sh** Better Make a Whole Lot of Money

For Andrew Young, being involved in business was often tied at least in part to the moneymaking ambitions of his son, Bo.

Andrew Young III, as Bo was named at birth, spent many years trying to avoid riding his father's coattails. That may have been in part due to the difficult media attention he received while a freshman at Howard University, when he was stopped by the police and, he said, beaten up. Bo changed colleges, then later changed again, and did not graduate.

After leaving school, Bo started many enterprises. The first, a vitamin marketing company, was run out of his father's basement in Southwest Atlanta. Bo partnered on that with Martin Luther King III, the son of the Civil Rights leader, who was a generation older and who had long been a family friend. Next, King III introduced Bo to a banker at the Long Island Savings Bank, and Bo went to work there as a mortgage broker. Next, he and another friend of King's started a company that marketed products like the Versa Bath Seat, a device that helped people move from wheelchairs to bathtubs. Then, through another King introduction, he got involved in running an envelope company. That business appealed to Bo because, as he put it, "I like businesses that people don't know about. You know, I don't need attention. I don't need to be famous." Bo also went on to work with Give Locally, a for-profit crowdfunding platform, and started a financial literacy company that marketed help for people needing to repair their credit.

Like Bo, Ryan Glover went to Howard for college, where he made advantageous friendships with, among others, a young Sean "P. Diddy" Combs and Kasim Reed, an Atlanta native who would go on to become mayor. When Ryan moved to Atlanta in the 1990s, he got into the music business right around the same time as Killer Mike was emerging as an up-and-coming rapper. Ryan wasn't a rapper, but he brought business skills to the table and founded a record label to produce music. He mentored rappers who wanted to protect themselves financially as they entered music deals, including Killer Mike.

Ryan was well into his career when he got involved with Bounce TV. After Noontime Records, he ran a men's suit company and then worked at Turner Broadcasting. These were comfortable years for Ryan—in 2007, at the time of his divorce, he was earning $162,000 per year. At Turner, he worked for Mark Lazarus, a white television executive, and alongside another television manager named Jonathan Katz, who was also white. All three left Turner around 2011 and reunited for Bounce TV.

Bounce TV was a joint idea of Ryan's and Katz's, Lazarus told us. Other Black-focused networks were on cable, and they felt there was a market for a free broadcast network, he said. Lazarus soon left for a senior role at NBC, and Ryan and Katz stayed on to launch Bounce. They had ambitions to take on established networks like BET.

Bounce needed to raise money to get going. And that's where Bo Young came in. Ryan turned to his then-next-door neighbor Bernard Parks Jr. and asked him if he could help bring in some prominent Black Americans as cofounders. Parks had grown up in Atlanta in a family well connected to the city's elite. His father, Bernard Parks Sr., had been a lawyer who worked with the city in municipal bond deals and was a law partner with Maynard Jackson, the Black mayor who preceded Andrew Young. Through their families, Parks Jr. and Bo Young were so close that Parks was the godfather of Bo's daughter, and Bo was the executor of Parks's will.

At first, according to Bo, Bounce TV looked for cash investors. It was pitching a 20 percent stake in the company for five million dollars. Bo brought in two wealthy white businessmen: William Wachtel, a lawyer who had long worked with his family and the Kings, and Steven Kristel, another one of Bo's former business partners (who would go on to name a restaurant in New York City after Bo). Bounce TV's founders held a pitch session for these friends of Bo and also the prominent Black Atlanta builder Herman Russell and his son, Jerome. The pitch flopped: none of the investors there signed on. As Bo put it, Russell was "not a shy man at all, and he unequivocally told them that he didn't see how they could make a dime in this business and that he liked to invest in things that he could hold and touch."

Soon, Ryan told Bo he would be happy to have founders who made no cash investment, as long as they were prominent. Ryan was interested in Bo's father and in Martin Luther King III. Bo was uncertain whether Bounce would make money, but his father saw the opportunity as a public service, feeling that the Black community needed better content featuring Black Americans. "The thing that kept resonating with him was that it was African-American-based content that was free [whereas BET cost money to watch], and that meant something—that meant a lot to him," Bo said. "It was for him to be able to help underserved markets—[it] is what he has given his entire life to."

The Youngs signed on. Their individual motivations reveal how father and son differed. After all, they also lived on opposite sides of town—Andrew in the Southwest, in a modest house, and Bo in Buckhead. Ryan was so excited about the prominent new "founders," who would also be board members, that Bounce TV publicly announced the Andrew and King involvement without King having received his advisers' sign-off, which caused a short-term kerfuffle. King eventually signed on.

Records filed in a court dispute showed further tensions. Facing extreme financial pressures due to a high-cost mortgage on his home, King was at risk of foreclosure and was desperate for a way to get money out of Bounce TV, Bo testified in a dispute over dispersal of their ownership stakes. Bo also worried that King was trying to force him to handle funds in a way that would get them into trouble with tax authorities. He and another person involved in the deal told the court that King held his Bounce TV stake in an LLC controlled by Bo to avoid having to share profits with his siblings, who were all bound by King family rules over profit sharing from efforts tied to the family name.

The bitterness that emerged from the Bounce TV deal was striking. When Bo was asked in a deposition if King was the kind of person who might engage in tax evasion, he said "absolutely," describing "his entitled arrogance and sense of 'I'm better than everybody else in the world because my daddy was Martin Luther King.'" (King was dropped from the case midway through it; a representative for King did not provide comments for this book.)

Bo's relationship with his longtime friend Bernard Parks also soured over the course of Bounce TV. Because he had initially brought Bo to the table with Bounce, Parks felt that he should be receiving part of the ownership stake that went to the Youngs and to King. He ended up suing Bo, claiming that Bo had promised him part of the company for his services. In the end, the court ordered Bo to pay Parks five hundred thousand dollars. Bo told us the complaint got extra attention because of the prominence of his father.

There was also tension between Bo and Ryan, according to the suit. As the company launched, Bo kept the focus on financial returns and expressed concerns to Ryan along the way—at one point saying, "Everyone and there [sic] Mama are worrying the shit out of me," according to the records in the case. At another point, Bo wrote, "This Bounce shit better make a whole lot of money."

Ryan, in turn, accused Bo of thinking, "Man I don't have time to be involved in no stupid ass Black tv company!!!"

When asked about these messages, Bo said emails between friends were sometimes casual like that. We asked him what drove him as a businessperson, and he said it wasn't about building up wealth to have lots of possessions. "For me, it's more for the free time. I mean, I want to make money so that I can have more free time, not so that I can have more stuff," he said. "For me to be able to pick my kids up from school and be at every soccer practice and every baseball game, every tennis match. That's what I care about." In court, he defended his business contributions, saying he had held meetings to pursue revenue opportunities outside television—for instance, with Bounce-branded internet, cell phones, prepaid debit cards, or insurance. In particular, he said he held meetings with MetaBank, the large prepaid card company, which was famous for the RushCard. (MetaBank would later invest in Greenwood.) Ultimately, Bo's deals didn't go anywhere, he said, because Ryan Glover was moving to sell the company.

Despite Bo's efforts, when Ryan was asked in court whether Bo Young had brought any business opportunities or investors to Bounce, he said not that he recalled. Bo Young "was my contact with his father when I needed Ambassador to perform a service," Ryan said.

Andrew Young had stepped off Bounce's board a few years after the company was launched, replaced by Bo, who had been a board adviser. As Bo explained, "It became apparent that I was pretty much making all the decisions."

Whatever the true division of power within Bounce, one strategy for success won out. In 2017, Bounce TV was sold as part of a $292 million deal to Scripps. The founders struck it rich: Andrew Young, Martin Luther King III, and Bo Young received $15.9 million, shared equally. A year later, when Bo was deposed in court about the deal, he said that he was holding his father's money in an investment account; the ambassador's money was being held in his son's name. "It is just sitting there earning interest?" the lawyer asked. "Yes," Bo said. And would it be paid to the ambassador, the lawyer asked. "If he asks for it," Bo said. And has he asked for it yet? "No," Bo said.

Ryan Glover, as cofounder of Bounce TV, made an even larger sum of money, but there were numerous other investors. In addition to Jonathan Katz, the white cofounder, there were nine other investors listed in the sales document. They included prominent Black entertainment figures, such as movie producers Will Packer and Rob Hardy and boxing manager Alan Haymon, and at least five white investors. Bounce's commitment to Black ownership seemed tepid. At one point, Ryan was asked in court if it was important that Bounce be minority-owned, and he said minority ownership "wasn't detrimental." When asked if he had had Bounce certified as minority-owned, Ryan said he had done that, but he could not remember which agency certified it.

Bounce TV was ultimately considered a success because it sold for a significant amount of money, delivering a good return to its investors. And there were other reasons to respect what Bounce had achieved. As we were carrying out our reporting on this in 2022, another Black-focused television network, the Black News Channel, founded in 2020, filed for bankruptcy. That was the network that featured *New York Times* columnist Charles Blow as a host after he called for a reverse migration to Atlanta. Clearly, it was no small feat to create a new network and successfully sell it, as Bounce had done. In addition, Bounce was successful in terms of its stated goal to create more Black-focused content. And from the standpoint of the Black-white wealth gap (which Bounce TV did not promise to address), it did make a few Black citizens of Atlanta wealthier.

No matter that Bounce was cofounded by white and Black Americans and sold to a company that was controlled and majority owned by white people. At least to Bo Young, what mattered was that money landed in the hands of Black Americans. "For me, there's no value in whether or not a company is majority Black," Bo Young told us, "as long as a bunch of Black people make money from it. And in most cases, it's almost better if it's not 'Black-owned,' because it makes it much harder to sell."

He pointed out that Black Americans have only so much wealth and that limiting people who could invest in Greenwood Bank to Black Americans would limit Greenwood's owners' upside. "People get caught in a lot of these things that have sentimental or ceremonial value," he said. "But when you look at the reality, like how many Black people got rich from it?—that's all that matters to me."

Had Bounce not been lucratively sold so quickly, it was likely that the founders would have also created a Bounce Bank, to complement the television network, Andrew Young told us. Their interest in banking had roots running back to Bounce, he said. But Greenwood's stated goals were different and more socially ambitious than those of Bounce. As time passed, and as Greenwood continued to take on new investors, we were wondering whether it remained majority-Black-owned, and at every turn, bank leaders declined to say. "I'm not at liberty to discuss that," Lynn Cherry, Greenwood's chief risk officer, told us. "Our founders are Black. Ownership takes on a different meaning because of the investments that we have. And so, unfortunately, I cannot answer that."

Outsourcing

As 2021 progressed, Greenwood was severely behind schedule in building its mobile app and website. Its customer waiting list had grown into the hundreds of thousands, and the company's leaders were concerned that they were going to miss their moment in the market if their technology wasn't built faster. So, they went looking for help.

They found it with a large technology outsourcing firm called

Robots & Pencils. Of Robots & Pencils' eighteen leaders, sixteen were white. (One, the head of quality assurance, was Black. And the head of talent was a woman of color.) The majority of engineers at Robots & Pencils were white.

In the wake of the racial reckoning of 2020, one of the metrics on which diversity advocates had been focusing when evaluating companies' commitments to diversity was the supply chain. Diversity advocates noted that lots of companies outsource parts of their businesses and buy supplies from outside companies. The racial makeup of these suppliers plays a role in who benefits financially from a company's business. Many Greenwood customers we spoke with told us they hoped their business with Greenwood was funding jobs for Black workers.

Robots & Pencils's chief executive officer, Tracey Zimmerman, told us her company did not have diversity metrics. "It's not something that we measure ourselves on," she said. "We're not that mature, we're not that big, we're not that formal."

As Robots & Pencils wrapped up its work for the bank, Greenwood began hiring Black engineers again. One new hire in the fall of 2021 was Umar Sayyad, a twenty-five-year-old software engineer. Sayyad was passionate about being a part of a Black-focused economy. He had personal ties to the idea. His father had moved to Sparta, Georgia, to run a Black community there that sold land only to Black Americans and had all businesses and services run and staffed by Black Americans. He wanted to emulate the ideals of his father. "It's Black banking," Umar Sayyad told us. "I'm a southern guy, born and raised in Atlanta, Georgia. So, having people look out for people who look like me sounds great. I felt like that's something that I can really put my skills into."

Soon after Sayyad started there, he began to think Greenwood was a mirage. Not only was the banking provided by white-run Coastal Bank, but the technology, it turned out, had also been built almost entirely by a white firm. "This is a company specifically targeting Black and Latinx people, but the people who are predominantly working on it were white," Sayyad told us. "Let's say you want to build the home, right? Now, you propose that home to be Black-built, right? But the people who built—the *agency* who built it are all white. You're giving your Black dollar to a white agency to build a Black home. Is it really, honestly a Black-owned home? It may be Black-owned, but is it for Black people and helping the Black community if you are circulating your dollar somewhere else?"

Greenwood's marketing claims still get Sayyad animated. "Once everyone hears from Killer Mike's podcast and everyone else how they're talking—'circulating the Black dollar, circulating the Black dollar' . . . No. We're not. It's nothing but a white bank."

The Exit Strategy

Sometimes the end of a story is tied to the start, and Ryan Glover's start on Greenwood dated back to his safari birthday party. There, he plotted, planned, and strategized Greenwood Bank with a technology executive named Paul Judge.

Judge, a Greenwood board member, was the wealthiest of the people involved in setting up Greenwood, one of the other founders would tell us. Not only had he sold an email security company for close to three hundred million dollars in 2006, but he also sold a web security company in 2009 and he owned the rights to a number of patents.

Though not as nationally famous as the other founders, Judge was a thought leader in the Atlanta technology scene, hosting *Shark Tank*-style investment meetups. He often shared his views on start-ups publicly. In terms of company exits—the occasion when a company's founders cash out on their work—Judge had said he learned some lessons after selling his company for three hundred million dollars. Soon, he saw a similar competitor sell for *eight* hundred million. It made him think, *How do you optimize the outcome?* In particular, he said, he wanted to know how to determine "Do you exit at a one-time multiple or a ten-time multiple?"

Greenwood's eventual "exit" could be a sale to a bigger company or an initial offering to go public. Or the founders could run the company for the long term and end up being paid out in profits over time.

Multiple investors told us that it was *not* likely Greenwood would be sold, at least not to a big bank. And their rationale was highly revealing: a large part of Greenwood's revenues, they said, were based on the interchange fees charged to merchants with each debit card swipe. Greenwood—like other fintech companies—was able to benefit from higher interchange fees than big national banks because it was partnered with a community bank (Coastal Bank). Years ago, in 2010, the federal government imposed limits on merchant fees charged by big banks, but the government exempted small banks—including many community banks—from the rule.

Fintech companies like Greenwood partnered with community banks specifically so they could share in these higher merchant fees. If Greenwood were sold to a large bank, it would no longer be able to charge those higher fees. That's why, investors told us, bluntly, the financial backers of Greenwood wouldn't be interested in selling Greenwood to a big bank.

The rubber had hit the road: Greenwood Bank, with all its focus on Buy Black and recirculating the dollar in the Black community, worked within a business model based on higher fees on merchants than those charged by big banks. In other words, when Greenwood customers decided to buy Black, if they used fintech debit cards (like Greenwood cards) to shop, the Black business owner would pay a hefty surcharge. Those Greenwood customers who were "recirculating the Black dollar" could bestow more dollars on Black businesses if they used a large bank's debit card.

In 2022, Ryan Glover updated us that Greenwood was going well, but he said that the Black community needed a lot of education on banking. He noted that many Black Americans, including him, simply didn't trust banks. He pointed out that when he built his home in the ritzy Buckhead neighborhood, it didn't occur to him to get financing. "And if I am in the position that I mistrust banks, certainly others who are not of my financing ilk think the same way."

But holding money in cash, he said, was not the way to build wealth. Greenwood, he said, could teach people to build wealth. We asked if he was thinking of Greenwood as a banking services company or as an education company, and he said, "Both." Then he interjected, "So, just so we're clear, I built Greenwood not as a charity in any way, shape, or form. I built Greenwood to make money."

CHAPTER 15

THE CUSTOMERS

The United States of America has had the world's largest economy for most of our history, with enough money to feed and educate all our children, build world-leading infrastructure, and generally ensure a high standard of living for everyone. But we don't.

—Heather McGhee, author of *The Sum of Us: What Racism Costs Everyone and How We Can Prosper Together*

It was April 1, 2022, and Tandreia Dixon finally made it off the Greenwood Bank waiting list. She was still working remotely out of her mother's modest home in the one-stoplight North Carolina town. She had worked and saved, worked and saved. Her plan was to save enough to go back to Atlanta and make another try at purchasing a home.

Feeling excited, Tandreia opened the Greenwood email. "'The wait is over. Apply for your account now,'" she read aloud. She clicked in, entered her name and other personal information, and then . . .

A slate of legal agreements and disclosures popped up. She glanced for a moment—"You know what, I can't read it," she muttered and started laughing. "I mean it's a bank. I hope they're not doing anything crazy."

And then: "'You're in the Greenwood family,'" she read out from the screen. "'Your spending account application is approved.'" She nodded and proclaimed, "That quick? That's a good thing." She kept reading and came upon a prompt: "'Upgrade to Greenwood Premium.'" She paused and decided to continue with Greenwood's standard plan. She didn't want extra fees. There was a background check running as she looked around the site, and then . . . boom! "I'm approved."

It all felt seamless to her. And simple. It gave her "cash app vibes," which she liked. As a technology person, she paid close attention to user interface and design. She smiled as she looked around the site. She saw a screen that would allow her to add money from another bank account. She saw a promo to enter a sweepstakes to win ten thousand dollars and noted to herself to apply. Tandreia was ready to go. Ready to transfer her money. Ready to spend with Greenwood. She smiled because this, to her, was an opportunity to keep improving her family's wealth. "Let's go to 'Move Money,'" she said.

Louise was sitting silently with Tandreia as she navigated the site. Tandreia's name had been the 536,537th on the waiting list, but so far, Greenwood had admitted only the top 100,000 from the list. Louise and Ebony had been bumped up because we were "friend-friends," as Ryan Glover had put it. We wanted to observe Tandreia's reaction to using the bank's website, and so, Louise gave her access link to Tandreia.

Now Tandreia was in, but she had skipped all the legal agreements and disclosures. Louise made a snap decision to intervene, feeling some responsibility for Tandreia. "Click on Agreements and Disclosures," Louise said.

Tandreia couldn't find it. She also couldn't find a search tool. Suddenly she started changing her mind about the interface. "They need to find a way to have that search there so you can go right to that," she noted. "They talked about financial literacy." Finding their disclosures, she said, should be easy.

Tandreia found the fees and the fine print in a lengthy PDF document and began to read. Immediately, she had a concern—about a policy that said customers could lose up to five hundred dollars if they lost their debit card. And then she read, "Coastal Bank."

Coastal Bank?

"I don't know anything about Coastal Bank," she said. She turned to Google for some research. "'Banking as a service'? Okay, okay." She thought it was an interesting concept. She saw that Coastal worked with neobanks. "Neobanks," she noted. "That's what Greenwood is. A neobank has no storefronts." She nodded confidently at first. Neobanks had been trendy topics on the financial advice podcasts she adored.

But then she read that Greenwood had no FDIC insurance. "I don't know what that is," Tandreia said. She turned to Google to learn.

Slowly, excitement turned to discomfort. Not FDIC-insured? Not able to protect her funds? She concluded, "I'm going to be honest, I'm going to keep them at a hundred," she said. She didn't want to put more than one hundred dollars into Greenwood at this point.

Phew. Without "going through the fine print," she said, "my mind would have been like 'Okay, this bank is founded by affluent Black men. I want to support them.'" But now she felt different. "I can't afford to just lose my money. I can't afford it," she said, getting agitated. "I'm working hard. I can't afford it now. We might need to get Killer Mike on the phone and talk about this. For real. I'm serious. We need to talk about this: What does it mean my money is not being backed by the bank? And I mean the conversation is about keeping dollars circulating within the community. The Black—Right? How are you protecting the dollar, brother?"

Tandreia made one hundred thousand dollars per year. What about the lower-income, unbanked people whom Michael Render had told us he wanted to serve? People like James Lovelace? Or people who worked at AutoZone, like Lecario Glass.

Six months after we first met Lecario Glass at the food pantry near Michael's childhood home, a lot had happened to Lecario: his scooter had been stolen, and he had changed jobs, lost his apartment, and moved back in with his mom. Though his new job required six hours of commuting on public transportation each day, the job change was good news—this one paid more and hurt his body less. At his old job at AutoZone, Glass said his body ached all over from his lifting batteries and other heavy items. AutoZone had given him a body brace to help. Still, the ten dollars an hour he had made did not feel worth it. He had been putting batteries into other people's cars while still being light-years away from owning his own.

Glass largely operated outside the traditional banking system. The closest he came to it was a Wells Fargo card, he said, which he never used. AutoZone had so many workers without bank accounts that the company paid him and others on Wisely cards, rather than with checks. Wisely cards can be used at an ATM to turn a paycheck into cash, or they can be used like a debit card to pay bills or for purchases. When Glass left AutoZone, he replaced his Wisely card by signing up for Chime.

Like many fintech apps, Chime offered a range of services, including checking accounts, instant loans, and early access to direct deposit payments. Its features appealed to people with complex financial histories and included a debit card with automatic savings features and overdraft protection. While Chime's checking accounts were free, its instant loans had high interest rates, sometimes more than 20 percent annually.

Glass also patronized Western Union, when he had paper checks to deposit, like a recent tax refund. It was something he'd seen his parents do all his life. Check cashing was big business: there were thousands of licensed check-cashing businesses across the country, and they had long been considered essential for people without bank accounts. Glass knew Western Union's check-cashing fees were high, but he wanted the cash in hand—not because he wanted to spend it, he said, but because he simply liked having cash around. It brought him a sense of security.

Glass seemed exactly the type of customer that Michael Render had said Greenwood Bank would like to help. As Michael said when Greenwood was launching, "Unbanked does not have to be synonymous with the poor, the dredge or the forgotten. . . . If you're from a check-cashing environment, you're not necessarily bound to poverty, as much as you need to learn some good habits young, so that you can learn and actually do banking." He and Greenwood's original (short-lived) president/chief technology officer, Aparicio Giddins, had talked about reaching unbanked people as a primary goal. They had emphasized this to several news reporters, including us.

But when we asked Glass about Greenwood more than two years after the bank was announced, he said he had never heard of it. The news of Michael Render's new banking services company had not reached the underbanked people at the food pantry next door to Michael's grandparents' house in Collier Heights.

James Lovelace also ran his financial life on Chime, and like Glass, he had not heard of Greenwood Bank. Lovelace told us he had never used payday loans or check-cashing services, but he was underbanked in the sense that he did not have a mortgage with a traditional bank.

Part of the issue may have been that Greenwood's management wasn't actually focused on the unbanked. Years into Greenwood's life, when we asked Michael Render if he was satisfied with its work for the underbanked, he urged us, please, to keep asking Ryan Glover and Ryan's assistant about it. He wanted us to refocus them on it.

Indeed, early research by Greenwood Bank found that its customer base was not the underbanked—rather, it was the middle class, Alex Harris, the early investor who had once worked at Chime, told us. Adam Davies, a former banker from Truist who worked on Greenwood's fund-raising, told us that the average credit score of people signing up for Greenwood was over 700.

To Bo Young, there was nothing wrong with this. Greenwood had to, first and foremost, "actually make money," he said. "We're not a charity. We're not a nonprofit. And, you know, I don't speak for Greenwood, but I mean, in speaking for myself as an individual, you know, the unbanked is somebody else's problem, not mine."

Vanessa Vreeland, another former Truist banker who raised money for Greenwood, put it bluntly: "You can't make much money from the unbanked."

Bo Young added that it's often white people who ask him about the unbanked, and that is tied to their negative impression of Black Americans. "I have this argument with my white friends all the time," he said. "When I think about Black people, I mean, I think about Oprah Winfrey. I mean, I think about Ken Chenault . . . You know, successful people." He said there are plenty of *middle- and upper-class* Black and Latino Americans who were not being well served by traditional banking who could be well served by Greenwood.

Bo continued, saying that helping the unbanked should not be on the shoulders of only Black-led companies. "If Chase Bank decides that they want to go out and give home loans in previously redlined communities . . . then, great," he said. "It doesn't have to be just Black people going to make a difference in a positive impact on the Black community. And I mean, based on . . . how Black people have been treated for the last four hundred years, I think white folks have more of an obligation than we do."

Greenwood had clearly made a shift in its first couple of years and reoriented itself in the direction of the upper middle class. One could say it was the proverbial pivot—many start-ups change direction as they get going—but this pivot potentially narrowed Greenwood's original mission. Greenwood pursued acquisitions aimed at Black professionals in the spring of 2022. One acquisition was the Gathering Spot, a networking community that met up in urban offices, and another was a career development platform called Valence.

Then, in October 2022, Greenwood began promoting a new offering: Elevate. Photos of Tahitian-style resorts and fancy wood-paneled offices accompanied copy previewing "our newest premium Greenwood offering," a membership option that would allow members to "travel in style" and to "take your career and lifestyle to the next level."

"It's always all about who you know," said a Greenwood Instagram post on the new offering.

Far from promising to help people get a leg up in banking, many of Greenwood's social media posts looked like ads for luxury travel. It was as if the lavish lifestyle that Ryan Glover and his wife showed off on their Instagram accounts was now being mimicked by his company. (As Ryan told us in one interview, "My wife and my family have no qualms with any luxury item purchases.")

Greenwood's shift to luxury didn't fully resonate with the public. The people we had met through Greenwood, whose stories, hopes, dreams, and disappointments had shed light on the nuances of the Black-white wealth gap, were not the people in whom Greenwood now seemed most invested. And these people—potential customers—were picking up on that.

We called Darrielle Poole, the mother of six and currently a billing worker in Durham, North Carolina, whom we spoke with in the spring of 2021 after seeing her in Greenwood's virtual meeting. She had been hopeful that a Black-run institution would be fairer to her than other banks, so that even if she received disappointing news, she wouldn't have to wonder about Greenwood's intentions.

A year and a half later, Poole was absorbed with life and had largely written off Greenwood Bank. Her identity had been stolen, and she was dealing with Bank of America on that. Her car had been stolen by drug users, and when the police returned it to her, she'd had to personally remove drug needles and traces of sexual activity from the interior. She was still worried about paying off her student loans for a degree she had never received. And even though her annual pay had gone up to sixty thousand dollars, banks were not increasing the size of the loans they were willing to offer her. She had worked toward buying her own home since 2009, when she and her family were evicted from an apartment following the financial crisis, and that dream of home-ownership seemed farther away than ever.

When we asked if she had more wealth than she'd had in 2009, she hesitated. "I want to say that [I'm] better off, because I make more. But if I'm honest, I don't know if that's the truth. Because I'm making more, and I'm spending more. And I still have pretty much the same assets, like cars and, you know, same material things," she said.

"I just feel like I'm just an outsider watching time go by and things get more costly," she said. Poole still received emails from Greenwood Bank regularly, she said, but she had not yet seen a strong enough reason to complete the sign-up process. What she wanted was a home loan, not an expensive luxury travel package.

Poole also didn't like how Greenwood had partnered with Coastal. "I think that the folks at Greenwood have great intentions on what they're trying to do, but I don't think that's the same as being an in-dependent group," Poole said. Having supported them because of the "racial inequality" in banking, she saw the partnership with Coastal as suspect. "I don't know. It's a little bit fishy," she said.

John McCullough, another potential Greenwood customer who at-tended the 2021 virtual gathering, thought Greenwood's actions were more than just a little bit fishy. He had come to Greenwood feeling burned by white-run banks, in particular Wells Fargo. There, in an ac-count mix-up shortly before Greenwood's launch was announced, he and his son were treated like "we were guilty until proven innocent," as he put it.

McCullough set up his Greenwood account in the fall of 2022, and he began shifting money into it. He had two jobs, and he arranged for one paycheck to automatically be split between his Greenwood account and an account at the Black-owned bank OneUnited. He didn't plan to do a lot of spending or make a lot of transactions—he thought he'd hold the money in those two banks to be able, eventually, to give it to his two-year-old granddaughter.

He wanted his deposits to help the Black community. "I really just did it to put money into an account, you know, so [the banks] would have money to go to mortgages," he said. "My thinking was, okay, if I put money into these Black-owned banks, then they would be able to loan money in the communities."

By the time he had deposited about $9,500 in Greenwood, he started having second thoughts because Greenwood was "backed by," as he described it, Coastal Bank. "It's a white-owned bank," he said. "Look it up."

With this insight into Greenwood's structure, McCullough said he couldn't figure out what value the fintech was adding to the lives of Black people. "I don't really know how or what the purpose of Greenwood is. I mean, can you go borrow money for a mortgage? Can you go to Greenwood to get a car loan?" The answer to both, at the time, was still no.

Even as Greenwood was promoting its Elevate program, Stephanie Muhammad, a spa owner in Alabama, was setting up her Greenwood account. At age sixty, Stephanie had long wanted to bank with a Black institution. She was part of the Nation of Islam, and that group's leader had talked about how important Black banking was. She had been on the waiting list, and they finally let her in, and she was really excited.

She moved $1,600 from Regions Bank into Greenwood Bank and set up some recurring direct deposits, for example, having her Social Security benefits deposited into her Greenwood account. It seemed like a new beginning after a difficult eighteen months. Her husband had died. That had meant moving out of his mother's house, where she had lived. He had left very little in terms of funds, and she was stuck with the debt they owed for their children's college (and for her own). She had moved in with her seventy-eight-year-old mother and brought along her daughter and granddaughter. Four generations in one rental.

Muhammad liked helping others when she could and would sometimes anonymously donate money to churches when there were children in need. She felt it was important to do that even when she was having trouble paying her own bills. She thought her Greenwood account would allow her to help the Black community while keeping her money safe. She trusted Greenwood Bank because she admired one of its founders. "I saw Andrew Young and, you know, that's what got me on board," she told us.

A few months later, she checked on her Greenwood account and saw that some of the money was gone. The account listed purchases she had not made. She called Greenwood's customer service right away, she said, but could not reach anyone for weeks. She was confused. "I'm used to banks handling things, when I give them a dispute, almost right away," she told us.

Finally, a customer service agent at Greenwood helped her make a claim and told her she would find out the results of the claim months later. In the meantime, payments that were supposed to be made from her account were missed. Her credit, already troubled from bills due after her husband passed away, took another hit. She worked out a deal to take money from her husband's estate to make short-term payments while she tried to sort out her account with Greenwood. "What am I supposed to do about my bill?" she said. As Muhammad told Greenwood customer service at the time in emails that we reviewed: "This has caused me to be two months behind on my car payment." She noted that she owed $1,080.20, and now, with a $54.00 late fee, she'd have to pay $1,134.20. "My most important creditor," she wrote, was "$299.00, that I had to borrow money twice to pay. I put money in your bank to secure it until *I* use it."

Muhammad's interactions with Greenwood went to the email account support@bankgreenwood.com. Muhammad told us she had never had an experience like this with "a bank."

We talked with Muhammad about fintechs and about Greenwood's banking partner, Coastal, none of which Muhammad recalled having heard anything about. "If I had known that," she said, "I wouldn't have gotten into it. I'm thinking Greenwood is a Black-owned bank. You know what I'm saying? The inspiration of it is a Black-owned city."

It would be months before Muhammad got her money back.

Then there was the recirculation of money that Greenwood had promised. There was still no sign of a lending program; as late as the spring of 2023, Eric Sprink of Coastal Bank told us he was eager to help Greenwood start a loan program, but that Greenwood had not moved forward with this.

Then there was Greenwood's most public recirculation effort, to help the small Black-owned businesses into which its customers' (Black) dollars would pour. Greenwood had promised to list Black businesses nationwide in its GreenBook database, to incentivize its debit card customers to spend at those businesses, and to dispense ten-thousand-dollar monthly business grants.

As of April 2022, the only Black businesses entered into the Green-Book were located in Atlanta, but by the end of our reporting in 2023, there were more than four thousand around the country. Still, a few of those businesses told us they were not seeing an influx of customers who mentioned Greenwood or its GreenBook. Latasha Whyte, the owner of Clean House of Atlanta, told us that she hadn't known her business was on Greenwood Bank's site. She said Black business owners like her needed more than business listings to succeed: they needed funding, loans, and pipelines that brought in lots of customers. She also cautioned against middlemen operations that take part of the profit or charge fees. She noted that in her first year in business, five years earlier, her housecleaning business participated in a Groupon promotion that gave such a big cut to Groupon that she operated at a loss across three hundred homes. "I did what I needed to do—I cleaned those homes," she said. But she said it was a warning against middlemen. "I want Black business owners to know." She asked what sort of cut Greenwood planned to take. (We did not know of any planned middleman fee for GreenBook listings, but we did know about the higher fees charged to merchants by fintechs like Greenwood.)

In addition to offering its GreenBook directory, Greenwood was donating money to Black-focused organizations like the NAACP each month.

A few years into Greenwood, it seemed clear the company's Green-Book listings and its monthly grants were simply not going to make a big dent in recirculation. There were more than two trillion dollars in cash in circulation in the U.S. economy. In addition, there was nothing in Greenwood's products that tied its customers' spending to Black-owned businesses; even in Greenwood's marketing, where the company urged people to shop Black, the examples they provided didn't always buttress the point. Social media posts showed people holding up Greenwood debit cards in front of places like Hudson Yards, a fancy new shopping area in Manhattan. The post read, "Keep your dollar circulating within the community with Greenwood." Which Black community would that be, we wondered, in the commercial area of Hudson Yards?

As 2022 was ending, dollars were circulating to Greenwood. In November, the company raised $45 million from an investor group led by Pendulum, a firm focusing on start-up founders of color. In the eighteen months since Greenwood's earlier investor round, more money had flowed into venture capital funds that had a focus on funding women and nonwhite people. The movement of funds to focus on diverse founders was real, for the time being.

The chief executive of Pendulum, Robbie Robinson, had worked as a wealth adviser to Barack Obama and his family. Of Greenwood, Robinson said he was excited to help the company to "equip our communities with the resources they have been systemically excluded from in the pursuit of economic opportunity."

But other than the Pendulum funding, the rest of the investors named in the round were not Black-led investment firms. Several big banks from the earlier round joined again. We had been told by people who had seen the financial documents that Greenwood was 50 to 70 percent Black-owned before this $45 million round—but given that many investors in this round were not Black, it was not clear if Greenwood would remain more than half Black-owned at the end of 2022.

Raising capital so soon was a surprise to some. But we had heard from former Greenwood employees that they had lost their jobs in the summer of 2022 because, they were told, the company was running low on money. The money in the latest fund-raising was needed in part to keep developing the product, investors said.

As Alex Harris, a Greenwood investor, explained to us, "The challenge for Greenwood was they announced that they were going to do this really early in their product history. These products take a long time to develop."

Still, Greenwood's investors seemed unbothered by the slow pace. "They are taking a very, very measured approach," said Adam Davies, the former Truist banker who went on to join a venture capital firm focused on diverse investments. "And I applaud them for this, because the last thing you want to do in a customer service business is have bad service, right? To have any issues with your product. And so, they've been incredibly deliberate about rolling out products cautiously."

In tandem with announcing the new fund-raising, Greenwood officially announced Elevate, the luxury membership program it had been teasing on its Instagram account. *American Banker* wrote, "It's something of a turnabout for this neobank, which was founded in 2020 to be a company that served the underbanked, especially Black people who were unable to obtain mortgages." The fee for Elevate membership would be two hundred dollars per month.

As Greenwood rolled out Elevate, the company came into the legal crosshairs of the State of California. The state's Department of Financial Protection and Innovation objected to what it saw as an improper use of the term *bank*, demanding that the company immediately stop using the word. "The word 'bank' has a certain connotation. And when people hear the word 'bank,' they assume certain things," Paul Yee, the senior counsel at the department, told us. "And that's not totally accurate for companies like Greenwood."

As all this played out in late 2022, Tandreia was still living at home in rural North Carolina. When we asked her about Elevate, she told us that Greenwood no longer felt "relevant" to her life. Spending as little as possible, she had managed to amass $52,000 in savings (outside of her retirement savings). She had a plan to move back to Atlanta in February. She would use $35,000 as a down payment to purchase a home and use the rest for moving and setup expenses. Her company was based in Atlanta, and though remote work was an ongoing option, she wanted to be back in the office in person. She was the only Black woman in a unit of forty people, she said, and she felt left out when colleagues socialized together in Atlanta. She missed her broader community there. Work itself, she said, was going well. As a solutions architect at Zuora, a subscription management software company, she consulted with several large brand-name content companies on how they might make more money. Homeownership finally seemed in reach.

One Friday in early December, Tandreia gave what she felt was one of the best presentations of her career. The chief technology officer for the client, a large streaming company, was there and gave her glowing praise at the end of it, Tandreia said. She felt proud and was eager to see her manager in her next meeting, because she felt sure she would receive praise.

The following week, Tandreia was laid off. Her manager told her it was not due to her performance, she told us. With her firing, Tandreia felt something uncharacteristic for her. Normally, she looked on the bright side. Normally, she had so much hope and was grateful for the things she had. Usually, she was the cheerleader in the room, inspiring other people. But on that day—when she was so close to moving back to Atlanta, when she had worked from a tiny home in rural North Carolina for sixteen months to save money—on that day, she felt angry. So angry.

CHAPTER 16

THE GAP PERSISTS

Not everything that is faced can be changed; but nothing can be changed until it is faced.
—James Baldwin, "As Much Truth as One Can Bear," 1962

As we neared the end of writing this book in 2023, we were invited onto a one-hour television special about wealth inequality. The host was a kind, smart white woman who was concerned about the Black-white wealth gap. There was a pattern to her questions: All the questions about Black people went to Ebony. All the questions about Wall Street, the economy, and white people went to Louise.

The experience bothered us only a little . . . until we started to hear from people who had watched the TV appearance: Why wasn't Ebony asked about the economy? Why wasn't Louise asked about Black people? Didn't you two report this book together, hand in hand? Didn't you both interview bankers, and didn't you both interview Black Americans?

The answer to the last three questions was yes. The discussion thrust us into a deeper conversation about why some people may perceive us differently from each other, about what actually *was* different. We sparred a little bit, and then the unstated became stated. "You're on the other side of the Black-white wealth gap from me," Ebony said, adding that even middle-class Black Americans like her felt the constraints of the gap. It was true. Such an obvious statement, but one that had not been made about us before. *You're on the other side from me.* It echoed for both of us.

After nearly three years of working together on this book, we understood a lot more about the Black-white wealth gap and a lot more about ourselves. We had worked together, as partners, examining the historic and present realities of the Black-white wealth gap. We had had lengthy discussions about so many chapters in history, about scores of datasets and academic papers, and we had walked alongside each other in on-the-ground reporting. We had cried together and cheered each other on.

After all this, it had become clear to us that, without interventions, the Black-white wealth gap will not close anytime in the near future. The gap is simply too big and tied to too many institutionalized practices. We saw it on the individual level as well: practically every time we called the people we had interviewed to check how they were doing, we heard of more setbacks, more barriers to their financial goals. Over time, this became discouraging, but it also galvanized us.

We were not the only ones. Ellora Derenoncourt, a young Princeton economist whose work we have featured throughout this book, had come into the academic spotlight by searching for answers about the Black-white wealth gap from chapters within history. Derenoncourt is a trailblazer in the field of economics not only because she is piecing together new datasets that bring important insights into the full American history of the Black-white wealth gap, but also because she is a Black female economist in a field dominated by white men.

Derenoncourt views the scarcity of Black people in her own field as a microcosm of problems society-wide. "This is an equity issue and a question of occupational segregation. Economics PhDs are highly remunerated. Why are Black students and students from other underrepresented groups interested in the social sciences more likely to matriculate in other fields? Somewhere along the way, many received the impression that economics was not the field for them," she has said. "An environment where people from different socioeconomic backgrounds have a voice has an entirely different feel from one where only elite strata are present."

Derenoncourt's academic rise—she moved into professorial roles in

July 2020 after her Harvard PhD, teaching at the University of California at Berkeley and then moving to an appointment at Princeton—occurred in parallel to an emotional conversation within her family. Derenoncourt's father, a Haitian immigrant, was a cardiac surgeon after serving in the U.S. Navy. Now retired, he called his children on the phone after the killing of George Floyd and cried with them. "After trying to save fifteen thousand lives and fighting like hell to save every life, I cannot tolerate having somebody obliterating somebody's life like that," he told them.

The family decided they wanted to band together for an online conversation about America's crisis. Proud to be Haitians, because of that country's historic revolt, when enslaved people there rose up for independence, the Derenoncourts hosted a public meeting on the Internet, with Ellora's father addressing medicine and policing, the family's oldest son discussing books he had published on Haiti's uprising, and Ellora discussing economic data. Brother and sister reminisced about a time at Harvard when students had occupied a building to protest its namesake, who had enslaved people. Of her research, Ellora's father said proudly that his daughter tries to "bring down the hammer with the info. They can't deny it, you know, when we have the four-one-one."

On the virtual gathering, Ellora played her role as the younger child, but she also stood out as the resident expert. She noted that social issues like policing are not often linked to economic research. "In economics, we typically don't look at some of these topics," she said. "Working on racial inequality, not many people do that . . . I had to kind of fight almost against my own training at Harvard, a predominantly white elite institution, to bring the numbers on this."

The academic is also personal.

By early 2022, after years of working to compile the historic Black-white wealth gap data, Derenoncourt and her co-authors were able to plot it on a graph and then run simulations to see how the gap might be closed. They found that the gap has remained large both because it started as such a large gap, but also because Black and white Americans have had different wealth accumulation patterns (saving and investing patterns) and because Black Americans have faced, and continue to face, discrimination and unequal treatment by many gatekeepers in society. Closing the gap would be an "uphill battle," she and her co-authors concluded, and if nothing changes in terms of income paid to Black Americans and their opportunities for saving, investing in stocks, and other advancement, then the Black-white wealth gap will *grow*, potentially quite dramatically over the coming decades.

What disappointing news: Derenoncourt's models showed that the Black-white wealth gap could get far worse. All this was playing out during the Covid-19 pandemic, a tumultuous time whose effects on wealth inequality were difficult to predict. On the one hand, the government provided hefty stimulus payments, which helped less-wealthy families. And companies and communities were introducing programs to help Black families. On the other hand, there were gains in the stock market, which would benefit the wealthiest families.

Meantime, still searching for hope, Derenoncourt's team looked at whether reparations could close the gap. It's well known that a Senate bill called H.R. 40 has been introduced in every Congress since 1989. It calls for creating a task force to study reparations for Black Americans. In addition to H.R. 40—named in a nod to the unfulfilled Reconstruction promise of forty acres—other proposals to pay back Black Americans include a GI Bill to compensate descendants of Black Americans who served during World War II and didn't get the GI benefits. These federal efforts, as of 2024, did not have widespread support in Congress. The strongest momentum for reparations since 2020 has been at the local level. Several local governments introduced trial guaranteed incomes and debated possible reparations programs. In Atlanta, the Fulton County Reparations Task Force released its report in early 2023 documenting past actions around convict leasing and also the use of eminent domain in Buckhead, which pushed Black residents out in the 1930s. The task force said it planned to investigate more examples of neighborhoods around Atlanta where people were pushed out by eminent domain. This occurred within weeks of the City of San Francisco's considering a proposal to pay $5 million apiece to Black Americans who descended from slavery, were incarcerated in the war on drugs, or were displaced from San Francisco by urban renewal in the mid-1950s. Around the same time, California's reparations task force recommended that $360,000 be paid to affected

Black people living there. At the end of 2023, New York's governor signed legislation creating a task force examining reparations. As of 2024, across the country, in cities large and small, there were scores of these sorts of local task forces. They were looking at the many reasons reparations may be owed, ranging from enslavement to redlining, the use of eminent domain for property seizure, and more.

Derenoncourt looked to math and simulations to examine reparations. She and her team used a hypothetical reparations amount of $267,000 per Black person—an estimate of the per-person share in the wealth gap between the total wealth of white Americans and the total wealth of Black Americans. (It's based on the assertion that Black Americans, in aggregate, should have wealth equal to their share of the population.) Derenoncourt and her team created a predictive model using the $267,000. It showed that those dollars, if paid, would nearly fully close the gap . . . but only for a short time. When we saw Derenoncourt in late 2022, she was disappointed but matter-of-fact. "It will open up again, you know, in the next few decades."

The Black-white wealth gap is dynamic, with many variables, inputs, and barriers, as you have seen in this book. An influx of cash to anyone is just a one-time influx, a windfall, but not permanent structural change. If the person still swims in a sea of discrimination, the influx won't make lasting change. If Black Americans were given an influx, the Black-white wealth gap would reemerge if it was still more difficult for Black people to get loans than it was for white people; if Black people were still arrested more than white people for the same alleged offenses; if Black people were promoted at work less than similarly talented white people; if Black people invested differently from white Americans; or, if Black people could not get access to the same types of relief as white Americans.

This is not to say reparations are not worth studying. It is more to point out that there are drivers in the Black-white wealth gap that would keep that gap open even beyond reparations. This is what makes the Black-white wealth gap different from the broader problem of wealth inequality for all Americans. "Overall wealth inequality—that's a social problem that needs to be dealt with," Derenoncourt told us. "But there is a gap in wealth by race that cannot be explained by things like income. So, you can focus on the poorest part of the income distribution for white Americans and Black Americans, and you will see vast differences in wealth. And that's really what needs to be part of the conversation, because wealth has to go somewhere from generation to generation.

"When we think about the racial wealth gap under slavery and just after," she continued, "that's what's being passed on generation to generation. And that's one of the main points we want to get across: Yes, we are just carrying this around. Okay. Wealth is very historical. It encodes history."

We are in a system of cycles of discrimination that, in turn, create and sustain patterns of personal behavior, belief systems, and government and business actions that keep the Black-white wealth gap alive and kicking. *We are all just carrying this around.*

*   *   *

In the spring of 2023, as we finished our reporting, we pulled court records to find out what had happened in the battle over James Lovelace's Atlanta home. Though his case and documents were strong, many rent-to-own deals ended in disappointment. Pro bono lawyers told us that victory for people living in those homes was rare.

But there it was. Victory.

In April 2022, Lovelace reached a settlement with Don Jacobs's business partner and the LLCs who held the title to Lovelace's home. James Lewis Lovelace III would now have full ownership rights to 547 Chappell Road, the home he had first moved into at age twenty-five in 2005.

We wanted to talk with Lovelace immediately, but his phone went straight to voicemail and his message box was full. His email address sent us a bounce-back. So, Louise got on a plane to Atlanta and then drove toward his house. Signs for "All Cash" car rentals, a used-tire shop, and Dollar General welcomed her to Bankhead, the neighborhood Lovelace called home and that had run in his family for generations. It was changing. She passed some nicer, new condominium buildings, built recently in anticipation of new corporate offices. Then she got to the Exxon station, where we'd last seen Lovelace's BBQ stand. It wasn't there, but it was still morning. BBQ sells better later on.

Driving in on Chappell, passing small homes, some boarded up, Louise looked up the hill, to the corner of Blyss Avenue. There was Lovelace's house. What once were mighty white columns on the little home were now crumbling. She saw peeling paint and black ash. It was shocking. Lovelace's house had been burned out. The front door was gone, replaced by metal bars. The front window was black. The paint was destroyed in most places. When Louise got out of her car to have a look, she saw remnants of gunfire on the ground. Around the corner, on Blyss, she looked up Lovelace's driveway. The BBQ smoker was gone. The ice-cream truck was gone, too. Nothing but big burnt wood beams, a red dumpster on its side, and loose trash on the ground.

"I am Atlanta, Georgia," Lovelace had once written on Instagram.

What had happened here?

Louise drove east on Route 78 and soon came upon Finley Avenue NW. She pulled over at the house that Frances Walker (James Woodall's great-grandmother) had grown up in and moved back into after leaving Jesse Day. This was the house where James's grandmother grew up, before moving to the projects. It was only 0.8 miles from Lovelace's house. It was boarded up, deteriorating. Soon, we would learn, an LLC would surprise Woodall's family by making a claim on the house and trying to force a sale of it.

As time passed, we didn't know exactly how to reach Lovelace, but we called his lawyers, we messaged him on social media, and we called his neighbors. We found a news story on the house fire that said it began around 1 a.m. on April 12. The fire department responded to a call, and firefighters rushed in, some falling through weak porch floor beams down into the basement. They pulled out a man, who was unnamed in the article, and took him to Grady Memorial Hospital.

The fire had occurred less than a week after Lovelace reached the settlement making him the owner of the house. We found postings on TikTok that he had made the day after the fire: he was still alive. In one reel, he does a walk-through of his burned home. He enters the side door, passes an orange couch and tattered tables; there is broken wood all over the floor. He looks out onto the porch, at the broken floorboards where the firefighters had fallen, at the dogwood tree in full bloom. The living room ceiling was destroyed, and you could see through to the floor above. In the reel, Lovelace clears debris off a table and pans his camera over his daughter's pink tricycle, which looks as bright as ever. He muted the sound on that video, but he soon posted another one, in which he tells people to follow their dreams. "There ain't nobody gonna believe in your dream for real, for real, but you," he says. "I've been showed so many times that your goal and your dream is your goal and your dream. Not theirs. So, stay in your lane and make sure you continue to follow and see it all the way out. Your dream and your goals. If you don't, they won't."

We also found two GoFundMe pages that Lovelace had put up asking for help after the fire. "I really don't ask anyone for anything, but this situation has mentally and physically drained me," he wrote. No one had donated.

The house on Chappell was becoming part of Lovelace's past. We found in public records that he sold it in January 2023, with a sale price of $100,000. It was not clear to his old lawyer or to us how much money he ended up with, given the new purchase price. (He had debt on the house and unpaid property taxes, his lawyer said; and there may have been other expenses.) We scoured public records and found new addresses for Lovelace. We mailed him certified letters with our photograph. We hoped he would call us back.

*   *   *

A couple of weeks after we traveled with Michael Render's family to the Crawford W. Long Museum, Michael called.

"I just wanted to thank you," he said. He said he appreciated our research and the invitation we'd given him to join the museum trip. We updated him that the museum had taken the findings on his family so seriously that they were discussing a first-ever exhibit on Long's Black descendants. History wasn't changing, but the documentation of it was. What had always been was now becoming recognized.

"I've known about my family's connections to Crawford Long since I was three years old," Michael said. "My aunt told me."

"I want to be clear," Louise told him. "We aren't describing your family as only enslaved people in Crawford Long's house. We are talking about a likely blood relationship."

"Yeah, of course," he said.

Michael Render, we'd heard, had his share of doubts about the banking company he cofounded, but he was already well known as one of the founders. It would be hard to do an about-face. His stated rationale from 2020 for being involved, to help the unbanked, seemed off message three years later. Greenwood simply was not a company focused on the unbanked. Michael still hoped that lending would become a source of community investment, but he continued to refer questions about helping the underbanked to his cofounder Ryan Glover and urged us to push Ryan to focus on it.

In addition, Michael had less Greenwood equity than the other founders: Andrew Young's family, Ryan, and the newcomer to company advertising, Paul Judge. Maybe it was because he didn't work there day-to-day, but Michael, the founder who was closest to being from the hood, was also the one getting less. When we asked him how he felt about this, he pointed out that Jay-Z was the most famous owner of the Brooklyn Nets basketball team despite having only a small percentage ownership. (Jay-Z has said publicly of his Nets stake, "The fact that I have any ownership in this franchise is fuckin' amazing," given that, as he noted, he grew up in the Brooklyn projects.) Michael also said, "None of the other banks that I helped [with the Bank Black movement] offered me any equity."

Michael hedged a bit on Greenwood in our final call. "I tell people, 'Hey, you don't have to have just one bank account—don't take all your money out of Bank of America,'" he said. "But find a small Black bank to do your Christmas savings, to do your retirement fund. . . . My retirement account is with Citizens Trust."

In the summer of 2023, Michael released his first solo album since back when he went bankrupt. It was a hit, and he went on tour. Called *Michael*, it was his most biographical album yet. It was truly something *of his own*. And he would go on to win three Grammys for it.

In the tour, he set up the stage as if for a funeral for his mother and grandmother. Onstage, he talked about working at AutoZone. He talked about crack cocaine ruining his community in the 1980s. "Fuck Ronald Reagan, fuck his wife, and fuck their entire administration for what they did to our communities," he said, playing audio about the Iran Contra hearings overhead. He talked about how much Ralph Lauren owed the Black and brown communities for dressing all their children in its Polo-branded clothes. And he talked about having mercy on addicts. These are "everyday people," he said. *Have some mercy.*

The crowd around us at the Apollo Theater was ecstatic. We were in Harlem, just a block from the old Freedom Bank headquarters, where Jackie Robinson once reigned. This is where we saw Killer Mike in his element. The men sitting in front of us cried and wiped each other's tears, as Michael rapped about his deceased mother and grandmother. "Oh my god, this is like church for real," one said as they embraced.

"Like a hole in my heart," Michael rapped.

*   *   *

By the spring of 2023, Brook Bacon felt the world had forgotten about his father's death. Money from the state of Georgia, even millions of dollars, couldn't really change that. A criminal case against the officer who killed Julian Lewis seemed unlikely. The video from the officer's dashboard camera had never been released. And without that video, Brook felt, there was little chance of getting a large public outcry for justice. Justice to him meant more than money—it meant seeing the officer penalized. Though we knew it would be difficult to watch, we filed a Freedom of Information Act request for the video, and we got it.

The footage began with the officer trailing Lewis's beat-up tan Nissan Sentra from a distance.

When the officer turned on his siren and drove in closer, Lewis turned on his right blinker, as if indicating that he would turn right soon. Within two minutes, he changed it to his left blinker, and he motioned out his window for the officer to follow him.

This was something we knew well: Black people are often told that when you are being pulled over by the police, motion for the officer to follow you to a safe, public place. The logic is that the encounter does not need to happen on a dark, dirt road where you are all alone.

The drive continued, and from the video standpoint, it seemed fairly calm. There was a handicap symbol on Lewis's license plate, looking right back at the officer. In that moment of the video, we felt Lewis looking right back at us.

Driving on a dirt road as time passed, Lewis picked up the pace. In the dash cam video, dirt flies up at the officer's windshield.

At five minutes, twenty-eight seconds of the video, the officer accelerated and rammed his car into the left bumper of Lewis's car, spinning the Nissan off to the left. By five minutes and thirty seconds, the officer was out of the car, yelling, "Up! Put your hands—"

BOOM! The noise came before the officer even finished his sentence. That was the bullet that killed Brook's father.

It all played out in less than two seconds while the unarmed Lewis was still sitting in his car.

The officer kept yelling, "Put your hands up, put your hands up, put your hands up! Let me see your hands!" Then the yelling turned to softer exclamations of "almighty" and "Jesus Christ." No point in yelling at a dead man.

The video is two hours long, but after those first minutes, there is little more to see because Lewis's car at that point was off camera. Cows moo in the background in between a few phone calls during which the officer said little more than "I had to shoot this man, and, you know, I'm just scared."

As of the printing of this book, it remained unclear whether prosecutors would take action. The Justice Department had said it would reexamine the closed case after the family's march for justice, but it did not release more information about it.

*   *   *

Wealth is not only money. There are less quantifiable forms of value within families—such as the pride parents have in their children's potential. A high-achieving child who acquires a strong education can lift a family's fortune in more sense than one, building on what his or her mother built and making all that hard work feel more worth it, paying forward debts rather than being dragged down by them.

It was that generational pride that we heard fracture in a primal scream one evening in March 2023, when Ebony called James Woodall's mother. Stephana had talked with Ebony numerous times, but the two had never discussed a key question in James's recent years: Why did he leave the NAACP?

"He had other professional opportunities," Stephana said.

Ebony was silent at first. She was coming off a day of numerous calls with NAACP officials in which people made it clear to her that they wanted us to stay away from telling James Woodall's story. As we called around, the organization sent a blast message to its leadership and told them to report any media phone calls about James Woodall back to headquarters.

"Stephana, it seems like there were other reasons," Ebony said.

And then the scream. Something clicked in his mother's head. She howled for her daughter and demanded, "*Why* did James leave the NAACP? *Why?*"

Shortly after that call, James called Ebony and said he was happy to pass along all the information about his departure. Throughout our reporting, James had been open with us, but we had not gotten the exact details on why the NAACP investigated him. That night, he sent over the documents.

Four days before Ebony called James's mother, the NAACP had suspended his membership in the organization. He had been gone from his role as the Georgia chapter's president for more than a year and a half, but suddenly, the NAACP was calling even his membership in the broader organization into question. As the organization's national president and CEO, Derrick Johnson, wrote to James, "the President and CEO suspended your membership after it was determined that your activities, behavior, and conduct were detrimental and inimical to the NAACP."

This was when we found out that James had been serving a controversial dual role in the organization: as unpaid volunteer president and as the state chapter's paid lobbyist. As the documents showed, this issue had come up in a complaint to the national organization about James in 2021, just when he and other local leaders were calling for change within the NAACP. We set about to determine what had actually occurred. It was at times uncomfortable for Ebony because she had a lifetime membership to the organization and was proud of the affiliation. Many storylines in this book, like the history of the pushback on redlining, show the NAACP doing admirable, important work. James Woodall's fallout with the organization shone a different kind of light.

At the heart of the issue was pay. The elite NAACP was divided, in some ways generationally, about what constituted paid and unpaid work. The NAACP's list of responsibilities for state presidents did not explicitly include lobbying, though promoting legislative policies that furthered the NAACP's goals was among the objectives of state chapters. Still, there was so much work involved in lobbying for positions the NAACP was trying to promote that James felt he was putting in work that was beyond his volunteer role. After more than six months of lobbying for the NAACP without compensation during 2020, James put forward an item to the NAACP's Georgia executive committee for the chapter to pay him a lobbyist a fee of $45,000. This came after he had spent about a year working brutal hours for the organization for free. Striking to us, as observers of James's leadership in the summer of 2020, was that his net worth, or wealth, was *negative* $66,800. This meant his wealth was likely below that of every other major character in this book. (James Lovelace, for instance, had higher wealth than James Woodall in the summer of 2020 because of the value of his house and because he had little debt.)

To understand the NAACP's concerns, we examined all the correspondence and also the complaint that had been filed about James. The NAACP's notice of the complaint said James had allegedly violated NAACP policies by improperly expensing a few small costs and, notably, by "serving as a Lobbyist while serving as an elected officer" and "receiving payments not approved by Executive Committee."

But James said the state's executive committee had approved his work and the lobbyist payment. Neither the NAACP's constitution nor its bylaws state that an elected officer cannot serve as a lobbyist for the NAACP. When we asked the NAACP's national office to show us a document with the rule that James allegedly broke, it did not. Moreover, the organization's press secretary told us it was up to the state executive committee whether and how to compensate officers. We called the people in the room during the Georgia state board meeting in March 2021. We learned that there were strong voices for and against the lobbyist arrangement. One voice in favor was Jasmine Younge, the executive director for Georgia at the time. "He's been lobbying, and he's been helping you, and he's gotten so far, farther than anyone else has established relationships," Younge reported to us that she told the group.

We spoke with four more people who were present at the vote in addition to Younge, and they told us that the group had, in fact, voted to approve a lobbyist payment. Two said that in March 2021, when the matter came back up in a heated way, the board voted again, and this time it approved the matter, with James identified as the lobbyist. Younge also told us that. "You guys approved this, knew that it was this," Younge told us she said, adding to us, "Really, it was a play on power. I think that there's a lot of jealousy there around his age."

As we called other NAACP officials to discuss the complaint against James, the story kept changing. At first, in 2022, Ebony was told by a national board member, Michael Curry, that it was "an indiscretion" and "bad judgment." But then, by 2023, NAACP officials had a different story, and several told us that James had breached NAACP policies. We kept calling around, and some at the NAACP then began to back away from definitive statements, even as they warned people who worked there not to talk with us. Despite the fact that the NAACP had suspended James's membership in 2023 and said, when notifying him of the suspension, that the organization had "determined" that his actions "were detrimental" to the NAACP, Edward DuBose, the NAACP leader running the investigation on James, later insisted to us that the jury was still out. He insisted that it was undetermined to us on March 13, 2023, and that was four days after the NAACP had notified James that he was suspended. DuBose's partner in the investigation, David Walker, told us, "We are not blaming anybody at this point."

Our call with Walker was on March 14, 2023, almost two years after James left his president post, and still, the matter was unresolved. "We are not accusing anybody. Here again, we are not at the point where we can say there was wrongdoing or not," Walker told us.

But the damage seemed to have already been done.

James left the whole experience feeling that his reputation had been severely harmed. He had worked his tail off and made a difference for Black residents of Georgia during 2020, but his wings at the NAACP and possibly elsewhere had been clipped. As this book was heading to print, we called him up to tell him that numerous people had told us that his version of the lobbyist story was true.

"I'm glad to know I'm not crazy," he said. "Thank you."

*   *   *

Tandreia Dixon's anger started to recede when she got to meet up with one of her heroes, the celebrity restaurant owner Pinky Cole.

Still out of work in early 2023, Tandreia remained at home in rural North Carolina with her mother. The $52,000 she had saved from her prior job for an eventual down payment on a home was slowly decreasing, as she used it for other expenses. She was exhausted and slept a lot the first few months after losing her job. This embarrassed her, because her mother was working at the family junkyard to support them both. Her mother told her to rest as much as she needed and not to worry.

Tandreia developed an idea for a new company she wanted to start. It was her third start-up attempt, and this time she wanted to get it in front of high-powered people. Cole had just started a project called American Sesh, where people could apply to meet with her and other entrepreneurs and develop their business ideas. Cole had become even more successful and famous as a Black businesswoman after raising $25 million in investment funds to scale up her vegan restaurant business. (The funds came from a Black-run investment firm and from the white restaurateur Danny Meyer.)

Tandreia applied to American Sesh and got in. In February, she flew herself to Atlanta and spent a half day in a room with Cole and dozens of other entrepreneurs, all of whom she felt were more seasoned than she was. Still, having that opportunity lifted her spirits again. The anger was gone, and her hope was back.

"Me in that room? As far as from a business perspective, I had the least experience out of everybody in the room," she said. "So, just the fact that I had the opportunity to be in with a lot of multimillionaires. Right? That says a lot about me. I have to continue living in these spaces. I know I'm destined for greatness. And I think it just did something for me on the inside, too."

When she returned home, Tandreia decided to create a gathering that could inspire people right where she grew up. She organized the first of what she hoped would become an annual conference for young people in eastern North Carolina. Called Tech Homecoming, her event invited people like her who had succeeded in technology to come back home to offer words of advice.

She still dreamed of getting back to Atlanta. She planned to run her start-up on the side while finding a job that would allow her to move back and purchase a home as soon as she could. She said she would be unlikely to use Greenwood Bank. She had lost her Greenwood debit card and had no interest in replacing it. She would use a big, well-established bank—not a new alternative that, she said, might be risky. She noted that Greenwood seemed to have changed direction. The people it would attract through its acquired company, the Gathering Spot, would be people making lots of money, she said. And she was concerned about Greenwood charging merchants higher fees on transactions, she said, noting that it didn't fit with helping Black businesses.

"I guess, if they have to find a way to make money. I'm not saying that it's right, but—" She paused. There is a battle, she explained, between "the social aspect, how you impact the society" and "the capitalist" side.

"I've heard a lot of my friends talk about the war between the two," she said. "It seems like Greenwood initially was trying to, you know, position themselves to be able to impact the community or brand themselves to do that. But I guess it didn't turn out that way."

Reflecting on two years of dialogue, Tandreia and Louise thanked each other for the inspiration. And then Tandreia shared a story she had never told us.

"My dad, he died of heart failure and kidney failure, but I think the worst part of it was just like the last two weeks of his life," she said slowly, taking herself back to January 2018.

It was the end of a difficult year of physical deterioration, but it wasn't his physical condition that made it so trying. It was his ideas, his dreams, his drawings of things he wanted to build. Tandreia often stayed overnight with him at the nursing home he was in. He would wake up at 2 a.m. some days and talk to her passionately about the things he still planned to accomplish.

"You know, my dad had issues with drugs and alcohol. Because of that, his physical health failed. But he was still full of life, still full of ideas, full of purpose. Yeah. He was dying full of purpose. And I just—I don't want to be that way," she said.

That's what was most sad to Tandreia. That he died still dreaming of things he had not accomplished.

"I want to live out my full potential," she said. "I want to live my dreams."

*   *   *

We continued following Greenwood's developments as we watched the broader picture change for the Black-white wealth gap. A backlash that had been brewing against diversity initiatives grew stronger through 2023 and into 2024. As the economy sputtered, job cuts hit the newly built-up diversity departments in corporate America. Start-up initiatives slowed. The initiative OneTen, for instance, founded by former CEOs Ginni Rometty, Ken Chenault, and Ken Frazier to create more jobs for Black workers, slogged on with a distant finish line. OneTen's chief executive told us a few months into 2023 (the initiative's first year) that OneTen had created 87,000 jobs. That meant there were 913,000 more to go to reach the initiative's goal of 1 million. By early 2024, OneTen had officially pivoted away from Black-focused initiatives and into equity initiatives for all groups of people. "There is diversity fatigue," said Debbie Dyson, OneTen's chief executive. "What we're doing can't be 'This is a diversity thing.'"

The broader public watched as cases tied to diversity moved toward Supreme Court rulings, and then, on a single day in 2023, the U.S. Supreme Court ruled against affirmative action, against President Biden's plan to forgive trillions of dollars in student debt, and in favor of allowing businesses not to serve people who don't conform to the business owner's religious beliefs. Being aware of racism—or being "woke"—had become political. The state of Florida approved a curriculum to teach schoolchildren that enslaved people had benefited by learning through their enslavement.

Emboldened by the Supreme Court's affirmative action ruling, groups opposing diversity jumped and suggested the case had ramifications beyond education. These groups and politicians began sending letters to Fortune 100 companies warning them that it would be illegal to consider diversity for supplier decisions or for hiring. They threatened to sue law firms for diversity-focused internships if the firms did not open the programs to white applicants. (The law firms quickly acceded.) They sued a diversity-focused venture capital fund for investing in founders in part because of their race. That VC firm, the Fearless Fund, had been an early funder in the Slutty Vegan restaurant chain run by Pinky Cole, one of Tandreia Dixon's role models.

Amid all this backlash, a battle within Greenwood exploded into public view in mid-July. Greenwood announced that one of the founders of the meetup company it had acquired in 2022, the Gathering Spot, would be leaving and that a white executive would be joining. Some customers posted online about being surprised to see "Black leadership replaced with someone who isn't a person of color," as one person wrote. This controversy was dwarfed when news outlets reported that the Gathering Spot's founders had filed a legal claim saying that Ryan Glover and Paul Judge had stiffed them and the Gathering Spot's investors out of five million dollars. And, the lawsuit claimed, Ryan and Judge had instead paid themselves personal bonuses. In a legal filing, Greenwood said that the terms of the company's merger deal providing for the five million dollars in bonuses had not been met.

Within a week, the parties had worked it out, and the Gathering

Spot's founders were back in the Greenwood fold. But the dispute stuck with some observers. "Watching (Black) capitalism destroy the amazing genius of the founders of @theGatheringSpot in real time is so humbling and a reminder that no tools of white supremacy will protect or save us," James Woodall wrote that weekend on Twitter. "May we one day have the courage to be free!"

Andrew Young told us that the outcome of the case was positive because the parties had come back together and made peace. (The peace was short-lived; Greenwood and the Gathering Spot split up again, for good, a few months later.)

It had been two years since we first started interviewing Andrew, back when Greenwood Bank was nascent. Now time had passed, and as we talked with Andrew more about Greenwood's commitment to the underbanked, to starting a lending program, and to closing the Black-white wealth gap, he demurred. "I have really let them use my name and my influence," he said. "I have had little or nothing to do with the actual day-to-day activities."

We relayed to Andrew that his son had told us white people should be the ones doing more to help close the Black-white wealth gap because, in Bo Young's view, they had caused it. Andrew didn't disagree, and he complimented his son, saying he was proud of his smarts.

So, we asked more broadly how Bo could say it *wasn't* the responsibility of Black people, too, particularly Black Americans who had found financial success? We noted, after all, that Andrew Young had spent his whole life working to help Black Americans.

Andrew interjected: "I have helped more white people in my political career than Black people." That was the nature of capitalism, he told us, and he believed in capitalism. The system meant that the people with the most money will keep getting the most money when you bring more money into the system. Now, at last, we saw whom Andrew had meant when he told us, "The pie gets bigger when you let other people in." The "you" was white Americans.

Did that bother Andrew? No, he said. It was just the way it was. He didn't think Black people should hunt for "statistical equality," he said, but just to have "equal opportunity to be the best that we can be."

We asked him if the Black-white wealth gap would ever be closed.

"That's a dream, that's not reality," he said. "Somebody named Andrew Young will never catch up with somebody named Rockefeller." The fight to equalize the money, he said, "that is a fight that I will not be able to engage in. I'm ninety-one now."

It had been 140 years since Andrew Young's grandmother Hattie Epps participated in the sit-in at DeGive's Opera House in Atlanta to call for equality. Her grandchild was resigned to an even longer wait.

Greenwood had marketed itself heavily as a salve for the Black-white gap and as a force for recirculating money to the Black community. Our investigation found that the bank was not immediately focused on struggling Black Americans and that its claims around recirculation were dubious, both in terms of the vendors Greenwood hired, the white-run bank that held its customers' deposits, and the idea that Greenwood was having much impact helping Black-owned businesses. If Greenwood had marketed itself as just another business out to make a buck, its customers would not have joined the bank's "mission." Greenwood would not likely have had as many customers. Pitching social justice change in its marketing had delivered for Greenwood.

As we were completing this book, Greenwood added a "marketplace" to its website where people are connected with external lenders. When we filled the form there to request a loan, it sent us to a payday lending company. That surprised us. We also found the marketplace offered to refinance student loans. When we called the bank's customer service in late 2023 to ask about getting a mortgage or a small business loan, the representative said that was still not possible. Within days, we saw that Greenwood had announced that it had helped line up a loan to a fish restaurant co-owned by Michael Render. The loan, from a white-run bank, was quickly criticized by people online. "How's the report on other small businesses," one person wrote. "I'd like to know about Charisse and her daycare; Charles and his wheelchair-modification business; Jacques and his building-supply company." And, capping off the announcements, Greenwood introduced an investment advisory service to let its customers trade stocks and ETFs. It offered a feature to identify Black-run companies. Greenwood's investing service was in partnership with a white-run brokerage firm. As for Greenwood's ownership, Ryan Glover said in early 2024 that the company was still more than half "minority owned," a vague description.

Meantime, Greenwood introduced a new tagline to its customer emails, continuing its racial gap promise: "Remember that every time you #SwipeGreenwood, you help close the wealth gap and create generational wealth in the Black community."

Will Greenwood ever deliver for the public? Or will its success be measured in upscale clientele and a big financial exit?

Regardless of how its founders choose to measure their company's worth, true public impact for Greenwood will be revealed in how the company helps people further down the economic ladder: the people who are underbanked; the people who are in debt; the people whose net worth is negative, even; the people for whom the Black-white wealth gap is a fire burning through their opportunities, hopes, and dreams.

*　　*　　*

One day as spring approached, Ebony's phone rang. It was James Lovelace. He had received our letter.

"How's your barbecue business going?" Ebony asked.

"Oh, I've been down for a while, but I started back up," he replied.

"Well, tell me this. How . . . how is your house?" Ebony asked.

"Oh, it's going well," he said.

"What do you mean?"

"Gone," Lovelace said. "I sold it."

"Are you happy?" Ebony asked.

"It's all right," he said. "I got what I could get."

"We saw it," Ebony said, then took a deep breath before continuing, "Did it catch on fire?"

"Yeah."

"I'm sorry. Were you living in it?"

"No. Not at the time."

The conversation continued, slowly, sadly. Lovelace, in a matter-of-fact voice, narrated what had happened.

On April 6, 2022, he and the LLC parties holding the title to his home reached an agreement. It wasn't a deal that Lovelace loved—he felt the higher purchase price he would pay them represented his essentially buying the house a second time—but he loved his house, and this seemed the best way to finally get title to it. Lovelace had a plan. He had decided, reluctantly, that he would not live there anymore. To generate wealth, he needed the house to be a money-making asset. He did his research and determined that if he renovated the rooms, he could use the home as an Airbnb property and earn about four thousand dollars per month. The house was so close to downtown Atlanta, he noted, that it should book well.

Five days after the settlement was reached, Lovelace also got his tax refund sent to him on Chime. He was with a friend and felt bad for her. She and her children were living in a hotel, he said. He took her shopping, bought her dresses, and got her a pedicure, he said. Later that day, the two had a dispute, and he said she tried to run him over with her car. Lovelace, at the time staying in another house, went inside to lie down. A bit later, his phone rang. It was his neighbor on Chappell Road. His house was on fire, and she said he should come immediately. Lovelace thought, *How is this possible?*

When Lovelace arrived at 547 Chappell Road at around 1 a.m., the fire was out and the homeless man staying with him had been taken to the hospital. It was Carl Phillips—the sixty-six-year-old partially blind man Lovelace had been taking care of. One of the starting points to ending homelessness, Rachel Reynolds of the homeless shelter that Carl Phillips used to visit told us, was for people in the shelter to find someone with whom they could have a healthy relationship. "For Carl, that was James . . . which is an amazing thing, that James did this for Carl," she said. Carl Phillips died in the hospital. Lovelace told us Phillips had become like an uncle to him.

Pretty much everything inside Lovelace's house was destroyed. The money he had invested didn't matter anymore. That day, he stood outside looking at the smoke. He thought of himself first seeing the house at twenty-five years old. He thought of how much of his life the house had become for him—almost twenty years. He talked to the police. He told them he thought he knew who had set the fire, and he identified the woman he had had a dispute with earlier that evening. She was on probation and wore an ankle monitor. The police were able to find her. The county charged her with first-degree arson, murder, felony murder, and willful infliction of physical injury on an elderly person.

Lovelace didn't have insurance on the house. He had tried to get it, but he had been told the home would need a new roof first. Given that there were people in court trying to take away his house at the time, he had been hesitant to spend money on a roof until he won the house.

Those first hours after the fire, Lovelace stood frozen in front of his burned-down home. "There wasn't anything I could do but just stand there in distress, because I knew I wasn't going to be able to fix it. I knew. I knew it was over," he said. "All the years I had been there and all the court I had been through—I even had to do a Chapter Thirteen. All that I tried to do. It just really went up in smoke with the fire."

Ebony looked for something positive, asking, "How have you come back from this, James? Have you bounced back?"

"It's been kind of rough," he said. "I got a little money back. Nowhere near what I was supposed to get for the place."

How much? About thirty-one thousand dollars. (We reviewed the real estate statement—that's what was left from the one-hundred-thousand-dollar sales price after he paid off the loan, the taxes, and some closing fees.)

"Did you feel bad selling it?" Ebony asked.

"I felt bad—I had been there since my twenties."

"So, are you . . . are you happy now?" Ebony asked.

"I'm—I'm alive," Lovelace replied.

The questions were more and more difficult. Ebony asked how much he had left from the thirty-one thousand, and Lovelace said about ten thousand dollars. He had paid off some debt with some of it, he said, and then there was the time back in jail—

"What do you mean?" Ebony asked. "You had to go back to jail?"

"They came and got me. They said I didn't go to a hearing," Lovelace replied. It was a hearing in the arson case. He was expected to be there, but he said he didn't get a subpoena for that and that he'd already gone to one hearing.

"So, James, are you telling me," Ebony said, "are you telling me that someone arrested you and put you in jail because of this fire?"

"Yes, they put me in jail because they said I didn't come to the hearing," he said.

The police arrested Lovelace on February 17, 2023. He was a material witness in the probation violation case for the woman suspected of burning down his house, and he had not shown up to a hearing. This had allowed the government to issue an arrest warrant. For this, Lovelace spent twenty-seven days in jail. He had to put up $1,850 in a bond. He also lost his earnings in that period and had to use some of his $31,000 from the house to cover his financial obligations while in jail.

Lovelace had been in jail the whole time we were trying to reach him. As soon as he was out, he received one of our letters and called us back.

"James, was the battle to keep your house worth it?"

"Yeah," he said.

His words were heavy.

"It will work out, I feel. It's just that an unfortunate event happened with that fire. That's the only downfall about it, because I was giving it my all," he said, then paused.

"You know, because it was my home, and I'd been there so long," he continued.

"So, it was worth it. Me keeping it. Just me keeping it, me being able to say *it was mine*."

AFTERWORD

*In recognizing the humanity of our fellow beings, we pay our-
selves the highest tribute.*

—Thurgood Marshall

Throughout our time working on this book, many people asked us
what should be done to finally bring about racial-financial equality.
We didn't come up with a miraculous solution, and that wasn't our goal
as journalists-professors. But in investigating the Black-white wealth
gap and the way it lurks within our society, we ended up with some
joint suggestions that we believe can help you in your own life.

On a personal level: When you see someone different from you,
look for common ground. Most people care about their children, their
families, their health, and their homes. See those through lines and
connections between your life and other people's. To take this idea
farther, if you see someone and you start to think they are a risk to
you, ask yourself whether they are, in fact, *at* risk. Is there something
you can do to help that person who is making you nervous? Have you
considered that they may think you are also a risk to them? Bring in a
tide of trust by lowering your guard first, by offering help, by offering a
hand. And finally, assume nothing based on someone's job or income.
Do not assume anything about why they are where they are. Keep in
mind that we swim every day in a sea of inequality, where meritocracy
is actually a function of privilege combined with hard work. The man
at the BBQ stand on the corner could be James Lovelace. The factory
worker who made your shirt could be Tandreia Dixon's mother. The

boy by the highway asking for money could be the future NAACP leader James Woodall.

We also suggest that readers who want to be a part of making a more equitable world find a way to partner with people who are from different backgrounds. Push yourself. If you run a business, can you run it with a partner from a different racial background or economic stratum? If you set up a community group, can you find a cohead who is different from you? Who are you mentoring and who is mentoring you? Who are your children spending time with? Are they seeing a broad world?

On a policy level, we provide suggestions here to help you think through what policies you choose to support, at work or in politics. These suggestions are predicated on your accepting two things: (1) that it's important to lift more Black families on the ladder of wealth and (2) that we do not want wealth gaps that are racialized or specific to demographics.

First, support more transparency into the wealth distribution in our country. While many people prefer privacy with regard to individual household wealth, regular economic releases of readily available anonymous data on wealth distribution, and routine coverage of this data by news outlets, would be helpful. Imagine a day of every month featuring "the jobs report," or GDP growth news alongside a "wealth report" examining where the wealth is accruing and where it is not. Also, push the companies you patronize and the places you work to be more transparent: What are their inclusivity goals? If a company markets itself as being focused on a particular demographic, probe more deeply: Who owns the company, whom does it employ? Who are its customers and suppliers?

Second, ask who benefits from new government or company policies. Push policymakers to ensure that benefits are being shared equally or, where appropriate, that they're reaching the people who they are intended to reach. Push policymakers in government and at companies to make benefits as inclusive as possible when it comes to the neediest people. And push for regular reviews to make sure that if one racial group is found to be benefiting more from certain policies, that programs are changed to reach needy people of other races. When you institute a policy, it's not enough to have good intentions—it's essential to follow up and see what's actually happening. (This is called "program evaluation" in the policy world.)

Because of historic injustices, Black Americans and other minority groups need extra follow-up. Think about how Black Americans did not receive full access to New Deal and GI benefits. One powerful framework for evaluation is "the Black Women Best" advocated by Janelle Jones, President Biden's first chief economist in the Department of Labor, and the first Black woman to hold that role. While in academia, Jones cowrote a paper proposing that the government use Black women as an economic barometer. If Black women did well under a policy, the paper argued, it would help bring more economic fairness to American communities.

We thought of Jones's paper again in 2022, when the television host Trevor Noah said in his farewell speech on *The Daily Show*, "If you truly want to learn about America, talk to Black women, 'cause unlike everybody else, Black women can't afford to fuck around and find out. Black people understand how hard it is when things go bad—especially in America, but anyplace where Black people exist, whether it's Brazil, whether it's South Africa, wherever it is. When things go bad, Black people know that it gets worse for them. Black women, in particular, they know what shit is."

To create inclusive policies, it is important to have people of different backgrounds in all levels of leadership in the government and in education, companies, and nonprofits. While it can't be assumed that someone from a particular background is representative of everyone of that background, it's important to have different perspectives in the room and to draw out all views in meetings and panel discussions.

Third, pay attention to conversations around risk and pricing. In business and in government, practices were developed more than one hundred years ago that supported charging higher prices to "riskier" people. Within capitalism, it makes sense that businesses want to be paid more for lending money to people who are less likely to pay them back. And it makes sense that businesses want to be paid more for selling products to consumers who may cost them more money to serve. That being said, this practice often leads to racially correlated results: Black people, as we have seen, are more likely to be charged more for things like auto insurance. Pay attention to these conversations in your business and in politics and ask whether there are other ways to share the risk that do not have such racial consequences. Ask whether there is room for the government or a third party to help defray the cost of that risk. In the case of higher pricing due simply to people living in poor areas, there seems to be a strong argument for system-wide actions that defray those costs. In the case of higher costs for people who have made financial mistakes, it's still a worthy question to ask: Are we trying to hold them back or help them move forward? How can we do the latter? Pay special attention in the overlooked case of people coming out of prison, who are often in debt.

Fourth, when someone says they want to close a wealth gap, ask "For which people?" A wealth gap, after all, has nuances throughout the distribution. Depending on which measures you look at, you could close some gaps without helping lots of people. With the Black-white wealth gap, for instance, if you measure all dollars in the hands of white Americans versus all dollars in the hands of Black Americans, concentrating more money in the hands of the wealthiest Black Americans is a way to close the gap. (Theoretically, you could put 13 percent of all American wealth in the hands of a small fraction of Black Americans, and that would equal their population-based share of American wealth.) So, if you want widespread change, ask more questions: Ask about the *who* as well as the how. Ask yourself whose opportunity you're fighting for.

Fifth and finally, be open to change. Do you want a more equitable world? This may mean that more affordable housing is built near your home. It may mean that the way your company decides who gets promoted will change. It may mean that the way your children's school handles grading is reevaluated, or even that their school's demographics change. Engage in these discussions with the goal of finding a path forward that opens doors for more people. Listen out for money-over-morals arguments, where people say they are in favor of something that is more inclusive but then back away for fear it will cost them money.

These suggestions are not policy prescriptions or solutions to the Black-white wealth gap—or any other wealth gap, for that matter. They are perspectives to take with you as you navigate our unequal world.

ACKNOWLEDGMENTS

This book was a massive project, and we have many people to thank. First, our editor at HarperCollins, Hollis Heimbouch, helped craft the vision and cheer us along the way. Thank you for your heartfelt belief in us and in the importance of our project. Also at Harper-Collins, we want to thank Rachel Kambury, Milan Bozic, Jenna Dolan, Heather Drucker, Jessica Gilo, and Trina Hunn. For early support at HarperCollins, we thank Sarah Reid. For additional superb editing, we thank Meghan Houser.

Our agent, David McCormick, of McCormick Literary Agency, was essential for the entire journey and especially our book proposal. Thank you to David and his associate Bridget McCarthy. A special thanks also to Elizabeth Shreve and Chris Artis of Shreve Williams Public Relations for your partnership in promoting the importance of this book.

This book was a research-heavy project, and we owe thanks to Sheelagh McNeill, Brandon Adams, Adam Orme, Rebecca Cruz, Betsey Cassone, and Katie Winograd. We also had helpful reporting assistance from Arianna Johnson, Amber Burton, and John Cooper. A special thank-you to Frances Smith for her brilliant illustrations and graphics. Thank you also to Roque Ruiz for additional help and to Jordan Mitchell for art we used online. Please check out the awesome portfolios of artwork online by Frances Smith and Jordan Mitchell. Links are on our website: www.15cents.info.

Thank you also to the Yale School of Management, where we teach the MBA course Race and Money in America: Contemporary Business Application. Dean Kerwin Charles, Edieal Pinker, Gabriel Rossi,

Tambira Armmand, and Professors Barry Nalebuff and Will Goetzmann have been exceptional guides in our teaching and research work. We appreciate the support of the Russell Sage Foundation, which welcomed us both to lecture about our book and where Louise was a visiting journalist. We also appreciate the *Wall Street Journal*, where we met and where we began work on this book.

Thank you to friends and colleagues who gave us helpful reads and feedback on revisions, including Lilly Armstrong, Vanessa Brown, Susan Chira, Guthrie and Jenny Collin, Nancy Edwards, Henry Ferris, Katherine and Clifton Hill, Stephanie Holloway and Leseliey Welch, Cassandra Spratling, Deborah Sontag, Billie Sweeney, John Stoll, and JT Thomas.

Thank you most of all to the people across the country who welcomed us into their stories. That includes people sometimes featured in only a few lines of this book who spent time with us. So many of your thoughts helped us shape this book. We hope you feel pride in your quotes throughout these pages. We are proud to have been able to tell detailed stories of Black families, adding to a historical canon that is still underrepresented.

Very special thanks and a place in our heart will forever remain for all of the major people featured in our book who spent countless hours with us, and also to their family members. We greatly appreciate the Renders (and the Blackmons and the Longs); the Youngs; the Glovers (and the Renties); the Woodalls (and the Days and the Robinsons); the Bacons (and the Lewises and the Kellys); the Dixons; and James Lovelace (and a special thank-you to his lawyer, Darrius Woods).

You all trusted us, and we appreciate that. Personal stories are among the most valuable currencies of life. You have enlightened us and our readers by sharing yours.

Ebony's Acknowledgments

After months of talking about our upcoming interview with Ambassador Andrew Young, Louise and I finally arrived, from New York and Kansas City, at the Georgia Public Broadcasting Building. June 15,

2021, was a hot Georgia day, and we had wondered whether, at age eighty-nine, Andrew would be super alert with us. We didn't know what to expect. In a wide-ranging interview, we discussed Andrew's ancestors, his activism, the Civil Rights Movement, mayoral and diplomatic work, and his most recent venture—Greenwood, a fintech company that provided banking services. He even asked us if we could help track down some history on his family, which you probably noted while reading this book.

Nearly two hours later, as we were wrapping up, he turned to me and said, "You've got a husband?" If I hadn't been so sad, I would have taken this as a compliment. It had been 126 days since my sweet partner, Terez A. Paylor, had died. Terez read an early version of our book proposal and encouraged and supported my writing the book with Louise.

At that moment, I was exhausted and still very deep in grief. Every day for more than a year after Terez unexpectedly passed away at thirty-seven, I had been buried in tasks pertaining to his estate—papers, emails, phone calls, meetings with lawyers and financial planners. Nothing prepares you to lose your person at the height of his or her career, and so I replied to Andrew, "He passed away three months ago. We were planning on getting married, yeah." My tears started. There wasn't a long silence before Louise started talking, turning what could have been an unbearably sad, awkward moment into a tribute to Terez.

"He was a great journalist, also, covered the NFL," she told Andrew. "Terez Paylor was her partner, and actually, at his funeral, it was extremely moving. The preacher of his funeral is involved in the national NAACP."

I whispered the preacher's name: "Wendell Anthony."

Louise continued: "And he talked at the funeral about how for Terez, he not only wrote about football but he really took a stand and explained in journalism why [Colin Kaepernick's] kneeling on the field—it was not an act of disrespect. That, really, he was standing up for what was right."

You are reading this book right now because Louise Story was my partner in writing it. And at times—such as when I went back to work full time and had to manage the things that suddenly appear on your plate after a sudden loss, the death of a loved one—she carried parts of it without me, as our lead writer.

During this multiyear journey, there have been people who opened doors and shared information that shaped this book. I am forever grateful to them. I appreciate everyone who shared their story, time, wisdom, and knowledge with us.

In September 2021, during the justice walk for Julian Lewis that his son, Brook Bacon, led, Louise and I had a memorable moment in our partnership. Days of that walk were so sticky and hot that our clothes clung to our bodies. Louise kept a close pace with Brook, learning every inch of his economic story. At times, I was inside the rest vehicle, a bus following along, with those who couldn't make the entire walk, and when nobody was looking, and sometimes when they were, I would cry on that bus, thinking of the life I would no longer have with Terez. Then I'd look out the window and see Louise at the front of the line, interviewing Brook. One of the drivers made a joke, asking if Louise and I were there to cover the walk or to be in it. And I explained immersive journalism to him. We were there, I explained, to fully understand what had motivated people to walk so many dozens of miles in the name of their loved one. Louise and I had to walk with them, or at least try, to fully understand their purpose, I said.

On that walk, I developed a deeper appreciation for the people who, decades earlier, had walked for my Civil Rights. Louise and I completed about half the walk—close to thirty miles over five days.

I have the deepest gratitude to Louise for her partnership in a project that I hope will be a defining moment for our careers and will spark needed conversation and action with regard to economic solutions for Black Americans. I also thank Louise's husband, who sacrificed time with her and supported this project.

For all our research into other people's ancestors, we had some gaps in knowledge about our own. My father's family was from Louisville in the 1900s, but in the 1800s, they were in Tennessee. As we looked at old records, I was surprised to find one branch in which two of my great-great-great-grandparents were identified as mulattoes. Odder still, these ancestors of mine had an older white man living in their household in

1870, when it was extremely atypical for a white person to live in a Black household. That white man had been wealthy before the Civil War, with a net worth of $88,000 in 1860. That white man was worth only $1,000 in 1870. I wondered if he was the father of one of my mulatto ancestors.

As Louise and I discussed this ancestry, I thought of my grand-mother Bessie Bond Reed, who descended from the mulatto ancestors. Bessie used to make the best cakes and even dresses for her grandchil-dren's dolls. Working on this book gave me a new understanding of our family and at which points in time they were more fortunate compared to some Black families. Bessie's husband, my grandfather Robert, for instance, fought in World War II. Unlike some Black Americans, he was then able to use the GI Bill to purchase a home in a suburb of Louisville. Bessie and Robert's homeownership provided stability for my grandmother after Robert died. And it set a goal for my family members to achieve homeownership. I thought often of that early homeownership in my family and its impact, just as I also thought of Black families with veterans who could not access those GI benefits because of racism.

I thank my family members for cheering for me—with a special emphasis on my aunts, a powerful delegation. Louise and I count among our supporters my aunt Sandra Reed Cowan, Grandma Bes-sie's daughter, who read an early version of this book; my aunt Kim Reed Hickman, Sandra's sister, who answered questions about our family tree; my aunt Angela Fields Johnson, my mother's sister; and my adopted "Aunt Vanessa." All four stayed the course with a lot of encouragement and love. I am also grateful to my maternal grand-mother, Helen, who, when I needed strength, told me, "You are my granddaughter," and there is power in that. And, of course, I thank with so much love and grace Terez's mom, my mother-in-law, Ava Paylor Elliott.

I'd also like to thank a fraction of the friends who have been ex-tremely helpful and supportive over the last few years and cheered on this project with words of encouragement. Those special friends include Leseliey Welch and Stephanie Holloway, Bill and Laurie Reiter, Me-keisha and Al Toby, Tasha Flournoy, Kiristen Jefferson, Tahman and Jennifer Bradley, Kortney and Frank King, Vahe and Cindy Gregorian, Charles Robinson, Tameka Robinson Bell, Delano Massey, Kate and Dave Butler, Russell Contreras, Amanda Barrett, Cory Schouten, Neysa Page-Lieberman, Victoria Cherrie, Krisha Tormes, Anna Munguia, Denise Farrar, Heather Carrington, Bridget Murphy, Ruby Bailey, Candace Buckner, Heather Ciras McCarthy, Abby Powers, Mará Rose Williams, Kathy Lu, Meghan Irons, Dr. Afi Scruggs, Dr. Lincoln Pettaway, Dr. Mary Bixby, Christine Wilson, Amie Parnes, Carol and Craig Schumer, Adrienne and Chris Albert, Charlayne Murrell-Smith, Carole Charnow, Kiona Sinks, Nicole Jacobs Silvey, Bob Kendrick, Joel Goldberg, Kisha Verdusco, Erika Brice, Tamarra Anthony, Joni Wickham, NaTika Rowles, Jon Lawrence, Bill and Terry Kole and Felecia Henderson. I appreciate you all and many others who were not named.

I acknowledge and thank all the journalists whom I have professionally worked with over the course of my career. One of my early mentors, Cassandra Spratling, a longtime Detroit journalist, was also an early confidential reader for us.

I have learned and grown in all my previous jobs, and that contributed to my skills on this project. A special thanks to my colleagues at the Marshall Project. I have such respect for our newsroom's work shining a light on the criminal justice and legal system. And to my friends and fellow board members at United WE (formerly, the Women's Foundation of Kansas City), I appreciate being united with you as United WE seeks to improve economic and civic opportunities for women.

My deepest love and thanks also extend to the Kansas City community, which has made me feel at home and welcomed after Terez's death. I appreciate the neighbors who brought me food, left notes on my door, and offered words of encouragement, as they knew I was working hard on this book. This community stretching across two states, Kansas and Missouri, has offered unwavering kindness and support.

I pray that everyone who reads this book will finish it with a deeper understanding of the wealth gaps in America and their impact historically and in the present day on Black Americans—especially those readers under fifty who are trying to improve their family's financial situation. May this information and education build upon the works of so many who come before us and lead those in power to make better and more just decisions for those who have been affected by past unjust actions.

Louise's Acknowledgments

When my daughter was born, Ebony was just joining my team at the *Wall Street Journal.* As we went through the Covid-19 pandemic, Ebony's face was one of the most common my daughter would see on the Zoom screen with me. A favorite memory I have of Ebony during the pandemic is when she hired a harpist to perform an online concert for a group of our colleagues. Everyone was so frazzled and tired, and Ebony had just the right idea for how to bring peace to our souls. My daughter sat on my lap for that concert. And when my daughter draws pictures for each member of our family, she often draws one for Ebony, too.

Ebony and I have been through thick and thin together, and I'm so glad to have had such a kind, insightful, forgiving, patient, and creative partner. It's been mainly easy, but when it hasn't been, our conversations helped us both stretch our thinking and learn more about what matters most.

I've always said I care a lot about fairness, and my work has long shone a light on unfairness in the world. But with this project, my understanding of fairness has been pressure-tested more than ever. Is fairness giving the same thing to everyone and expecting the same thing from everyone? I've realized it's not that simple. In the race of life, not everyone starts at the same point, and not everyone is wearing the same shoes. Perhaps winning the race of life is not about being first, leaving others in the dust. Perhaps it's about crossing the finish line holding someone else's hand, someone different from you, someone you met on the path and enjoyed the journey with.

I have many people to thank for helping me reach the point where I could carry out this book. First of all, Ebony. Even in the saddest of times, you are strong and graceful. I admire you and appreciate your steadfast friendship. Whether it was when I was sick in the Atlanta Whole Foods, or relaxing on the beaches of Corsica, or on a corporate Zoom, you told the world about me, "She's my friend." Thank you. I wish more than anything that Terez could have read this book—I know he has been watching out for us.

Some more thank-yous:

From my childhood in Florida, I want to thank my classmates from the Lake Sybelia Elementary School, which was located on the border of Maitland and Eatonville, a historic Black community. While I am sure there were undercurrents I was unaware of, I felt in elementary school that white and Black children were friends, peers, and of equal value. I am grateful for that early exposure, for the literature of Zora Neale Hurston, and for the teachers of Lake Sybelia, especially Marva Hall Taylor, my fourth-grade teacher, who told me about being a daughter of sharecroppers and who performed with me in the play *Big River*.

Also from my childhood, I want to thank the Central Florida theater and opera community, where I witnessed a welcoming environment for the LGBT community in the 1980s and where, as an actor, I learned to stand in other people's shoes. I especially thank Robin Jensen, my opera teacher, and Novie Greene, my voice teacher.

I had an amazing education, and I am grateful for all my teachers every step of the way. I owe a special thanks to Missy Baker for developing my writing skills. And to Barry Nalebuff at the Yale School of Management, who taught me to think differently in helpful ways and who spotted my business acumen.

In journalism, I have had a lot of mentors, and I'm lucky for that. In particular, I want to thank Marcia Chambers, Steven Brill, Sylvia Nasar, Gretchen Morgenson, Larry Ingrassia, Jill Abramson, Deborah Sontag, James B. Stewart, Dean Baquet, and Matt Purdy. I learned a lot from the great editors Christine Kay, Paul Fishleder, Winnie O'Kelley, and Tim O'Brien while at the *New York Times*. I so enjoyed working with investigative reporting colleagues Ginger Thompson, Michael Luo, Stephanie Saul, David Barstow, Walt Bogdanich, James Glanz, Andrea Elliott, and Jo Becker, and the great 2014 Innovation Team members Amy O'Leary, Andrew Phelps, Adam Ellick, Adam Bryant, Elena Gianni, Ben Peskoe, Jon Galinsky, Charles Duhigg, and A. G. Sulzberger. I am also grateful for my friends from Dow Jones, especially Rajiv Pant, Ramin Beheshti, Smita Pillai, Suzi Watford, Karl Wells, Jonathan Buckley, Josh Stinchcomb, Guthrie Collin, Christina Van Tassell, Kamilah Mitchell-Thomas, Eleanor Breen, and Will Lewis.

Longtime friends are so important, and those special people include the Armstrongs, the Hills, the Haleys, the Kegley-Koles, the Hilewiczes, the Praids, Chris Fabian, Adam Ellick, the Kochi-Cselles, the Zeira-Leiths, and my high school Wildcat cross-country team. I especially appreciate Monica Hickey for all the special times running with her around New York City. During the pandemic and while we were starting this book, I appreciated the friendships of Kabir Seth, Jason Jedlinski, Dion Bailey, Lydia Serota, Leslie Yazel, Ross Fadely, Mike Finkel, John Schimmel, Fernando Turch, Thomas Williams, Anthony De Rosa, Kevin Dubouis, Krista Schmidt, Stephen Wisnefski, Shazna Nessa, Francesco Marconi, Emily Anderson, and others currently and formerly at the *Wall Street Journal*. In recent years, I have appreciated the friendships of all of the Brumbergs, Alex Wallace, the Porcellis, the Collins, Arielle Tepper, Dylann Craig Germann, Josh Steiner, Irina Novoselsky, Andrea Douglas, Hannah Granade, Beril Pekin, Angelina Lipman, Isora Bailey, and all the superpower mothers and the teachers at my children's schools. I appreciated my fellow board members of the Community Word Project and the Prison Journalism Project. I appreciated the team working with me over the years in my home: Gloria, Amelia, Meriem, Mouna, Heydi, Betsey, Shazam, Carmel. I also appreciated the scholars at the Russell Sage Foundation, and I learned from the work of people there, including Scott Allard, Elizabeth Ananat, Jennifer Chudy, Phil Garboden, Colin Gordon, Jennifer Klein, Trevon Logan, Terry Maroney, Natasha Quadlin, Adam Reich, Eva Rosen, Lara Shore-Sheppard, Jennifer Silva, JT Thomas, Mignon Moore, and Anna Louie Sussman.

This book taught me to look differently at my personal roots. I was born in Atlanta, in the Crawford Long Hospital, and I heard about the city's history from my father, also an Atlanta native. My father was the first in his family to attend college. He was brilliant, hardworking, and kind. I looked up to him and admired his self-made success. While writing this book, I realized that Emory, where he attended medical school, admitted its first Black student only a few years before my father went there on scholarship. For as "self-made" as my father was, he had the advantage of being white. I realized: had he been Black and a few years older, he could not have taken the path he took. That would have affected my life and the advantages I have had.

The first Black student at Emory University School of Medicine was Hamilton Holmes. A road named after him runs on the west side of Atlanta and intersects Collier Drive, where Michael Render grew up (and where the Berean Outreach Ministry food pantry is located). Michael Render: I learned about Hamilton Holmes—and I came to understand that even my self-made dad was privileged—because of you.

I hold my mother and my father on high. Purer people there could not be. They gave me unwavering support, and they always believed in me and my siblings. They also showed me what it meant to be kind to everyone, always. I am so grateful to them both. I thank my siblings, too, as well as my in-laws.

For more than twenty years, my husband has been my co-pilot. Thank you, my sweet homme, for making my dreams your own and for caring so much about my desire to make a positive impact on the world. I cannot believe how lucky I am.

I've dedicated this book to my children. I hope that reading it inspires you to find your own ways to make the world better.

NOTES

The authors of this book conducted several hundred in-depth interviews. Quotations that are not sourced in the endnotes are from interviews conducted for this book, generally by one of the two authors. The authors use "we" throughout the book because the project was a partnership, but most interviews were not conducted by both of them. These interviews occurred in the years 2020 through 2023. Facts that are not sourced are either commonly known facts or are from subjects' social media posts or are from the authors' interviews. The book draws on extensive historical records, where name spellings and dates of birth sometimes vary. In these instances, the authors have made best efforts to use the name spellings that the subjects and their families preferred.

EPIGRAPH

xi   back marked "insufficient funds": Martin Luther King Jr., "I Have a Dream" speech, Washington, D.C., August 28, 1963.

PREFACE

xv   "showed up here at Grady": "RIT Activated to Help Three Firefighters Caught in Floor Collapse in Atlanta (GA) Fire," FirefighterNation.com, April 12, 2022.

xix   turned down only 28 percent: Shawn Donnan et al., "Wells Fargo Rejected Half Its Black Applicants in Mortgage Refinancing Boom," Bloomberg, March 11, 2022.

xxii   "police brutality and systemic inequity": James Woodall and Mark Ellingsen, *Wired for Racism? How Evolution and Faith Move Us to Challenge Racial Idolatry* (Hyde Park, N.Y.: New City Press, 2022), pp. 9–10.

xxv   Black students had not: Emory University School of Medicine, where Louise Story's father earned his medical degree, did not admit Black students until 1963.

INTRODUCTION: THE BLACK-WHITE WEALTH GAP

1   "wealth" as the reason: Nina Banks, *Democracy, Race and Justice: The Speeches and Writings of Sadie T. M. Alexander* (New Haven, Conn.: Yale University Press, 2021), p. 4.

3   Black-white gaps have improved: "On Views of Race and Inequality, Blacks and Whites Are Worlds Apart," Pew Research Center, June 27, 2016.

4   and it includes race: Edward N. Wolff and Maury Gittleman, "Inheritances and the Distribution of Wealth or Whatever Happened to the Great Inheritance Boom?" Working Paper No. 445, U.S. Bureau of Labor Statistics, U.S. Department of Labor, January 2011.

4   gap since 1989: In addition, on occasion we use the Survey of Income and Program Participation from the U.S. Census Bureau.

4   the University of Bonn: Ellora Derenoncourt, Chi Hyun Kim, Moritz Kuhn, and Moritz Schularick., "Wealth of Two Nations: The U.S. Racial Wealth Gap, 1860–2020," *The Quarterly Journal of Economics*, September 1, 2023.

4   median white family: Ana Hernández Kent and Lowell R. Ricketts, "The State of U.S. Wealth Inequality," Federal Reserve Bank of St. Louis, May 23, 2023.

5   the 2022 government survey: The Survey of Consumer Finances is carried out every three years. The next survey data year will be 2025, and the release of that data will be in the fall of 2026.

5   Black wealth was $211,600: These are all in 2022 dollars. Data pulled from the Data section of the Federal Reserve website, updated October 18, 2023. Historic data also reviewed in Neil Bhutta et al., "Changes in U.S. Family Finances from 2016 to 2019: Evidence from the Survey of Consumer Finances," *Federal Reserve Bulletin* 106, No. 5 (September 2020). The Black-white wealth ratio also came out to 15.5 in 2022 when using median figures from the Federal Reserve's Survey of Consumer Finances. The median Black family in 2022 had $44,100 compared to the median white family's level of $284,310.

5   average for white families: These are all in 2022 dollars. Data has been pulled from the Data section of the Federal Reserve website, updated October 18, 2023. Historic data also reviewed in Ana Hernández Kent and Lowell R. Ricketts, "Racial and Ethnic Household Wealth Trends and Wealth Inequality," Institute for Economic Equity, Federal Reserve Bank of St. Louis, November 29, 2022. Note that when averages, rather than medians, are used, the ratio of Black wealth to white wealth is just slightly higher, but virtually the same as of 2022. In 2022, the average Black family had 15.54 percent of the average white family's wealth. The median Black family had 15.51 percent of the median white family's wealth. In some years, the average is higher than the median, because with averages, the highest level of wealthy families pulls up the numbers. In tandem with the 2007 housing collapse and recession, the Black-white wealth ratio for median families dropped for several years. In recent years, that ratio has been coming back up to the levels of the late 1990s. The ratio of the average Black and white families' wealth, however, has remained flat the last decade, and has not recovered ground lost after 2007. With both measures (the mean and the median), the gap remains very large consistently over the past several decades.

6   that year had no wealth: Survey of Income and Program Participation from the U.S. Census Bureau. As analyzed in Rakesh Kochhar and Mohamad Moslimani, "Wealth Surged in the Pandemic, but Debt Endures for Poorer Black and Hispanic Families," Pew Research Center, December 4, 2023.

6   work lower-paying, blue-collar jobs: William A. Darity Jr. and A. Kirsten Mullen, *From Here to Equality: Reparations for Black Americans in the Twenty-First Century* (Chapel Hill: University of North Carolina Press, 2022), pp. xii.

7   "policy ideas come up": Derenoncourt quoted in Marissa Michaels, "Economics Professor Ellora Derenoncourt Discusses New Center on Inequality," *Daily Princetonian*, November 11, 2021.

7   Survey of Consumer Finances: Another important data source was Monroe Nathan Work's, the *Negro Year Book* (Tuskegee, Ala.: Negro Year Book Publishing Company, editions 1912–1938).

10   with the following framework: We expanded this framework from Charles Tilly, *Durable*

Inequality (Berkeley: University of California Press, 1999). The suggestion that we incorporate Tilly's categories and add the term *expropriation* came from Colin Gordon, a professor of U.S. history at the University of Iowa.

11 was recorded in 2023: In the fall of 2023, when the Federal Reserve released the 2022 Survey of Consumer Finances, there was some debate on whether there was progress toward closing the Black-white wealth gap. The median values of that gap have been improving since 2013, and, indeed, in 2022 they went up to 15.5 percent (they had been at 12.8 percent in 2019). This puts the median figures at their highest level since 2001. That said, the gaps of both the median and the average levels of Black and white families improved in the late 1990s to levels above this and then fell in the early 2000s. The median started improving in 2013, while the average kept falling. In 2022, the gaps for the mean and median wealth levels reached the same level (15 percent). It is unclear after 2022 whether the Black-white wealth ratio will continue to go up for either the median or the mean. If the median continues going up at the rate that it did from 1989 to 2022, the Black-white wealth gap would converge to 1:1 in 291 years (in the year 2314). If the median continues to go up at the rate it did from 2013 to 2022, the Black-white wealth gap would converge to 1:1 in 120 years (in the year 2143). If the median continues going up at the rate it did from 2019 to 2022, the Black-white wealth gap would converge to 1:1 in 91 years (in the year 2114).

13 the Black-white wealth gap: Lily Batchelder and Greg Leiserson, "Disparities in the Benefits of Tax Expenditures by Race and Ethnicity," U.S. Department of the Treasury, January 20, 2023.

15 lowest homeownership rate: The U.S. Census Bureau data showed Black homeownership at 45.7 percent in August 2023, below the homeownership rates for white, Latino, and Asian people. This data did not include Native Americans. U.S. Census, "Current Population Survey/Housing Vacancy Survey," U.S. Census Bureau, August 2, 2023.

15 rate of white Americans: U.S. Bureau of Labor Statistics, "Labor Force Statistics from the Current Population Survey," U.S. Bureau of Labor Statistics, Department of Labor, September 2023.

15 average white household: Aditya Aladangady and Akila Forde, "Wealth Inequality and the Racial Wealth Gap," *FEDS Notes*, Board of Governors of the Federal Reserve System, October 22, 2021.

15 as are white Americans: "Survey of Consumer Finances (SCF)," Board of the Governors of the Federal Reserve System; and Neil Bhutta et al., "Disparities in Wealth by Race and Ethnicity in the 2019 Survey of Consumer Finances," *FEDS Notes*, Board of Governors of the Federal Reserve System, September 28, 2020.

15 than white college graduates: Melanie Hanson, "Student Loan Debt by Race," Education Data Initiative, January 16, 2023.

15 33 percent of white Americans: This report tracked outcomes over six years, so it was unclear whether students finished after six years had elapsed. D. Shapiro et al., "Completing College: A National View of Student Completion Rates—Fall 2012 Cohort," National Student Clearinghouse Research Center, December 2018.

16 wipe away their debts as often as white Americans: Paul Kiel and Hannah Fresques, "Data Analysis: Bankruptcy and Race in America," ProPublica, September 27, 2017.

16 generated by tracked companies: U.S. Census Bureau, Nonemployer Statistics and Annual Business Survey, 2017.

16 law, and many other fields: Valerie Wilson, Ethan Miller, and Melat Kassa, "Racial Representation in Professional Occupations," Economic Policy Institute, June 8, 2021.

16 around 4,000 FDIC-insured banks: "Minority Depository Institutions Program," Federal

Deposit Insurance Corporation, October 16, 2023; and "Statistics at a Glance," Federal Deposit Insurance Corporation, October 16, 2023.

16 as it is for white Americans: Megan T. Stevenson and Sandra G. Mayson, "The Scale of Misdemeanor Justice," *Boston University Law Review* 98, No. 731 (March 2018): p. 759.

16 rate of white Americans: "Police Shootings Database 2015–2023: Search by Race, Age, Department," *Washington Post*, October 16, 2023.

16 lending practices in the area: Dylan Purcell, "Violent Blocks and the Legacy of Redlining in Philadelphia," *Philadelphia Inquirer*, September 16, 2021.

17 1930s Minneapolis zoning map: "Mapping Inequality: Redlining in New Deal America," Digital Scholarship Lab, University of Richmond, December 2015.

17 Cup Foods, the corner store: Deena Winter, "Cup Foods Clerk Regrets 911 Call on George Floyd; Chauvin Body Cam Footage Played in the Third Day of Trial," *Wisconsin Examiner*, April 1, 2021.

17 and about 21 percent Black: This data was reported with a small margin of error on either side, which is why we use "about" in the text. U.S. Census Bureau, American Community Survey, 2016–2020, City of Minneapolis website.

17 "African blood or descent": Greg Miller, "When Minneapolis Segregated," Bloomberg, January 8, 2020.

17 rate among Black residents: Miller, "When Minneapolis Segregated."

18 forty acres of land: Henry Louis Gates Jr., "The Truth Behind '40 Acres and a Mule,' 100 Amazing Facts About the Negro," PBS.

19 "generations ago": Dylan Jackson, "Atlanta Has the Highest Income Inequality in the Nation, Census Data Shows," *Atlanta Journal-Constitution*, November 28, 2022.

CHAPTER 1: MEET GREENWOOD BANK

23 "Remember that every time": Greenwood Bank email advertisement, July 14, 2023.

24 for Elton John: Samantha Leal, "Why This Luxe South African Safari Lodge Is the Ultimate Abode," *DuJour*, 2020.

24 on social media: @mr.mthornton, Instagram post, March 14, 2020.

25 Berean Outreach Ministry: "Berean Outreach Ministry Center," Berean SDA Church, March 7, 2022.

27 get a license to ride it, or insurance: In many places, scooters require a driver's license and insurance. However, some drivers may not be aware of this.

27 "is now absent a bank": Michael quickly added that there was one, lonely banking outpost still on the west side, a Citizens Trust Bank, a longtime Black-owned bank based in Atlanta. All quotes by Michael Render, unless otherwise cited, are from one of the authors' interview with Michael Render. (This is the case with all people quoted in this book: when a citation is not included, the quote is from an interview with the books' authors.)

28 fall over the next decade: "Minority Depository Institutions List." FDIC website, updated quarterly.

28 "well-being of the world": Frederick Douglass, "To the Depositors of the Freedmen's Savings & Trust Co.," White House Historical Association, originally published in Douglass's newspaper the *New National Era*, June 25, 1874.

29 bank founded in 1921: Willard C. Lewis, "Citizens Trust Bank," New Georgia Encyclopedia, October 30, 2021.

29 the Black banking movement: In 2017, Wells Fargo introduced a sixty-billion-dollar program aimed at increasing Black American homeownership. It is unclear if this was tied to the Black bank movement or to the sixty-million-dollar Black mortgage program Michael

mentioned to us. "Wells Fargo Commits to Increase African American Homeownership," Wells Fargo Newsroom, February 28, 2017.

CHAPTER 2: MICHAEL RENDER AND THE FRACTURING OF A CITY

33 mayor of Baltimore, 1910: Michael H. Wilson, "The Racist History of Zoning Laws," Foundation for Economic Education, May 21, 2019.

33 George Floyd was killed: Jay Croft, "Killer Mike Urges Atlanta Protesters 'Not to Burn Your Own House Down' in Emotional Plea," CNN, May 30, 2020.

34 ". . . and apartheid ended": "T.I., Killer Mike Join Mayor Keisha Lance Bottoms in Condemning Violence in Atlanta Protests," 11Alive.com, May 29, 2020, YouTube video.

34 "You won't regret it": Stuart Emmrich, "'It Is Your Duty Not to Burn Your Own House Down'—Killer Mike's Powerful Message to Atlanta Protestors," *Vogue*, May 30, 2020.

35 "don't know how to express": Ment Nelson [@mentnelson], Twitter, May 29, 2020.

35 "tries to detain one of you": @PunchXD, "Killer Mike, usually I respect you but not this time," Twitter, May 30, 2020.

35 rural areas of the state: Alton Hornsby Jr., *A Short History of Black Atlanta, 1847–1993* (Montgomery, Ala.: E-book Time, 2015).

35 only about 2,500: Hornsby, *A Short History of Black Atlanta*.

35 lived in Atlanta as of 1863: Hornsby, *A Short History of Black Atlanta*.

36 in Atlanta in 1864: Maurice J. Hobson, *The Legend of the Black Mecca* (Chapel Hill: University of North Carolina Press, 2017), p. 12.

36 public figures and businesspeople: Hobson, *The Legend of the Black Mecca*, p. 12.

36 "feeds Anglo-Saxon hearts": Quoted in Gunnar Myrdal, *American Dilemma: The Negro Problem and Modern Democracy* (Piscataway, N.J.: Transaction Publishers, 1944), p. 1354.

36 "essential to mutual progress": Bernice Tell, "Separate Yet One: Booker T. Washington's Atlanta Compromise Displayed at Library," Library of Congress, Washington, D.C.

37 "who out-raced her": W. E. B. Du Bois, *Three African-American Classics* (Garden City, N.Y.: Dover Publications, 2007), p. 214.

37 state university in 1961: Amanda Nash, "Hamilton Holmes," New Georgia Encyclopedia, August 19, 2005.

37 into a new home: Samuel L. Adams, "Bombing Probe Shows No Tenseness in Area," *Atlanta Daily World*, February 28, 1956.

38 months after purchasing it: Clerk's Office, Georgia Superior Court, Deed to Land Lot 207 of the 14th District of Fulton County, Georgia, February 4, 1956, Box 3081, p. 689; and Atlanta Title Company, Title No. 172, p. 665. Box 3108, p. 150.

38 purchased a new home: Adams, "Bombing Probe Shows No Tenseness in Area"; and Clerk's Office, Georgia Superior Court.

38 one-story 1,056-square-foot white house: Zillow listing, February. 2, 2024.

38 the Hightower Road divide: Clerk's Office, Georgia Superior Court, Deed to Land Lot 207 of the 14th District of Fulton County, Georgia, October 29, 1954, Box 2937, p. 26.

39 40 percent of Atlanta's population: LeeAnn Lands, *The Culture of Property: Race, Class, and Housing Landscapes in Atlanta, 1880–1950* (Athens: University of Georgia Press, 2009), p. 234.

39 between 1880 and 1906: Rebecca Burns, *Rage in the Gate City: The Story of the 1906 Atlanta Race Riot* (Athens: University of Georgia Press, 2006), p. 27.

39 Black or white renters: Lands, *The Culture of Property*, p. 32.

39 single-race neighborhoods in the city at the time: Lands, *The Culture of Property*, p. 29.

39 "aesthetics and property control": Lands, *The Culture of Property*, p. 2.

39 "to get some niggers": Burns, *Rage in the Gate City*, p. 121.

39   been hard-earned, were destroyed: Burns, *Rage in the Gate City*, pp. 118–43.

40   "into Atlantans' collective experience": Burns, *Rage in the Gate City*, p. 176.

40   editions of the *Atlanta Daily World*: Alexa Benson Henderson, "Heman E. Perry and Black Enterprise in Atlanta, 1908–1925," *Business History Review* 61, No. 2 (Summer 1987): pp. 217, 240.

40   to "prominent citizens": Burns, *Rage in the Gate City*, p. 145.

40   not come to fruition:: Burns, *Rage in the Gate City*, p. 146.

41   "premises of white owners": "Boundary Lines Set for Negroes," *Atlanta Constitution*, October 12, 1910.

41   onto largely Black blocks: "Baltimore Tries Drastic Plan of Race Segregation," *New York Times*, December 25, 1910.

41   Atlanta looked for other means: Ronald Bayor, *Race and the Shaping of Twentieth Century Atlanta* (Chapel Hill: University of North Carolina Press, 1996), p. 54.

41   zoning ordinances in 1916: "Zoning," [Online] *Encyclopedia of Cleveland History*, Case Western Reserve University, June 29, 2018.

42   evangelist for the practice: Joan Cook, "Harland Bartholomew, 100, Dean of City Planners," *New York Times*, December 7, 1989.

42   colored people and boardinghouses: "Expert Shows Benefits of a Zoning Law," *Chicago Commerce*, October 18, 1919.

42   New York City's zoning committee: "Village of Euclid v. Ambler Realty Co.," [Online] *Encyclopedia of Cleveland History*, May 12, 2018.

42   a plan in Cleveland: Robert Harvey Whitten and Frank Rabold Walker, *The Cleveland Zone Plan: Report to the City Plan Commission Outlining Tentative Zone Plan for Cleveland* (Cleveland, Ohio: City Plan Commission, 1921).

42   wrote to Atlanta officials: Richard Rothstein, *The Color of Law: A Forgotten History of How Our Government Segregated America* (New York: Liveright, 2017), p. 46.

42   "white and colored race": Robert H. Whitten, *The Atlanta Zone Plan: Report Outlining a Tentative Zone Plan for Atlanta*, City of Atlanta City Planning Commission, 1922, p. 10.

42   Whitten's map broke up: "Tentative Zone Plan," map, City of Atlanta City Planning Commission, 1922.

42   race-based zoning was illegal: Bowen et al. v. City of Atlanta (1924), 125 S.E. 199 Ga. 145.

42   woman named Alice Link: "Two Attacks Made on City Zoning Law," *Atlanta Constitution*, May 25, 1924.

42   Supreme Court ruling: "Two Attacks Made on City Zoning Law."

43   new Black resident's porch: "Blast Rocks Sells Ashby Area: Housing Fracas Continues in Friday Midnight Blast," *Atlanta Daily World*, June 1, 1947.

43   knocked out by a bomb: "Blast Rocks Sells Ashby Area."

43   "money can't change your color": "Terrorists Blast 3 Homes," *Afro-American*, June 7, 1947.

43   1951 in Cicero, Illinois: "Cicero Segregation Riot," *St. Louis Post-Dispatch*, June 22, 1951; and Rothstein, *The Color of Law*, p. 145.

43   1952 in Richmond, California: Roy Wilkins, "The Watch Tower," *California Eagle*, March 13, 1952; and Rothstein, *The Color of Law*, pp. 139–40.

43   1954 in Shively, Kentucky: "Jurors Inspect Wade-Home Damage During Silent Sightseeing Trip," *Courier-Journal*, December 7, 1954; and Richard Howlett, "Louisville Remembers a Tumultuous Time 60 Years Ago," WBUR, December 1, 2014.

43   1957 in Levittown, Pennsylvania: "Negro Is Defiant on Buying House," *Chattanooga Daily Times*, August 17, 1957; and "Samuel Snipes, 99, Dies; Lawyer for First Black Family in Levittown, Pa.," *New York Times*, January 10, 2019.

43   when they moved in . . . in 1985: Bettie Winston Baye, "100 Pray, Sing at Blacks' Firebombed Home," *Courier-Journal*, July 5, 1985.

44   As Ethington Lewis: Ethington T. Lewis, "Oral History Interview of E. T. Lewis, Clip 1 of 1," Booker T. Washington High School, Atlanta, Ga., March 14, 1979.

44   an interview in 1979: Lewis, "Oral History Interview of E. T. Lewis, Clip 1 of 1."

44   the time, was "Just Us": Josh Green, "Wandering Around Just Us, Atlanta's Smallest Neighborhood," Curbed Atlanta, September 20, 2016.

44   in a stately mansion: "2019 Vision Plan Mozley Park," Park Pride, June 28, 2020.

44   a Black-focused newspaper: Kevin M. Kruse, *White Flight: Atlanta and the Making of Modern Conservatism* (Princeton, N.J.: Princeton University Press, 2005), pp. 62–65.

45   "Negro or Mongolian Race": Shelley v. Kraemer, 334 US 1 (1948).

45   race-based restrictions: John Paul Stevens, *Five Chiefs: A Supreme Court Memoir* (New York: Little, Brown, 2011), p. 69.

45   William Weatherspool: Cynthia Jennings, "Rev. Dr. W.W. Weatherspool, Former Pastor of Mount Olive Baptist Church," Showcasing the Residents of Southview Cemetery, n.d.

45   percent of white Atlantans: Nathan Glazer and Davis McEntire, *Studies in Housing and Minority Groups: Special Research Report to the Commission on Race and Housing* (Los Angeles and Berkeley: University of California Press, 1960), p. 35.

46   not open to Black buyers: "Atlanta Whites Protest Pastor in Neighborhood: Governor Brought into Row," *Pittsburgh Courier*, February 26, 1949.

46   would "protect our homes": "Mayor Tries to End Row over Negro Home Limits," *Atlanta Constitution*, February 15, 1949.

46   had to be brought in: "Atlanta Whites Protest Pastor in Neighborhood."

46   put it at the time: "Mayor Tries to End Row over Negro Home Limits."

46   "or surely becoming Black": Kruse, *White Flight*, p. 79.

46   "idea of community integrity": Kruse, *White Flight*, p. 80.

46   people left Georgia farmland: Andrew Wiese, *Places of Their Own* (Chicago, Ill.: University of Chicago Press, 2004), p. 179.

47   "not to occur again": Wiese, *Places of Their Own*, p. 193.

47   "new 'Gentleman's Agreement Line'": Kruse, *White Flight*, p. 82.

47   "week by week": Kruse, *White Flight*, p. 82.

47   "white and Negro communities": Kruse, *White Flight*, p. 86.

48   didn't want him there: Kruse, *White Flight*, p. 85.

48   a few years earlier, in 1954: Clerk's Office, Georgia Superior Court, Deed to Land Lot 207 of the 14th District of Fulton County, Georgia, October 29, 1954, p. 26.

48   and a "cement finisher": *Atlanta City Directory*, 1910s, Fulton County City Records.

48   become a nurse: 1950 U.S. Federal Census.

48   Collier Heights, with a total of 1,700: Lydia A. Harris, "Brick by Brick: Atlanta's Collier Heights," *Southern Spaces*, April 20, 2016.

48   "damn thing about it": Wiese, *Places of Their Own*, p. 187.

48   "Blacks had bought the land": Wiese, *Places of Their Own*, p. 187.

48   "UNLESS THE WHITE MAN SELLS": Betsy Riley, "A Separate Peace: Collier Heights," *Atlanta Magazine*, April 30, 2010.

49   "regardless of any decision": Riley, "A Separate Peace: Collier Heights."

49   sold their homes to Black buyers: Glazer and McEntire, *Studies in Housing and Minority Groups*, p. 34.

49   farther from the city's center: Wiese, *Places of Their Own*, p. 187.

49   recalled Minnette Coleman: Quoted in Christopher Johnson, "The Epic of Collier Heights," *99% Invisible* podcast, aired December 7, 2021.

50   "this Deep South metropolis": Al Kuettner, "Atlanta Has an Answer to Negro Housing," United Press International, July 17, 1958, as cited in the National Register of Historic

Places Inventory—Nomination Form for Collier Heights Historic District, National Park Service, U.S. Department of the Interior, filed May 15, 2009.

50 ranch-style home in Collier Heights: Wilma Dykeman and James Stokely, "New Southerner: The Middle Class Negro," *New York Times*, August 9, 1959.

50 "grumble about taxes": "Races: A Lift in Living," *Time*, September 21, 1959.

51 "had in Collier Heights": Quoted in Riley, "A Separate Peace: Collier Heights."

51 Collier Heights soon afterward: Quoted in Johnson, "The Epic of Collier Heights."

51 "but [it] sounds cool": Druzella Denise Clonts, Funeral Booklet, 2017.

51 forgot his love": Clonts, Funeral Booklet.

52 arrested for petty crimes: DeKalb County Judicial Records.

52 hard sacrifice on her: Michael Render, aka Killer Mike, vocalist, "Motherless," 2023, on *Michael*.

52 rapped about the abandonment: Michael Render, "Motherless."

52 a dependent child: DeKalb County Judicial Records.

53 grits, eggs, and bacon: "Bettie Clonts" obituary, Legacy.com, March 5, 2012.

53 their hair in order: "Bettie Clonts" obituary.

53 the 1906 racial attacks: Henderson, "Heman E. Perry and Black Enterprise in Atlanta, 1908–1925."

54 called "defiant" behavior: Luke McCormick, "Hear Killer Mike's Fiery 'R.A.P. Music': The MC Runs Us Through His New LP," *Spin*, May 7, 2012.

54 "leaders of the crooks": Album cover, *R.A.P. Music*, 2012, Williams Street.

54 the group as radical: "Min. Farrakhan and Killer Mike on the Duty of Hip Hop Artists," Media Network, September 18, 2021, YouTube video. For an article about antisemitic statements, see Sophie Tatum, "Nation of Islam Leader Farrakhan Delivers Anti-Semitic speech," CNN, February 28, 2018.

CHAPTER 3: ANDREW YOUNG AND FINANCE FOR THE FREEDMEN

57 "to only be: halfway free": Andrew Young: "Freedman's Bank 150th Anniversary," C-SPAN, January 7, 2016.

57 *"to desegregate the money"*: "Freedman's Bank 150th Anniversary" [emphasis added by authors].

58 "world in which we live": "Freedman's Bank 150th Anniversary."

58 a Black bank: Marcus Anthony Hunter, "Black America's Distrust of Banks Rooted in Reconstruction," *Chicago Reporter*, February 22, 2018.

58 help them with "thrift": Carl R. Osthaus, *Freedmen, Philanthropy, and Fraud: A History of the Freedman's Savings Bank* (Champaign: University of Illinois Press, 1976), pp. 1–2.

58 Military Savings Bank in South Carolina: Reginald Washington, "The Freedman's Savings and Trust Company and African American Genealogical Research," *The National Archives: Prologue Magazine* 29, No. 2 (Summer 1997).

58 into law in March: Washington, "The Freedman's Savings and Trust Company and African American Genealogical Research."

58 surrendered in Appomattox, Virginia: Sarah Pruitt, "Why the Civil War Actually Ended 16 Months After Lee Surrendered," History.com, September 1, 2018.

59 back to Black Americans: "Freedman's Savings and Trust Company Charter and By-Laws," 1865, Library of Congress, Washington, D.C.

59 "the country to deposit": Claire Célérier and Purnoor Tak, "Finance, Advertising and Fraud: The Rise and Fall of the Freedman's Savings Bank," Proceedings of the EUROFIDAI-ESSEC, Paris, December Finance Meeting, 2022, SSRN Library, June 17, 2022.

59 their money in the bank: Washington, "The Freedman's Savings and Trust Company and African American Genealogical Research."

59 "not discussed around children": Walter Young, "The HistoryMakers Video Oral His-

tory Interview with Dr. Walter Young," The HistoryMakers, October 12, 2006, and December 13, 2006.

59 left those lines blank: U.S. Federal Census Records and Freedman's Bank Records.

60 branches around the country: Jay Sager, "Historical Echoes: The Legacy of Freedman's Savings and Trust," Liberty Street Economics, Federal Reserve Bank of New York, February 10, 2017.

60 like speculative new companies: Sager, "Historical Echoes."

60 than other contemporary banks: Célérier and Tak, "Finance, Advertising and Fraud."

60 "the FREEDMAN'S SAVINGS BANK": "The Freedman's Savings and Trust Company," New National Era, June 22, 1871, p. 4, as cited in Célérier and Tak, "Finance, Advertising and Fraud," p. 4.

60 white employers in New Orleans: 1870 Census.

60 the District of Columbia: Célérier and Tak, "Finance, Advertising and Fraud."

60 more than $57 million: Washington, "The Freedman's Savings and Trust Company and African American Genealogical Research."

60 advantage of the bank: Jonathan Levy, Freaks of Fortune (Cambridge, Mass.: Harvard University Press, 2012), pp. 129–43.

61 by selling war bonds: Levy, Freaks of Fortune, p. 113.

61 banks under their supervision: "Freedman's Bank Demise," U.S. Department of the Treasury.

61 show of confidence: See "Minority Banking Timeline" tab on website for Partnership for Progress: A Program for Minority-Owned Institutions from the Board of Governors of the Federal Reserve System.

61 on June 29, 1874: "The Freedman's Savings Bank: Good Intentions Were Not Enough; A Noble Experiment Goes Awry," Office of the Comptroller of the Currency, March 14, 2019.

61 the time it collapsed: "The Freedman's Savings Bank: Good Intentions Were Not Enough."

61 of their outstanding balances: Eric Foner, Reconstruction: America's Unfinished Revolution, 1863–1877 (New York: Harper Perennial, 2014), p. 532, as cited in Yong Kwon, "Unpaid Debt: The Freedman's Bank and the Abandonment of Black America," Cabinet Magazine, October 13, 2020, and "Old Freedmans [sic] Bank Failure Is Near Wind-Up," Chicago Defender, August 8, 1914.

61 profitable in the near future: Frederick Douglass, "To the Depositors of the Freedmen's Savings & Trust Co.: Notice Published in the 'New National Era' from Frederick Douglass upon the Bank's Failure," June 25, 1874, White House Historical Association.

61 "others have injured them": Douglass, "To the Depositors of the Freedmen's Savings & Trust Co." [emphasis added by authors].

62 "a mere animal existence": Douglass, "To the Depositors of the Freedmen's Savings & Trust Co." [emphasis added by authors].

62 "the white man's milk": "Freedman's Bank Demise."

63 "the bank's frontline employees": Célérier and Tak, "Finance, Advertising and Fraud," p. 6.

63 going to white people: Célérier and Tak, "Finance, Advertising and Fraud," p. 6.

63 but not reinvested there: Douglass, "To the Depositors of the Freedmen's Savings & Trust Co."

64 Black Americans served by the bank: Luke C. D. Stein and Constantine Yannelis, "Financial Inclusion, Human Capital, and Wealth Accumulation: Evidence from the Freedman's Savings Bank," Review of Financial Studies 33, No. 11 (November 2020).

64 misleading marketing and overstatements: Claire Célérier and Purnoor Tak, "The Impact of Financial Inclusion on Minorities: Evidence from the Freedman's Savings Bank," PDF, April 12, 2021.

64   largely to white people: Célérier and Tak, "Finance, Advertising and Fraud," p. 5.

64   "has never yet made good": W. E. B. Du Bois quoted in Marcus Anthony Hunter, "22 Million Reasons Black America Doesn't Trust Banks," Salon, February 18, 2018.

64   "to the disaster of [the Freedman's Bank]": Booker T. Washington quoted in Hunter, "22 Million Reasons Black America Doesn't Trust Banks."

65   "to handle his business": "The President's Message," *Chicago Defender*, December 10, 1910.

65   20 percent of his deposit: "Old Freedmans [*sic*] Bank Failure Is Near Wind-Up."

65   rights of enslaved people: Walter Young, "The HistoryMakers Video Oral History Interview with Dr. Walter Young."

65   the light-skinned Creole community: Timothy McNulty, "Spokesman to Nations, Back Home He's Andrew," *Chicago Tribune*, August 29, 1977.

65   sister, the census for that year shows: 1880 Census records.

65   It took until 1883: A. Young, "To the Depositors of Freedman's Bank, that Failed 1874," *Afro-American*, July 22, 1905.

65   unclaimed deposits from the bank: Young, "To the Depositors of Freedman's Bank, that Failed 1874."

65   three-year-old Daisy: Federal Census Records.

66   their religion and their god's will: Megan J. Wolff, "The Myth of the Actuary: Life Insurance and Frederick L. Hoffman's 'Race Traits and Tendencies of the American Negro,'" National Center for Biotechnology Information, *Public Health Reports* (2006).

66   price on white lives: Sharon Ann Murphy, "Slave Insurance," entry in [Online] Encyclopedia Virginia, February 1, 2021.

67   50,000 to 650,000 in just ten years: Morton Keller, *The Life Insurance Enterprise, 1885–1910* (Cambridge, Mass.: Belknap Press/Harvard University Press, 1963), p. 8, as cited in Wolff, "The Myth of the Actuary."

67   burials and death expenses: J. Marquis, *The Metropolitan Life: A Study in Business Growth* (New York: Viking Press, 1947), p. 55, as cited in Wolff, "The Myth of the Actuary."

67   unaware of this discrepancy: Benjamin Wiggins, *Calculating Race: Racial Discrimination in Risk Assessment* (Oxford, UK: Oxford University Press, 2020), p. 29.

67   states passed similar bills: Wiggins, *Calculating Race*, p. 32.

67   "to circumvent such policies": Wiggins, *Calculating Race*, p. 32.

67   "'to disease and death'": Frederick Hoffman, "Vital Statistics of the Negro," *Arena*, 1892, as cited in Wolff, "The Myth of the Actuary."

67   headquarters and hired him: Wolff, "The Myth of the Actuary."

68   "with the field today": Wolff, "The Myth of the Actuary."

68   "of the statistical method": Wolff, "The Myth of the Actuary."

68   to other poor, "immigrant" groups: Wolff, "The Myth of the Actuary."

68   brought in Black clients: Wiggins, *Calculating Race*, pp. 23, 33.

68   not accept Black people as customers: Jessie Wright-Mendoza, "How Insurance Companies Used Bad Science to Discriminate," JSTOR Daily, September 17, 2018.

68   retract the paper: The association's president at the time was Susan Athey, a Stanford University economist, and the publication officers were Kristine Etter and Doug Quint.

69   born in 1860, in Franklin, Louisiana: Federal Census and Social Security Records.

70   among those who benefited: Walter Young, "The HistoryMakers Video Oral History Interview with Dr. Walter Young."

70   New Orleans from Atlanta: Federal Census and Probate Records. Note that the 1900 Census says they married in 1891, but Young's probate filing says it was 1888, as does the 1930 Census.

70   and they were arrested: "An Interesting Case that Occurred at DeGive's Opera House Last Night," *Atlanta Constitution*, February 4, 1883.

70   for violating the Civil Rights Act: "The Civil Rights Law: Manager L. DeGive Arrested for Its Violation," *Atlanta Constitution*, September 28, 1883.

71   moot at that point: "Case Decided: October 15, 1883," *Landmark Cases*. C-SPAN.

71   "now preparing to sow pens": Frank S. Young, "The Great Bulk of the Planting Is Completed, but a Little Rain Is Needed Too," *Times-Picayune*, May 9, 1894, p. 16.

71   the Odd Fellows: "Colored Pythians: Grand Lodge Ends Session by Electing Officers," *Times-Picayune*, June 4, 1908; "To Attend Grand Lodge: Colored Odd Fellows from Here Will Go to Lake Charles Meet," *Times-Picayune*, July 27, 1916; and "Knights of Honor Elect," *Times-Picayune*, August 31, 1917.

71   be chartered in Georgia: Henderson, "Heman E. Perry and Black Enterprise in Atlanta, 1908–1925," p. 237.

72   local news item put it: "Negroes Organize Business League," *New Orleans Item*, July 8, 1910; and "Negroes Form League."

72   chain of Black banks:: "Negroes Organize Business League"; and "Negroes Form League."

72   over to white ownership: Henderson, "Heman E. Perry and Black Enterprise in Atlanta, 1908–1925," p. 236.

72   "swore vengeance on him": Henderson, "Heman E. Perry and Black Enterprise in Atlanta, 1908–1925," p. 236.

73   focused on Black customers: "Douglas Life of New Orleans Pays Dividend," *Pittsburgh Courier*, February 1, 1936; and Death Certificate of Frank Smith Young. Note: The company name is spelled with one *s* in these documents. However, its name might actually have been spelled "Douglass," with two *s*'s, as Douglass Life Insurance Company was a prominent Black insurer at the time.

73   land in Franklin worth $2,000: Frank S. Young Probate Filing, 1940, 16th Judicial District Court, Parish of St. Mary, Louisiana.

CHAPTER 4: RYAN GLOVER AND THE HISTORIC GREENWOOD

74   "he is on equality with you": Quote in Gary Zellar, *African Creeks: Estelvste and the Creek Nation* (Norman: University of Oklahoma Press, 2007), p. 192.

75   "whether white, red, or Black": David A. Chang, *The Color of the Land: Race, Nation, and the Politics of Landownership in Oklahoma, 1832–1929* (Chapel Hill: University of North Carolina Press, 2010), chap. 3.

75   around the year 1800: The location and year given for Renty Rentie's birth are based on information from a descendant, but are not verifiable against government records, which cite later dates and locations tied to Renty Rentie and his wives and children. That said, there is a Slave Register from 1813 to 1834 that contains an individual the Rentie family and others on Ancestry.com believe to be Renty Rentie. That record is from the National Archives of the UK Kew, Surrey, England, Office of the Registry of Slaves and Slave Compensation Commission Records.

75   to an 1833 census: David Zuber, "Trail of Tears (1831–1850)," *BlackPast*, February 9, 2022.

76   enslaved by the tribe: Zuber, "Trail of Tears (1831–1850)."

76   "beast who came along": Robert Warrior, *The World of Indigenous North America* (New York: Routledge Taylor and Francis, 2015), p. 533.

76   of five thousand miles apiece: Zuber, "Trail of Tears (1831–1850)."

76   Morris, around 1847: Federal Census Records and other government records. Note: Morris Rentie's birth year is stated as 1847 or 1846, in various documents.

76 alongside the Native Americans: Chang, *The Color of the Land*, chap. 3.

76 sixteen enslaved people as of 1860: 1860 Slave Schedule.

76 care of the livestock: Grace Kelley, "Interview #7306: Louis Rentie," Indian-Pioneer History Project for Oklahoma, Works Progress Administration, 1937, p. 476.

76 back for the journey: Zellar, *African Creeks*, p. 172.

77 "or suitably provided for": 116th Congress, House Resolution 1514, Introduced March 5, Congress.gov, 2019.

77 the U.S. Supreme Court: Jack Healy, "Black, Native American, and Fighting for Recognition in Indian Country," *New York Times,* September 8, 2020.

77 "in this new territory": Wells quoted in Victor Luckerson, "The Promise of Oklahoma," *Smithsonian Magazine,* April 2021.

77 as late as 1900: Luckerson, "The Promise of Oklahoma."

77 from across the South: Hannibal B. Johnson, *Acres of Aspiration: The All-Black Towns of Oklahoma* (Fort Worth, TX: Eakin Press, 2020).

77 horses, goats, and sheep: Kelley, "Interview #7306: Louis Rentie," p. 474.

77 "home already on it": Kelley, "Interview #7306: Louis Rentie," p. 474.

77 former owner, John Yargee: "Search the Dawes Rolls, 1898–1914," Dawes Rolls, Oklahoma Historical Society, n.d.

78 "to leave their homes": Quoted in Chang, *The Color of the Land*, chap. 3.

78 Americans across different tribes: Chang, *The Color of the Land*, chap. 3; and Muskogee County Genealogical and Historical Society, *Muskogee County Genealogical and Historical Society Quarterly* 25, No. 4 (2008).

78 Nashville Normal and Theological Institute: Zellar, *African Creeks*, p. 172.

78 founded just after the war: Jalen Blue, "A Blaze of History: A Prominent Black University that Endured Two Fires Once Was Located on the Peabody Campus," News, Vanderbilt University, November 7, 2019.

78 enslaver, the tribal chief: Zellar, *African Creeks*.

79 "of land and money": Quoted in Chang, *The Color of the Land*, chap. 3.

79 Black tribe members 40: Chang, *The Color of the Land*, chap. 3.

79 "Negro race in the [Creek] Nation": Zellar, *African Creeks*, p. 191.

79 "on equality with you": Quoted in Zellar, *African Creeks*, p. 192.

79 written by Warrior Rentie: Quoted in Zellar, *African Creeks*, p. 192. The tension grew so much that in 1901, there was a conflict in town known as the "Crazy Snake Uprising." Tribal members who opposed allotment started seizing land from members who supported it, prompting the federal government to send in troops to help quash the uprising and jail many of the members who led it. See Kenneth W. McIntosh, "Crazy Snake Uprising," The [Online] Encyclopedia of Oklahoma History and Culture.

80 "We believed in allotment": Kelley, "Interview #7306: Louis Rentie."

80 "an eye to the future": Kelley, "Interview #7306: Louis Rentie."

80 each received 160 acres: Kelley, "Interview #7306: Louis Rentie."

80 white settlers in 1898: "Native Americans (1836–1907)," Tulsa Preservation Commission, May 19, 2015.

80 10,000 acres in total, our research found: "Search the Dawes Rolls, 1898–1914."

80 a benefit for citizens: Michael L. Lanza, *Agrarianism and Reconstruction Politics: The Southern Homestead Act* (Baton Rouge and London: Louisiana State University Press, 1990), p. 3.

81 of those 1.5 million families were Black: "Sharecropping, Black Land Acquisition, and White Supremacy (1868–1900)," World Food Policy Center, June 13, 2022.

81 the "Negro Homestead Bill": Lanza, *Agrarianism and Reconstruction Politics*, p. 23.

81 "and they want land": Quoted in Lanza, *Agrarianism and Reconstruction Politics*, p. 21.

81   of Indiana concurred: Lanza, *Agrarianism and Reconstruction Politics*, p. 101.

81   continue to grow cotton: Lanza, *Agrarianism and Reconstruction Politics*, p. 25.

81   could even give away the titles to it: Lanza, *Agrarianism and Reconstruction Politics*, pp. 97–99.

81   timber agents to police the matter: Lanza, *Agrarianism and Reconstruction Politics*, pp. 104–9.

81   repeal the law altogether: Lanza, *Agrarianism and Reconstruction Politics*, p. 113.

81   only four thousand Black families: W. E. B. Du Bois, "The Negro Landholder of Georgia," *Bulletin of the Department of Labor* VI, No. 35 (July 1901): p. 648.

81   went to white people: Lanza, *Agrarianism and Reconstruction Politics*, p.128.

82   "of the United States": Luckerson, "The Promise of Oklahoma."

82   "self-assertive, they are aggressive": Quoted in Zellar, *African Creeks*, p. 234.

82   "portion of the territory": "Negro Business in the Indian Territory," *Topeka Plaindealer*, February 10, 1905.

82   1907 study of Black banks across the country: W. E. B. Du Bois, *Economic Co-operation Among Negro Americans* (Atlanta, Ga.: Atlanta University Press, 1907). Note: Early news reports also called the bank the Creek Citizen's Realty Bank and Trust Company. See also "Still Another Enterprise," *Muskogee Comet*, June 16, 1904.

83   "quarter of a million dollars": "Negro Business in the Indian Territory."

83   880 acres of land: Warrior Rentie's immediate family would have had more like 1,600 acres of land, because he and his wife had eight children, and each member of the family would have received 160 acres. But the newspaper writing about his bank may have been unaware of this.

83   incipient state of Oklahoma: Zellar, *African Creeks*, p. 241.

83   to the Justice Department: Zellar, *African Creeks*, pp. 250–51.

83   imposed on Native Americans: "Five Civilized Tribes Status of Allotments," H.R. 15641, May 27, 1908.

84   "Black wealth in the region": Luckerson, "The Promise of Oklahoma."

84   coercion of Black Americans to leave town: Luckerson, "The Promise of Oklahoma."

84   oil found on her land: Steve Gerkin, "The Unlikely Baroness," *This Land*, March 24, 2015.

84   12.5 percent in royalties: Gerkin, "The Unlikely Baroness."

84   her white guardian became rich: Gerkin, "The Unlikely Baroness."

84   on the children's parcels: Tonya Bolden, *Searching for Sarah Rector: The Richest Black Girl in America* (New York: Abrams Books for Young Readers, 2014), p. 25; and Gerkin, "The Unlikely Baroness."

84   they were supposed to protect: "Andrew J. Smitherman: A Pioneer of the African American Press, 1909–1961," The Free Library, 2010.

84   "the race they have so grossly wronged": KalaLea, host, "The Rise of Greenwood," *Blindspot*, Season 2, Episode 2 (The History Channel and WYNC Studios, June 4, 2021).

85   "day you will die": "Andrew J. Smitherman: A Pioneer of the African American Press, 1909–1961."

85   lived in a rental home: Federal Census Records; and "Index to Probates and Guardianships," Muskogee County, Oklahoma, 1907–1930.

85   she still needed a guardian: "Index to Probates and Guardianships."

85   for thirty thousand dollars a year: Rentie v. Commissioner, 21 B.T.A. 1230, United States Board of Tax Appeals, Docket No. 33782 (1931).

85   1939, at age thirty-five: Federal Census Records.

85   oil wells on Rentie-owned land: *The Oil & Gas Journal* 19, No. 35 (January 28, 1921).

86   for several Rentie children: "Can Job-Holder Be a Guardian? Suit Will Tell," *Muskogee Times-Democrat*, October 26, 1922.

86 funding for Smitherman's organization: "Andrew J. Smitherman: A Pioneer of the African American Press, 1909–1961."

86 Business, he said, "was swinging": "Black Wall Street Music Project / Morris Rentie Sr.," MyInfoTechFAME, January 4, 2021, YouTube video.

86 all-Black town called Rentiesville: United States Congress, "H.Res. 435 (117th) Recognizing the 100th Anniversary of the 1921 Tulsa Race Massacre," introduced May 25, 2021, Govtrack.us; see also Amy Latham, "Rentie Grove's Demise," *Tulsa World*, February 16, 1997. The exact family lines between this William Rentie and the other Renties featured in these pages is unclear, but they have been reported to be related. See also Arthur Lincoln Tolson, "The Negro in Oklahoma Territory, 1889–1907: A Study in Racial Discrimination" (PhD diss., University of Oklahoma, 1966).

86 neighborhood on the Tulsa city border: Christa Rice, "Looking Back at Oklahoma's All-Black Community of Rentie Grove," Explore Claremore History, February 9, 2022. Note: Rentie Grove sat along the border of Tulsa and a town now called Jenks and may have extended into both places.

87 "up to nineteen times": Quoted in KalaLea, "The Rise of Greenwood."

87 flooded the streets of Greenwood in retaliation: Jeremy Cook and Jason Long, "How the Tulsa Race Massacre Caused Decades of Harm," *The Atlantic*, May 24, 2021.

87 three hundred people were murdered: Aaron Morrison, "One Hundred Years After Tulsa Race Massacre, the Damage Remains," Associated Press, May 25, 2021.

87 "been frightened to death": Quoted in Tim Madigan, "Remembering Tulsa: Marking the Centennial of the Tulsa Race Massacre," *Smithsonian Magazine*, April 2021.

88 trapped by white attackers: Lee Anna A. Jackson, "Tulsa, 100 Years Later: Black Wall Street Remembered," *Essence*, May 31, 2021.

88 like nearby Rentie Grove: Alicia Odewale, "#TulsaSyllabus Has Arrived," Aliciadodewale .com, June 19, 2020; and @AliciaOdewale, "In case anyone is curious how my course 'Archaeology of Black Heritage in Oklahoma' is doing . . . ," Nitter, September 18, 2021.

88 his family fled Oklahoma: Mark Spencer, "A. J. Smitherman: A Crusading Editor Pays a Heavy Price," *Philadelphia Tribune*, February 6, 2021.

88 multiple towns in Florida: Gillian Brockell, "Tulsa Isn't the Only Race Massacre You Were Never Taught in School. Here Are Others," *Washington Post*, June 1, 2021.

88 "in the control cities": Cook and Long, "How the Tulsa Race Massacre Caused Decades of Harm."

89 ended up in low-level jobs: Cook and Long, "How the Tulsa Race Massacre Caused Decades of Harm."

89 by 1925, he owned a car: "Rev [*sic*] Frederick Hill Behn Sr.," Find a Grave, September 27, 2008; and Federal Census Records.

89 for his family's rights: "Rev [*sic*] Frederick Hill Behn Sr."

89 family reunion guidebook, adding that: "Rev [*sic*] Frederick Hill Behn Sr."

89 "received his money": "Rev [*sic*] Frederick Hill Behn Sr."

89 the surname "Rentie": This research involved obtaining the Dawes Commission allotment cards for Morris, Katie, and their children (including Delilah) and then geolocating those plots on present-day maps. Once present-day addresses and parcels were obtained, the research focused on the ownership history of those plots. One critical book used in identifying the plots was E. Hastain, *Hastain's Township Plats of the Creek Nation* (Muskogee, Ok.: Model Printing Company, 1910).

90 to his "youngest children": "Rev [*sic*] Frederick Hill Behn Sr."

90 eventually grow up: Letha Bennett Draft Card and Federal Census Records.

90 but to white people, decades ago: Dawes Commission cards; Hastain, *Hastain's Township Plats of the Creek Nation*, local property records; and Federal Census Records. In addition, there were two lawsuits from Morris and Katie Rentie over their properties while Morris and Katie were alive, but those suits do not focus on Delilah Rentie's land. See Wilson v. Rentie (1926), O.K. 984; and Rentie v. McCoy, Case Number: 2961 (1912).

90 talking to us: Following journalism ethics, we did not pay Ryan, but we found it interesting to have received the request. No one else in our book requested that, including people of far lesser means.

92 holders by February 2020: Nidhia Sebastian, "The Story of Chime, the Leading Digital Banking Company in the US," Timesnext, September 27, 2020.

93 In early 2021: Anna Irrera, "Digital Banking Startup Greenwood Raises $40 Million from Big Banks," Reuters, March 25, 2021.

93 predatory lending and other mortgage issuance violations: E. Scott Reckard, "SunTrust to Pay Nearly $1 Billion to Settle Mortgage Abuse Allegations," *Los Angeles Times*, June 17, 2017; and Russell Grantham, "BB&T Bank Pays $83 Million to Settle Federal Loan Complaint," *Atlanta Journal-Constitution*, September 30, 2016.

93 its founding in 1891: "SunTrust Bank History," Truist Newsroom.

93 the investment for Truist: Vreeland left Truist in 2022 to create a venture capital firm focused on investing in diverse founders. Her firm is called Vree Ventures.

93 called Pathward Financial: The company did not discuss Greenwood with us, but a person who has seen Greenwood's cap sheet, a document detailing ownership, identified Meta-Bank as an investor.

94 eventually, a financial settlement: Liz Moyer, "RushCard to Settle Prepaid Card Suit for $19 Million," *New York Times*, May 13, 2016.

CHAPTER 5: JAMES WOODALL AND THE FEDERALLY FUNDED GAP

95 Federal Emergency Relief Administration, Atlanta office: Quoted in Douglas L. Smith, *The New Deal in the Urban South* (New Orleans: Louisiana State University Press, 1988), p. 233.

95 "conversation for so long": Quoted in Ernie Suggs and Nedra Rhone, "When Daily Life Is 'Exhausting,'" *Atlanta Journal-Constitution*, June 5, 2020.

96 "of their white counterparts": Quoted in Suggs and Rhone, "When Daily Life Is 'Exhausting.'" And the fact that the percentage of Black Americans in prison is five times the percentage of white Americans in prison is verified here: E. Ann Carson, "Prisoners in 2021—Statistical Tables," U.S. Department of Justice: Office of Justice Programs: Bureau of Justice Statistics, December 2022.

96 "doesn't feel that way": Quoted in Suggs and Rhone, "When Daily Life Is 'Exhausting.'"

96 "this country burning down": Quoted in Suggs and Rhone, "When Daily Life Is 'Exhausting.'"

96 "have been protesting": James Woodall, Facebook, May 31, 2020.

96 officer to be fired: James Woodall, Facebook, June 5, 2020.

96 determinedly, in his collared shirt and Covid-19 mask: Malachy Browne, Christina Kelso, and Barbara Marcolini, "How Rayshard Brooks Was Fatally Shot by the Atlanta Police," *New York Times*, June 14, 2020.

97 arms to block traffic: Chandler Thornton, "Georgia NAACP President Calls for Atlanta Police Chief to Be Terminated," CNN, June 13, 2020.

97 "silence of our friends": Quoted in Thornton, "Georgia NAACP President Calls for Atlanta Police Chief to Be Terminated."

97 "until they do their job," he called out: Quoted in David Wickert, Greg Bluestein, and

Alexis Stevens, "Thousands of Demonstrators at Georgia Capitol as Legislature Reconvenes," *Atlanta Journal-Constitution*, June 15, 2020.

98   served in World War I: "Walter Jonah Walker," found through search of "U.S., Lists of Men Ordered to Report to Local Board for Military Duty, 1917–1918."

98   only in his thirties: 1930 U.S. Federal Census; 1920 U.S. Federal Census; and 1910 U.S. Federal Census.

98   a fourth-grade education: 1940 U.S. Federal Census.

98   the 1930 Census noted: 1930 U.S. Federal Census.

99   had completed the second: Ancestry.com.

99   per white child: U.S. Office of Education reports, as cited by Raymond Bernard, "Consequences of Racial Segregation," *The American Catholic Sociological Review* 10, No. 2 (June 1949), p. 86.

99   compared to Black students: Patricia Sullivan, *Lift Every Voice: The NAACP and the Making of the Civil Rights Movement* (New York: The New Press, 2009), p. 92.

99   a co-owner of Sears: Julius Rosenwald Fund, "School Money in White and Black," quoted in Buell G. Gallagher, *American Caste and the Negro College* (New York: Columbia University Press, 1938), p. 119.

99   than that for white babies: Gunnar Myrdal, *An American Dilemma* (New York: Harper and Brothers, 1944), p. 162.

100   to about 10.7 billion dollars: Price Fishback and Valentina Kachanovskaya, "The Multiplier in the States During the Great Depression," *Journal of Economic History* 75, No. 1 (March 2015), p. 130. The total federal funds spent on major relief programs from 1932 to 1939 in 2015 dollars was $41.7 billion. The $10.7 billion—also in 2015 dollars—is for the WPA, FERA, and CWA programs.

100   far more relief than rural Black residents: Ira Katznelson, *When Affirmative Action Was White* (New York: W. W. Norton, 2005), p. 37.

100   "administrative practices and standards": Quoted in Richard Sterner, *The Negro's Share: A Study of Income, Consumption, Housing, and Public Assistance* (New York: Harper and Brothers, 1943), p. 14, cited in Katznelson, *When Affirmative Action Was White*, p. 37.

100   "that stinks to heaven": Quoted in Smith, *The New Deal in the Urban South*, p. 233.

101   "Negroes to fall through": Quoted in Dona Cooper Hamilton and Charles Hamilton, *The Dual Agenda* (New York: Columbia University Press, 1998), p. 30; and also Katznelson, *When Affirmative Action Was White*, p. 48.

101   "of the economic scale": Quoted in Derrick Johnson, "Viewing Social Security Through the Civil Rights Lens," *The Crisis*, NAACP, August 14, 2020.

101   Black-owned businesses were concentrated: Ernie Suggs, "29 Reasons to Celebrate Black History Month: No. 11, Auburn Avenue," *Atlanta Journal-Constitution*, January 4, 2017.

101   "of the Civil War": Cited in Smith, *The New Deal in the Urban South*, p. 233.

102   all Americans owned homes: Ta-Nehisi Coates, "The Case for Reparations," *The Atlantic*, June 2014.

102   the newspaper wrote: Todd M. Michney and LaDale Winling, "New Perspectives on New Deal Housing Policy: Explicating and Mapping HOLC Loans to African Americans," *Journal of Urban History* 46, No. 1 (2020).

102   "something quite so valuable": Quoted in Michney and Winling, "New Perspectives on New Deal Housing Policy."

102   HOLC's old correspondence: Michney and Winling, "New Perspectives on New Deal Housing Policy."

102   "no facility for photographing": Michney and Winling, "New Perspectives on New Deal Housing Policy."

103   "as he is employed": Michney and Winling, "New Perspectives on New Deal Housing Policy."

103   the 2020 study found: Michney and Winling, "New Perspectives on New Deal Housing Policy."

103   favored the west side of town: Michney and Winling, "New Perspectives on New Deal Housing Policy."

103   "of Negro homeownership": Quoted in Michney and Winling, "New Perspectives on New Deal Housing Policy."

103   and the Fourth Ward: Michney and Winling, "New Perspectives on New Deal Housing Policy."

103   the Ebenezer Baptist Church: Suggs, "29 Reasons to Celebrate Black History Month: No. 11, Auburn Avenue."

104   "interest of the city": Atlanta Real Estate Board 1922 annual report, as cited in Mark Pendergrast, *City on the Verge: Atlanta and the Fight for America's Urban Future* (New York: Basic Books, 2017), p. 76.

104   the 1920s, the neighborhood: It was called the Fourth Ward until the 1950s, when it became the Old Fourth Ward.

104   was 61 percent: Karen Ferguson, *Black Politics in New Deal Atlanta* (Chapel Hill: University of North Carolina Press, 2002), p. 164.

104   "city's worst slums": Michney and Winling, "New Perspectives on New Deal Housing Policy."

104   got going in earnest: "Mapping Inequality."

105   had "different racial groups": "Mapping Inequality."

106   "population have been separated": Frederick Babcock, *The Valuation of Real Estate* (New York: McGraw-Hill, 1932), p. 91 [emphasis from authors].

106   "a reduction in values": Cited in Rothstein, *The Color of Law*, p. 65 [emphasis from authors].

106   "desirability, utility and value": Housing and Home Finance Agency, *Underwriting Manual: Under Writing and Valuation Procedure Under Title II of the National Housing Act*, United States Federal Housing Administration, Washington, D.C., November 1936 [emphasis added by authors].

106   against "adverse influences": Housing and Home Finance Agency, *Underwriting Manual: Under Writing and Valuation Procedure Under Title II of the National Housing Act*, United States Federal Housing Administration, Washington, D.C., February 1938.

106   "(the FHA) does not benefit": Michney and Winling. "New Perspectives on New Deal Housing Policy," p. 155.

106   rare Black-owned insurer: Sullivan, *Lift Every Voice*, 77; and Cheryl Oestreicher, "History of the Atlanta Branch of the National Association for the Advancement of Colored People," Emory Scholar Blog, Emory University, April 7, 2011.

107   "persons of African descent": Letter from Roy Wilkins to Robert C. Weaver, June 11, 1938.

107   practices at the FHA: Letter from Robert C. Weaver to Roy Wilkins, June 15, 1938.

107   "is a mixed population": Letter from Dream Homes Owner to Walter White, NAACP, October 3, 1938.

108   "placed in their path": Letter from Roy Wilkins to Stewart McDonald, October 12, 1938.

108   to the FHA administrator: Letter from M. Thompson to Roy Wilkins, October 17, 1938.

109   lending policies of those institutions: Letter from M. R. Young to Roy Wilkins, October 18, 1938.

109   for underwriting loans: Letter from Thurgood Marshall to Stewart McDonald, November 18, 1938.

109   its own. The document: Housing and Home Finance Agency, *Underwriting Manual: Under Writing and Valuation Procedure Under Title II of the National Housing Act*, United States Federal Housing Administration, February 1938, sec. 2, para(s), pp. 226, 228.

109 40 percent were homeowners: William J. Collins and Robert A. Margo, "Race and Home-ownership: A Century-Long View," *Explorations in Economic History* 38, No. 1 (2001): pp. 68–92.

110 "of previous residents in the area": Arthur M. Weimer and Homer Hoyt, *Principles of Urban Real Estate* (Berkeley: University of California Press, 1939), p. 370.

110 "of the Caucasian race": Cited in Wendy Plotkin, "1920s–1950s Appraisal Views on Racial Effects on Value," Orbital Communications, September 1, 2003; and Weimer and Hoyt, *Principles of Urban Real Estate*, p. 140.

111 in World War II: Kerry Pleasant, "Honoring Black History World War II Service to the Nation," U.S. Army, February 27, 2020.

111 Woodall's great-grandfathers, Ernest Woodall: Ernest Woodall's draft card, in family's possession.

111 and Jesse Day: Jesse Day's draft card, in family's possession.

111 limbo with no pay: George Q. Flynn, "Selective Service and American Blacks During World War II," *The Journal of Negro History* 69, No. 1 (Winter 1984).

111 Black volunteers at all: Flynn, "Selective Service and American Blacks During World War II," p. 20.

112 kept separated by race: Thomas A. Guglielmo, "Desegregating Blood: A Civil Rights Struggle to Remember," PBS, February 4, 2018.

112 "treated as he is now": Quoted in "American Negroes and the War," *Harper's Magazine*, April 1942.

112 "What are you fighting for?": "I Had Come Face to Face with Evil: Leon Bass Talks About His Experiences of Racism," video, Facing History & Ourselves, April 12, 2022; and "Universal Declaration of Human Rights," Facing History & Ourselves, last updated November 13, 2019.

112 "to live *half American*?": Quoted in Bryan Greene, "After Victory in World War II, Black Veterans Continued the Fight for Freedom at Home," *Smithsonian Magazine*, August 30, 2021; and James G. Thompson, "Should I Sacrifice to Live 'Half-American?," *Pittsburgh Courier*, January 31, 1942, p. 3.

112 the United States in the war: Matthew Delmont, "Why African-American Soldiers Saw World War II as a Two-Front Battle," *Smithsonian*, August 24, 2017.

113 were looking for jobs: "The GI Bill of Rights: An Analysis of the Servicemen's Readjustment Act of 1944," *Social Security Bulletin*, Social Security Administration, July 1994.

113 the entire federal budget: *Congress and the Nation: 1945–1964* (Washington, D.C.: Congressional Quarterly Service, 1975), p. 1335, as cited in Kathleen Frydl, *The GI Bill* (Cambridge, UK: Cambridge University Press, 2011), p. 3.

113 veterans like Vester Robinson: Vester Robinson's service record.

113 The Woodalls: Ernest Woodall's draft card.

113 there were about seven thousand: Glenn T. Johnson, Dean of Men, Atlanta University, February 2, 1946, as cited in Frydl, *The GI Bill*, p. 252.

113 million Black serviceman overall: Tyler Bamford, "African Americans Fought for Freedom at Home and Abroad During World War II," National WWII Museum, New Orleans, La., February 1, 2020.

113 "of Georgia Tech center": Glenn T. Johnson, as cited in Frydl, *The GI Bill*, p. 252.

114 act of white supremacy: Quoted in Flynn, "Selective Service and American Blacks During World War II," p. 17, as cited in Frydl, *The GI Bill*, p. 252.

114 white veterans but not Black: American Council on Race Relations, "Summary," *Survey of Community Veteran Information Centers*, March 1946, Folder: Veterans, Box 67, Papers of Harry S. Truman, Harry S. Truman Library, p. 7, as cited in Frydl, *The GI Bill*, p. 246.

114 "the program is administered": Frydl, *The GI Bill*, p. 256.

115 "as poor financial risks": Frydl, *The GI Bill*, p. 237.

115 barred sales to Black buyers: Steven F. Lawson, ed., *To Secure These Rights: The Report of President Truman's Committee on Civil Rights* (Washington, DC: United States Government Printing Office, 1947), p. 14, as cited in Frydl, *The GI Bill*, p. 254.

116 to nonwhite families: Katznelson, *When Affirmative Action Was White*, p. 140.

117 for his health benefits: Greene, "After Victory in World War II, Black Veterans Continued the Fight for Freedom at Home."

117 the Democrats would continue: Philip Bump, "When Did Black Americans Start Voting So Heavily Democratic?" *Washington Post*, July 7, 2015.

118 for a robbery in 1943: Felony sentence, September 22, 1984, The State v. Jessie [*sic*] Day, No. A69945, Superior Court of Fulton County, State of Georgia (hereafter cited as: The State v. Jesse Day, since Jesse is the name spelling that Jesse and his family preferred.).

118 charged him with bastardy: The State v. Jesse Day.

118 in which six million: "The Great Migration (1910–1970)," National Archives, June 28, 2021.

119 and he beat Frances: The State v. Jesse Day.

120 duplexes, opened in 1964: Michelle E. Shaw, "Bulldozers Begin Razing Bowen Homes Housing Project," *Atlanta Journal-Constitution*, June 9, 2009.

120 for crime and poverty: "Last Housing Project in Atlanta Nears Demise," Associated Press, July 27, 2009.

120 of rapper Shawty Lo: Don Trapstar, "Bowen Homes," [Online] Urban Thesaurus, May 25, 2009.

120 and boxer Evander Holyfield: Douglas C. Lyons, "Evander Holyfield: Coping with Sudden Success," *Ebony*, January 1991, pp. 48–52.

120 programs in and out: "Finding Aid for Bowen Homes Records," Atlanta Housing Archives, The Housing Authority of the City of Atlanta, May 2019.

121 "require some public purpose": Warren L. Dennis, "The Community Re-Investment Act of 1977: Its Legislative History and Its Impact on Applications for Changes in Structure Made by Depository Institutions to the Four Federal Financial Supervisory Agencies," Working Paper No. 24 (1978), Credit Research Center, Krannert Graduate School of Management, Purdue University.

121 accessible to Black Americans: This is relevant to a 2022 discussion of the CRA: Michael West, "Re: Community Reinvestment Act Notice of Proposed Rulemaking," Devotion USA, August 5, 2022.

121 a court in California: Regents of the University of California v. Bakke, 438 US 265 (1978).

122 money in a neighborhood: U.S. Congress, 95th Congress, 1st Sess., 1977, *Congressional Record*, Vol. 123, Part 14, p. 17630.

122 Stephana turned eighteen: Harold and Charlotte Woodall divorce agreement.

123 graduate was $29,669: Mark Kantrowitz, "Who Graduates with Expensive Student Loan Debt," *Student Aid Policy*, December 14, 2015; and spreadsheet of National Postsecondary Student Aid Study data provided to authors by Mark Kantrowitz.

124 up to 60 percent: "Student Borrowing in the 1990s," *ACE Issue Brief*, Center for Policy Analysis, American Council on Education, November 2001.

124 55 percent in 1984: "College Enrollment and Work Activity of 1994 High School Graduates," U.S. Bureau of Labor Statistics, Department of Labor, June 1, 1995.

124 "debt load and repayment": Fenaba Addo, "Parents' Wealth Helps Explain Racial Disparities in Student Loan Debt," Federal Reserve Bank of St. Louis, March 29, 2018.

124 than what they had borrowed: Melanie Hanson, "Loans for Undergraduate Students," *Condition of Education*, National Center for Education Statistics, 2023.

124 postpone purchasing a home: Hanson, "Student Loan Debt by Race."

125 higher, at 59 percent: "IPEDS: Graduation Rates component," National Center for Education Statistics, Winter 2020–2021.

125 less than fifty thousand dollars a year: Mark Kantrowitz, "Shocking Statistics About College Graduation Rates," *Forbes*, November 18, 2021.

126 impersonating a police officer: Court of Appeals of Georgia, Robinson v. State (2015), No. A14A2206, April 14, 2015.

126 sentences plus sixty years: Christian Boone, "DNA Evidence Sends Serial Rapist to Life in Prison," *Atlanta Journal-Constitution*, June 25, 2010.

127 whistleblowing about the police: Georgia Injustice Project website.

127 him via letters: Georgia Justice Records; and letter from Jonathan Robinson sent to authors via a relative.

128 segregated from white residents: Sonam Vashi, "Atlanta's Section 8 Tenants Have Trouble Finding Good Housing," *SaportaReport*, January 7, 2019.

128 to serving 3.5 million families: Specialist in Housing Policy, "An Overview of the Section 8 Housing Programs: Housing Choice Vouchers and Project-Based Rental Assistance," PDF, Congressional Research Service, last updated February 7, 2014.

128 the area's median income: "An Overview of the Section 8 Housing Programs."

128 rents were going up: "Federal Rental Assistance Fact Sheets," Center on Budget and Policy Priorities, January 19, 2022.

129 be shot in 2020: Aimee Ortiz, "What to Know About the Death of Rayshard Brooks," *New York Times*, November, 21, 2022.

129 first school district in the country in nearly four decades: Linda Jacobson, "Loss of Accreditation Rocks Georgia District," *Education Week*, August 29, 2008.

131 way to rebuild credit: Bev O'Shea, "Credit Privacy Number: A CPN Is a Scam, Not a Solution," NerdWallet, August 31, 2020.

132 Cody died from Covid-19: "Demorris Cody," Obituary, Donald Trimble Mortuary, Inc.

132 "what it meant to him": "A Celebration of the Life and Legacy of Demorris Cody," Celebration of Life, July 8, 2020, YouTube video.

132 "that's a beautiful thing": "A Celebration of the Life and Legacy of Demorris Cody."

CHAPTER 6: BROOK BACON AND THE PERCEPTION OF RISK

133 "convince congregants to take out subprime loans": Michael Powell, "Bank Accused of Pushing Mortgage Deals on Blacks," *New York Times*, June 6, 2009.

133 of the year: "Police Shootings Database 2015–2023: Search by Race, Age, Department," *Washington Post*, October 16, 2023.

133 to protect their neighborhood: Richard Fausset, "What We Know About the Shooting Death of Ahmaud Arbery," *New York Times*, August 8, 2022.

134 car into a ditch: Alyssa Lukpat, "$4.8 Million Settlement Reached in Trooper's Fatal Shooting of a Black Driver," *New York Times*, April 3, 2022.

134 charges against the officer: James Woodall, post about the murder of Julian Edward Roosevelt Lewis, Facebook, August 12, 2020.

135 more *at risk* than *a risk*: For more on the concept of being "at risk" versus "a risk," see Benjamin Wiggins's excellent book, *Calculating Race: Racial Discrimination in Risk Assessment*.

135 revisit the case: Azi Paybarah, "No Indictment for Former Georgia Trooper Who Shot and Killed a Black Motorist," *New York Times*, June 29, 2021.

135 local white militias: This was not a hyperbolic warning. In the months after Lewis was killed, his family and lawyers had demonstrated in front of a small city hall to call for the

release of the patrol car video from the officer who had shot Lewis. About one hundred people came to the demonstration—and were joined by about a dozen white men with high-powered rifles who had come from out of town to "protect the city," as local news coverage put it. The white men stood on the rooftops of buildings around town holding the rifles as they watched the demonstrators.

138 rent to pay: 1920 U.S. Federal Census.

139 records in the 1880s: Georgia, U.S. Property Tax Digests, 1793–1892.

139 in his fifties: 1900 U.S. Federal Census.

139 Tuskegee Institute in Alabama: In 1985, Tuskegee Normal and Industrial Institute became Tuskegee University.

139 Martin Luther King Jr. parade: Lisa Parker, "Rev [sic] Martin Bacon," Find a Grave, October 5, 2019.

140 far back as the 1760s: Geneanet Community Trees Index, Ancestry.

140 formed in 1803: U.S. Passenger and Immigration Lists Index and Census Records.

140 hold on to their land: "Land Act of 1804," Ohio History Central.

140 to college by 1854: U.S. School Catalogs, 1765–1935, Ancestry.

141 58.5 to 1: 1870 U.S. Federal Census.

141 wealth gap was nearly 60 to 1: Ellora Derenoncourt et al., "Wealth of Two Nations."

141 also list education levels: 1930 U.S. Federal Census; and 1940 U.S. Federal Census.

143 Sistine Madonna, circa 1513: Shalagh Bacon, Instagram post.

143 less than 4 percent Black: "Nashua, New Hampshire Population 2023," World Population Review, 2023.

143 said at the time: Shalagh Bacon, Instagram.

146 putting zero dollars down: Suffolk County Property Records.

146 had sold for $39,250: Zillow.

146 parts of the country: Lisa Williams and Kenya Hunter, "Here's How Much of Their Income Mass. Residents Have to Fork Over for Their Mortgage, by City," WGBH, July 19, 2019; and Barry Bluestone, Chase Billingham, and Tim Davis, "The Greater Boston Housing Report Card 2008," Center for Urban and Regional Policy, Northeastern University, October 2008.

147 "Harlem gets pneumonia": Quoted in Stephanie Strom, "Failed Dreams—The Collapse of a Harlem Bank; Freedom Bank's Demise: A Trail of Risky Loans and Fast Growth," New York Times, December 3, 1990.

147 a national Harris Poll: This survey was conducted online within the United States by the Harris Poll on behalf of this book from October 18 to 25, 2022, among 4,052 adults age eighteen and older. The sampling precision of Harris online polls is measured by using a Bayesian credible interval. For this study, the sample data is accurate to within +/- 1.9 percentage points using a 95 percent confidence level.

148 it was 11 percent: Signe-Mary McKernan et al., "Less than Equal: Racial Disparities in Wealth Accumulation," Urban Institute, April 2013.

149 in association fees: Complaint, June 8, 2006, Trustees of the Canterbury Village Condominium Trust v. Taneeta Bacon; New Century Mortgage Corporation, Civil Action No. 2006-00065796, District Court Department West Roxbury Division, Commonwealth of Massachusetts.

149 second-largest subprime mortgage issuer: Julie Creswell and Vikas Bajaj, "Home Lender Is Seeking Bankruptcy," New York Times, April 3, 2007.

150 "like a trash novel": John Gallagher, "Insider E-Mails: Wall Street Pushed Bad Detroit Mortgage Loans," Detroit Free Press, January 26, 2015.

150 "Sorry to be flip. . . .": Gallagher, "Insider E-Mails."

150 Black neighborhoods at that time were subprime: Office of Policy Development and Research, "Unequal Burden: Income and Racial Disparities in Subprime Lending in America," U.S. Department of Housing and Urban Development, February 22, 2008.

151 borrowers had subprime loans: Office of Policy Development and Research, "Unequal Burden: Income and Racial Disparities in Subprime Lending in America."

151 reforms after this late 1990s report: Office of Policy Development and Research, "Unequal Burden: Income and Racial Disparities in Subprime Lending in America."

151 than lower-income white families: "Lower income" defined as those making thirty thousand dollars or less per year. Emily Badger, "The Dramatic Racial Bias of Subprime Lending During the Housing Boom," Bloomberg, August 16, 2013.

152 qualified for a prime loan: Taneeta did not reply to our inquiries on the topic of her foreclosure, though we discussed it with Brook.

152 debt on her minivan: U.S. Bankruptcy Court, District of Massachusetts, Bankruptcy Petition No. 06-14293, November 17, 2006, Document 1.

152 from 101 to 19: Bluestone, Billingham, and Davis, "The Greater Boston Housing Report Card 2008."

152 her 2005 monthly income: New Century Mortgage Corporation, Civil Action No. 2005-00116120, August 30, 2005.

152 "less than 8.3%": Taneeta Bacon's mortgage statement, in her possession.

152 loans like Taneeta's: Nathalie Baptiste, "Staggering Loss of Black Wealth Due to Subprime Scandal Continues Unabated," *The American Prospect*, October 13, 2014.

152 the City of Baltimore: Baptiste, "Staggering Loss of Black Wealth Due to Subprime Scandal Continues Unabated."

153 Black Americans "mud people": Powell, "Bank Accused of Pushing Mortgage Deals on Blacks."

153 worth dropped 16 percent: Christopher Famighetti and Darrick Hamilton, "The Great Recession, Education, Race, And Homeownership," Economic Policy Institute, May 15, 2019.

153 Americans lost 36 percent: The amount of housing wealth lost depended in part on where people lived, as wealth in different parts of the country dropped more than in others. Latino homeowners and Asian American homeowners lost more housing wealth than many Black homeowners due to the former's prominence in the Southwest and West Coast, where real estate prices dropped more sharply.

153 she filed for bankruptcy: U.S. Bankruptcy Court, District of Massachusetts, Bankruptcy Petition No. 06-14293, March 1, 2007.

155 of fornication in 1944: Georgia, U.S. Central Register of Convicts, 1817–1976, Ancestry.

155 participating in the lottery: Georgia, U.S. Central Register of Convicts, 1817–1976.

155 two inches thick: Pauli Murray, *States' Laws on Race and Color and Appendices* (Cincinnati: Women's Division of Christian Service, 1951).

156 midwestern states: Equal Justice Initiative, *Lynching in America: Confronting the Legacy of Racial Terror*, Equal Justice Initiative, 2017.

156 "perpetrator for a crime": Equal Justice Initiative, *Lynching in America.*

156 Inman Park: Jim Auchmutey, "Atlanta Gets New Monument to History," *Atlanta Journal-Constitution*, June 15, 2009.

156 among other manual jobs: Douglas A. Blackmon, *Slavery by Another Name: The Re-enslavement of Black Americans from the Civil War to World War II* (New York: Anchor Books, 2008), p. 341.

156 been outlawed, Blackmon wrote: Blackmon, *Slavery by Another Name.*

156 chief executive of American Express: "James D. Robinson III."

156 firms in the world: Jeffrey Kutler, "The Fintech Finance 40: James D. Robinson III and James D. Robinson IV," *Institutional Investor*, January 15, 2018.

156 "and history is messy": The relative was Rodney Mims Cook Jr.

157 nine months in 1917: Darity and Mullen, *From Here to Equality*, pp. 11–12.

157 much money before being incarcerated: Two thirds of people in jail say they made $12,000 or less annually before going to jail, according to Michelle Alexander, *The New Jim Crow: Mass Incarceration in the Age of Colorblindness* (New York: The New Press, 2010), p. 194.

157 job search a priority: Christy Visher, Sara Debus-Sherrill, and Jennifer Yahner, "Employment After Prison: A Longitudinal Study of Releasees in Three States," Urban Institute Justice Policy Center, October 2008.

157 unemployment rate of 27.3 percent: Lucius Couloute and Daniel Kopf, "Out of Prison and Out of Work: Unemployment Among Formerly Incarcerated People," Prison Policy Initiative, July 2018.

157 rate of 5.8 percent: Couloute and Kopf, "Out of Prison and Out of Work."

158 incarcerated white women: Couloute and Kopf, "Out of Prison and Out of Work."

158 had *no* criminal record: Devah Pager, *Marked: Race, Crime, and Finding Work in an Era of Mass Incarceration* (Chicago, Ill.: University of Chicago Press, 2007); and Brooke Kroeger, "When a Dissertation Makes a Difference," *New York Times*, March 20, 2004. The Second Chance Act movement in 2018 sought to block employers from asking about criminal histories, but not all states passed laws supporting this. See "Second Chance Act," National Reentry Resource Center.

158 and Latino-white wealth gaps: Chris Burrell, "State Commission Calls for Dismantling Structural Racism In Mass. Prisons, Jails," WGBH, January 4, 2023.

158 for many people: Alexander, *The New Jim Crow*, p. 7.

158 cities had criminal records: Alexander, *The New Jim Crow*, p. 8.

159 "waged against our communities": Alexander, *The New Jim Crow*, p. xxiii. Alexander also explained that while most arrests are for nonviolent crimes, a higher proportion of people in jail are there for violent crimes because those offenses bring longer terms. But she pointed out that arrests for nonviolent crimes also affect the trajectories of people's lives.

159 five times the rate of white Americans: Ashley Nellis, "The Color of Justice: Racial and Ethnic Disparity in State Prisons," The Sentencing Project, October 13, 2021.

159 population was 38.4 percent: "Inmate Race," Federal Bureau of Prisons, last updated May 6, 2023.

159 13.6 percent of the U.S. population: "Quickfacts: Population Estimates," U.S. Census Bureau, July 1, 2022.

159 as having "second-class status": Alexander, *The New Jim Crow*, p. ix.

159 60 percent of the state's prison occupants: Carl Vinson, "Georgia Criminal Justice Data Landscape Report," Public Welfare Foundation.

159 were enslaved in 1850: Gregg Kennard, post about attending "Decriminalizing Race & Poverty: Clint Smith in Conversation with James Woodall" Zoom event, Facebook, September 21, 2021. This statistic is only compared to the number of enslaved people who were over the age of fifteen. Also some people criticize this comparison as misleading because the United States population is larger now than it was in the early and mid-1800s. Still, the raw numbers are comparable and are commonly cited.

160 police three years prior: Julian Lewis Correctional Records.

160 ended up getting out early: Lewis Correctional Records.

160 with possession of cocaine: Lewis Correctional Records.

160   and for domestic violence: Lewis Correctional Records.

160   until August 27, 2020: Lewis Correctional Records.

160   was still on parole: Lewis Correctional Records.

161   when Brook appeared in court, he said: Indeed, the incident did not appear in public records.

CHAPTER 7: THE BANKRUPTCY GAP

163   *Souls of Black Folk*: W. E. B. Du Bois, "The Souls of Black Folk," *Three African-American Classics* (Garden City, N.Y.: Dover Publications, 2007), p. 257.

163   studio album, called *PL3DGE*: Mitch Findlay, "Killer Mike Celebrates 10 Years of 'Pl3dge,'" *Hot New Hip Hop*, May 17, 2021.

163   "we still muthafuckin' slaves": Emanuel Wallace, "Killer Mike: Pl3dge," RapReviews.com, May 24, 2011; and Michael Render, "That's Life II," *Pl3dge*, May 17, 2011.

163   have made it: Render, "That's Life II."

163   "standing next to Warren Buffett": Render, "That's Life II."

164   "dollar he's ever got": Kathy Iandoli, "Killer Mike Reveals that He Believes He Could Get Killed for His Lyrics," *HipHopDX*, April 28, 2011.

164   father, dropped out: "Killer Mike: Jay Z Called Big Boi & Said I Want . . . You Can't Out Smooth Dre & You," B High Atl, 2022, YouTube video.

164   time dealing crack: "Killer Mike Unleashes 'Monster," *Billboard*, March 10, 2003; and Joe Coscarelli, "Killer Mike, Atlanta's Rap Journeyman, Is at the Peak of His Powers," *New York Times*, May 19, 2023.

164   "for a reason": Several years later, a news article described Michael as a leader, not as a rapper. Michael likes to share that his father sent his son the article and apologized, saying, "The man in this article is who I've always seen you as." Michael Render's Instagram account.

165   on a Jay-Z album: "Killer Mike: Jay Z Called Big Boi & Said I Want . . . You Can't Out Smooth Dre & You."

165   "I wanted *mine*": "Killer Mike: Jay Z Called Big Boi & Said I Want . . . You Can't Out Smooth Dre & You."

165   father for child support: Michael Lee Render, the father of Killer Mike, did not respond to multiple inquiries from the authors about this.

165   Michael wasn't paying all the child support: Summons for Michael Render, Civil Action No. 2004-CV87914, March 21, 2011, Superior Court of Fulton County.

165   and $78,008 in debt: U.S. Bankruptcy Court, Northern District of Georgia (Atlanta), Bankruptcy Petition No. 11-76733-mhm, Document 14, filed October 28, 2011 (hereafter cited as: Document 14, Bankruptcy Petition No. 11-76733-mhm).

165   "I was on my ass": Jordan McDonald, "Rapper and Netflix Star Killer Mike Says This Was His Best Business Decision—and Warren Buffett Agrees," CNBC, March 20, 2019.

165   "that slavery's abolished (shit)": Killer Mike, "Ju$t," YouTube video.

166   portion of the population: Leslie E. Linfield, "2010 Annual Consumer Bankruptcy Demographics Report: A Five Year Perspective of the American Debtor," Institute for Financial Literacy, September 2011.

167   debts reorganized or relieved: Sarah S. Greene, Parina Patel, and Katherine Porter, "Cracking the Code: An Empirical Analysis of Consumer Bankruptcy Outcomes," *Minnesota Law Review*, No. 101 (2017): p. 1031.

167   8 percent of white families: Federal Reserve 2019 Survey of Consumer Finances, as an-

alyzed by McKinsey and Company; and Shelley Stewart III et al., "The Economic State of Black America: What Is and What Could Be," McKinsey Global Institute, June 17, 2021.

167 and a $300 shotgun: Document 14, Bankruptcy Petition No. 11-76733-mhm; and U.S. Bankruptcy Court, Northern District of Georgia (Atlanta), Bankruptcy Petition No. 11-76733-mhm, Document 1, September 14, 2011 (hereafter cited as: Document 1, Bankruptcy Petition No. 11-76733-mhm).

167 it had been repossessed: That was later disputed by the trustee who said the car had been sold for $3,000.

167 a white-run conglomerate: Document 14 and Document 1, Bankruptcy Petition No. 11-76733-mhm.

167 owed in child support: Document 14 and Document 1, Bankruptcy Petition No. 11-76733-mhm.

167 had married in 2006: Izzy Casey, "Sweet Details About Killer Mike's Relationship with Wife, Shana Render," YourTango, October 15, 2020.

168 in the filing: U.S. Bankruptcy Court, Northern District of Georgia (Atlanta), Bankruptcy Petition No. 11-76733-mhm, Document 16, November 8, 2011, Trustee's Objection.

168 or relief was granted: U.S. Bankruptcy Court, Northern District of Georgia (Atlanta), Bankruptcy Petition No. 11-76733-mhm, Order of Dismissal.

168 for her cell phone: U.S. Bankruptcy Court, District of Massachusetts, Bankruptcy Petition No. 06-14293, Document 1, November 17, 2006.

168 "worth holding on to": U.S. Bankruptcy Court, District of Massachusetts, Bankruptcy Petition No.07-11428. Document 21, March 29, 2007.

168 complete credit counseling: U.S. Bankruptcy Court, District of Massachusetts, Bankruptcy Petition No. 06-14293, Motion of Chapter 13 Trustee to Dismiss.

169 if given the chance: U.S. Bankruptcy Court, District of Massachusetts, Bankruptcy Petition No. 07-11428, Document 21, March 29, 2007.

169 would resolve her debts: U.S. Bankruptcy Court, District of Massachusetts, Bankruptcy Petition No. 07-11428, Document 48, July 25, 2007.

169 the motion was granted: U.S. Bankruptcy Court, District of Massachusetts, Bankruptcy Petition No. 07-11428, Dismissed August 20, 2007.

169 resold for $247,000: Zillow.

170 and bankruptcy, has said: Quoted in Leslie A. Pappas, "Bankruptcy Racial Disparities Poised to Add to Pandemic Pain (1)," Bloomberg Law, August 31, 2020.

170 "most instances, Black people": Quoted in Pappas, "Bankruptcy Racial Disparities Poised to Add to Pandemic Pain (1)."

170 plans, according to research: Greene, Patel, and Porter, "Cracking the Code."

170 University of California, Irvine: Porter was a professor at the University of California, Irvine, when the research came out in 2017. A Democrat, she later became a member of the House of Representatives for a district in Orange County, California.

170 2007 Consumer Bankruptcy Project: The Consumer Bankruptcy Project, an ongoing national survey begun in 1981, is conducted across a sample of bankruptcy cases.

170 or having had prior bankruptcies: Greene, Patel, and Porter, "Cracking the Code."

171 the court is setting: Bronson Argyle et al., "Explaining Racial Disparities in Personal Bankruptcy Outcomes," Consumer Financial Protection Bureau, March 2023.

171 plan for relief: Case 11-76733-mhm in U.S. Bankruptcy Court, Northern District of Georgia (Atlanta) "Chapter 13 Trustee's Objection to Confirmation & Motion To Dismiss," filed November 8, 2011; December 13, 2011, letter from Render's attorney to the Trustee;

Exhibit 1 in the December 13, 2011, filing in the case; and Item #5 Repossession item in the Bankruptcy Form 6 Schedule.

171 have their cases dismissed: Argyle et al., "Explaining Racial Disparities in Personal Bankruptcy Outcomes." For Chapter 7 bankruptcy, a far quicker process with less discretion as to the actions that can be taken, scholars found that qualities other than race explained the disparities.

171 bankruptcy trustees were white: Argyle et al., "Explaining Racial Disparities in Personal Bankruptcy Outcomes."

171 no Chapter 13 trustees were Black: "Trustee Information," U.S. Bankruptcy Court, Northern District of Georgia (Atlanta).

171 the U.S. Trustee Program: The U.S. Trustee Program is an arm of the U.S. Justice Department that manages the nationwide trustee offices.

171 "is apparent," he said: Cliff White, "Remarks of Director Cliff White at the 2021 Annual Conference of the National Association of Bankruptcy Trustees," 2021 Annual Conference of the National Association of Bankruptcy Trustees, Washington, D.C., August 26, 2021.

172 stacks the odds against them: Greene, Patel, and Porter, "Cracking the Code."

172 the gradual repayment plans: Paul Kiel and Hannah Fresques, "How the Bankruptcy System Is Failing Black Americans," ProPublica and *The Atlantic*, September 27, 2017.

172 those in Chapter 7: Kiel and Fresques, "How the Bankruptcy System Is Failing Black Americans." ProPublica and *The Atlantic* used the dominant race within zip codes as a proxy for the race of filers.

172 to keep their cars: Edward E. Morrison, Belisa Pang, and Antoine Uettwiller, "Race and Bankruptcy: Explaining Racial Disparities in Consumer Bankruptcy," *Journal of Law and Economics* 63, No. 269 (2020).

172 give them lower interest rates: Pappas, "Bankruptcy Racial Disparities Poised to Add to Pandemic Pain (1)."

173 regular monthly foreclosure sales: Pappas, "Bankruptcy Racial Disparities Poised to Add to Pandemic Pain (1)."

173 for not paying it: Ashley Simpo, "Op-Ed: Why the Taboo of Child Support and Black Families Still Sparks Heated Debates," BET, November 4, 2019; and Eleanor Pratt, "Child Support Enforcement Can Hurt Black, Low-Income, Noncustodial Fathers and Their Kids," Urban Institute, June 15, 2016.

173 "once they get locked up": Miller v. Deal, 295 Ga. 504, 761 S.E. 2d 274 (Ga. 2014), as cited in Matthew Clarke, "Poor Parents Fail to Pay Child Support, Go to Jail," Prison Legal News, September 2, 2016.

173 his child support debt: Russ Bynum, "Man Shot by Police Had Much to Celebrate in Recent Months," Associated Press, April 11, 2015.

174 also Michael's distant cousin: Blackmon is Michael's mother's cousin. Blackmon's father is a brother of Michael's mother's mother, Bettie Hawthorne Clonts.

175 pervasive in most other places: Charles Toutant, "'It's Hard to Have a Discussion About This': The Uncomfortable Truth About Setting Tort Damages," *New Jersey Law Journal*, March 29, 2022.

176 study of syphilis: "Tuskegee Patient Medical Files Numerical by Patient Number," National Archives at Atlanta, January 13, 2021.

CHAPTER 8: TANDREIA DIXON AND THE GENERATIONAL WEALTH HUSTLE

177 and businesswoman, 1918: "Annie Malone and Madam C. J. Walker: Pioneers of the African American Beauty Industry," Smithsonian National Museum of African American History and Culture; and "Madam C. J. Walker (Sarah Breedlove) (1867–1919)," *Jim Crow Stories*, PBS Thirteen.

178 "I will be a multimillionaire": Tandreia Dixon's Instagram account.

178 First, a nearly ten-minute video: Eliott C. McLaughlin, "Three Videos Piece Together the Final Moments of George Floyd's Life," CNN, June 23, 2020.

178 white police officer: Rachel Treisman, "Darnella Frazier, Teen Who Filmed Floyd's Murder, Praised for Making Verdict Possible," NPR, April 21, 2021.

178 in Central Park: Melody [@melodyMcooper], video, Twitter, May 25, 2020.

178 man carrying Swarovski binoculars: Sarah Maslin Nir, "How 2 Lives Collided in Central Park, Rattling the Nation," *New York Times*, June 14, 2020.

178 police violence in 1965: Photo of Charles Everett, a cousin of Tandreia Dixon's, at a Black Lives Matter protest in Washington, D.C.

179 three million dollars in seed funding: Chauncey Alcorn, "Killer Mike's New Black-Owned Bank Receives 'Tens of Thousands' of Account Requests in Less than 24 Hours," CNN, October 11, 2020.

179 of people within days: Alcorn, "Killer Mike's New Black-Owned Bank Receives 'Tens of Thousands' of Account Requests in Less than 24 Hours."

181 Black heads of families: Du Bois, "The Negro Landholder of Georgia," p. 648.

181 26 percent in 1920: For comparison, about half of white farmers owned their farms throughout this period.

181 high profit margins in this era: Du Bois surveyed Georgia farm owners in 1898–99 and found that of 271 families, 80 percent made no profit from their farming, and in fact, many had incurred debt. Du Bois, "The Negro Landholder of Georgia," p. 648.

182 historians have estimated: Andrew W. Kahrl, "Black People's Land Was Stolen," *New York Times*, June 20, 2019.

182 "the ownership of land": Du Bois, "The Negro Landholder of Georgia," p. 648.

182 featured Black business districts: There was a white-led attack on Black businesses in Wilmington in 1898 that damaged much of the area and killed one dozen to three hundred Black people, according to estimates. Vince Winkel, "CoastLine: The 120th Anniversary of Wilmington's 1898 Coup," WHQR, November 7, 2018.

182 in the late 1800s: Kahrl, "Black People's Land Was Stolen."

183 "not accessible to them": Joy DeGruy, *Post Traumatic Slave Syndrome: America's Legacy of Enduring Injury and Healing* (Milwaukie, OR: Uptone Press, 2005), p. 105.

183 Atlanta to General Sherman: Thomas H. Martin, *Atlanta and Its Builders: A Comprehensive History of the Gate City of the South* (Springfield, Mass.: Century Memorial Publishing Company, 1902), pp. 613, 623.

183 as an Atlanta newspaper wrote in 1902: "Negro Preacher Insane," *Atlanta Journal-Constitution*, April 18, 1902 [emphasis added by book authors].

183 three weeks after arriving: Robert Epps's Mental Hospital Records, Georgia Department of Archives and History [emphasis added by book authors].

184 The mid-1850s: Ephram Dixon's birth year varies in different records, ranging from 1850 to 1862. His name is also sometimes spelled Ephraim. Many names in the book can be found in government records with multiple spellings.

185 owned their home, mortgage free: 1920 U.S. Federal Census.

185 paid for the land in 1901: Ephram and Laura Dixon Property Deeds, 1903–1932.

185 in someone else's home: 1930 U.S. Federal Census.

185 from overly high tax assessments: "The Power to Destroy: Property Tax Discrimination in Civil Rights-Era Mississippi," *Journal of Southern History* 82 (August 2016): pp. 579–616.

185 Other historians: Kenneth K. Baar, "Property Tax Assessment Discrimination Against Low-Income Neighborhoods," *The Urban Lawyer* 13, No. 3 (1981): p. 333406; and Rothstein, *The Color of Law*.

185 as developers came in: Lizzie Presser, "Their Family Bought Land One Generation After Slavery: The Reels Brothers Spent Eight Years in Jail for Refusing to Leave It," ProPublica, July 15, 2019. The incident occurred in Daufuskie, an island in South Carolina.

185 taxes were not paid: Bernadette Atuahene and Christopher Berry, "Taxed Out: Illegal Property Tax Assessments and the Epidemic of Tax Foreclosures in Detroit," *UC Irvine Law Review* 9, No. 847 (2019).

185 Law School professor: Atuahene and Berry, "Taxed Out."

186 compared to white homeowners: Carlos F. Avenancio-León and Troup Howard, "The Assessment Gap: Racial Inequalities in Property Taxation," PDF, January 2022.

186 "to the advantage of developers": Quoted in Presser, "Their Family Bought Land One Generation After Slavery."

187 Jenkins lost it all: Roy Reed, "Blacks in South Struggle to Keep the Little Land They Have Left," *New York Times,* December 7, 1972.

187 four or five hundred thousand dollars apiece: Kahrl, "Black People's Land Was Stolen."

187 due to the threat of eminent domain: Rachel Garbus, "Bagley Park Is a Monument to Buckhead's Historic Black Communities—and a Reminder of the Racism that Drove Them Out," *Atlanta Magazine,* March 13, 2023.

187 had four children: North Carolina, U.S. Marriage Records 1741–2011.

188 breaking and entering, a felony: Court Records for Samuel Dixon.

189 drug possession in 2006: Court Records for Samuel Dixon.

191 even the playing field: "Fulton County Reparations Task Force," Fox News 5, October 12, 2021.

191 more in investor funding: "Fintech Startup Greenwood Raises $40 Million in Funding to Provide Black and Latino Banking Services," PRNewswire, March 25, 2021.

191 Greenwood virtual gathering: Greenwood Virtual Hangout. April 8, 2021.

194 Greenwood customer-to-be, Clive Davis: John Casmon and Clive Davis, "How To Break into Multifamily Investing with Clive Davis, Episode 237," *Target Market Insights* podcast, Multifamily Insights, YouTube video, October 23, 2020.

194 "once in a lifetime": Eminem, "Lose Yourself," *8 Mile,* Shady Records, 2002.

196 "there is no progress": Aparicio (Reese) Giddins and Kasha Giddins, "HLP: Dealing with Injustice—A Needed Conversation," *The Harried Life Podcast,* June 1, 2020.

196 such as payday loans: "People of Color and Low-Income Communities Are Disproportionately Harmed by Banking and Financial Exclusion," Joint Economic Committee Democrats.

196 Black as of 2021: "Action #3—Representation," Google, *Diversity Annual Report,* 2022.

196 1,548 people were Black: Goldman Sachs, *EMEA Diversity and Inclusion 2020 Report.*

196 IRS call center jobs: *FY19 Annual Report to Congress,* Office of Minority and Women Inclusion, Department of the Treasury, 2020.

197 Latino Americans, 19 percent: U.S. Census Bureau.

197 According to the Bureau of Labor Statistics: "Labor Force Characteristics by Race and Ethnicity, 2020," Report 1095, U.S. Bureau of Labor Statistics, November 2021.

197 Black and Latino workers: "Labor Force Characteristics by Race and Ethnicity, 2020."

197 of weekly pay levels: "Labor Force Characteristics by Race and Ethnicity, 2020."

198 less than white Americans: Whether Latinos or Black Americans earn less compared to each other varies from job to job. And in a twist, Asian Americans often earn more per week than white Americans, though there is income inequality within the Asian American population.

200 "help you keep safe": "No Contact Kit by Dixon Brands [ad]," Jake Walch, November 30, 2020.

200 "getting on your clothes": "No Contact Kit by Dixon Brands [ad]."

201 gap would predict: Tiffany Howard and the Center for Policy Analysis and Research, "The State of Black Entrepreneurship in America: Evaluating the Relationship Between Immigration and Minority Business Ownership," Congressional Black Caucus Foundation, April 2019, p. 14.

201 options as white borrowers: For instance, a National Community Reinvestment Coalition study in 2020 found that Black and white people walking into banks to apply for Paycheck Protection Program loans experienced different levels of encouragement to apply for those loans, were offered different products, and were provided with different information by bank representatives. More information can be found here: "Despite Gaping Holes in Government Data, Tests Show PPP Borrowers Faced Discrimination," National Community Reinvestment Coalition, July 15, 2020.

201 Asian Americans reported the same: Tiffany Howard and the Center for Policy Analysis and Research, "The State of Black Entrepreneurship in America," p. 14.

202 rival soft drink to Coca-Cola: Draeke Weseman, "Crip-a-Cola: From Gang to Brand?" *Duets Blog*, January 30, 2019; and "Killer Mike Helps Gangs Become Successful Business Owners," Tru Dreadz, April 17, 2019.

202 "the establishment," Michael said: *Trigger Warning with Killer Mike*, Season 1, Episode 3, Netflix, 2019.

202 "yourself basic economics": @SheBeEverywhere, "Killer Mike at Black Bank Event at OneUnited Miami," July 31, 2016, YouTube video.

202 "have a conversation": @SheBeEverywhere, "Killer Mike at Black Bank Event at OneUnited Miami."

203 *money circulation in the Black community*": "About," Greenwood Bank website [emphasis from book authors].

203 before leaving the community: "About," Greenwood Bank website; "How Dollars Circulate in Black Communities," Greenwood Bank website, January 25, 2021; and "Black Wall Street History: The Tulsa Race Massacre of 1921," Greenwood Bank website, January 18, 2021.

204 "gap for Black communities": "About," "How Dollars Circulate in Black Communities," and "Black Wall Street History," all at Greenwood Bank website.

204 within the Black community: "About," "How Dollars Circulate in Black Communities," and "Black Wall Street History," all at Greenwood Bank website.

204 linked to an article: Kimberly Fain, "The Devastation of Black Wall Street," JSTOR Daily, July 5, 2017.

204 the *Atlanta Black Star*: Christina Montford, "6 Interesting Things You Didn't Know About 'Black Wall Street,'" *Atlanta Black Star*, December 2, 2014, updated January 31, 2017.

204 from a 2011 story: "What Happened to Black Wall Street on June 1, 1921?" *San Francisco Bay View National Black Newspaper*, February 9, 2011.

204 "leaves the Black community in 15 minutes": "What Happened to Black Wall Street on June 1, 1921?"

204 CNBC published them: Tom Huddleston Jr., "'Black Wall Street': The History of The Wealthy Black Community and the Massacre Perpetrated There 100 Years Ago," CNBC, last updated May 28, 2021.

204 So did the *Boston Globe*: "Tulsa's Black Wall Street Was Once 35 Blocks of Wealth. Now It's Two," *Boston Globe*, November 1, 2022.

204 *New York Times DealBook*: Michael Render, "Fund Black-Owned Banks that Renew Opportunity," *New York Times DealBook*, December 9, 2020.

205 U.S. currency later on: Loren Gatch, "Local Scrip in the USA During the 1930s: Lessons

for Today?" Presented at the Conference on Monetary Regionalisation, September 28–29, 2006.

205 "for the next stamp": Bruce Champ, "Stamp Scrip: Money People Paid to Use," Federal Reserve Bank of Cleveland, April 1, 2008.

205 in exchange for goods: Bryan Carl Bjorklund, "Saving Local Communities Using Scrip Money to Fight the Great Depression in North Central Iowa" (PhD diss., University of Northern Iowa, 2017), p. 88.

205 keep money circulating around town: Bjorklund, "Saving Local Communities Using Scrip Money to Fight the Great Depression in North Central Iowa."

205 rather than being spent elsewhere: Rebecca Mqamelo, "Community Currencies as Crisis Response: Results from a Randomized Control Trial in Kenya," Frontiers.

206 there until the 2010s: Eric Fleischmann, "A Brief Look Back at Ithaca Hours," The Anarchist Library, July 23, 2022.

206 nonprofit that administers the currency: "Blockchain Hits Main Street," BerkShares, April 2022.

206 cryptocurrency BerkShares: "Western Massachusetts Challenges the U.S. Dollar," Berk-Shares, n.d.

206 thirty days in Asian communities: "How Dollars Circulate in Black Communities."

206 "in the Black community": Alcorn, "Killer Mike's New Black-Owned Bank Receives 'Tens of Thousands' of Account Requests in Less than 24 Hours."

206 from the Selig Center for Economic Growth: "How Dollars Circulate in Black Communities."

206 fact-checking of these data points: Brookie Madison, "Does a Dollar Spent in the Black Community Really Stay There for Only Six Hours?" Truth Be Told, December 22, 2015.

207 from the mid-1990s: The story by Brookie Madison said the data was in Brooke Stephens, *Talking Dollars and Making Sense: A Wealth Building Guide for African-Americans* (New York: McGraw Hill, 1997), p. 18.

207 "Where would you get that from": Madison, "Does a Dollar Spent in the Black Community Really Stay There for Only Six Hours?"

207 *"wealth within Black communities"*: "How Dollars Circulate in Black Communities" [emphasis from book authors].

208 for a Greenwood account: "How Dollars Circulate in Black Communities."

208 helped create with the Crips: Jay-Z, vocalist, "Entrepreneur" by Pharrell Williams, 2020.

208 the cofounder of Twitter: Jakob Rodriguez, "Killer Mike Announces Jay-Z as a Partner in Crip-a-Cola, Blood Pop," KSAT, August 26, 2020.

209 the Crip-a-Cola company: Rodriguez, "Killer Mike Announces Jay-Z as a Partner in Crip-a-Cola, Blood Pop."

CHAPTER 9: THE SO-CALLED BLACK DOLLAR

210 Martin Luther King Jr., 1967: Martin Luther King Jr., "Beyond Vietnam," in *A Time to Break Silence: The Essential Works of Martin Luther King, Jr., for Students* (Boston: Beacon Press, 2013), pp. 92–93.

210 "just wanna be agreed with": Michael Render [@killermike] post of books he is reading, Instagram, June 25, 2020.

211 "hidden gold mine": Armistead S. Pride and Clint C. Wilson II, *A History of the Black Press* (Washington, D.C.: Howard University Press, 1997), p. 243.

212 haven't talked since: When we asked about his interactions with Ball, Michael declined to elaborate, and this phone call was recounted to us solely by Ball.

212 "attractive audiences for marketers": Stuart Elliott, "A Channel Reflects the Reshaping of TV Demographics," *New York Times*, February 26, 2013.

213 "corporate ad buyers": Jared A. Ball, *The Myth and Propaganda of Black Buying Power* (Chum, Switzerland: Palgrave Macmillan, 2020), p. 4.

215 that state ended slavery: "Freedom's Journal," Newspapers, PBS.

215 page to abolition efforts: Editors of Encyclopaedia Britannica, "The North Star," *Encyclopaedia Britannica*, November 11, 2016.

215 newspapers had been established: "Freedom's Journal."

215 Black-owned daily in 1932: Pride and Wilson, *A History of the Black Press*, p. 228.

215 Lincoln University historians found: Pride and Wilson, *A History of the Black Press*, p. 228.

215 working journalists were Black: Pride and Wilson, *A History of the Black Press*, p. 229.

216 "intensify white prejudices": *The Essential Kerner Commission Report* (New York: Liveright, 2021).

216 5 percent of newsroom jobs: Pamela Newkirk, "The Not-So-Great Migration," *Columbia Journalism Review* (May/June 2011).

216 and coverage of race: Paul Farhi and Sarah Ellison, "Ignited by Public Protests, American Newsrooms Are Having Their Own Racial Reckoning," *Washington Post*, June 13, 2020.

216 "city became majority nonwhite": Farhi and Ellison, "Ignited by Public Protests, American Newsrooms Are Having Their Own Racial Reckoning."

216 "painful day-to-day workplace experiences": The New York Times Company, "Making a More Diverse, Equitable, and Inclusive New York Times."

217 using the uppercase for years: Elahe Izadi, "Why Hundreds of American Newsrooms Have Started Capitalizing the 'B' in 'Black,'" *Washington Post*, June 22, 2020.

217 In the 1920s, the NAACP: Pride and Wilson, *A History of the Black Press*, p. 233.

217 "in the 'lower case'": Quoted in Izadi, "Why Hundreds of American Newsrooms Have Started Capitalizing the 'B' in 'Black.'"

217 *African American* led the way: Izadi, "Why Hundreds of American Newsrooms Have Started Capitalizing the 'B' in 'Black.'"

218 "capitalizes the 'B' in Black": Sarah Glover, "One Thing Newsrooms Can Do: Capitalize 'B' When Reporting About the Black Community," *Amsterdam News*, June 11, 2020.

218 news outlets did so as well: The National Association of Black Journalists also recommended that the *W* in *white* be capitalized, saying that "whenever a color is used to appropriately describe race then it should be capitalized, including White and Brown." News organizations did not capitalize *white*, saying it was not a culture or ethnicity, and so we have followed that guidance in this book.

219 Black Panther Party in the 1960s: Study by Guy B. Johnson, as cited in Pride and Wilson, *A History of the Black Press*, p. 231; and "History of *The Crisis*," NAACP, February 11, 2022.

219 as part of their coverage: Pride and Wilson, *A History of the Black Press*, p. 266.

219 "Black Civil Rights crusade": Enoc P. Waters, "About Recapturing a Fading Mission," *Editor and Publisher*, March 12, 1977, as cited in Pride and Wilson, *A History of the Black Press*, p. 234.

219 a "hidden gold mine": Pride and Wilson, *A History of the Black Press*, p. 243.

219 the buying "power" of Black consumers: Cited in Ball, *The Myth and Propaganda of Black Buying Power*, p. 17.

220 Florida television executive: Mike Snider, "Black News Channel Will Launch Broadcasting in New York on January 6, 2020," *USAToday*, November 6, 2019.

221 "still progress to be made": Pascal Archimède, "Gary Wordlaw, 'Orchestra Conductor' of Black News Channel TV," Nofi Media, March 24, 2020.

221 a defense against "systemic oppression": Vynessah Dasher, "The Black Dollar: A Substantial Defense Against Systemic Oppression," Black News Channel, 2020.

222 "over the world": Archimède, "Gary Wordlaw, 'Orchestra Conductor' of Black News Channel TV."

222 "had not fled them": Charles M. Blow, "We Need a Second Great Migration," *New York Times*, January 8, 2021.

CHAPTER 10: BLACK BANKING AND CIVIL RIGHTS

223 Freedom National Bank, 1971: "Address by the Honorable Samuel R. Pierce, Jr. Before the Houston Real Estate Association on January 15, 1971." Transcript located on St. Louis Federal Reserve website.

223 Greenwood Bank really was: "Dear Killer Mike: Greenwood bank exposed!?!?" The Poor Black Man, December 12, 2020, YouTube video.

224 "list of Black banks": FDIC Minority Depository Institutions List, FDIC website.

224 the Nasdaq in 2018: Donovan Jones, "Coastal Financial Readies $38 Million IPO," Seeking Alpha, July 11, 2018.

224 the following year: "Investor Presentation," Coastal Financial Corporation, October 27, 2022.

224 all were white: Coastal's website included names and photos of its top ten executives in January 2023. After the authors of this book asked about diversity at the top, the number of people featured on the site was reduced to three. Sprink, the chief executive of Coastal, said in an interview for this book that there were more people "of minority status" lower down in the company.

225 he has said: Amelia Pollard and Max Reyes, "Silicon Valley's Hottest Money Apps Depend on Old-School Banks," *Bloomberg Businessweek*, October 29, 2021.

225 in the country: Rica Dela Cruz and Xylex Mangulabnan, "US Banks Had More Female Employees in 2021, Only 10 as CEOs," *S&P Global Market Intelligence*, December 6, 2022.

225 banks in the country: FDIC Minority Depository Institutions List. FDIC website.

226 only sixteen Black-owned banks: FDIC Minority Depository Institutions List.

226 Ryan Glover's ancestors: Du Bois, *Economic Co-operation Among Negro Americans*.

227 program at Talladega College: "Young, Andrew," The Martin Luther King, Jr. Research and Education Institute, Stanford University.

227 a businessman, Dunbar McLaurin: Louis Lomax, "Dr. Aubre Maynard: The Man Who Saved Dr. Martin King," *Afro-American*, October 4, 1958.

227 segregation in public schools: "Brown v. Board of Education," History.com, last updated January 11, 2023; and New York Public Library website description of McLaurin family collection, 1948–1973. The case McLaurin won in the Supreme Court was called *McLaurin v. Oklahoma State Regents*, 339 U.S. 637.

227 him a "business wizard": "GI Business Wizard Dunbar McLaurin of Oklahoma," *Ebony*, December 1949, p. 43, as cited in David W. Levy, *Breaking Down Barriers: George McLaurin and the Struggle to End Segregated Education* (Norman: University of Oklahoma Press, 2020), p. 66.

227 Black-focused bank in Houston: "Banker Dunbar S. McLaurin Suicide Victim in N.Y. Home," *Jet*, July 26, 1973, p. 6.

227 called Riverside National Bank: It would later be called Unity National Bank of Houston, which, as of 2020, still existed, though it was struggling financially. Naomi Snyder, "Texas' Last Black-Owned Bank Hasn't Made a Profit in 3 Years. But There's Hope," *Houston Chronicle*, last updated July 4, 2020.

227 "start a bank in Harlem": "Banker Dunbar S. McLaurin Suicide Victim in N.Y. Home," p. 6.

228 to Black depositors: Mehrsa Baradaran, *The Color of Money: Black Banks and the Racial Wealth Gap* (Cambridge, Mass.: Belknap Press/Harvard University Press, 2019), p. 77.

228 by John Rockefeller Jr.: Dunbar National Bank was unrelated to Dunbar McLaurin.

228 run by Black Americans: "Staff of the Dunbar National Bank, Harlem, NY, 1930," *Harlem World*, September 11, 2016.

228   a decade in 1938: Baradaran, *The Color of Money*, p. 80.

228   "loaned to white customers": Baradaran, *The Color of Money*, p. 78.

228   of his briefcase: *Hearing Before the Subcommittee on Financial Institutions Supervision, Regulation and Insurance of the Committee on Banking, Finance and Urban Affairs House of Representatives*, 101st Congress, (1990), p. 85.

228   "ghetto economics": Dunbar McLaurin, "Ghediplan: Ghetto Economic Development and Industrialization Plan," *The Human Resources Administration of the City of New York*, April 1968.

228   to the Black community: *Hearing Before the Subcommittee on Financial Institutions Supervision, Regulation and Insurance of the Committee on Banking, Finance and Urban Affairs House of Representatives*, p. 23.

228   build its office: "Address by the Honorable Samuel R. Pierce, Jr. Before the Houston Real Estate Association on January 15, 1971," transcript located on St. Louis Federal Reserve website.

228   to join Freedom Bank: Jackie Robinson, *I Never Had It Made* (New York: HarperCollins, 1972), p. 184.

229   "fight on our hands": Robinson, *I Never Had It Made*, p. 184.

229   "needs of Harlem people": Robinson, *I Never Had It Made*, p. 184.

229   "not to be trusted": Robinson, *I Never Had It Made*, p. 184.

229   Southern Christian Leadership Conference: "Dr. King's Group Meeting in Alabama," *Atlanta Constitution*, September 25, 1962.

229   destroyed by arson in Georgia: "Rebuilding of Negro Churches Started in Terrell and Lee," *Atlanta Journal*, July 4, 1963.

229   ". . . we cannot turn back": "Chanting Freedom Songs, Negroes March in Capital," *Macon News*, August 28, 1963.

229   "Freedom! Freedom! Freedom!": "Chanting Freedom Songs, Negroes March in Capital."

229   when jailed in the South: Martin B. Cassidy, "Beyond the Dream: Remembering King's Visit to Stamford," *Stamford Advocate*, September 7, 2013.

229   lieutenant at Camp Hood: Arnold Rampersad, *Jackie Robinson: A Biography* (New York: Ballantine Books, 1997), pp. 100–105.

229   "thing for our country": Peter Golenbock, *Bums: An Oral History of the Brooklyn Dodgers* (Garden City, N.Y.: Dover Publishing, 1984), pp. 222–24.

229   "freedom rider before freedom rides": Quoted in Chris Lamb, "Spring Training," *American Legacy* 13, No. 1 (Spring 2007): pp. 14–20, as cited in Bryan Steverson, "Journey to Justice: The Converging Paths of Jackie Robinson and Dr. Martin Luther King Jr.," *Jackie Robinson: Perspectives on 42*, Society for American Baseball Research, March 19, 2021.

229   "movement was Jackie Robinson": Quoted in Bob Nightengale, "Contracts Need Good Home," *USA Today Sports Weekly*, August 31–September 6, 2016, p. 20, as cited in Steverson, "Journey to Justice."

230   "using his prize funds": "Dr. King Is Depositor at Freedom National," *Amsterdam News*, December 18, 1965.

230   recall, great "public relations": William Hudgins, interviewed by Julieanna L. Richardson, April 15, 2002, HistoryMakers Digital Archive, A2002.057, Session 1, Tape 4, Story 4.

230   King's "anti-capitalist feelings": King quoted in Michael K. Honey, *To the Promised Land: Martin Luther King and the Fight for Economic Justice* (New York: W. W. Norton, 2018), p. 28.

231   about six hundred other people: Cheryl Renee, "Civil Rights Activist Andrew Young Reflects on Selma March," WTVM, last updated March 8, 2015.

231   a photo on his office wall: Renee, "Civil Rights Activist Andrew Young Reflects on Selma March."

231   been in the North: Aldon D. Morris, *The Origins of the Civil Rights Movement: Black Communities Organizing for Change* (New York: The Free Press, 1984), p. 123.

232 distributed in Black neighborhoods: A. Philip Randolph and Bayard Rustin, "How the Civil-Rights Movement Aimed to End Poverty," *The Atlantic*, February 2018.

232 "this nation was founded": Quoted in Randolph and Rustin, "How the Civil-Rights Movement Aimed to End Poverty."

232 "poverty conditions," he wrote: Jordan Weissmann, "Martin Luther King's Economic Dream: A Guaranteed Income for All Americans," *The Atlantic*, August 28, 2013.

232 "Black man made America wealthy": Honey, *To the Promised Land*, p. 19.

232 "as it now stands in the United States," he said: Quoted in Honey, *To the Promised Land*, p. 122.

233 or new jobs programs: Honey, *To the Promised Land*, p. 124.

233 his book *My Song*: Harry Belafonte, *My Song: A Memoir of Art, Race and Defiance* (New York: Vintage, 2012), p. 328.

233 "capitalist, and I'm not": Belafonte, *My Song*, p. 328.

233 "get to the promised land": Martin Luther King Jr., "I've Been to the Mountaintop," Speech, April 3, 1968.

234 "to have an 'insurance-in'": King, "I've Been to the Mountaintop."

234 "poor at some level": Belafonte, *My Song*, p. 328.

234 "means to 'save humanity'": Vincent Harding's "The Vocation of the Black Scholar and the Struggles of the Black Community," 1974, as cited in Andrew J. Douglas and Jared A. Loggins, *Prophet of Discontent: Martin Luther King Jr. and the Critique of Racial Capitalism* (Athens: University of Georgia Press, 2021), p. 82. Vincent Harding was a Black historian who authored King's "Beyond Vietnam" speech and worked with the King family on the memorial center after King's death.

234 the King family: The King Center was called the Martin Luther King Jr. Memorial Center from 1968 until 1978, when it was renamed the Martin Luther King Jr. Center for Nonviolent Social Change.

234 "the center's philanthropic backing": Douglas and Loggins, *Prophet of Discontent*, p. 75.

235 South Africa's apartheid government: Belafonte, *My Song*, p. 335.

235 on April 4, 1968: "Assassination of Martin Luther King Jr.," Martin Luther King, Jr. Research and Education Institute, Stanford University.

235 "bunch of twelve-year-olds," Andrew recalled: Quoted in Bill Hutchinson, "At 86, Andrew Young Recalls Horror of Witnessing Moment Martin Luther King Jr. Was Assassinated in Memphis," ABC News, April 3, 2018.

235 he was "still clowning": "Young, Andrew," Martin Luther King Jr. Research and Education Institute, Stanford University, March 12, 1932.

236 to create some jobs: "Poor People's Campaign," Martin Luther King Jr. Research and Education Institute, Stanford University.

236 "Blacks on the other": Belafonte, *My Song*, p. 328.

236 and then, in 1981: "Biography Andrew J. Young," Andrew Young School of Policy Studies, Georgia State University.

236 "to own the restaurant": Greenwood [@Greenwood], post of this quote by Andrew Young, Instagram.

236 "going to be a capitalist": Malcolm X, "Malcolm X at the Audubon Ballroom," Speech, December 20, 1964, from Teaching American History.

237 "piece of the action": Richard Nixon, "Accepting the Republican Nomination," *PBS Primary Source*, 1968; for more context, see "Black Capitalism: Mostly an Empty Promise," *Time*, July 9, 1973.

237 "as easily as whites": Robert L. Allen, *Black Awakening in Capitalist America: An Analytical History* (Garden City, N.Y.: Anchor, 1969), p. 153, as cited in Robert E. Weems Jr. and Lewis A. Randolph, "The National Response to Richard M. Nixon's Black Capitalism

Initiative: The Success of Domestic Detente," *Journal of Black Studies* 32, No. 1 (September 2001): pp. 66–83.

237   mortgage to their church: Suzanne M. Snell, "Harlem's Freedom National Bank—Exploiters or Soul Brothers?" *Harvard Crimson*, July 5, 1966.

238   "maintain, they help themselves": Snell, "Harlem's Freedom National Bank—Exploiters or Soul Brothers?"

238   a more integrated economy: Weems and Randolph, "The National Response to Richard M. Nixon's Black Capitalism Initiative," pp. 75–77.

238   strong supporters across racial lines: Roy Innis, chairman of the Congress of Racial Equality (CORE), was a Black leader at the time who was strongly promoting the idea of a more independent Black economy.

239   in developing countries: "The Black Sector Answers," *New York Times*, August 22, 1971.

239   board of directors, Robinson: Robinson, *I Never Had It Made*, p. 185.

239   Black-led bank founded in 1948: "Why Carver," Carver Federal Savings Bank, n.d.

239   "You are in serious trouble": Robinson, *I Never Had It Made*, p. 191.

239   "instruments of economic development": Andrew F. Brimmer, speaking before the Joint Session of the 1970 Annual Meetings of the American Finance Association and the American Economic Association, as cited in Pierce, "Address by the Honorable Samuel R. Pierce Jr."

239   one hundred million dollars into minority banks: Pierce, "Address by the Honorable Samuel R. Pierce Jr."

239   less stable than older ones: Pierce, "Address by the Honorable Samuel R. Pierce Jr."

240   "pinnacle of the white financial world": "Brother Dunbar Simms McLaurin," *Sphinx* 59, No. 3 (1973): p. 54.

240   "'piece of the action'": Pierce, "Address by the Honorable Samuel R. Pierce Jr."

240   "in New York City": Pierce, "Address by the Honorable Samuel R. Pierce Jr."

240   "less like an area for exploitation": Quoted in Robinson, *I Never Had It Made*, p. 189.

241   "an utterly risky philosophy": Robinson, *I Never Had It Made*, p. 190.

241   loans being written off: Robinson, *I Never Had It Made*, p. 190.

241   "balance had to be struck": Robinson, *I Never Had It Made*, p. 196.

241   that met with frustration: "Banker Dunbar S. McLaurin Suicide Victim in N.Y. Home," p. 6.

241   "massaging your ego": "Economist's Speech Stresses Success for Black Business," *Harvard Crimson*, December 16, 1971.

241   of building a Black business: "Banker Dunbar S. McLaurin Suicide Victim in N.Y. Home."

241   save the Black bank: Charlayne Hunter, "Ailing Freedom National Bank Gets a New Chief," *New York Times*, October 3, 1974.

241   early in his career: Hunter, "Ailing Freedom National Bank Gets a New Chief."

241   National and Citizens Trust: Hunter, "Ailing Freedom National Bank Gets a New Chief."

241   from going into business: Hunter, "Ailing Freedom National Bank Gets a New Chief."

242    $1 million in stock: Reginald Stuart, "Refinancing Set by Freedom Bank," *New York Times*, July 4, 1975.

242   Freedom National was white: *Hearing Before the Subcommittee on Financial Institutions Supervision, Regulation and Insurance of the Committee on Banking, Finance and Urban Affairs House of Representatives*, p. 86.

242   sizable profit each year: *Hearing Before the Subcommittee on Financial Institutions Supervision, Regulation and Insurance of the Committee on Banking, Finance and Urban Affairs House of Representatives*, p. 25.

242   proxy fight for it: John F. Berry, "Freedom Bank Is Target of a Bitter Proxy Fight," *Washington Post*, June 17, 1982.

242   oil refinery in Arizona: *Hearing Before the Subcommittee on Financial Institutions Supervi-*

sion, Regulation and Insurance of the Committee on Banking, Finance and Urban Affairs House of Representatives, p. 79.

242   360 banks would fail: *Hearing Before the Subcommittee on Financial Institutions Supervision, Regulation and Insurance of the Committee on Banking, Finance and Urban Affairs House of Representatives*, p. 4.

242   banks would be minority banks: *Hearing Before the Subcommittee on Financial Institutions Supervision, Regulation and Insurance of the Committee on Banking, Finance and Urban Affairs House of Representatives*, p. 287.

242   attack at age forty-six: Craig Wolff, "Travers J. Bell Jr., 46, Founder of Only Black Firm on Exchange," *New York Times*, January 27, 1988.

242   individual stock ownership program: Andrew L. Yarrow, "Freedom Bank's Failure Hits Harlem Like a Death in the Family," *New York Times*, November 12, 1990.

242   "it's a terrible blow": Rangel and Abiodun quoted in Yarrow, "Freedom Bank's Failure Hits Harlem Like a Death in the Family."

242   "of Black people": Abiodun's surname was not printed in Yarrow's article. It may have been the poet Abiodun Oyewole, but authors have not found confirmation of that.

243   "Harlem loses," she said: Quoted in Yarrow, "Freedom Bank's Failure Hits Harlem Like a Death in the Family."

243   to purchase Freedom Bank: *Hearing Before the Subcommittee on Financial Institutions Supervision, Regulation and Insurance of the Committee on Banking, Finance and Urban Affairs House of Representatives*, p. 42.

243   to avoid investment flight: *Hearing Before the Subcommittee on Financial Institutions Supervision, Regulation and Insurance of the Committee on Banking, Finance and Urban Affairs House of Representatives*, p. 2.

243   was also saved: *Hearing Before the Subcommittee on Financial Institutions Supervision, Regulation and Insurance of the Committee on Banking, Finance and Urban Affairs House of Representatives*, pp. 5–6.

243   said at the hearing: *Hearing Before the Subcommittee on Financial Institutions Supervision, Regulation and Insurance of the Committee on Banking, Finance and Urban Affairs House of Representatives*, p. 8.

243   "the community," Siebert said: *Hearing Before the Subcommittee on Financial Institutions Supervision, Regulation and Insurance of the Committee on Banking, Finance and Urban Affairs House of Representatives*, p. 88.

244   "supervisors terminated its life": *Hearing Before the Subcommittee on Financial Institutions Supervision, Regulation and Insurance of the Committee on Banking, Finance and Urban Affairs House of Representatives*, p. 201.

244   "cold, Harlem gets pneumonia": Quoted in Strom, "Failed Dreams—The Collapse of a Harlem Bank; Freedom Bank's Demise."

244   seventeen in 2022: FDIC Minority Depository Institutions Lists 2001 and 2022.

245   on Black banking: Tim Todd, *A Great Moral and Social Force: A History of Black Banks* (Kansas City, MO: Federal Reserve Bank of Kansas City, 2022).

247   bank in Atlanta: Bailey was on the advisory board of Citizens Trust Bank, a Black-owned bank in Atlanta.

CHAPTER 11: PUSHING FOR CHANGE, FROM THE INSIDE

249   Toni Morrison, *Jazz*: Toni Morrison, *Jazz* (New York: Vintage, 1992), p. 208.

249   "seen in a generation": "Equality and Inclusion Discussion Featuring Georgia NAACP President James Woodall," Georgia Chamber, July 23, 2020, YouTube video.

249 "to make a difference": "Equality and Inclusion Discussion Featuring Georgia NAACP President James Woodall."

249 "That's community. 'Com—unity'": "Equality and Inclusion Discussion Featuring Georgia NAACP President James Woodall." James used the phrase "you know" numerous times in this quote and we have cut out that phrase so that the quote is more easily understood.

250 "worker to senior executives": "Equality and Inclusion Discussion Featuring Georgia NAACP President James Woodall."

250 economic value within the next five years: Dana M. Peterson and Catherine L. Mann, "Closing the Racial Inequality Gaps: The Economic Cost of Black Inequality in the U.S.," Citi Global Perspectives and Solutions, September 2020.

251 college NAACP chapters in Georgia: "Executive & Ad Hoc Committees Staff," NAACP Georgia State Conference, listed online with no date. His biography is also covered in contemporaneous news sources, such as Al Hackle, "Woodall Kicks Off District 160 Campaign," *Statesboro Herald*, August 20, 2016.

251 lead Georgia's NAACP: "Georgia Elects Youngest State President in NAACP History," *NAACP Dekalb*, October 2019.

251 1996 to 2004: Kweisi Mfume became a congressman in Maryland in 2020. He left the NAACP in 2004 after an allegation of sexual harassment. The next year, he acknowledged he had had an affair with a subordinate. The NAACP paid a financial settlement to the accuser. Addy Baird, "The NAACP Paid $100,000 to a Woman Who Accused Him of Sexual Harassment. Now He's Likely Headed to Congress," *Buzzfeed News*, February 25, 2020.

253 helped fund it with one hundred million dollars: Candy Cheng, "Merck CEO Ken Frazier and Ginni Rometty Start Groundbreaking Initiative to Give 1 Million Black Americans Without College Degrees 'Family-Sustaining' Corporate Jobs by 2030," Insider, December 10, 2020.

253 killing of George Floyd: Cheng, "Merck CEO Ken Frazier and Ginni Rometty Start Groundbreaking Initiative."

253 "wealth in this country": Cheng, "Merck CEO Ken Frazier and Ginni Rometty Start Groundbreaking Initiative."

253 "will not be silent": Quoted in Kevin Stankiewicz, "'There Is No Middle Ground'—Black CEOs Urge Companies to Oppose Restrictive Voting Laws," CNBC, March 31, 2021.

254 of Black households do: Lenore Palladino, "The Contribution of Shareholder Primacy to the Racial Wealth Gap," Roosevelt Institute Working Paper, February 2020.

254 owned just $0.38 trillion: Palladino, "The Contribution of Shareholder Primacy to the Racial Wealth Gap."

255 to have stock to increase that wealth: Fabian T. Pfeffer, Sheldon Danziger, and Robert F. Schoeni, "Wealth Levels, Wealth Inequality, and the Great Recession," Russell Sage Foundation, June 2014.

255 "preferential rates across the income distribution": "Disparities in the Benefits of Tax Expenditures by Race and Ethnicity," U.S. Department of the Treasury, January 20, 2023.

256 removed from the people involved: "New 'RHOA' Star Tanya Sam Accused of Stiffing Employee out of $7K Bonus," RadarOnline, December 11, 2018. The case was *Cheryll Bolden v. Tanya Sam, Paul Judge et al.*, Case Number 18M97452, September 12, 2018, DeKalb County Court.

256 people of color: Bloomberg examined 88 of the S&P 100 companies and counted Hispanic, Asian, and Black people as people of color. These 88 companies added 323,094 jobs in 2021, and 302,570 went to these groups of people, the examination found. Companies analyzed included Apple, Walmart, Wells Fargo, and many other large companies.

256 reform legacy organizations to be more inclusive: Jeff Green et al., "Corporate America Promised to Hire a Lot More People of Color. It Actually Did," Bloomberg, September 25, 2023.

257   Annie E. Casey Foundation: James Woodall Resignation Letter, May 23, 2021. Obtained by this book's authors.

257   to diversity and equality: Tracy Jan, Jena McGregor, and Meghan Hoyer, "Big Business Pledged Nearly $50 Billion for Racial Justice after George Floyd's Death. Where Did the Money Go?" *Washington Post*, August 23, 2021. This book's authors have obtained NAACP documents that show donations in 2020 and 2021. There were $29 million in donations to one NAACP unit, known as the empowerment funds, in 2021. There were $9 million in donations to other NAACP funds that year. The donations were higher in 2020, totaling $73 million in contributions and grants, plus other revenue lines.

259   flood of donations: Letter to Derrick Johnson, NAACP CEO, and Leon W. Russell, chairman of the NAACP board, "Re: Grievances of Membership & Units, NAACP," signed "State Conference Presidents and Unit Presidents."

260   "remain on the battlefield": James Woodall Resignation Letter, May 23, 2021.

261   Brook said at the time: Records in Georgia back to 1990 did not include an amount more than $4.8 million, news reports at the time said. Alyssa Lukpat, "$4.8 Million Settlement Reached in Trooper's Fatal Shooting of a Black Driver," *New York Times*, April 3, 2022; and Jozsef Papp, "Settlement Reached with State of Georgia in Death of Julian Lewis, According to Law Firm," *Augusta Chronicle*, March 31, 2022.

262   upon getting the settlement: The initial settlement funds were split evenly between him and his father's widow, after hefty legal fees were taken out.

CHAPTER 12: THE BLACK WALL

263   President Abraham Lincoln: Lincoln quoted in Edmund Kirke, "A Suppressed Chapter of History: Conversations About War and Peace with Abraham Lincoln," *The Atlantic*, April 1887.

263   "and the political process": "Killer Mike Honored by Georgia Senate as 'Outstanding Ambassador,'" ARTISTdirect.

263   "equitable distribution of water": "Killer Mike Honored by Georgia Senate as 'Outstanding Ambassador.'" Michael Render's quote was reprinted in Georgia Senate Resolution 315 in March 2017.

265   Britain was blocking that: Jonathan Levy, *Ages of American Capitalism: A History of the United States* (New York: Random House, 2021), p. 65.

265   "backs to commercial prosperity": Levy, *Ages of American Capitalism*, p. 29. Settlers in the American colonies enslaved Native Americans and Africans. And they imported white Americans as indentured servants (who could purchase their freedom and emerge from slavery in ways unavailable to Black Americans). But African slavery over time became the main source of slave labor in the United States.

265   British and enslaved: Levy, *Ages of American Capitalism*, p. 31.

265   of African origin: Levy, *Ages of American Capitalism*, p. 30.

265   "African and Afro-descendent people": Levy, *Ages of American Capitalism*, p. 29.

265   of the country's exports: Coates, "The Case for Reparations."

265   in the United States: "Slavery, United States," Library of Congress, Washington, D.C., March 18, 2011.

266   were "worth" four billion dollars: Catarina Saraiva, "Four Numbers that Show the Cost of Slavery on Black Wealth Today," Bloomberg, March 18, 2021.

266   "all other assets combined": David Blight, interviewed by Terry Gross, "Historian Says '12 Years' Is a Story the Nation Must Remember," NPR, October 24, 2013.

266   shifted to private ownership: Editors of Encyclopaedia Britannica, "Enclosure," *Encyclopaedia Britannica*, February 25, 2013.

266   fifths of a person: Editors of Encyclopaedia Britannica, "Three-fifths compromise," *Encyclopaedia Britannica*, August 23, 2023.

267   "humanity: their agency": Wiggins, *Calculating Race*, p. 11.

267   merged into J.P. Morgan: Clyde W. Ford, "Op-Ed: Founding Fathers as Founding Debtors: How Some of Them Used Slaves as Collateral," *Los Angeles Times*, July 1, 2021.

267   Brown Brothers Harriman: Roger Lowenstein, "The Wall Street Capitalists Who Put Morals Above Money," *New York Times*, May 19, 2021.

267   Wells Fargo: Ford, "Op-Ed: Founding Fathers as Founding Debtors."

267   pledged as "collateral": Matthew Korfhage, "Hamilton Fans Rejoice: The National Bank He Conceived Will Become a Museum in Philadelphia," *USA Today*, July 13, 2023.

267   13,000 enslaved people as collateral: Makebra Anderson, "JPMorgan Chase & Co. Admits Links to Slavery," *Final Call*, February 9, 2005.

267   North and to Europe: Edward E. Baptist, *The Half Has Never Been Told: Slavery and the Making of American Capitalism* (New York: Basic Books, 2014), p. 247.

268   family of London: "Stephen Duncan correspondence, 1817–1877," Louisiana State University–Special Collections, *Archivegrid*; and "Francis Surget Letters, 1860," Collection Number: 04793-z, University of North Carolina at Chapel Hill, Southern Historical Collection, Finding-Aids-Lib-UNC.

268   Edward Baptist has written: Baptist, *The Half Has Never Been Told*, p. 232.

268   in the country: Thomas L. Scott, "9 of the Biggest Slave Owners in American History," *Atlanta Black Star*, December 23, 2014; and Martha Jane Brazy, "Stephen Duncan," *Mississippi Encyclopedia*, April 19, 2018.

268   "I ever seen": Edith Wyatt Moore, "Interview with Charlie Davenport, Natches, Mississippi," in *Federal Writers' Project 1936 to 1938: Slave Narrative Project*, vol. 9, *Mississippi*.

268   Arkansas and Florida: Baptist, *The Half Has Never Been Told*, p. 247; Emile P. Grenier, "The Early Financing of the Consolidated Association of the Planters of Louisiana," *LSU Scholarly Repository* (1938); and Michael G. Schene, "Robert and John Grattan Gamble: Middle Florida Entrepreneurs," *Florida Historical Quarterly* 54, no. 1 (1975): p. 8.

268   Brothers in Alabama: Baptist, *The Half Has Never Been Told*, p. 352.

268   including Barings Bank: Reginald C. McGrane, "Some Aspects of American State Debts in the Forties," *American Historical Review* 38, no. 4 (July 1933), p. 676.

269   "'the least labor'": Reginald C. McGrane, "Some Aspects of American State Debts in the Forties," p. 676.

269   enslaved seventy-six people: National Register of Historic Places Inventory—Nomination Form for Render Family Homestead, National Park Service, United States Department of the Interior, filed January 30, 1984.

269   worked as contract laborers: "James Render House, Circa 1832, Greenville," Vanishing Georgia, April 14, 2022.

269   enslaved person was collateral: Collection 1960–023, Historical Society of New Mexico Collection, Box 8326, Folder 41, 1828, October 28, Mortgage on Slaves Bought by Samuel Wooton from James Render, Wilkins County, GA.

269   as late as 1900: 1900 Census, Dollie and Jim Render.

269   land for $1.1 million: Zillow.

269   "I stand in solidarity," he wrote: Michael Render [@killermike], Instagram, July 28, 2020.

270   up until 2015: Matthew Brown, "Fact Check: United Kingdom Finished Paying Off Debts to Slave-Owning Families in 2015," *USA Today*, June 30, 2020.

270   pay off the debt: Thomas Craemer, "There Was a Time Reparations Were Actually Paid Out—Just Not to Formerly Enslaved People," UConn Today, March 5, 2021.

270   people they had enslaved: The District of Columbia Compensated Emancipation Act (12 Statutes at Large 376), adopted April 16, 1862.

270   three hundred dollars per enslaved person: Darity and Mullen, *From Here to Equality*, p. 100. Those payments are in 1862 dollars. Three hundred dollars would be worth around $140,000 in 2010s dollars.

270   "plundered and abused them": Quoted in Tera W. Hunter, "When Slave Owners Got Reparations," *New York Times*, April 16, 2019.

271   South continued to fight: Darity and Mullen, *From Here to Equality*, p. 102.

271   "always be subordinate": "T.I., Killer Mike Join Mayor Keisha Lance Bottoms in Condemning Violence in Atlanta Protests," YouTube.

271   the University of Georgia: Ernie Suggs, "Descendants of Confederate VP Want His Statue Out of U.S. Capitol," *Atlanta Journal-Constitution*, August 25, 2017.

271   U.S. Capitol's Statuary Hall: Kery Murakami, "Views Differ Over Confederate Vice President Statue," *Valdosta Daily Times*, September 5, 2017.

271   "equitable to their owners": L. W. Nevius, *The Discovery of Modern Anesthesia: By Whom Was It Made? A Brief Statement of Facts* (New York: GW Nevius, 1894), p. 14, as quoted in Henry Connor, "Crawford W Long—Still an Enigma," *Proceedings of the History of Anesthesia Society* 34 (July 2–3, 2004).

272   "to control and influence": Frank K. Boland, "Crawford Williamson Long and the Discovery of Anesthesia," *The Georgia Historical Quarterly* 7, No. 2 (June 1923): p. 140.

272   while he was traveling: J. Jacobs, "Some Personal Recollections and Private Correspondence of Dr. Crawford Williamson Long" (Atlanta, GA: Wellcome Library, 1919; pamphlet WZ 6:29:7), pp. 8–9, as cited in Connor, "Crawford W Long—Still an Enigma," pp. 61–68.

272   Athens, Georgia, were enslaved people: "The Lived Experiences of Enslaved People in Athens, GA," Death and Human History in Athens. Nearly half of people in Athens were enslaved in 1860 according to this source. Please note that John Henry Long's birth date is stated as 1860 in some records, as in the 1850s in others, and, in his death record, it stated that he was born in 1849.

272   ages of sixteen and thirty-seven: 1860 Slave Schedule.

272   but no father: Death certificate for John Henry Long, registered June 4, 1951, North Carolina State Board of Health.

273   his profitable drug business: Frank Kells Boland, *The First Anesthetic* (Athens: University of Georgia Press, 1950), pp. 118–19.

CHAPTER 13: TWO ATLANTAS

276   Alabama State University, 1984: "Andrew Young Urges: Save, Invest and Vote," *New Journal and Guide*, July 18, 1984.

278   lower-income levels: Patrick Bayer and Kerwin Kofi Charles, "Divergent Paths: A New Perspective on Earnings Differences Between Black and White Men Since 1940," *Quarterly Journal of Economics* 133, no. 3 (August 2018): pp. 1459–1501.

278   as a U.S. congressman: Andrew Young was in Congress January 1973 to January 1977, and he was ambassador January 1977 to September 1979.

279   "of resentment early on": Yancey quoted in Andre Jackson, "Atlanta: A Hard Push for Minority Business," *St. Louis Post-Dispatch*, October 2, 1990.

279   discrimination against white people: Jackson, "Atlanta: A Hard Push for Minority Business."

279   gender of their employees: Andrew Young, Harvey Newman, and Andrea Young, *Andrew Young and the Making of Modern Atlanta* (Macon, Ga.: Mercer University Press, 2016), p. 110.

280   municipal bond book: Cassidy Sparks, "Bernard Parks Jr. Explains the Legacy of Atlanta," *Rolling Out*, February 10, 2019.

280   to redress "past discrimination": Young, Newman, and Young, *Andrew Young and the Making of Modern Atlanta*, p. 124.

280   at Historically Black Colleges and Universities: Quoted in Young, Newman, and Young, *Andrew Young and the Making of Modern Atlanta*, p. 126.

280   miss out on any opportunities: Jackson, "Atlanta: A Hard Push for Minority Business."

280   "both qualitative and anecdotal": Jackson, "Atlanta: A Hard Push for Minority Business."

281   "only ones making money": Quoted in Pamela E. Foster, "Young Criticized as Soft on Black Business," *New Pittsburgh Courier*, December 16, 1989.

281   cut in the 1980s: The Reagan administration cut funding on federal poverty programs. See "Looking Back on the Young Years," *Atlanta Journal-Constitution*, December 31, 1989.

281   dollars, by some counts: Jessica White, "Young Returns to Share His Global Vision," *Chautauquan Daily*, August 6, 2012.

281   then, the 1996 Summer Olympics: "Looking Back on the Young Years."

281   "do with a peanut": Quoted in Art Harris, "Mr. Atlanta: Andy Young as Cheerleader for the City, He's Forged an Unprecedented Alliance Between Black Voters and White Money," *Washington Post*, July 16, 1988.

282   sharing enough of the buck: "Looking Back on the Young Years." John Wesley Dobbs was a Black leader in Atlanta in the early 1900s and the grandfather of Maynard Jackson. He liked to say that Black Americans needed the ballot, the buck, and the book. Young, Newman, and Young, *Andrew Young and the Making of Modern Atlanta*, p. 127.

282   "needs of the city's poor": "Looking Back on the Young Years."

282   second highest in the country: Newark, New Jersey, had the highest poverty rate in 1989. See "Looking Back on the Young Years."

282   that decade were low paying: "Looking Back on the Young Years."

282   the city's poor people: Harris, "Mr. Atlanta: Andy Young."

282   Williams said in 1988: Joan Vennochi, "Controversy, Candor Stalk Andrew Young," *Boston Globe*, March 17, 1988.

282   the city's contracting office: Foster, "Young Criticized as Soft on Black Business."

282   "had limited job skills": Young, Newman, and Young, *Andrew Young and the Making of Modern Atlanta*, 125.

282   back national poverty programs: Amy Wallace, "Housing Plan Met with Skepticism. Mayor Has Always Neglected the Issue, Critics Say," *Atlanta Journal-Constitution*, August 28, 1989.

283   chance at obtaining a mortgage: Bill Dedman, "Atlanta Blacks Losing in Home Loans Scramble," *Atlanta Journal-Constitution*, May 1, 1988. The *Journal* and the *Constitution* were sister papers at this time, but they both ran these stories in the series about redlining.

283   not lending to them: Editorial Board, "Redliners Should Do Business Fairly, or Not at All," *Atlanta Journal-Constitution*, May 6, 1988.

283   "invested in the banks": Editorial Board, "Redliners Should Do Business Fairly, or Not at All."

283   "loaned to white customers": Baradaran, *The Color of Money*, p. 78.

283   "economic withdrawal makes sense": Quoted in Editorial Board, "Redliners Should Do Business Fairly, or Not At All."

283   give a strong response: Bill Dedman, "Black Legislators Seek to Probe Loan Pattern with State Bank Chief," *Atlanta Journal-Constitution*, May 6, 1988.

283   not just Black areas: Quoted in Bill Dedman, "City Hall Clout Could Sweeten Home-Loan Pot," *Atlanta Journal-Constitution*, May 4, 1988.

283   "grown—almost despite them": Quoted in Dedman, "City Hall Clout Could Sweeten Home-Loan Pot."

284 "poisons the whole city": Quoted in Dedman, "City Hall Clout Could Sweeten Home-Loan Pot."

284 five years in prison: Wallace, "Housing Plan Met with Skepticism."

284 funding, but not Atlanta: Wallace, "Housing Plan Met with Skepticism."

284 dilapidated or without plumbing: Wallace, "Housing Plan Met with Skepticism."

284 were in substandard condition: Wallace, "Housing Plan Met with Skepticism."

284 money to Black homeowners: "Housing Programs Set for Moderate-Low Income Families," *Atlanta Daily World*, June 16, 1983.

284 to downtown Atlanta: Donna Williams Lewis, "More Whites Needed Downtown, Mayor Says," *Atlanta Journal-Constitution*, February 10, 1987.

284 "by the federal government": Quoted in Wallace, "Housing Plan Met with Skepticism."

284 "all of our citizens": Quoted in Larry Copeland, "Mayor Full of Praise in Last Address. Housing and Crime Only Negative Areas He Notes," *Atlanta Journal-Constitution*, January 4, 1989.

284 house Atlanta's citizens: Copeland, "Mayor Full of Praise in Last Address."

285 the 1930s and '40s: It was in Bankhead that a woman had to sue the city in the 1920s to be allowed to rent her house to Black renters and where there were numerous bomb attacks on houses purchased by Black people in 1946. See chapter 2 of this book.

285 house, built in 1925: Zillow.

286 sold with traditional mortgages: Joel Kurth, "Land Contracts Trip Up Would-Be Homeowners," *Detroit News*, February 29, 2016.

286 bank initiated a foreclosure: In re Lovelace, No. 19-59346-LRC (Bankr. N.D. Ga. Aug. 2, 2021); and Fulton County Property Records for 547 Chappell Road NW.

286 responsibility to honor that: In re Lovelace, No. 19-59346-LRC.

286 went through foreclosure: In re Lovelace, No. 19-59346-LRC.

286 public housing complexes: Stephanie Garlock, "By 2011, Atlanta Had Demolished All of Its Public Housing Projects. Where Did All Those People Go?" *Bloomberg*, May 8, 2014.

286 not to come back: "Olympics—Atlanta 'Cleanup' Includes One-Way Tickets for Homeless," *Seattle Times*, March 22, 1996.

286 "into the city": Dan Immergluck, *Red Hot City: Housing, Race and Exclusion in Twenty-First Century Atlanta* (Oakland: University of California Press, 2022), p. 43.

287 "of existing, lower-income residents": Immergluck, *Red Hot City*, p. 44.

287 more than 250,000 foreclosures: Michael E. Kanell, "Economy Healed, but Atlanta's Scars from Recession Remain," *Atlanta Journal-Constitution*, December 20, 2017.

287 in reaction to the crisis: Evan Cunningham, "Great Recession, Great Recovery? Trends from the Current Population Survey," U.S. Bureau of Labor Statistics, April 2018.

287 rose to 16.8 percent: "Great Recession, Great Recovery? Trends from the Current Population Survey." Monthly Labor Review. U.S. Bureau of Labor Statistics. April 2018.

287 not go to college: Timothy Smeeding, "Income, Wealth, and Debt and the Great Recession," Russell Sage Foundation and Stanford Center on Poverty and Inequality, October 2012.

288 offering it as rent-to-own: Fulton County Property Records, Installment Purchase Land Contract, Deed Book 62317, p. 567.

288 owner of 547 Chappell: In re Lovelace, No. 19-59346-LRC.

288 "all of those properties": Quoted in Russell Grantham, "Investors Scoop Up Omni Homes," *Atlanta Journal-Constitution*, March 27, 2010.

288 rent-to-own properties: Immergluck, *Red Hot City*, p. 158.

288 said at the time: Quoted in Gerry Shih, "Foreclosure Frenzy Dismays Aspiring Homeowners," *New York Times*, December 12, 2009.

289 "than traditional bank qualifications": "Private 'Hard Money' Loans," Stonecrest Financial.

289 as he kept paying: James Lewis Lovelace III v. I Buy Everything, LLC, Gerald R. Col-

lins, and CSB Logistics, LLC, Chapter 13 Filing, Case 19-59346-LRC (hereafter cited as: Lovelace Chapter 13 filing), Appendix A.

289 purchased it for $5,576: Fulton County Quit Claim Deeds, Corrective Quit Claim Deed, Deed Book 48434, October 9, 2009, p. 138.

290 closer to nine months: Fulton County, Georgia, Jail Records, Booking Numbers 1229816, 1122854, 0629379, and 1235616.

290 trouble with the police: Fulton County, Georgia, Jail Records show one eleven-day period in May 2014 for parole violation and battery, but other than that, nothing after 2013.

290 in the Atlanta area: Zachary Hansen, "American Dream for Rent: Investors Zero in on Black Neighborhoods," *Atlanta Journal-Constitution*, February 9, 2023.

290 between 2006 and 2021: Fulton County Property Records.

291 of his loan back to Stonecrest: Lovelace's lawsuit against the LLCs that purchased the loan/house from Stonecrest says that he should have had a balance of $20,263 when the house was transferred in the summer of 2018. James Lewis Lovelace Chapter 13 filing, Exhibit A.

293 new types of buyers: Immergluck, *Red Hot City*, p. 101.

293 $5,000 the entire year: Lovelace Chapter 13 filing, Official Form 107, filed July 15, 2019.

293 around $20,000 that year: Lovelace Chapter 13 filing, Official Form 107.

293 was $47,953 per year: This is the amount of income that the U.S. Department of Justice Trustee Program considered to be the median for the state of Georgia for cases filed between May 1, 2019, and October 1, 2019. Lovelace's bankruptcy filing was within that period.

293 "I am Atlanta, Georgia," he wrote: James Lovelace Instagram account.

293 earn $40,336 that year: Lovelace Chapter 13 Filing, Official Form 106I, Filed May 13, 2022.

294 "Chappell Road," he called her: James Lovelace Instagram account.

294 high in tension between the two men, Lovelace said: Jacobs told us that he tried to evict Lovelace, and he agreed that there was high tension in the hearings.

294 the federal government in 2021: The Paycheck Protection Program (PPP) was run by the Small Business Administration as part of pandemic-related stimulus. PPP Loan.info.

294 "really makes the money": "How Don Jacobs Went from Pro Sports to Pro Entrepreneurship," Blog Talk Radio, 2016.

294 and deposit account fraud: Fulton County, Georgia, Inmate Records. Jacobs told us that these arrests were for innocent mistakes caused by his naïveté.

295 walk from Lovelace's house: Josh Green, "Microsoft's Game-Changing Westside Project Is Rumbling to Life," *Urbanize Atlanta*, April 11, 2022.

295 hundred thousand dollars apiece: Josh Green, "Project with $700K+ townhomes in Bankhead, as Seen from Above," *Urbanize Atlanta*, October 10, 2022.

295 not share that information: U.S. Bankruptcy Court, Northern District of Georgia (Atlanta), Bankruptcy Petition No. 19-05340-LRC, filed January 27, 2020; and In re Lovelace, No. 19-59346-LRC.

296 "disclosed everything we had": Freeman said providing all disclosures in land sales is their general practice. He did not provide proof of what they did in the case of the property at 547 Chappell Road.

296 Jacobs himself "had millions": Jacobs in an interview said that Lovelace doesn't know him well enough to know his net worth, and indeed, we saw that Jacobs had filed for bankruptcy, and he concurred, saying he's "human."

296 "tell Mr. Lovelace": He moved in 2019 to working at the Atlanta Volunteer Lawyers Foundation and finished his work for Lovelace from that job.

296 his own thirty-year-old car: Lovelace, Chapter 13 filing, Official Form 107.

296 by the public pool: "Atlanta Closes All Public Pools for 'Operational Assessment,'" *Atlanta Journal-Constitution*, July 25, 2021.

297 known as the Arden house: "Featured Properties," Dorsey Alston Realtors; and Agence France-Presse, "In One Wealthy Atlanta Suburb, A Plot to Secede from the City," October 29, 2022. The Jollys held multiple parties for political causes. Their party for secession, where $450,000 was said to be raised, was in May 2021.

297 creator of modern Buckhead: The insurance executive was named James Dickey Sr. See Thornton Kennedy, "Dickey Home Central to Buckhead's History," *Northside Neighbor*, November 9, 2016.

297 "official[ly] filing for divorce": [@billywhiteusa], post about fund-raiser, Instagram, May 6, 2001.

298 "make substantial savings": Sophia Dodd, "Buckhead Annexation," Atlanta History Center, *The UnderCurrent on Medium*, September 12, 2022.

298 "Buckhead City" exploration study: John Ruch, "Group Promoting Buckhead Cityhood Seeks Money for Polling to See If the Public Agrees," Rough Draft Atlanta, January 20, 2021.

298 were identified as backers: Thomas Wheatley, "When the Going Gets Tough, These Buckhead Residents Get Secession Fever," *Atlanta Magazine*, April 15, 2021.

298 public pension funds: Tamar Hallerman and J. D. Capelouto, "Bill White Says Scrutiny of Finances, Business Dealings Unwarranted," *Atlanta Journal-Constitution*, February 11, 2022.

298 it would remain masked: White told the *Atlanta Journal-Constitution* in May 2021 that donors to the Buckhead secession effort had been promised anonymity. J. D. Capelouto, "From Big Apple to Buckhead: Fundraiser Grows War Chest for Cityhood Push," *Atlanta Journal-Constitution*, June 10, 2021.

299 "all the money we need": Quoted in Capelouto, "From Big Apple to Buckhead."

299 496,000 residents: U.S. Census Bureau; J. D. Capelouto and Jennifer Peebles, "What Would 'Buckhead City' Look Like? We Crunched the Numbers," *Atlanta Journal-Constitution*, April 25, 2021.

299 of Atlanta's property taxes: Howard Husock, "Secession in Atlanta?" *City Journal*, May 19, 2022.

299 Black Americans in Atlanta: The racial demographics of Buckhead in 2021 were 74 percent white, 11 percent Black, 8 percent Asian, 5 percent Latino, and 2 percent "Other." Capelouto, "From Big Apple to Buckhead."

300 had increased that year: Crime, by some measures, increased in 2021 compared to 2020, but then would decrease some in 2022 (after our interview with White). Whether the crime was bad in Buckhead was a hotly debated topic. Cameron McWhirter, "In Atlanta's Buckhead Neighborhood, Rising Crime Fuels Move to Secede," *Wall Street Journal*, January 20, 2022; and La'Tasha Givens, "Verify: Is Crime Down in Atlanta's Buckhead Neighborhood?" 11Alive, December 13, 2022.

301 of Atlanta, James W. English: This is the mayor we highlighted in chapter 6, who was involved in convict leasing. English also founded a bank in Atlanta that eventually became part of Wells Fargo.

301 introduced a resolution for the Peyton Wall: David Pendered, "Rodney Mims Cook, 1924–2013: Recalled as a Friend by Atlanta Councilmember Michael Julian Bond," *SaportaReport*, January 15, 2013.

301 ordered the barrier torn down: Lois Carlisle, "Atlanta's Berlin Wall," Atlanta History Center, May 14, 2021.

301 family received after his father: Pendered, "Rodney Mims Cook, 1924–2013."

302 a European castle: Fulton County Property Records; Rodney Mims Cook website; and May 2010 Circa Meeting notes.

302 losing a wealthy neighborhood: Brentin Mock, "The Baton Rouge Secession Attempt that Could Defund the Police," Bloomberg, August 9, 2022.

302 to form a new state: Jeff Goertzen, "This Graphic Shows How San Bernardino County Could Become a State," Sun, October 10, 2022.

302 majority-Black area, called Mableton: Rachel Garbus, "From Sandy Springs to Mableton: New Majority-Black Cities Are Changing the Atlanta Cityhood Story," Atlanta Civic Circle, March 16, 2022.

302 revenue of $38 million by 2012: Sam Rosen, "Atlanta's Controversial 'Cityhood' Movement," The Atlantic, April 26, 2017.

302 "Black [and] less well-off": Mark Niesse, "New Cities Could Further Split Atlanta Region," Atlanta Journal-Constitution, February 21, 2015.

303 prominence of Black voters: Husock, "Secession in Atlanta?"

303 "live within our limits": Kevin M. Kruse, White Flight: Atlanta and the Making of Modern Conservatism (Princeton, N.J.: Princeton University Press, 2005). pp. 247–48.

303 county court system: "Frequently Asked Questions and Answers on the Buckhead City Issue," Committee for a United Atlanta.

303 at a press conference: @BuckheadCity, "Real Buckhead City, Georgia, Voters and Business Owners Speak Out in Support of Our Cityhood Plan. Grassroots Advocacy Group," Facebook, January 29, 2022.

304 candidate named Devonta Sullivan: "Buckhead City Fundraiser—Get the Facts. Get Involved," Happening Next.

304 funder of his nonprofit: John Ruch, "Meet the 'Prison Dr.,' the Youth Mentor Pledged $1.25M by the Buckhead City Committee," SaportaReport, January 18, 2022.

305 for the movement entirely for free: Hallerman and Capelouto, "Bill White Says Scrutiny of Finances, Business Dealings Unwarranted," Atlanta Journal-Constitution, February 11, 2022.

305 "big green breasts," Wolfe wrote: Tom Wolfe, A Man in Full (New York: Dial Press, 2001), p. 26.

305 spoken out against secession: J. D. Capelouto, "Hearings Set for Buckhead Cityhood Bill During Special Session, Lawmakers Say," Atlanta Journal-Constitution, September 29, 2021.

306 convict work camps: Garbus, "Bagley Park Is a Monument to Buckhead's Historic Black Communities"; and Task Force Advisory Board, "Fulton County Reparations Task Force Report: April 2021–January 2023," Fulton County Government, January 12, 2023.

307 to intimidate Black residents: "Bagley Grew Black Community in Heart of Buckhead," WordPress.

307 far below market value: Task Force Advisory Board, "Fulton County Reparations Task Force Report: April 2021–January 2023"; the Research Update #2: Bagley Park from the Task Force; Susan M. Conger, "Historic Bagley Park (Frankie Allen)," Heritage Preservation Program at Georgia State University, December 9, 2008; and Tom Lasseter, "The Slaves Built That," Reuters, June 28, 2023. Susan Conger's paper notes that some researchers attribute the name Bagley Park to someone named Charley Bagley, who, Conger wrote, may have been the same person as William Bagley.

307 the grocer William Bagley: Garbus, "Bagley Park Is a Monument to Buckhead's Historic Black Communities."

309 "American Dream for Rent": Brian Eason, "American Dream for Rent: About This Investigation," Atlanta Journal-Constitution, February 9, 2023.

309 of all single-family homes: Brian Eason and John Perry, "American Dream for Rent: Investors Elbow Out Individual Home Buyers," Atlanta Journal-Constitution, February 9, 2023.

309 than in white areas: Hansen, "American Dream for Rent."

309 traded private equity firm: Peter Grant, "Blackstone Bets $6 Billion on Buying and Renting Homes," Wall Street Journal, June 22, 2021.

309 renting out homes: Matthew Goldstein, Jennifer Ablan, and Lauren Tara LaCapra, "Exclusive: Ex-Goldman Mortgage Chief Plans Foreclosed Home Fund," Reuters, July 19, 2012; and Kellie Cowan, "Renters Recall 'Nightmare' Experiences with Corporate Landlord Progress Residential," Fox 13, March 7, 2022.

309 individual homeowner could obtain: Eason and Perry, "American Dream for Rent."

310 "moved in as renters": Quoted in Eason and Perry, "American Dream for Rent."

310 "the single-family home": "Metro Atlanta Is Ground Zero for Corporate Purchases, Locking Some Families into Renting," *Atlanta Journal-Constitution,* February 16, 2023.

310 just 1.4 percent: Hansen, "American Dream for Rent."

310 "just no denying it": Quoted in Hansen, "American Dream for Rent."

CHAPTER 14: A WHOLE LOT OF MONEY

312 chairman, Freedom National Bank: Robinson, *I Never Had It Made,* p. 268.

313 "the next Ray Kroc": Kroc, the early CEO of McDonald's, is credited with growing it into a major fast-food chain. (Note that he did not found McDonald's, but rather, purchased it in 1961.)

314 beaten up: Bo's father and other Civil Rights leaders immediately held a press conference berating the police, but then a D.C. superior court cleared the police officers of the charges, saying they had done their jobs and that Bo had been out of line. Courtland Milloy, "Bo Turned Dad's Clout on Good Cop," *Washington Post*, December 13, 1992; and Andrew Brownstein, "Abuse of Police Power Alleged in D.C. Officers' Assault Trial," *Washington Post*, November 13, 1992.

314 and did not graduate: Andrew Young III Deposition, September 17, 2018, Bernard Parks v. Andrew Young III, AY3 LLC, Martin Luther King III, Andrew Young II, Civil Action No. 2017-CV-296153, Superior Court of Fulton County, State of Georgia (hereafter cited as: Bernard Parks v. Andrew Young III et al.).

314 been a family friend: Andrew Young III Deposition, Bernard Parks v. Andrew Young III et al.

314 running an envelope company: Andrew Young III Deposition, Bernard Parks v. Andrew Young III et al.

314 "I don't need to be famous": Andrew Young III Deposition, Bernard Parks v. Andrew Young III et al.

314 to repair their credit: His company was called National Credit Educational Services.

314 to become mayor: Jon Lafayette, "Glover Puts Bounce in New Network's Step: Comedy, Music Videos, Boxing and Concerts on Tap for Year-Old Venture," *Broadcasting & Cable*, April 16, 2012.

315 earning $162,000 per year: Ryan Glover Divorce Settlement, 2007, 2007-CV-129272, Fulton County Courts.

315 the executor of Parks's will: Verified Complaint, October 4, 2017, Bernard Parks v. Andrew Young III et al., pp. 6–7.

315 New York City after Bo: "Bo's Kitchen and Bar Room," *Manhattan Sideways*.

315 "could hold and touch": Andrew Young III Deposition, Bernard Parks v. Andrew Young III et al.

316 "his entire life to": Andrew Young III Deposition, Bernard Parks v. Andrew Young III et al.

316 King eventually signed on: Ryan Glover Deposition, September 4, 2018, Bernard Parks v. Andrew Young III et al.

316 tied to the family name: Andrew Young III Deposition, Bernard Parks v. Andrew Young III et al.; and Verified Complaint, Bernard Parks v. Andrew Young III et al.

316 "was Martin Luther King'": Andrew Young III Deposition, Bernard Parks v. Andrew Young III et al.

317 ended up suing Bo: Verified Complaint, Bernard Parks v. Andrew Young III et al.

317 to pay Parks five hundred thousand dollars: Greg Land, "Both Sides Cheer $500K Verdict Against Andrew Young III over Sale of TV Network," Daily Report, Law.com, March 8, 2019.

317 "whole lot of money": Verified Complaint, Bernard Parks v. Andrew Young III et al., p. 16.

317 "stupid ass Black tv company!!!": Verified complaint, Bernard Parks v. Andrew Young III et al., p. 16.

317 for the RushCard: Andrew Young III Deposition, Bernard Parks v. Andrew Young III et al. Note: The RushCard, affiliated with record executive Russell Simmons, ran into controversy when customers couldn't get their money out.

317 moving to sell the company: Andrew Young III Deposition, Bernard Parks v. Andrew Young III et al.

317 "to perform a service": Ryan Glover Deposition, Bernard Parks v. Andrew Young III et al.

318 "all the decisions": Andrew Young III Deposition, Bernard Parks v. Andrew Young III et al.

318 $292 million deal to Scripps: David Lieberman, "E.W. Scripps Agrees to Pay $292M for Bounce, Grit, Escape & Laff Networks," Deadline, August 1, 2017. The Scripps deal included multiple networks, among them Bounce. Scripps had purchased 5 percent of the company years earlier.

318 received $15.9 million, shared equally: Andrew Young III Deposition, Bernard Parks v. Andrew Young III et al.

318 yet? "No," Bo said: Andrew Young III Deposition, Bernard Parks v. Andrew Young III et al.

318 remember which agency certified it: Ryan Glover Deposition, Bernard Parks v. Andrew Young III et al.

318 filed for bankruptcy: Eventually BNC was sold to Allen Media Group and merged into theGrio website.

320 woman of color: Robots & Pencils website.

321 number of patents: "About," Paul Judge website; Robert McMillan, "Secure Computing to Buy CipherTrust," ComputerWorld, July 12, 2006; and Google Patent Database.

321 "a ten-time multiple": Scott Henderson and Paul Judge, "Paul Judge on the Art of the Exit," Hypepotamus, July 30, 2013.

322 exempted small banks: The Durbin Amendment in the 2010 Dodd-Frank Wall Street Reform and Consumer Protection Act.

CHAPTER 15: THE CUSTOMERS

323 "But we don't": Heather McGhee, The Sum of Us: What Racism Costs Everyone and How We Can Prosper Together (New York: One World, 2021), p. 13.

325 Greenwood at this point: As described earlier in this book, deposits with Greenwood were held in Coastal Bank, and Coastal was FDIC-insured. In this scene, Tandreia was reacting to the fact that Greenwood itself was not FDIC-insured.

326 20 percent annually: Andrew Dunn, "Chime Loan Review: Instant Loans and Early Paycheck Access," CreditKarma, November 4, 2022.

326 "you can learn and actually do banking": Penny Crosman, "A 'Platform Built by Us and for Us': Black Leaders Start Neobank," American Banker, October 8, 2020.

328 on the new offering: Greenwood [@Greenwood], "Travel in Style" post, Instagram; and Greenwood [@Greenwood], "Advance Your Career" post, Instagram.

333 circulation in the U.S. economy: "U.S. Currency in Circulation," U.S. Currency Education Program.

333 on start-up founders of color: Greenwood, "Correcting and Replacing Greenwood Raises $45 Million Funding Round Led by Pendulum and Announces Elevate, a New Career and Lifestyle Membership," Business Wire, December 1, 2022.

333   they have been systemically: *Systemically* is the word Robinson used. This is not a typo.

333   "pursuit of economic opportunity": Greenwood, "Correcting and Replacing Greenwood Raises $45 Million." Other investors in this round included Cercano Management, Cohen Circle, and the George Kaiser Family Foundation.

334   Greenwood officially announced Elevate: Miriam Cross, "Greenwood Launches Upscale Benefits with a $200 Monthly Fee," *American Banker*, December 9, 2022.

334   stop using the word: Settlement Agreement, "The Commissioner of Financial Protection and Innovation v. Greenwood, Inc.," December 21, 2022.

334   "like Greenwood": Ryan Glover would later tell a reporter that the agreement with the California agency had little impact on Greenwood's trajectory. Emmanuel Felton, "What Happened to Wall Street's Post-Floyd Bet on Black Banking," *Washington Post*, January 3, 2024.

CHAPTER 16: THE GAP PERSISTS

336   James Baldwin: James Baldwin, "As Much Truth as One Can Bear: To Speak Out about the World as It Is, Says James Baldwin, Is the Writer's Job as Much of the Truth as One Can Bear," *New York Times*, January 14, 1962. This quote comes from this article in the *Times*, but it was also incorporated in the film and book *I Am Not Your Negro*, both of which were based on Baldwin's writings, including his unfinished book about the Civil Rights leaders Medgar Evers, Malcolm X, and Martin Luther King Jr. That book was to be called *Remember This House*.

337   "only elite strata are present": Jakob Brounstein, "Interview with Incoming Faculty Member Ellora Derenoncourt," Newsroom, Berkeley Economics, University of California, Berkeley.

338   her father said: @Thorobred Books, "Family Meeting Hosted by Frantz D. w/ Economist Ellora Derenoncourt and Frantz Derenoncourt, MD," YouTube, June 9, 2020.

339   dramatically over the coming decades: Derenoncourt et al., "Wealth of Two Nations," p. 29.

339   reparations for Black Americans: Juana Summers, "A Bill to Study Reparations for Slavery Had Momentum in Congress, but Still No Vote," NPR, November 12, 2021.

339   the GI benefits: "Clyburn, Moulton Reintroduce Legislation to Provide Black WWII Veterans and Their Descendants with Long Overdue GI Bill Benefits," James E. Clyburn website press releases, February 28, 2023.

339   possible reparations programs: In Evanston, Illinois, reparations were passed in 2021, but two years later, not much had been paid out. Emmanuel Felton, "A Chicago Suburb Promised Black Residents Reparations. Few Have Been Paid," *Washington Post*, January 9, 2023. In terms of Universal Basic Income experiments, variations on this idea had been tried by 2023 in places including Chicago (Jonathan Weisman, "$500 a Month, No Strings: Chicago Experiments with a Guaranteed Income," *New York Times*, February 13, 2023) and in Stockton and Compton, California (Abby Vesoulis and Abigail Abrams, "Inside the Nation's Largest Guaranteed Income Experiment," *Time*, September 16, 2021; and Rachel Treisman, "California Program Giving $500 No-Strings-Attached Stipends Pays Off, Study Finds," NPR, March 4, 2021).

339   in the 1930s: In addition to the task force continuing its work evaluating reparations for the Black people who lost land in Buckhead, there were two other developments there that are relevant to events in this book. In 2023, the Buckhead secession movement shut down and Bill White moved away after the state did not pass legislation to push the secession process forward. Also, after the efforts of Elon Osby (William Bagley's granddaughter), Bagley Park in Buckhead got its name back. It is now called Historic Bagley Park, and in 2022, a sign with the new name was installed.

339   mid-1950s: "San Francisco Proposes Reparations, Includes $5 Million for Eligible Black People," PBS, March 14, 2023.

339 paid to affected Black people living there: Katherine Donlevy, "California Task Force OKs Reparations Plan That Could Cost State $800B," *New York Post*, May 7, 2023.

340 examining reparations: Michelle Watson, "New York Governor Signs Law Establishing Reparations and Racial Justice Commission," CNN, December 19, 2023.

340 of the population: This reparations amount has been proposed by scholars William "Sandy" Darity and Kirsten Mullen in their book *From Here to Equality*, p. 264. They stated that overall household wealth in the U.S. in 2018 was $107 trillion and that Black Americans, at 13 percent of the population, should have $13.91 trillion of that. In 2018, they said, Black Americans held 3 percent of wealth, so they would need 10 percent more, which was $10.7 trillion. That amount divided by 40 million Black descendants of slavery would be $267,000 per person.

340 only for a short time: Derenoncourt et al., "Wealth of Two Nations."

341 title to Lovelace's home: "Notice of Motion to Approve Settlement," Case Number 19-59346-LRC, U.S. Bankruptcy Court, Northern District of Georgia (Atlanta), April 6, 2022.

342 found postings on TikTok: James Lovelace [@jameslewislovel4/], "Minor set back for a Real Major come back [*sic*]," TikTok, April 13, 2022.

343 "you don't, they won't": James Lovelace [@jameslewislovel4/], "Take control of your own destiny, you the only one that can," TikTok, May 25, 2022.

344 "ownership in this franchise is fuckin' amazing": Quoted in George Packer, *The Unwinding: An Inner History of the New America* (New York: Farrar, Straus and Giroux, 2013), p. 258.

346 more information about it: A grand jury had declined to indict the officer in 2021. Azi Paybarah, "No Indictment for Former Georgia Trooper Who Shot and Killed a Black Motorist," *New York Times*, June 29, 2021. After the March for Justice Walk that year, the Department of Justice said it was examining the killing in consultation with the FBI, but nothing public happened over the next couple of years. "U.S. Attorney's Office, FBI Examining Screven County Death," Press Release, U.S. Attorney's Office, Southern District of Georgia, September 20, 2021.

347 broader organization into question: In December 2022, James Woodall sent a letter to the NAACP providing written responses to all the points in the original complaint. He picked up the matter in December 2022, he told us, because he felt people around the organization were harming his reputation and he regretted that there had been no hearing or opportunity for him to reply to the allegations. He told us he did not hear back in response to his December 2022 letter and that the next he heard was in March 2023, when the suspension was declared. We have reviewed all these letters. The NAACP's press secretary declined to discuss the case with us.

347 "inimical to the NAACP": Letter from NAACP president Derrick Johnson to James Woodall, March 9, 2023.

348 fee of $45,000: Article X Petition against the Georgia NAACP Leadership, March 15, 2021.

348 a few small costs: Article X Petition. One of the few expense allegations in the complaint involved money provided by the Sapelo Foundation. We called Christine Strigaro, the director of that foundation at the time, and she told us she had no issues with the way James Woodall had spent its funds.

348 "approved by Executive Committee": Letter from NAACP to James Woodall, April 1, 2021.

349 lobbyist payment: In addition to these four people, one other NAACP official who was briefed on the matter said that both votes did occur, and that James was identified as the lobbyist in the second vote. In addition, Younge, who is quoted in our book, attended the meetings, and she confirmed that, by the second vote, the voters knew James was the lobbyist. (Younge was not on the executive committee, so she is also not counted among the four voters we cite.) Note: We did not count James Woodall himself among the four people who confirmed the first vote or among the two who confirmed the second vote.

350 Walker told us: In December 2023, when we reached out again, Edward DuBose, cohead of the investigation, told us the investigation had concluded, but he would not say the finding. The NAACP's press secretary declined to provide more detail. James Woodall told us the organization had not replied to him about their conclusion.

351 might be risky: Silicon Valley Bank had failed recently, and that was part of what was on her mind.

352 "'This is a diversity thing'": Dyson quoted in Steve Lohr, "How a Diversity Initiative Changed Course with the Times," *New York Times*, January 22, 2024.

353 one person wrote: @kiacomedy wrote on Greenwood's Instagram post about the change, July 15, 2023.

353 not been met: Ryan Wilson, as representative of TGS Sellers v. Paul Judge and Ryan Glover, Case Number 2023CV382534, July 11, 2023; and Itoro N. Umontuen, "The Gathering Spot and Greenwood Are Embroiled in Fierce Legal Battle," *Atlanta Voice*, July 19, 2023. Note: The Gathering Spot founders sued in February 2023, Greenwood's team countersued in June 2023, and the Gathering Spot team sued again in July 2023.

354 in the Greenwood fold: In December 2023, the Gathering Spot and Greenwood would split apart again.

355 "building-supply company": @thelandbaroness posted in the comments on Greenwood's Instagram post on December 21, 2023.

356 more than half "minority owned": Ryan Glover, quoted in Felton, "What Happened to Wall Street's Post Floyd Bet on Black Banking?" *Washington Post*.

357 died in the hospital: Alexis Stevens, "Atlanta's 2022 Homicide Victims," *Atlanta Journal-Constitution*, January 19, 2023.

358 an elderly person: Superior Court of Fulton County Georgia, Case Number 22CP209128, Indictment, August 11, 2023. The woman accused in this case submitted a handwritten note to the judge that she did not commit the crime.

358 some closing fees: "Settlement Statement," U.S. Department of Housing & Urban Development, File Je-23-1011, 547 Chappell Road NW, January 26, 2023.

359 put up $1,850 in a bond: Lovelace's bond payment confirmation said $1,850 in the bond and $45 for a sheriff's fee. He told us he paid $2,100 in total. There may have been other fees. The court's findings of fact said the bond was $1,500. The assistant prosecutor on the case confirmed to us that Lovelace paid a bond. He was provided with a free lawyer under a "counsel of indigent person" order, as the court called it. Some of the money was refunded to him when he later returned to testify and fulfilled his material witness obligation. "Order: Findings of Fact," Indictment No: 19-B-02548-5, Superior Court of Gwinnett County, Georgia, March 23, 2003; and "Bail Payment Confirmation 8156966408," Superior Court of Gwinnett County, Georgia, March 16, 2023; also note, Gwinnett County records say Lovelace was subpoenaed in November 2022. See "Motion to Compel," Indictment No. 19-B-02548-5, but he insisted to us he had been to a hearing and didn't know he had to go to another.

AFTERWORD

361 "we pay ourselves the highest tribute": Thurgood Marshall, written in Furman v. Georgia (1972).

363 an economic barometer: Kendra Bozarth, Grace Western, and Janelle Jones, "Black Women Best: The Framework We Need for an Equitable Economy," Roosevelt Institute, September 2020.

INDEX

ABOUT THE AUTHORS

Louise Story is a prizewinning investigative journalist who spent more than fifteen years at the *New York Times* and the *Wall Street Journal*, where she was a top masthead editor. Her investigative reporting has led to the largest kleptocracy forfeiture in U.S. history; a multibillion-dollar settlement in the derivatives market; and to Goldman Sachs's SEC settlement following the 2008 financial crisis. Louise's film *The Kleptocrats* aired on the BBC, Apple, and Amazon. She teaches at the Yale School of Management.

Ebony Reed is a seasoned journalist who has led coverage and operations at the *Plain Dealer* in Cleveland, the *Detroit News*, the Associated Press, and the *Wall Street Journal*. She is the chief strategy officer at the Marshall Project, a news outlet focused on the justice system, and teaches at the Yale School of Management.